The Great Pyramid – The Inside Story
A Five Thousand Year Old Mystery Solved

Front cover image copyright Maximillion69/Shutterstock.com

ISBN-13 978-1482787344

ISBN-10 1482787342

www.thegreatpyramidstory.net

This book is dedicated to the memory of my father from whom I inherited my curiosity for all of life's mysteries.

"All truth passes through three stages. First it is ridiculed. Second it is violently opposed. And third it is accepted as being self-evident."

Arthur Schopenhauer.

Contents

Line Illustrations

Acknowledgements

Special thanks go to my wife, my son and daughter and to my two grandchildren for their input and practical assistance without which this book would never have been published. I would also like to thank other family members (they know who they are) for their kind support and assistance in getting my work into the public domain. Thanks also to my Copy Editor Ian McCulloch for bringing his skills to my manuscript and to Andrew Bayuk for posting his wonderful photographs of the pyramids on his website www.guardians.net which was an invaluable source of information. On that same note, I would like to thank all those who maintain websites dedicated to the dissemination of knowledge with special thanks to those who specialize in ancient cultures and ancient structures, for I would have made little progress without this wonderful resource. I would also like to thank Bonnie M. Sampsell, Graham Hancock, Robert Bauval, Professor Giulio Magli, Thomas Brophy, John Anthony West, Christopher Dunn, Adrian Gilbert, J. Douglas Kenyon, Christopher Knight and Robert Lomas, Peter Lemesurier, Robert and Olivia Temple, Alan Alford and all those intrepid seekers of truth who laid the groundwork for my discoveries at Giza. I am indebted to you all. Finally, it would be remiss of me not to mention some of those who have made great contributions to our understanding of the pyramids at Giza and who are no longer with us. W.M. Flinders-Petrie and Charles Piazzi Smyth are two names that instantly spring to mind but there are many others too numerous to mention who have made great contributions to our understanding of these structures.

Introduction

My first impression as a young child of the Great Pyramid was one of wonder and awe, as I'm sure it was for most boys of my age. As I got older, I became intrigued by the complexity of its inner passages and chambers and I was curious as to their purpose. For as long as I can remember, I have always been curious as to how things worked and how they were made and the Great Pyramid was no exception. But I was completely puzzled as to how this structure had been put together, for in those early days, I did not know enough about the structure to figure out how or why any of its features had been created. Like most people of my generation, I had become conditioned to think of the Great Pyramid as a tomb that was commissioned by a specific king in a specific time period. There seemed to be no doubt about it for everyone seemed to agree that this was the case.

I believe that this is probably one of the main reasons why so many of us are drawn back to this structure time and time again, for as I got older, I realized that so much of what I had been told about the Great Pyramid simply did not make sense. Deep down inside I knew that the pyramids at Giza couldn't have been built in the manner we were told, or for that matter, used for the purposes we had been led to believe. If there was a link between its passages and chambers it certainly wasn't an obvious one, but it was impossible to believe that its corridors had been created for the purpose many Egyptologists believed them to have been created. It was this deep desire to get to the bottom of this puzzle that kept drawing me back to this enigmatic structure.

I've lost track of the times I've wandered the Giza plateau and trekked around and within its pyramids – not physically, but mentally, for I have never been to Egypt – so why it should have been on yet another of those mental wanderings I do not know... but that's when it happened, one day I simply turned left instead of right and found myself viewing a feature of the pyramid from another perspective... and it hit me like a thunderbolt. Instantly, I knew for certain that I had found the key that we had all been searching for... the key that would unlock the secrets of the Great Pyramid. I immediately realised that this key would provide me with most of the clues I needed to solve the many riddles associated with this structure. But my mind was now racing as I tried to put some of the features of the structure into context in light of this new information. Yet at the same time, I couldn't believe that this had happened to me. I had no idea how many people had wrestled with this problem over many decades and got nowhere. Could I really be this lucky?

It didn't take very long to verify that I had indeed found the key to how this structure had been put together for the discovery had by now changed my whole perception of the structure. I now understood why its chambers and passageways had been created and it was so far removed from the orthodox perception of this structure that it is hard to believe that so many could have been so wrong about it. However, knowing why its chambers and shafts had been created was not the whole story, for I needed to know how they had been created in order to discover how the structure had been put together. That had been my objective for many years – for decades – and I couldn't – wouldn't – settle for anything less now that I possessed the key to its construction. However, I realised that I couldn't possibly tell the world why the ancient builders had created these chambers, shafts and passageways if I couldn't prove how and why they had been created, for academics and pyramid enthusiasts alike would simply refer to my revelations as yet another theory and dismiss them out of hand if I couldn't prove my case.

But this was not a theory this was a discovery... a realisation that we had completely misinterpreted the features of this structure. However, I knew that if I was ever going to get academics and pyramid enthusiasts the world over to take my findings and my conclusions seriously I had to prove beyond the shadow of a doubt that I truly had discovered the secrets of the ancient pyramid builders. And there was only one way I could do that, I would have to reconstruct the Great Pyramid block by block, from the ground up, in order to show how and why its chambers, shafts and all of its features had been created. That was the only way that I could prove conclusively that I had indeed made such a staggering discovery.

This is my reconstruction of this great monument based on the many discoveries I have made at Giza and elsewhere since I discovered the key – the "Rosetta Stone" of pyramid construction – and gained access to the secrets of the ancient pyramid builders. I can guarantee that not only will my reconstruction of this structure change your whole perception of the pyramids and the people who built them it will also change your perception of archaeology, for, based on my findings, Egyptologists seem to have been as much in the dark about the construction of the Great Pyramid as most of us. Welcome to the real world of the ancient pyramid builders and the Great Pyramid as you've never seen it before.

Chapter One

Preparation

Before we begin work on our reconstruction of the Great Pyramid, I would just like to point out that the Great Pyramid was not the first structure to be constructed on the Giza Plateau. In fact, construction work had been going on for many decades on the plateau before the ancient builders came to build the Great Pyramid on this site. Although I had studied these structures for many years prior to making my breakthrough, I was completely taken aback when I discovered the extent of the infrastructure that had to have been put in place on the plateau before the ancient builders began to build.

What also became apparent very soon after I discovered the secret of pyramid construction was the great difference in the climate when these structures were under construction as there was undoubtedly a great deal of precipitation in this area at this time. This will come as no surprise to those of you who are familiar with the work of John Anthony West and Robert M. Schoch Ph.D. as they have pointed out that there is considerable evidence to suggest that the Sphinx and the Sphinx Enclosure in particular, show signs of extensive water erosion. This would seem to indicate that the Sphinx could be much older than Egyptologists believe it to be. In light of my more recent discoveries at Giza, I now believe that the pyramids here are also much older than Egyptologists believe them to be.

I refer to my initial breakthrough throughout the pages of this book as a discovery but it was in fact the sudden realization that we had misinterpreted a major feature of the Great Pyramid. In doing so we failed to understand what this structure was all about for it is this feature more than any other that was the key to understanding how the Great Pyramid was constructed. Before we begin to reconstruct the Great Pyramid, we must also be fully aware of the tremendous amount of work that went into preparing the site as the construction of the pyramid could not have begun until all of the subsurface work was complete. Long before the builders began to set down the first course of the Great Pyramid, they created an extensive network of tunnels and a chamber within the bedrock itself, the subterranean chamber. The tunnel network is much more extensive than what has been discovered so far but I don't doubt that the builders began work on this network of tunnels at the top end of what we now refer to as the descending corridor. As you may be aware, when this tunnel had reached the required depth, the builders extended it further and created a horizontal section of the tunnel that extended as far as what would become the south wall of the subterranean chamber. The chamber was then carved out of the bedrock here.

The walls and floor of the subterranean chamber would have been more or less as we see them today when it was complete. However, much of the great pit that now exists in the middle of the floor of this chamber was excavated in more recent times. On the south wall of the chamber, and offset from the opening to the horizontal corridor on the north wall, there is the opening to the short horizontal tunnel that extends for 40 metres or so beyond the south wall of the chamber. This tunnel comes to an abrupt end. The floor level of the chamber is a metre or more below the floor level of the horizontal tunnels in the north and south walls of the chamber.

When the builders prepared the base (foundation) for the structure they did not create a level platform over this thirteen acre site as there was simply no point in removing a great volume of limestone from the foundation level then putting it back where it had come from when they began to install the lower courses of the structure. Much of the mound that existed here prior to the construction of the pyramid could be incorporated into the lower courses of the structure and that is exactly what the builders did. However, a good proportion of limestone was also removed from this area as a chamber was carved out of the bedrock on top of the mound and a vertical shaft excavated down through the bedrock from the floor of this chamber (a chamber that had no roof at that stage of the construction). This vertical shaft extends almost to the lower end of the descending corridor and a recess was cut into the west wall of the descending corridor (the wall on the right going down) that intersected this vertical shaft near the bottom end of the corridor. All of these shafts, corridors and chambers had to be created before construction work could begin on the Great Pyramid for they all played a vital role in the construction process itself.

When all of the tunnelling work was over and the base of the structure had been prepared, the builders were then ready to begin installing the first course of the structure, the foundation course. However, a great deal of infrastructure was still needed before the builders could transport the first of the limestone blocks to the site.

The transportation system

There has been much speculation as to why the pyramid builders suddenly began to build pyramids using large blocks of limestone and many Egyptologists and pyramid enthusiasts have wondered what the catalyst had been for the emergence of new pyramid designs at this time. I had long been of the opinion that canal barges had been used to transport the masonry to the sites of these new, fully integrated pyramids but it was only when I discovered the key to the construction of these pyramids that I realized that it was the transportation system itself that had been the catalyst. Canals had been used to transport building materials prior to the advent of large stone pyramids but these had simply been extensions of the River Nile. That was not the case though when the builders began to construct pyramids using large stone blocks since these pyramids were constructed on much higher ground away from the river.

So what changed? What new development enabled the pyramid builders to construct pyramids using large blocks of limestone? The answer, the catalyst, was the invention of the canal lock. The builders realized that if they could tap into, or create, a water source at a higher elevation to feed a canal system, then not only could loads be transported over great distances, they could also be transported up to much greater elevations. If you can transport building materials up to the bedrock of a plateau, then you can build much larger pyramids from much larger blocks of stone on solid foundations.

The ancient pyramid builders didn't just stumble upon the canal lock however and then begin work on the large, stone built pyramids at Giza. The canal lock had been in existence for a very long time before the pyramid builders began to survey the Giza Plateau with a view to constructing a whole complex of pyramids, temples and the many satellite structures there. By the time they came to install the infrastructure at Giza the canal builders had become absolute masters of this craft for they had by then constructed two large, stone built, fully integrated pyramids at Dashur and created an extensive canal system and water resource on the west bank of the Nile prior to the construction of the pyramids at Giza. The canal system they created at Giza was almost certainly an extension of this earlier system for the pyramid builders would, in all probability, have originally constructed a dam and created a water reservoir that had the capacity to cope with the demands that would later be made on it when construction work began at Giza. (The canal system on the west bank of the Nile may actually have been extended south from Giza to Dashur for a canal system undoubtedly existed at Giza when the Sphinx was carved out of the bedrock on the east side of the Giza Plateau. The Sphinx is thought to be much older than the pyramids at Giza.)

People living in the Nile Valley had been using canals long before the builders of the pyramids at Dashur came to construct these new style pyramids from large blocks of stone, with the water source for these canals coming from the River Nile itself. It was only when they tapped into a water source at a higher elevation, or they created one by constructing a dam, that things changed and by incorporating locks into the canal system, this form of transportation was no longer restricted to the low lying fertile areas that flanked the Nile. Large loads could now be transported up and onto the more stable bedrock that was to be found at higher elevations away from the river. This bedrock was the perfect foundation for large, stone built pyramids.

The invention of the canal lock, in conjunction with these water reservoirs, not only made it possible to transport large loads up to greater elevations, for the pyramid builders realised that with some ingenuity the canal lock could be used to much greater effect. Locks could be incorporated into the pyramid structures themselves and barges could be used to transport building materials up and onto the platforms of these new style pyramids. That, in a nutshell, is what happened at Dashur. That is what made it possible for the very first time to build fully integrated pyramids using large blocks of limestone.

When the ancient pyramid builders eventually came to position the Great Pyramid on the Giza Plateau, they had already constructed a number of these large stone pyramids by then with these new style pyramids evolving to become highly complex structures, none more so than the Great Pyramid itself. When we study the layout of the Giza Complex and the positions of the many structures on the plateau it is obvious that the ancient pyramid builders intended to create the largest pyramids that it was possible to construct on this site given the limitations of the site and the elevation of the feeder canal on the west side of the plateau (assuming of course that the configuration of the three principal structures here is meant to mimic the three stars of Orion's Belt).

The greatest difficulty for the builders when they came to construct the two largest pyramids here was that the pre-existing, single channel, feeder canal on the west side of the plateau was inadequate, for it would have taken far too long to construct these two gigantic structures using only a single channel canal. What was needed was a dual channel canal where a continuous stream of barges could transport masonry to these structures, where their passage was unhindered by the need for empty barges to be transported in the opposite direction. Such a system was created at Giza prior to the construction of the two largest structures here, with the small, single channel canal acting as the feeder canal when both of these structures were under construction. However, this dual channel supply canal would have taken a great deal of time and resources to construct, and if we accept that the structures at Giza were constructed to a predetermined plan, then it is inconceivable that the builders of this transportation system constructed the Great Pyramid before the Middle Pyramid at Giza.

We often hear Egyptologists talk about earth ramps and the accommodation for workmen on the plateau but there is little mention of the logistics involved in the transportation of such massive quantities of limestone to each of the structures on the plateau, or mention of the phenomenal amount of planning that was required before the first limestone block was set in place at any of these construction sites. The failure on the part of Egyptologists to understand what it really took to build these massive structures meant that we were completely in the dark as to the infrastructure that was needed to put the pyramids and all of the peripheral structures into their respective positions on the plateau.

The construction of the dual channel supply canal would have been a major civil engineering project that would have taken a very long time to complete. For this reason, its builders would undoubtedly have taken the shortest, most practical route to the north side of the Middle Pyramid from the canal basin below the escarpment on the north side of the Great Pyramid. The construction of the Middle Pyramid could not begin until the supply canal was in place, but the canal builders could not take the most direct route from the top of the escarpment to near the mid-point on the north side of the Middle Pyramid since the greater part of this dual channel canal would be utilised during the construction of both the Middle Pyramid and the Great Pyramid. A large section of the dual channel supply canal was used for the transportation of masonry to the site of the Great Pyramid after the Middle Pyramid had been completed therefore the supply canal had to be routed through the foundation of the Great Pyramid. If the Great Pyramid had been constructed first however, and the supply canal had been routed around this structure later, it would have consumed 25-30% more resources at least with a similar increase in the time it would have taken to complete the canal infrastructure. Later, as we make our way up through the lower levels of the Great Pyramid, you will come to realize that the pyramid builders always chose the most efficient means and methods at every stage of this construction. That is why I am one hundred per cent certain that the Middle Pyramid would have been constructed before the Great Pyramid as it was the most logical, cost effective and quickest way of doing it.

You will see from the drawings (Figs.1a & 1b) on the next page what I believe to have been the true course of the dual channel supply canal. It originated in the canal basin below the escarpment north east of the Great Pyramid and a series of locks were then built up the face of the escarpment. The dual channel canal then turned south and it was extended almost as far as the opening above the descending corridor on the foundation of the Great Pyramid (this opening was well within the northern perimeter of the Great Pyramid's foundation at this time). The next section of the canal to be constructed lay in a south-westerly direction from the area around this opening to the descending corridor. This section of the canal was extended as far as the opening to the lower descending corridor on the north side of the Middle Pyramid. After the Middle Pyramid had been completed however, this section of the dual channel canal was then decommissioned prior to the construction of the Great Pyramid. That was the lie of the land when construction work began on the Great Pyramid above the foundation level and a constant stream of barges would have transported the first of the many millions of limestone blocks that make up the body of this structure to the construction site.

A common belief was that the stepped core of these structures was constructed first and then the outer casing blocks were installed on each level. Contrary to what we have been told by many experts over the years, the first blocks to be installed on the foundation of

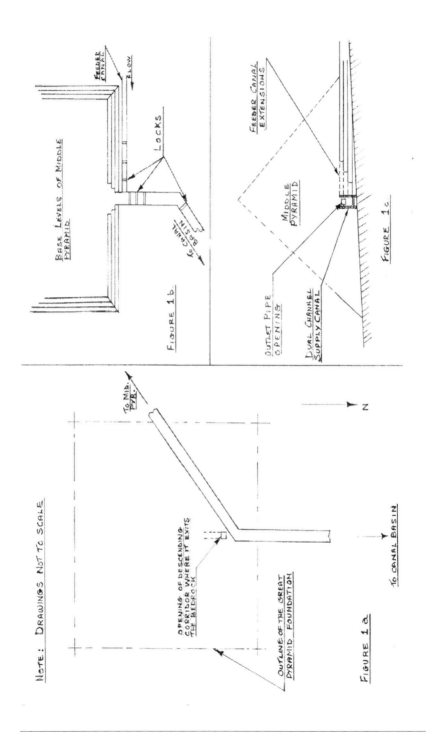

NOTE: DRAWINGS NOT TO SCALE

To Mid. PYR.

N

OPENING OF DESCENDING CORRIDOR WHERE IT EXITS THE BEDROCK

OUTLINE OF THE GREAT PYRAMID FOUNDATION

To CANAL BASIN

FIGURE 1a

FEEDER CANAL

FLOW

LOCKS

BASE LEVELS OF MIDDLE PYRAMID

To Canal BASIN

FIGURE 1b

FEEDER CANAL EXTENSIONS

MIDDLE PYRAMID

OUTLET PIPE OPENING

DUAL CHANNEL SUPPLY CANAL

FIGURE 1c

the Great Pyramid were the outer casing blocks. In fact, the very first blocks installed on the foundation level would have been the corner blocks and the corner blocks would have been the first blocks to be installed on every subsequent course of the structure. The surveyors had to ensure that the structure was square and the orientation of its sides correct before they installed the foundation course and every course thereafter, therefore the outer casing blocks had to be installed first on each course before the vast bulk of the core masonry on these levels.

The most difficult task when building a true pyramid is in maintaining the pyramid shape as it is built up. The secret to doing that is to accurately survey the structure on each and every level. You can't do that if you construct the core of the structure first as it is the accuracy of the outer casing that determines whether or not you succeed in building a true pyramid or not. The builders of these structures were not infallible, they made mistakes, and when we look at the action the builders took to remedy their mistakes and ensure they did not occur again, it is only then that we can fully appreciate the importance that the builders placed on accurate surveying. The builders fully understood that if they got the perimeter casing right on each level then it was a simple enough task to keep the core masonry in check. The first few courses of the Great Pyramid would have taken a very long time to complete with each course being little different to the previous one as they all covered such an enormous area. The only internal feature created within the body of the structure at this early stage of the construction was the descending corridor. This subterranean pipe had to be extended up through the first sixteen courses of the pyramid at a 26 degree angle from the horizontal. However, a considerable time would have passed before the builders got around to extending this pipe up through the structure for they had to establish the perimeter walls on the first few courses of the structure before they could begin to build up its core.

Unlike the sides of the Middle Pyramid at Giza, the Great Pyramid actually has eight sides. It is not apparent to the eye but each of the four sides of the Great Pyramid is made up of two halves, these veering inward towards a mid-point on each side that is approximately one metre behind the sightline from corner to corner at ground level. The mid-point is only offset by about a metre from true but the casual observer on the plateau today is unlikely to notice this slightly concave appearance of its sides as it is only really noticeable under certain light conditions. There has been some speculation about this odd feature in the past but there is only one reason that it exists and that was to enable the surveyors of the structure to get a clear sightline from corner to corner on each level of the structure as the pyramid took shape. As I alluded to earlier, the builders made some mistakes along the way and somehow, during the construction of the Middle Pyramid, the corners of the structure got out of alignment and the structure began to twist. The problem wasn't discovered until a number of courses had been installed, by which time it was too late to correct the error. The only remedy was to bring the corners of the structure back into alignment as the next few courses of the structure were installed. This ensured that the four corners of the structure at ground level would be aligned with those on the capstone (the pyramidion) when it was finally installed on top of the Middle Pyramid. When the builders came to construct the Great Pyramid however, they incorporated this design feature into the structure to ensure that the surveyors always had a clear sightline from corner to corner in a bid to avoid the difficulties they had encountered earlier. It makes perfect sense that the pyramid builders would make this change to the design of the structure after encountering difficulties when constructing the Middle Pyramid. When it was believed that the Great Pyramid was constructed before the Middle Pyramid however, this only confused the issue and added to the speculation as to the purpose of this feature.

Establishing the perimeter walls

The outer casing blocks that were originally installed in the Great Pyramid were much deeper on their undersides than the standard limestone blocks used to build the core structure. Although these blocks had one angled face they would undoubtedly have been much heavier than the standard rectangular core blocks. I mentioned earlier that a section of the dual channel supply canal cut across the foundation level of the Great Pyramid from the northern perimeter, to the top opening of the descending corridor and then to a point on its western perimeter. When the builders first began to transport the casing blocks for the foundation level onto the site they may have made use of the dual channel canal system to transport much of the casing blocks for the western perimeter wall out to this boundary. The western extremity of the dual channel canal would by this time, have been just outside the western perimeter of the foundation level.

The section of this canal that had been extended all the way to the midpoint on the north side of the Middle Pyramid would have been dismantled after the Middle Pyramid had been completed. This would have taken place prior to the construction of the perimeter wall here as the supply canal had cut across what was now about to become the western wall of the foundation course of the Great Pyramid. The landings would have been the foundation level and the sleds and casing blocks for the western perimeter would have been discharged directly from the barges onto the foundations here. Where the canal crossed the northern perimeter of the foundation the sleds would have been discharged directly onto the foundation level here also. There would have been no ramps at these locations, for the builders would have cut a deep channel out of the foundation level where the canal cut across the foundation of the Great Pyramid and the sleds would have been offloaded directly onto the foundation level from the barges. (I have been unable to confirm that the builders cut this deep channel out of the bedrock here prior to the installation of the outer casing blocks on the foundation level.) I believe that this would have been the option chosen by the builders for the casing blocks were extremely heavy, although wooden rollers would possibly have been used under the sleds to make transportation easier since some of these sleds had to be hauled a considerable distance at this stage of the construction.

There was however, no pre-existing supply canal on the south and east sides of the structure when work began on the Great Pyramid. It is possible that the builders cut a single channel out to these perimeters prior to the start of the construction. By using rollers under the sleds however, it is quite possible that the casing blocks for the east and south walls were simply hauled from the canal barges as near as possible to these boundaries and hauled across the foundation level to the perimeter on the east and south sides of the structure.

The first blocks of the Great Pyramid to be put in place were the corner casing blocks. These first limestone blocks would have been transported on sleds, pulled either by teams of men, or by draught animals. The sleds could also have been hauled over rollers to reduce friction and ease their passage on the way to their intended destinations but as we know almost nothing about the people of this time, it's impossible to say for certain just what methods they employed to do some of the tasks on the project. A great deal of time would certainly have been spent ensuring that the four corner blocks on the foundation level were perfectly aligned before the mortar on their undersides had set. When all four corner blocks were in place however, the builders would then have begun to install the first of the casing blocks, working from each of these corner blocks towards the mid-point on each side of the structure.

The builders had to nudge each of the casing blocks into position so that the adjoining faces of the adjacent blocks were only a few millimetres apart and that was no simple matter given the weight of these blocks. It is one thing to pull a limestone block along with ropes to somewhere near to its final position but it is impossible to move a large block weighing several tons very small distances in an accurate manner by pulling it with ropes that will always have some give in them. Sir W M Flinders-Petrie remarked that he could not put the blade of his pocket knife into the gaps between the casing blocks of the Great Pyramid, some of which were still in place at the beginning of the twentieth century. To be so precise when positioning blocks, a more controllable method of movement had to have been employed by the builders.

If you want to move a heavy object and have some degree of control over the distance it has to move, then the best way to do so is by employing leverage or Newtonian principles. By using an object that a force can be applied to, kinetic energy can be used to move a much larger object. A simple battering ram wielded by a few experienced men soon becomes an extremely accurate instrument in skilled hands and I have no doubt that just such an instrument was used to nudge the casing blocks of the Great Pyramid into position. It may have been a simple ram that could be picked up by a few men and used whenever and wherever it was needed, or it may have been a more substantial ram suspended from a wooden frame. Either way, it was almost certainly a ram that was used to manoeuvre the limestone casing blocks into their final positions as the distance a block is moved is easily controlled using this implement. It is also possible that the builders used levers at some point, or in conjunction with the ram, but I believe it was much more likely that they favoured the ram to move the limestone blocks as it could be used in almost all situations. It was portable and didn't need any preparatory work before it was wielded. Levers, on the other hand, needed to have some immovable object placed in a position to act as a pivot for their use.

The limestone blocks would have been placed on a bed of wet lime mortar when they were hauled from the sleds. This mortar would seal the joints between the casing blocks when it dried out but when it was wet, it acted as a lubricant, making it much easier for the builders to manoeuvre the heavy blocks of limestone into position. However, each casing block would not have been nudged from one end until the opposite end came up against the face of the adjacent block as it would have been impossible to obtain such small gaps (joints) between the casing blocks if they had been installed in this manner. In this case each casing block would have been set down much further back from the edge of the perimeter than the corner block, or the casing blocks already installed, with the adjacent end faces aligned with one another. The block to be installed would then have been nudged or levered forward until its angled outer face was in alignment with the outer face of the adjacent block (and the angled face of the blocks in the course below on all subsequent levels). It was only by using this method that the gaps between the blocks could be kept to an absolute minimum and by using the ram on the back (inward) face of each block there was no possibility of the smooth outer faces and sharp edges of the blocks being damaged during these installations.

I mentioned earlier that the sides of the Great Pyramid were angled inward towards a centre point on each side that was a metre or so behind the sight line; it therefore stands to reason that the end faces of the corner blocks had to have been angled ever so slightly inward in order for the blocks that butted up against them to be aligned with the offset centre point on each side of the structure. When the first of the casing blocks was nudged into position, it is most likely that one of the faces to be joined had a thin film of mortar applied to it prior to the block being nudged forward. When the mortar had set, the builders would have had a perfectly sealed joint.

In setting the mid-point of each side a metre back from the sightline from corner to corner on each side the builders had effectively split each side of the structure into two halves. This would have made it much easier to spot any casing blocks that were out of alignment over this shorter distance. When each of the two sections was complete in the core masonry behind the casing blocks there was a gap between the two blocks nearest to the centre of each side. This was a much smaller gap than the standard length core block and small limestone blocks were installed in this gap. All of the casing blocks from the Great Pyramid have long since been hauled away but the two casing blocks nearest the centre point of each side, the last two casing blocks to be installed, would undoubtedly have been butted up against one another and the midpoint would have been clearly defined on the outer casing of the structure. There would have been no small blocks fitted between these casing blocks as there would have been no gap here to fill when each side was complete. What we do know is that a number of much smaller limestone blocks were used to fill in the gaps in the centre of each row of rectangular limestone blocks in the rows immediately behind the casing blocks. This may also have been the case in one or two rows behind these, but eventually, after a number of rows of limestone blocks had been installed behind the outer casing blocks on each level, the builders would have dispensed with this practice.

When the perimeter wall had been completed on the foundation level, the builders would have then installed a complete row of standard rectangular blocks all around the inner perimeter of the structure. The depth of the underside of the outer casing blocks was much greater than the standard sized rectangular blocks used to build up the core of the structure, so it was only when two complete rows of blocks had been installed all around the perimeter on the foundation course of the structure that the casing blocks on the next course could be installed. The installation of the casing blocks in the second course of the structure would not have taken nearly so long as the first and the pace now picked up considerably.

So far, the builders have been able to transport masonry right onto the foundation level of the structure on barges and then transport that masonry out to a number of points on the perimeter of the foundation on sleds. From the landings, the limestone blocks had been hauled along the perimeter to their final destinations. That all changed now. Due to the construction of the perimeter wall on the foundation level, the water level was increased and these waters now poured out into the great pond the builders had created when they completed the perimeter walls of the structure. This water poured up the descending corridor into the pond demonstrating the true purpose of the descending corridor. It was a water supply pipe. When the builders had been busy tunnelling under the foundations of the Great Pyramid they not only created the descending corridor and the subterranean chamber, they also created an inlet pipe that we have yet to discover. This pipe possibly originates somewhere near the middle of the north side of the middle pyramid and it extends all the way to somewhere near the subterranean chamber. Although the opening at the inner end of this pipe has been blocked up, it is undoubtedly near to the subterranean chamber as the water from this inlet pipe would have poured into this chamber. (The other large pyramid, the Middle Pyramid at Giza, has its inlet and outlet pipes on the same side of the structure – the north side.)

The Great Pyramid had its inlet and outlet pipes on different sides of the structure and the reason the inlet pipe originates near to the openings on the north side of the middle pyramid is all to do with the elevation. The opening to the inlet pipe had to be at a much greater elevation than the opening at the outlet in order to have a natural flow of water through the piping system. The piping system had been created in order to supply water to the ponds within the structure and to the dual channel supply canal on the north side of the structure. Water had to flow through this piping system naturally and up the descending corridor for as long as possible as the lower courses of the structure were built up and at least until the mouth of the descending corridor had reached the sixteenth level of the structure, where we see it today. Only by having the opening on the inlet pipe at a higher elevation than the outlet of the descending corridor on the sixteenth course of the structure, would water have flowed through the piping system to feed the supply canal on the north side of the structure.

After the perimeter wall had been established on the foundation course, barges entered through a gap in the north perimeter wall as they transported the outer casing blocks for the second course into the structure and then across the pond to the perimeter walls. These blocks would have been discharged directly onto the top of the foundation course. These casing blocks formed the next course of the perimeter wall but if the builders had completed more of the foundation course before they'd installed these blocks, then they would have had to move them a much greater distance to the perimeter of the structure when they were unloaded from the barges. However, with only two rows of blocks in place in the foundation course, the casing blocks on the second level had only to be nudged a short distance into their final positions after the corner blocks had been installed on this level.

The builders set a precedent here when they installed the outer casing blocks on the second level after only two rows of blocks had been installed in the first course of the structure. This was how the perimeter walls on all levels for some time after would have been established. Therefore, after the third row of limestone blocks had been installed all around the inner perimeter on the foundation course, the first row of standard rectangular blocks would have been installed on the next level up. The base of the perimeter wall on this level was then wide enough to support the outer casing blocks on the third level.

The pattern of the construction now changed slightly for they could not go on extending the perimeter wall up to ever greater heights indefinitely without building up the core levels of the structure. A series of locks had to be constructed on the north side of the structure as the lower courses of the structure were built up and the perimeter wall below the opening on the northern perimeter where the barges entered and exited the structure had also to be built up as the core levels were built up. The gap in the northern perimeter wall where barges entered the pond on each of the levels had to be closed at some point and now that the perimeter wall on the second course was wide enough to support the outer casing blocks in the next course up, the builders would have gone on to complete the first course of the structure and close the gap in the northern perimeter wall on the foundation level. The sides of the lock here, on the north side of the structure, would also have been extended upwards each time the gap was closed on each level of the perimeter wall.

The gap in the second course of this wall was now the access point for the barges as water poured up and out of the mouth of the now extended descending corridor into this pond on the first level up. Once more, the builders would have gone on to establish the perimeter wall on the third course of the structure and then, just as they had done earlier, bolstered the perimeter wall on this level and the one below by installing another row of rectangular limestone blocks all around the inner perimeter on these levels. They then went on to complete the second course of the structure after the perimeter wall was wide enough to support the outer casing blocks in the fourth course of the structure and further extended the descending corridor up to this level.

This was the pattern of the construction all the way up to the sixteenth level. The builders continued to extend the descending corridor up through the structure and as each course was installed, the upper opening of this corridor crept nearer to the northern perimeter of the structure. This corridor (pipe) had to be extended up through all the lower courses of the structure as this was the feeder pipe for the supply canal on the north side of the Great Pyramid. However, after just a few courses had been completed, the builders created a junction in this pipe. This is where the ascending corridor branches off in the opposite direction. The builders then had two feeder pipes to extend up through the courses of the structure and water would have flowed out of both of these pipes into the ponds as the next few courses of the structure were built up.

As mentioned earlier, the outer casing blocks had to be installed on each level first as it would have been impossible to install these casing blocks at a later stage of the construction. It was only by installing the outer casing blocks, that the builders could accurately survey the structure at each stage of its construction to ensure that a true and accurate pyramid shape was actually being produced. I can only say that we were very naive to have believed that it could ever have been otherwise.

Once the pattern of construction had been established, it would have been repeated over and over again as each of the lower levels of the structure was built up. It would have taken the builders a very long time to construct the lower courses of the Great Pyramid as there was such a great volume of limestone blocks installed on each of these lower levels. Even with such a fast method of transportation, they still had to complete each level of a structure that had a thirteen acre footprint. The difference in the size of the platforms at this lower level would have been almost imperceptible and with almost no variation in the layout of these platforms, it would have been a very long and monotonous process building up these lower levels. Having created an enormous pond within the perimeter walls on each level, the builders gradually reduced the size of each pond as they installed block after block on each platform, working from the perimeter walls back towards the centre of the structure. The last few operations on these levels would have seen the installation of the blocks around the mouth of the descending and ascending corridors before the gaps in the north wall of the structure were closed on these levels.

Angular oddities

One of those seemingly odd features of the Great Pyramid is the method used to extend the descending and ascending corridors up through the lower courses of the structure. The masonry that surrounds these corridors is tilted at the same 26 degree angle as the corridors themselves so as to maintain a box structure around these shafts. Although this has been the subject of some speculation, there is a simple enough reason as to why the sections above and below the corridors, and therefore the sides of the corridors, were constructed in this way. As you will soon discover, both of these pipes had to cope with considerable pressure at later stages of the construction. If the builders had simply projected the corridors up through the horizontal layers of the pyramid, inbuilt weaknesses would have occurred as the builders would have had no control over where the 26 degree top and bottom faces of the corridors intersected the vertical and horizontal joints in each course. Setting the blocks around these pipes at the same 26 degree angle was simply the best way to overcome this difficulty and to ensure a uniform standard of construction that would cope with the water pressure and its rate of flow.

When the base levels had been completed up to the top of the mound, the chamber commonly referred to as the 'grotto' was created out of the recessed pit that had been excavated at the top of the well shaft before construction work had begun. When the pond above the level of the top of the mound had to be flooded, water would have poured down into this pit and the well shaft if the builders had not taken measures to ensure that this did not happen. To avoid this unwelcome intrusion, the builders had to seal the top of the chamber by placing a roof over it. They then cut an opening in the roofing slab for access. When they put the next course of limestone blocks on top of this roof, they extended the access shaft up through this course of limestone to ensure that its opening was always one course above the level of the water in the pond. This they did on all subsequent courses of the structure until they had no need to extend it any further.

The access shaft to the grotto had to be created so that men could gain entry to this chamber when the pyramid was under construction. This chamber was in fact the pump room and the pump operators gained access to this chamber via this access shaft. However, as you are no doubt aware, the builders did not simply extend this access shaft straight up through each course of masonry since it was imperative that the shaft terminated at a specific location within the structure. The main reason why this access shaft snakes its way up to the lower end of the grand gallery was for communication. The builders had to give instructions to the pump operators at the later stages of the construction. But that is ahead of us; we don't need to concern ourselves with the operation of the pump at this stage of the construction.

When the opening at the top end of the descending corridor neared the perimeter wall on the north side of the structure, a huge flooring slab was installed. This flooring slab is 2.3 metres thick and 10 metres wide. This formed the floor of the descending corridor here. The slabs on the topside of the descending corridor are also impressive at 2.6 metres thick and 3.6 metres wide. These slabs also lie at a 26 degree angle above the descending corridor and form its roof here. It would have been an impressive enough feat just to cut, dress and move these enormous slabs, but to install them in the pyramid at a 26 degree angle to the horizontal was an extraordinary feat. Impressive as this was, I think it unlikely that these enormous slabs of limestone were transported very far. I believe that these slabs would have been quarried on the plateau itself from the area around the mound that lies within the perimeter walls of the structure. The top of the mound was about 10 metres above the base of the Great Pyramid and there was a ready source of limestone here when the foundation of the Great Pyramid was being prepared. I think that it is most probable that the basement sheet (flooring slab) and some of the larger limestone blocks, beams and slabs used at this stage of the construction (up to the level of the original entrance) were quarried from the area around the mound when the foundation for the Great Pyramid was being prepared. The basement sheet and the slab installed above the descending corridor had to be hoisted up to their final positions some fifteen or more courses above ground level, it would have been much easier to raise these slabs up one course at a time from one of the stepped levels of the mound using hydraulic power and barges than it would have been to transport them from a quarry some distance away. We know that the builders of the pyramids at Giza transported granite from quarries at Aswan, but granite is a much stronger material than limestone. I therefore don't believe that the builders would have risked transporting the flooring slab any great distance if it could be avoided as this very wide flooring slab could easily have been fractured in transit. After the ponds had been created however, it would have been a fairly simple matter to quarry the flooring slab and the roofing slab from around the mound in the middle of the pond and float them off on barges.

After thirteen or fourteen courses of the structure had been installed, the basement sheet was installed. This limestone slab would have been transported over to the area where it was to be installed near to the opening in the north perimeter wall. The water level would then have been decreased and the slab lowered onto supporting piers on either side of the barge. When the slab had been installed on these piers, the supporting structure underneath the slab would then have been built up and completed before the casing blocks were installed in the perimeter wall on this level.

That more or less completed the floor of the descending corridor. However, no sooner had the basement slab been installed, than the builders blocked up the opening at the top end of the descending corridor. This in fact had been the reason why the builders installed this massive slab of limestone here. When all the supporting masonry had been built up below the basement sheet to fully support it, two large limestone beams were slid down the basement sheet to block the opening at the top of the descending corridor. These beams were the same height as the corridor but they were much longer than the width of the corridor and they butted up against the limestone face on either side of the opening to the corridor. (I realize that there is no obstruction at the top end of the descending corridor today, but please bear with me here and accept for the moment that the builders had good reason to block this pipe at this stage of the construction; all will soon become clear.)

When the two blocking stones had been installed, another large limestone slab was placed on top of these limestone beams. The underside of this slab was aligned with the roof of the descending corridor and the installation of this slab would have extended the roof of the corridor had it not been blocked up. As it was, it simply added more weight on top of the blocking stones.

Through the door

The threshold of the Great Pyramid's original doorway today, marked by the 10 metre long flooring slab, is sixteen courses and 17 metres up from ground level. This was the first major milestone of the construction for there had been very little variation in the build pattern of each course up to this stage and none at all on the exterior faces of the pyramid. Now, with the installation of the flooring slab (also known as the 'basement sheet') and the blocking stones, that was about to change.

The builders now had two distinct corridors (pipes) within the structure; the descending corridor, the greater part of which had been excavated out of the bedrock long before the construction of the pyramid had begun, had now been extended all the way up through the structure almost to the northern perimeter, before being plugged. A few courses up from the foundation level, a junction had been formed within this corridor and the ascending corridor was created. It had been extended up from this junction to the inner platform, now on the sixteenth course of the pyramid, and water flowed out of this pipe into the ponds. When we look at the original doorway of the Great Pyramid today, we can see that the builders installed massive (double) limestone gables some distance above the opening to the descending corridor. As the next few courses of the structure were installed above the sixteenth level, the builders built up the platforms on either side of the opening on the northern perimeter wall to support these gables. However, they did not build up the floor level of the area below these gables as the supply canal was extended into the structure here from the lock on the north side of this opening. This channel was extended as far as the bottom end of (what would become) the grand gallery as the next few courses of the structure were built up. The reason that this opening is so wide on the north side of the Great Pyramid is because it was a dual width channel that was extended almost all the way to the bottom of the grand gallery. (The Great Pyramid is the only pyramid that I am aware of that had a dual width channel on its north side extended into the structure.) Water had been flowing up the ascending corridor from the moment the builders plugged the top end of the descending corridor and it was through this pipe that water flowed up and into the dual width supply canal.

20

An area in the centre of the structure had not been built up as the walls of the channel had been built up at this stage of the construction and the builders now had a recess in the floor of the inner platform. The floor of this recess is the floor of the chamber we know today as the Queen's Chamber. However, I will refer to this chamber from now on as the lower chamber as its more common name is grossly misleading (it is the lower of the two principal chambers created within the body of the structure).

The floor of the inlet channel may have been stepped up from the doorway to the level of the mouth of the ascending corridor as we see it today. As the courses had been built up the ascending corridor in turn had been extended until its opening was just one course below the floor level of the horizontal passageway. The channel therefore, may not merely have been extended straight into the pyramid on the sixteenth level its floor level may have increased by one or two steps along the channel eventually reaching its highest elevation at its inner extremity, one course below the floor level of the horizontal passageway.

The pond in the centre of the structure had become very small now for it was really only that space within the lowest courses of the walls of the lower chamber that could be regarded as a pond now. However, that was all that was needed here, since the method of building up the platforms of the structure changed dramatically after the horizontal passageway had been created. Although barges could still enter the structure at this stage of the construction, they were confined to the inlet channel and could navigate only as far as the north end of the horizontal passageway. But that was as far as they needed to go for now, as a docking station had been set up here in the passageway on the far side of the opening to the ascending corridor, with the floor at the north end of the horizontal passageway becoming the landing point for the limestone blocks. It was here that the cargo had to be discharged from barges at this stage of the construction for the elevation of the supply canal could be increased no further.

The shafts in the north and south walls of the lower chamber were originally channels cut into the top surface of the second course of blocks in the walls of this chamber, these blocks were also set back from the other blocks in the sidewalls by about 15 centimetres. It was only when the next course of limestone blocks (the third course) was installed in the sidewalls of this chamber that these channels became shafts. These shafts, as you probably know, extend back into the structure for a few metres before they turn upwards and they were extended up through the structure to a point well above the level of the upper chamber (King's Chamber).

The walls of the lower chamber could not be built up any higher than this third course in the areas near these shafts at this stage of the construction, as this chamber now became a central distribution hub. It was from here that all the limestone blocks to build up the courses above this level would be hauled up to the platforms for some time to come. However, I've got a bit ahead of myself here, so I'd better explain how this was achieved.

There was a fundamental change in the way that building blocks were transported up to the platforms now. Up to this stage of the construction, the limestone blocks had been transported into the structure and then on to their final destinations on barges. However, this now became a four stage process as the barges could proceed no further than the top opening of the ascending corridor at the inner end of the entrance tunnel, the limestone blocks had to be discharged here onto the floor of the horizontal passageway. The horizontal passageway was just beyond the top opening of the ascending corridor and it was here that the limestone blocks were offloaded onto the floor of the passageway one block at a time. (The floor level of the horizontal passageway was just below that of the decks of the barges when they were grounded here).

The objective at the next stage of the operation was to propel the limestone blocks along the horizontal passageway and on into the partially constructed lower chamber from this docking station. The blocks, which were unloaded onto the floor of the passageway in the area between the two ramps at the bottom of the grand gallery (the ramps are only just noticeable at this point as they are only two blocks high) were hauled and / or pushed from the decks of the barges into the passageway. A lock had been installed at the inner end of the inlet channel and as the water level increased in this lock, the pressure built up behind the block sitting in the horizontal passageway. The block was then pushed from behind and the pressure of the build-up of water behind it ensured that its momentum was maintained all the way along the passageway. At the far end of the passageway, a sled or trolley had been placed in position below the step here, and as the block hit the buffer on the back of this sled / trolley, its momentum would have carried both the sled and the block forward, out of the passageway, and on into the lower chamber. The water that had built up behind the block would then have surged into the chamber as the block cleared the passageway.

It was at this point, when I discovered what the horizontal passageway had been designed for, that I realised why the niche in the east wall of the lower chamber had been created. This was the 'safe area' for the men working in the partially constructed lower chamber at this stage of the construction. The workmen here needed a place of safety when the limestone blocks on the trolleys exited the horizontal passageway. They would stand inside this recess until the limestone block had cleared the passageway and the water behind it had surged into the chamber. The floor level of the niche was originally one block higher than it is today and it would have had a step up to this level also. (The floor here and the back of the niche had been excavated in medieval times with the lower block and step having been removed during those excavations, giving the impression that its floor had been on the same level as the floor of the lower chamber.) However, if we visualise the niche as it is today and imagine the floor level at the height of the first course, we can clearly see that the niche is perfectly proportioned to accommodate two people of normal stature standing side by side in this recess.

This safety area would have been a necessary requirement for the two men working on the floor of the lower chamber as they needed a safe haven to get out of the path of the block and trolley as it exited the passageway. The limestone block and its trolley would have come out of the horizontal passageway at some speed and, as the block cleared the passageway, the large volume of water that had built up behind it would then have surged into the chamber. The workmen would have been at serious risk of injury from the sled and in danger of being knocked off balance by the force of the water had they not had this place of safety. The niche was therefore a necessary feature of the lower chamber with a practical purpose during the construction of the Great Pyramid.

The water level in the lower chamber now could never drop below the level of the floor in the horizontal passageway as the water couldn't escape from this depression in the middle of the structure. The horizontal passageway was about 60 cm higher than the floor level in the chamber. The water level in the chamber would also have increased considerably after each block exited the horizontal passageway and the water behind it surged into the chamber. This was very fortunate indeed as the builders needed to exploit these ever changing water levels within the chamber in order to raise the limestone blocks up off of the deck of the trolley. The next task was to hoist these blocks up and onto the sidewalls of the chamber and a specially modified shadouf was undoubtedly the mechanism used in this confined space to hoist the limestone blocks up onto the sidewalls of the lower chamber. For those of you not familiar with this lifting device, it is simply a beam secured to a central column with a counterweight at one end. The free end of the beam can be pulled downward by the operator(s) and a load can then be attached to this end of the beam. When the beam is released by the operator, the counterweight at the other end of the beam hauls the load up off the ground. The beam can also be swivelled so that the load can be deposited on a landing or on a barge, for instance. It was a specially modified version of this simple machine that was used to hoist the limestone blocks up onto the sidewalls of the lower chamber.

As the builders began to build up one stepped platform after another on all sides of the lower chamber, they created ramps on either side of the partially constructed chamber and it was on these ramps that the limestone blocks were hauled up to the platforms now under construction. The ramps began a metre or more back from the edge of the sidewalls in the chamber and they were extended up through the courses of the structure at the same angle as the shafts (approximately 39 degrees) as the platforms were built up. The ramps were positioned directly above the shafts that originated in the sidewalls of the chamber. Plenty of lubrication was needed on the ramps and that was the purpose of the shafts; they were water pipes. Water was pumped up these pipes to the platforms when the water level in the lower chamber exceeded the level of the shaft openings in the lower chamber; it poured out onto the platforms and down the ramps to lubricate them when the hand pumps were operated in the chamber.

Looking at the drawing on the next page (Fig. 2) showing the overhead view of the structure when it was just two courses above the floor level of the lower chamber, we can clearly see the inlet channel and the horizontal passageway that leads to the partially constructed lower chamber. From the gap in the north wall of the pyramid, a long channel leads inward to the opening at the top of the ascending corridor. At this stage of the construction you can also see

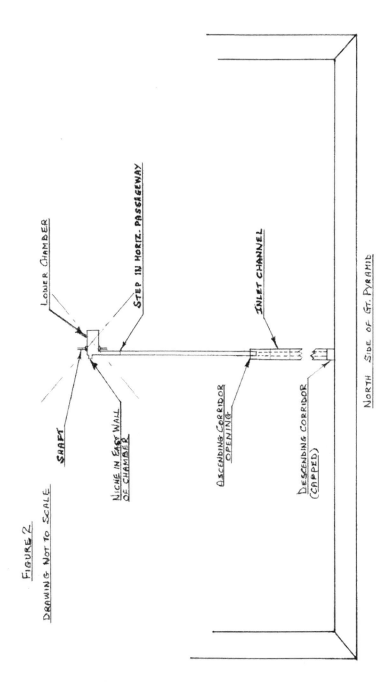

FIGURE 2

DRAWING NOT TO SCALE

LOWER CHAMBER

STEP IN HORIZ. PASSAGEWAY

INLET CHANNEL

SHAFT

NICHE IN EAST WALL OF CHAMBER

ASCENDING CORRIDOR OPENING

DESCENDING CORRIDOR (CAPPED)

NORTH SIDE OF GT. PYRAMID

the channel (horizontal passageway) that extends from the opening at the top of the ascending corridor to almost the midway point of the inner platform. This channel is only two courses deep here over most of its length but it drops down to the level of the floor of the rectangular depression in the centre of the platform before it reaches this depression. The rectangular depression in the centre of the platform is, of course, the beginnings of what was later to become the lower (Queen's) chamber. The floor level of this rectangular depression in the platform is one course below the floor level of the narrow channel that we know today as the horizontal passageway. You will notice that the deeper part of this channel only extends back about 5 metres from the chamber to the step near the end of this 40 metre long passageway. The floor of the horizontal passageway suddenly drops almost 60 centimetres here and this step was regarded as one of those weird anomalies that keep cropping up in the Great Pyramid. However, it was simply because we hadn't understood the function of the internal features of the pyramid that these features became anomalies in the first place. If we'd had a better understanding of the structure we would have been better able to understand why these features had been created. By transporting the limestone blocks into the distribution hub at the centre of the structure, and then hauling that masonry up to the platforms that were under construction, the builders were able to extend, what were now becoming, the perimeter platforms of the structure. These were built up to an elevation beyond the elevation of the upper chamber, almost certainly to an elevation somewhere around the level of the top of the stack (my term for the so called relieving chambers above the upper chamber). The shafts (water pipes) were not extended any further than this since there was no benefit to be gained by pushing the perimeter platforms up beyond this level at this stage of construction. What Egyptologists now refer to as 'doors' at the top end of these blind shafts are simple non-return valves that were operated from the lower chamber by means of a wire. These valves would have been closed by the pump operators after water had been pumped up to a small reservoir at the top of the ramps. (The small bronze artefact found in one of these shafts by Waynman Dixon is the handle that was attached to the lower end of the control wires of one of these valves.)

The construction of the pyramid became very complex at this stage. Limestone blocks were now being hoisted up onto the sidewalls of the lower chamber, three courses up from its floor, by the shadouf. Another method of hauling limestone blocks must also have been employed here as the limestone blocks had then to be hauled up the ramps on either side of the chamber to the platforms under construction. When the sidewalls had been built up until they were three courses high and the builders began to hoist masonry up onto these sidewalls, the blocks had to be hauled up to the platforms from this level. After the blocks had been lifted up onto the sidewalls of the chamber, they were pushed back from the edge of the wall a metre or so, until they came up against a limestone ramp which had been created when the next course of masonry had been installed. When the limestone blocks had been pushed back onto the ramps, some method of hauling these blocks up the ramps must have been employed.

I cannot say for certain just what type of mechanism the builders used to haul the limestone blocks up these increasingly longer slopes but I suspect that it would have been a windlass type mechanism. I know that mainstream Egyptologists are unlikely to accept that such a mechanism could have been in use during this early period, but when you fully discover just how far advanced the people who built the Great Pyramid really were, I'm sure you would agree that this wasn't beyond their capabilities by any means. In fact, as we progress through this book, I'm certain that you will fully realize just what it took to put the Great Pyramid on the plateau for there were some astonishing engineering feats undertaken by these ancient builders. With the possible exception of W. M. Flinders-Petrie and a few others, Egyptologists have consistently failed to understand what it took to create these phenomenally complex structures. Some of their theories have been extremely naïve, showing little or no understanding of basic building principles. This is not surprising however, given that engineering and construction are not their fields of expertise, but despite their lack of experience in these fields, many Egyptologists speak with such conviction and certainly give the impression that they have some great understanding of these structures. They do not.

I am unsure as to which method the builders implemented to haul the limestone blocks up the ramps. It may simply have been oxen or onagers (wild asses) that were used. There was certainly enough distance between the top of the ramps and the outer perimeter of each platform at the outset, at least until the ramps were about as long as the platform was wide, for this to have been possible. As the distance between the top of the ramps and the outer perimeter decreased however, the hauling operation could easily have been broken down into two or three parts, with more animals being hitched to the drag line at regular intervals. (Onagers were being used to pull chariots in Sumer in the middle of the third millennium B.C.E.)

This is certainly the simplest solution and for that reason alone I don't think we can rule it out; but nor can we rule out the possibility that a windlass was used to haul these blocks up the ramps on either side of the lower chamber. Irrespective of the method used to haul the limestone masonry up to the perimeter platforms however, I certainly believe that draught animals would almost certainly have been used on the platforms themselves to haul the limestone blocks on wooden sleds from the top of the ramps to their final destinations. However, if the sleds had been placed on rollers, or trolleys had been used, then these could easily have been hauled across the platforms by just a few men.

I thought I knew my way around the Great Pyramid fairly well but when I began to do more research for this project I realized that all was not as I had perceived it to be. It was probably because I wasn't paying enough attention to the small details in the early days of studying this structure due to my fascination with the big picture. I had certainly overlooked some of the more important details. When admiring the skill with which this enormous structure had been put together, small details didn't seem to matter too much; however, when I began to mentally reconstruct the Great Pyramid, the small details began to matter a great deal. So just in case you have been labouring under the same misconceptions about the structure as I was, I will point out my folly before we take a look at the partially constructed Great Pyramid at this stage of our reconstruction.

I'd known for a long time that the sides of the Great Pyramid are oriented to the four cardinal points. Unfortunately I had also believed that the descending and ascending corridors, and therefore the horizontal passageway and grand gallery, were on the centre line of the pyramid, the north-south axis. Although it is true that the two main chambers within the body of the pyramid straddle the north-south axis, the access to both of these chambers from their entry passageways are at the extreme eastern end of the chambers. The entry corridors therefore can't be aligned with the north-south axis of the structure. The main doorway of the Great Pyramid is actually situated 7.5 metres east of the north-south axis on the north face of the structure (left of centre). Therefore the descending and ascending corridors, as well as the horizontal passageway and the grand gallery, are all situated more than 7 metres east of the north-south axis of the pyramid, as are the double gables on the north side of the structure. As I was later to discover, this offset to the east of the north-south axis was a crucial part of the pyramid design, but it didn't seem to make a lot of sense when I set out to reconstruct the Great Pyramid. It was only later that I realized the reason for this offset. Let us take a look now at the partially constructed lower chamber again.

The walls of the horizontal passageway were formed within two courses of limestone. After the two courses that form the walls of the horizontal passageway were complete, the builders then installed the limestone beams that form the roof of the horizontal passageway as the next course of the structure was put in place. The floor of the gallery however, would only have been built up by one or two more courses at this stage of the construction as it could not be built up beyond the level of the top of the sidewalls in the lower chamber. A clear channel was needed through to the lower chamber for the heavy limestone beams that form the gabled roof of this chamber to be transported into the inner area after the central distribution chamber (the partially constructed lower chamber) was no longer required.

You will see from the drawing (Fig. 3) on the next page that each of the limestone courses that have been installed since the central hub was established in the partially constructed lower chamber, are stepped upward and outward from this hub. This is how the structure was built up from here and why I refer to the platforms at this stage of the construction as perimeter platforms, for a great hollow was being created in the centre of the structure as the perimeter platforms were built up. The blocks on either side of the horizontal passageway are angled down to the floor level of the inlet channel at the northern end of the passageway. As you are no doubt aware, these are the beginnings of the ramps that form part of the floor of the grand gallery. The slot between the ramps that extends all the way to the top of the gallery could not yet be created but this would be created when further courses were added to the floor of the gallery. The walls of the grand gallery were also taking shape as the

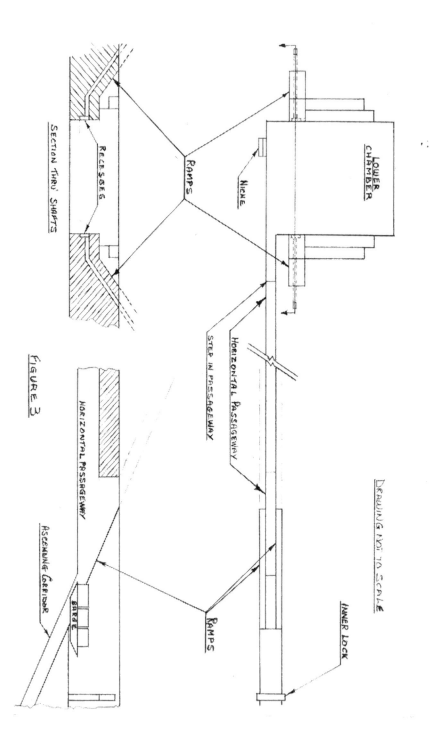

SECTION THRU' SHAFTS

RECESSES

RAMPS

NICHE

LOWER CHAMBER

STEP IN PASSAGEWAY

HORIZONTAL PASSAGEWAY

DRAWING NOT TO SCALE

INNER LOCK

FIGURE 3

HORIZONTAL PASSAGEWAY

ASCENDING CORRIDOR

RAMPS

BARGE

structure was being built up on either side of the channel, these walls having been built up from the floor level of the horizontal passageway.

A metre or so beyond the face of the north and south walls of the lower chamber, and three courses up from the floor level of the chamber, ramps were taking shape. The openings at the top of the shafts on the platforms on the north and south sides of the chamber are a metre or more back from the top edge of these ramps. You will see from the drawing that the ramp and the shaft (water pipe) on the north side of the lower chamber are just west (left) of the west sidewall of the grand gallery (the one on the right when standing at the bottom of the gallery looking up). As I mentioned earlier, the floor of the grand gallery that is now just a few courses above the floor of the horizontal passageway wasn't fully built up as the gallery sidewalls were built up. It could only be built up after the builders had completed the first phase of the construction of the perimeter platforms. When the perimeter platforms had been built up to somewhere above the 70th course of masonry from the central hub, work in the chamber stopped, and the shadouf was then dismantled and removed from the chamber. When the water level in the channel was increased, barges were then used to transport masonry into the central area. The floor level of the grand gallery was then built up as the walls of the lower chamber were built up.

You will see from the drawing (Fig. 3) that when five courses of limestone blocks had been installed above the floor level of the lower chamber, the west end wall of the chamber and both of its corners were built up as the perimeter platforms were built up. But the areas of the sidewalls above where the shafts are situated couldn't be built up beyond the third course of the chamber walls, as it was in these areas that the limestone masonry, used in the construction of the perimeter platforms, was placed on the landings. The shafts and the ramps on the north and south sides of the chamber were in use until the inner stepped levels and the perimeter platform had reached an elevation where there was nothing to be gained by pushing it any higher (somewhere above the 70th course). Only then could the builders build up the sidewalls of the lower chamber and complete them as the hub was no longer required. We should note here, before we begin to build up the walls of the chamber, that the horizontal passageway opens into the lower chamber at its east end. When we begin to create the channel up the centre of the floor in the grand gallery (between the ramps) it will take the exact same path as the horizontal passageway, eventually ending up somewhere above the roof of the lower chamber at its east end. Taking the limestone blocks into the structure and then building up the platforms of the structure in this odd configuration, thus creating a bowl shaped inner area, may seem an odd way to build up the structure but not when we look at the bigger picture. Right from the start, the builders had installed the outer casing blocks on the foundation level as this was the only way to ensure that the structure could be surveyed accurately. As they went on to build up the next few levels of the structure, they did so in the exact same manner as they had begun; they installed the outer casing blocks on each level first. However, it was not only their need to accurately survey the structure at each level of the construction that led them to install the casing blocks on each level before they installed the vast bulk of the limestone blocks on each of these levels, this was simply the only way that it was possible to install these outer casing blocks; these blocks couldn't be installed at a later stage of the construction. When the builders later took the casing blocks into the structure and then transported them up to the perimeter platforms, they were simply continuing with the strategy they had employed from the beginning of the construction. In other words, they simply had to build up the perimeter platforms in this manner as it was the only way that they could install the outer casing blocks on each level of the structure before the vast quantity of standard limestone blocks that make up the bulk of the structure could be installed. By taking the outer casing blocks into a central distribution hub and then hauling them up to each of the levels, the builders continued to ensure that the structure was accurately surveyed at each stage of its construction.

When the perimeter platform had reached the optimum elevation, the focus of the construction shifted back to the area at the bottom of the grand gallery. The builders would have already made some use of the lock they had established at the inner end of the entrance tunnel by this stage, but they were about to make much more use of it now when they moved onto the next stage of the construction. Before we move on though, I would just like to make a point here with regard to the lower chamber. The builders had used the recess in the floor in the centre of the inner platform as the distribution hub when the perimeter platforms were being built up but the builders could so easily have built up the levels of the inner structure from the floor level of the lower chamber after it ceased to function as a hub. They did not do so. Had they done so, there certainly would have been no lower chamber to be seen in the Great Pyramid today. But the fact that the builders went on to create a chamber here at all after they had made a great deal of use of this space at the heart of the structure intrigued me and I realized that this chamber only existed because it had to have served some other purpose. As we are only too aware, after work on the perimeter platforms had ceased, the builders did go on to create the lower chamber in this area. The only conclusion that I could draw from the fact that there is a chamber here at all, is that it had to have been required at some later stage of the construction since the builders went to an awful lot of trouble to create it. To be accurate, we can't really say that the chamber itself served a dual purpose as the chamber was incomplete when it had been used as a distribution hub. Technically speaking, it would not have been regarded as being a chamber at all at this stage of the construction. We can, of course, say that the recess that had been created at the centre of the structure did perform a dual purpose, as its walls were later extended upward and a roof installed to create an enclosed space here with one single entry point. This is the enclosed space commonly referred to as the "Queen's Chamber" today but I prefer to use the term lower chamber as the customary name is grossly misleading; its other purpose was not as a burial chamber for any queen of Egypt.

As you will discover later, this chamber was not created for a queen; it was created for another purpose altogether and the clue to its function was the sealing of the shafts in the sidewalls of the chamber. For it to function as the builders intended, this chamber had to be air tight, except for the one opening (the horizontal passageway). That is why the openings to the shafts on the north and south walls were sealed up. These shafts (water pipes) had been needed when this area served as a distribution hub but the shafts had to be sealed when the chamber was completed because the builders needed to create an airtight chamber at this location as it would play its part in later phases of the construction. Since we have still to complete our reconstruction of this chamber however, we will take a look at what role the completed chamber played in the grand scheme of things later.

When the lifting mechanism had been removed from the lower chamber, the builders then concentrated all of their efforts on completing the walls and roof of the chamber and building up the floor of the gallery and the inner area above the lower chamber. The completion of the sidewalls of the lower chamber was a straightforward operation and it should not have presented any problems for the builders. After the lifting apparatus had been removed from the chamber two 15 cm thick limestone slabs would have been installed in front of the two recessed blocks in the sidewalls. This brought these blocks flush with the other blocks in the sidewalls and sealed the shafts (water pipes) at their lower ends. The sidewalls would then have been built up to their full height prior to the installation of the gabled roof. (The barges had a clear passage through to this area and water could be pumped up the ascending corridor to increase the water level in this inner area. The water level would have been controlled by means of the lock at the inner end of the inlet channel.)

When the walls of the chamber had been built up to their full height, the course above the top of the sidewalls (as we see them today in the lower chamber) would have been installed. The limestone blocks on this course would have been stepped back from the edge of the sidewalls of the chamber to create a ledge along the top of both sidewalls. It was this ledge on either side of the chamber that supported and retained the lower ends of the limestone gables when they were put in place. No ledge was created above the west end wall of the chamber as the masonry that forms the end wall here had simply to be extended upward another two or three courses. (The inner platform at the west end of the chamber would have been built up slightly prior to the gables being installed as a landing was needed here when the gabled roof was being installed.) This wall provided a buffer at the west end of the chamber when the limestone beams (pre-formed gables) were being hauled up into the vertical position. The inner platform at the east end of the chamber however, could not be built up until this gabled roof had been installed.

We will transport our limestone beams right into the chamber on barges when we come to put the roof on the lower chamber but we have to leave the reconstruction of the chamber roof for now and take a look at what was happening elsewhere on the structure when the perimeter platforms had been under construction. We need to go back out to the grand doorway to get a handle on how the structure developed on this north side of the pyramid as we pushed those perimeter platforms higher from the central hub. We will take a look at this in the next chapter.

Chapter Two

The tunnel

Anyone standing in front of the original doorway of the Great Pyramid today can't fail to notice the enormous double gables above the entrance to the descending corridor. The most striking thing about this entrance is the great size of these gables, installed some distance above the rather small opening to the descending corridor. This is all a bit perplexing as the gables are a considerable distance above the entrance to the descending corridor and they plainly serve no purpose relative to this opening. This entrance should not be confused with the opening a few metres to the right of the opening to the descending corridor and some courses lower; this entrance was excavated by Caliph Al-Ma'mun in 820 C.E. The tunnel entrance excavated by the caliph in the 9th century is the entry point for visitors to the Great Pyramid today. When the caliph began his excavations here, the double gables above the entrance to the descending corridor were almost certainly still well hidden behind the smooth limestone outer casing of the structure. It was possibly only after the great earthquake of 1301C.E. that the double gables above the entrance to the descending corridor became visible. (It is thought that most of the original casing stones of the Great Pyramid had been shaken loose at this time and thus provided the builders of Cairo with a ready supply of quarried limestone for many centuries to follow.)

Another misconception that is commonly believed is that Al-Ma'mun was unaware of the original entrance to the descending corridor, more than 7 metres east of the north-south axis, when he began his excavations in the middle of the north side of the pyramid. An early account has the descending corridor hidden behind a door that could be swung open; the same account states that the position of the doorway had been long forgotten by the time the caliph began his excavations and he therefore decided to tunnel into the pyramid from the mid-point on the north side. Having been fortunate enough to have his tunnel intersect the ascending corridor, the caliph went on to excavate around the granite plugs, gaining access to the inner chambers and passageways. Although the caliph did indeed excavate his way into the Great Pyramid by such a route, this story of his good fortune is purely a fictional one. The Caliph knew exactly where he was going with his tunnel before he began his excavations here. With hindsight, it is now obvious that we should have given the original entrance much more consideration since the opening to the descending corridor is so out of proportion with the two massive gables above it that it makes no sense at all to link one with the other. Why then install such huge gables above such a small opening?

The descending corridor is a tunnel, a pipe just over a metre square, that plunges down through the lower courses of the pyramid and then on down through the bedrock at 26 degrees to the horizontal all the way to the subterranean chamber. The subterranean chamber is more than a hundred metres from the opening to the descending corridor on the north face of the structure. On the face of it, the doorway is over-engineered to say the least, but when we also consider that the descending corridor plunges steeply down from the doorway through the lower courses of the structure, there is even less of a reason to assume that the double gables have any connection whatsoever with the descending corridor. The fact that the double gables are above the entrance to the descending corridor does not indicate that they had been installed here to relieve the pressure above this corridor. On the contrary, these gables are in fact the first of a series of double gables that formed the roof of a grand entrance tunnel that was extended right into the heart of the structure. This tunnel was on the same axis as all of the corridors and the grand gallery, so it was no coincidence that its entrance was above the opening to the descending corridor. As we discovered earlier, the descending corridor, and the ascending corridor, were in fact water supply pipes. Water flowed up through these pipes to the ponds and the supply canal on the north side of the Great Pyramid from the depths of the subterranean chamber. When we installed the basement slab at the grand entrance we blocked up the opening to our descending corridor, diverting the water supply up the ascending corridor, just as the ancient builders had done before us. This then became the supply pipe to feed the inner ponds, the supply canal and the locks on the north side of the structure.

In chapter one, we discovered that the grand doorway was in fact the point where the supply canal entered the pyramid. From this entrance, a channel was created all the way to the mouth of the ascending corridor and to the bottom of (what eventually became) the grand gallery. The floor of this channel may have been stepped up by one or more courses over its length until it was just one course below the level of the floor in the horizontal passageway. The limestone blocks used to build up the courses above the entrance tunnel and the doorway were then unloaded from the barges at this docking station at the north end of the horizontal passageway and propelled along the passageway and on into the lower chamber, the distribution hub. This masonry was then hoisted up onto the sidewalls of the chamber before being hauled up ramps to the perimeter platforms as they were built up. The ramps on either side of the lower chamber run parallel with the shafts (water pipes) below, which in turn were extended up from this area to somewhere above the 70th course of masonry. It was from here that the outer (perimeter) platforms were built up to the level where the shafts (water pipes) that originated in the lower chamber end.

It is a long way up to the 70th course of the structure from the basement sheet at the entrance to the inlet channel (on the 16th level) but it was to this level that we pushed our perimeter platform using this delivery system. In short, in order to transport limestone through the channel and then propel it along the horizontal passageway to the lower chamber, we needed to keep this channel open. In order to do that, and continue with the construction of the perimeter platform on the north side of the structure, we had to construct a gabled roof above the channel, just as the original builders had done at least four and a half thousand years ago.

You may not be convinced that this was the route along which the masonry was transported at this stage of the construction and I understand just how difficult it is to accept this fact at this moment in time, as I was not certain at this stage of my original exploration as to where this might lead. What we have to bear in mind though is that the most difficult problem to overcome when building a smooth sided pyramid on this scale is getting the building blocks up onto the platforms, an operation that becomes more difficult with the completion of each course. The ancient builders had solved that problem a long time before they came to build the Great Pyramid after they discovered that it was impossible to install the large casing stones on pyramids constructed of large blocks of limestone after the core blocks had been put in place (and it was impossible to accurately survey the structure). They got around this little difficulty by taking the masonry into a hub at the very centre of the structure and from this hub the masonry was hauled up ramps to the platforms under construction. Getting the masonry up and onto the platforms was not the only consideration, as the builders also had to take account of the fact that the smooth outer casing blocks had to be installed first on each level before the core blocks could be installed behind them. This was the only way that they could accurately survey the structure to ensure that they were constructing a true and accurate pyramid. Transporting the limestone blocks into a central hub before hauling them upward and then outward to the perimeter of each platform, was a truly inspired idea on the part of the designer of the structure. This meant that the limestone blocks were distributed from the central hub to every point on the perimeter of each platform by the shortest possible route. Using this method there was no requirement to haul limestone blocks from one side of the structure to the farthest fringes of each platform. (In all truth, it was the methods of transportation employed at this stage of the construction, and the routes taken, that was inspired, for the builders had no option but to take the building material into the structure before it was hoisted up to the platforms.)

I had some difficulty visualising the Great Pyramid at various stages of its construction because, as you have discovered by now, its construction was far from straightforward. I will therefore endeavour to paint as full a picture as possible for you at all stages of our reconstruction and recap regularly to help you visualise the ever changing landscape within the perimeter of the structure. Once we move on to the next stage of the project however, we will get a better understanding of how some of the internal features of the structure were created and discover why they were created. Hopefully the picture will be much clearer by the end of this chapter.

I must warn you though, as the structure becomes ever more complex, so do the solutions that the builders employ to overcome some of the difficulties they encounter. There are some really big surprises ahead, for not only are there many more phenomenal feats of engineering, but the way in which these builders used every ounce of their intellect and abundant practical skills to overcome almost insurmountable problems, left me in absolute awe of them at times. In fact, long before I reached the top of the pyramid, I had begun to question everything that I had ever been told about this structure. By the time I got to the top, it was by then patently obvious that no one, Egyptologists included, had any real understanding of how these magnificent structures had been put together.

In order for the north side of the pyramid to be built up along with the rest of the structure from the level of the inlet channel, the channel simply had to be bridged. If the channel was to continue to be the supply route for the building materials for some time to come, then the tunnel roof would have to sustain the tremendous weight of the masonry above it for as long as the inlet channel was in use. Long before the start of the construction of the Great Pyramid, the dual channel canal had functioned as a two-way transport system. When the construction of the Great Pyramid reached the sixteenth course, a permanent opening was created in the perimeter wall on the north face of the pyramid. This opening then became the entrance to a channel / tunnel that was extended all the way into the structure as far as the bottom of the grand gallery as the next few courses of the structure were built up. This channel was wide enough to accommodate two barges side by side (the middle pyramid does not have this feature) and also wide enough for barges to enter and exit the structure simultaneously. That is the reason why the grand doorway was so large and why we see these double gables only on the north side of the Great Pyramid as this is the only pyramid where a dual width supply canal was extended into such a structure (as far as I am aware of). Quite simply, the gables we see today at the doorway are the first of many double gables that continue all the way back into the pyramid as far as the bottom of the gallery. This in itself clearly explains why such massive gables were needed here. They were not installed here to support the load of the masonry above the opening to the descending corridor; they were installed above the channel to support the massive weight of the masonry above the entrance tunnel when the pyramid was under construction.

With hindsight, we should have suspected that the gables we see at the doorway were just the first of many gables since the 52 degree angle of the north face of the pyramid had ensured that there would never be excessive weight above the opening to the descending corridor. On the other hand, the gabled roof of the entrance tunnel that the builders created here was put under ever increasing pressure the farther into the structure it was extended and that is why such massive gables were needed.

The gables

The next task then is to install the double gables above the doorway and then to repeat this operation with the gables behind those that we can see at the doorway. This continues until we have created a gabled roof above the channel all the way to the bottom of (what will become) our grand gallery. This was a very tricky operation that was fraught with danger for the men who put the gabled roof on the inlet tunnel. Fortunately for us, we only have to take a look at the complexity of the operation here and that involves no physical danger whatsoever.

I must point out before we begin to install the gables, that the builders would have begun this operation when the platform was no more than two or possibly three courses above the top of the sidewalls of the inlet channel at each section of the channel. The upper gables had to be installed after the lower gables had been hauled up into the vertical position. It is therefore logical to assume that the builders would have begun the operation to install the first of the lower gables when the height of the platform on either side of the channel was at the optimum height for the installation of the upper gables (this will soon become clear). The height of the gabled roof in the tunnel had to be stepped up in stages, possibly two or three, along its length to maintain a minimum clearance height in the tunnel. Therefore one or two step-ups were created on the ledges above the sidewalls to coincide with the step-ups in the floor of the tunnel. These step-ups made the task of installing the lower gables a much easier one.

The builders would have begun this operation by taking two barges, with one large limestone beam on the deck of each barge, into the channel on the north side of the structure. The two barges would have been positioned alongside one another and the water level in the channel would have been increased until the underside of the limestone beams was slightly above the level of the ledges on either side of the channel (these ledges support the gables). Some distance from the tunnel entrance, the ledges on the top of the sidewalls step up to the level of the next course of the structure. The builders would have made use of this step(s) on either side of the channel during the operation to hoist the gables up into the vertical position.

The barges carrying the large limestone beams that would form the first of the lower gables came into the channel with (what would soon become) the bottom ends of the gable legs entering the channel first. The builders would almost certainly have begun this operation to raise the gables up into the vertical position at the innermost step-up on the ledges above the sidewalls of the channel and then they would have worked their way back to the main entrance from here. The limestone beams would have been raised up off the deck of the barges on two hardwood beams, or possibly metal rails, and this would have reduced the friction when the limestone beams had to be manoeuvred on the decks of the barges to form the 'A' shape of the gable. The barges would have been manoeuvred along the channel as far as the innermost step-ups on the sidewalls until the bottom ends of the legs were almost parallel with these steps. At this stage in the operation the bottom ends of the legs of the gable would have been levered and hauled outward over the ledges on either side of the channel until they touched the sides of the ledges. In carrying out this operation, it was inevitable that the opposite ends of the limestone beams would have moved some distance in the opposite direction, inward, and toward each other. When this gap at the top ends of the two legs was closed (the peak of the gable) the 'A' shape of the gable was formed, albeit in the horizontal plane. This very first gable to be installed may have been lying at 90 degrees to its eventual position at this stage of the operation, but that is what was required here, since the lower gables were hoisted up into the vertical position fully formed.

The raising of the gables was an operation that required the use of both brute strength and hydraulic power to safely ensure that the gables ended up in the vertical position (like those that we see today above the grand doorway). The first task was to loop a heavy rope over the peak of the gables and harness the ends of the rope to heavy oxen on either side of the channel. This is my personal interpretation, but once again, the builders may have used a windlass type of winding mechanism on either side of the channel instead of using heavy oxen. Irrespective of how they hauled the gables up into the vertical position, they would almost certainly have wound anchor ropes around two wooden beams anchored behind some strategically placed limestone blocks. Men would have taken up the slack on these ropes and kept a constant tension on them as the gable was hauled and pushed up into the vertical position. This was to ensure that the gable did not go crashing down into the channel if something went wrong with the lifting operation. However, the gables would not have been hauled up into the vertical position from the horizontal position they would have been tilted until they were at about a 30 degree angle from the horizontal before the hauling operation would have begun.

When the legs of the gable had been splayed out until its lower ends were above the ledges on either side of the channel, the water level would have been decreased slightly until the lower ends of the limestone beams became grounded on the ledges. It was only the top ends of the gable that was now supported by the barges as the wooden support beam would have been removed from the leading ends of the barges at this stage of the operation. The water level in the channel was now increased and the barges began to slowly raise the top end (the apex) of the gable upwards. There was a limit as to how high this end of the gable could be raised using this method, but if there had been a good clearance between the underside of the limestone beams and the decks of the barges, it was certainly possible to raise the top end of the gable high enough for the hauling operation to begin. It would have required a tremendous effort to haul these massive gables up into the vertical position and it's possible that draught animals were used on the platforms here in some capacity or other. Once again though, we have no way of knowing what methods the original builders employed here as they hauled the lower gables up and into the vertical position; we can only speculate as to the methods used based on what had to be achieved.

As the builders slowly hauled the gables upright, another rope would have been looped over the apex of the gables. This rope was looped over the opposite side of the apex from the rope already in position there. This rope would have been used to check the forward movement of the gable as it neared the vertical position. Once again, the ends of this rope would have been wound around a heavy wooden beam (anchored by limestone blocks) two turns or more, and slowly paid out as the gable was hauled up to the vertical position (by placing a steady tension on these ropes they would have checked the forward movement of the gables if they had begun to lurch forward). As each of the gables was hauled up, they pivoted on the bottom edge of each leg nearest to the ledge, but at some point near the end of this operation, the weight of the gables would have shifted and they would have tended to lurch forward if the beam had not been held in check. The anchor ropes were used to check the forward motion of all the gables when the weight shifted during the lifting operation. This prevented them from lurching forward violently for they could easily have done some damage, or ended up at the bottom of the channel if their forward movement had not been checked at this stage of the operation. Later, after the first of the gables had been installed, this forward movement had still to be checked as the weight of the gable shifted for the adjacent gables could have sustained some damage if the gables being installed had been allowed to slam into them.

Using the forces of water, man and possibly beast, the first of the gables would have been slowly hauled up to the vertical position with the legs of the gable hard up against the steps on the ledges on either side of the channel. After the first gable had been installed, the builders would have repeated this operation with each gable that they installed as they worked their way back towards the opening of the entrance tunnel / channel. The last of the lower gables to be installed in this section of the tunnel roof was the one that we can see at the grand doorway of the Great Pyramid today. After this, the longest section of the gabled roof to be put in place, the procedure changed slightly as the builders had then to take the heavy limestone beams through the tunnel they had created before they could begin to install the remaining lower gables above the channel at its inner end. When the last of these gables had been installed, the tunnel roof was complete all the way to the bottom of (what would soon become) the grand gallery. Each of the gables in this last (inner) section of the entrance tunnel would have been installed in exactly the same manner as the very first gable installed above the channel, but these gables would have been hauled up into the vertical position in the opposite direction from those installed in the first section of the tunnel. The peaks of these gables would have been hauled up into the vertical position in the direction of the grand doorway. The first gable to be installed in this section of the tunnel therefore would have been hauled up against the very first gable installed in the entrance tunnel, with this gable acting as the buffer stop as the gable was hauled up into the vertical position. This being the case however, all of the limestone beams used to form the lower gables in the inner section of the tunnel had to have been transported through the tunnel with the ends that would form the apex of the gables, at the leading ends of the barges in this instance.

After the barges were in position and the water level had been increased so that the legs of the beams could be splayed out at the lower end to form the "A" shape of the gable, the procedure would have been exactly the same as I described earlier when we installed the very first gable. In this section of the tunnel, the builders would have worked their way back towards the bottom end of the grand gallery and not to the grand doorway as they installed each gable. Eventually, they would have installed the last of the lower gables above the channel and completed the entrance tunnel.

Although I have just described how the lower gables would have been installed throughout the length of the tunnel, the builders would, in all probability, have begun to install the upper gables on the tunnel roof not long after the first of the lower gables had been installed. They may in fact have begun to install the upper gables in the first section of the tunnel after only two or three of the lower gables had been installed. We also have to remember here that at this stage of the construction, work on the perimeter platforms would probably have been on-going when the gabled roof was under construction; therefore the order of construction of the double gabled roof on the inlet tunnel may have been dictated to some extent by the work being undertaken on the perimeter platform in this area. A great deal of forward planning would have been necessary in order to ensure that any disruption of the work on the perimeter levels was kept to a minimum. But the platform on either side of the channel had to be built up in conjunction with the installation of the upper gables as the legs of these upper gables had to be bolstered by the masonry on these levels. Unlike the installation of the lower gables, each of the massive limestone beams that formed the upper gables had to be hauled from their barges and onto the platform on the side of the channel where they were to be installed before they could be hauled into place. It would have taken a great deal of effort to move these massive beams a very small distance and that is why I have no hesitation in saying that all of these limestone beams would have been transported into the entrance channel and then hauled onto the platforms on either side of the channel, before any of the lower gables had been installed. This was the only way to ensure that these beams could then be raised up and through the vertical position to form the upper gables from the positions they occupied on the platforms here. It would have taken a great effort to haul these beams any distance therefore they would have been offloaded from the barges onto the limestone platforms at exactly the position where they would later be hauled up and through the vertical position before they came to rest on top of the lower gables.

The limestone beams that were used to form the upper gables would have been supported on hardwood or metal rollers on the decks of the barges to make it easier to haul them on and off the decks of these barges. Landings would have been built up above the ledges on either side of the channel and the limestone beams would have been hauled from the barges onto the limestone platforms. More rollers would have been placed under the beams as they were hauled onto the platforms. Unlike the installation of the lower gables, these massive beams had to be raised one at a time and then jacked up until the apex of the upper gable was directly above the lower gable. In planning an operation like the one I am about to explain, the builders would have to have come up with a method that was both achievable and as safe as possible for those about to undertake this work. It was a very dangerous operation but a very well planned one. The installation of the massive double gables along the full length of the channel was quite possibly the most dangerous of all the operations undertaken on this project. But you don't have to take my word for it; you can make up your own mind after we've installed our own double gables.

As I mentioned earlier, each section of the upper gable installations had to be coordinated with the construction of the platforms on either side of the channel. The installation of the first of the double gables would have probably taken place not long after the first two or three lower gables had been installed; three gables side by side, for instance, would have provided a very stable base for the first of the upper gables. I would assume that the builders would have been anxious to get the operation to install the gabled roof of the structure under way as quickly as possible since it would have taken a very long time to install both the lower and upper gables above the channel. Work on the perimeter platforms would have been curtailed when the gabled roof of the entrance tunnel was under construction but the perimeter platform on the north side of the structure could not be built up beyond the elevation of this roof until the gabled roof of the tunnel was complete.

The platform on either side of the lower gables had to be higher, probably two courses above the height of the ledge that the lower gables were installed on. A gulley had to be created on either side of the lower gables to accommodate the lower ends of the limestone beams that comprise the upper gables as they were hauled up into the vertical position, tipped over, and then lowered into position on top of the lower gables (Fig. 4). This operation would

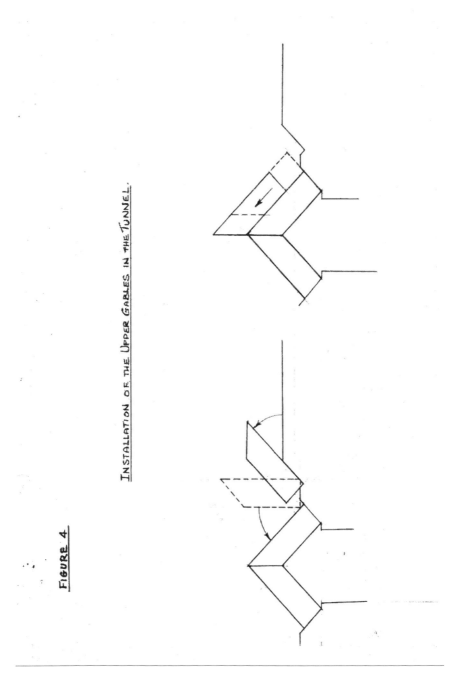

FIGURE 4

INSTALLATION OF THE UPPER GABLES IN THE TUNNEL.

have begun with the tilting of the limestone beams; the edge of the platform here would have been cut away so that it sloped downward into the gulley that had been created on either side of the lower gables. The ledge at the bottom of the gulley that temporarily supported the limestone beams as they were hoisted up into the vertical position and then tipped over was not a flat landing like the ledge used to support the lower gables. It had a ridge running along the centre of the gully. The sides of this ridge were angled to accommodate the lower ends of the limestone beams before and after they were manoeuvred into position on top of the lower gables. The top of the ridge along the gulley was flat and this ridge would have been the pivot for the lower ends of each of the limestone beams as they were hauled up to the vertical position, then beyond the tipping point, before being lowered into position on top of their corresponding lower gables. That was only the first part of the operation though, because the limestone beams had still to be jacked up until the top end of the beam was positioned right above the apex of the lower gable. That was no easy operation either so we'd best take a closer look at what was involved in both of these manoeuvres.

Prior to being installed, each limestone beam would have been manoeuvred until it had almost half its length overhanging the sloping edge of the platform. The beam was then tilted and, as the top end of each beam was raised up off the platform, the beam would have slid the short distance down the slope until the lower end of the beam came to rest against the sloping face on the side of the ridge in the gulley nearest to the platform. You will see from the drawing (Fig. 4) on the next page how this operation was executed. At this stage in the operation, a number of ropes had then to be attached to the top end of the beam. The first of these ropes was looped over the top of the beam and the ends of the rope were most probably fastened to a windlass, or possibly two or more draught animals, on the platform on the opposite side of the channel. This was the rope that was used to haul the beam up into the vertical position.

A second rope would then have been looped over the top end of the beam and the ends of this rope would have been looped over and around a very stout wooden beam. This rope and the wooden beam would have been part of the braking system to check the forward movement of the limestone beam after it had been hauled up and through the vertical position. When the tension on both ends of this rope was then slowly eased, the beam would have been lowered into position on top of its corresponding lower gable. I am sure that most of us are familiar with the principle where, if a rope is wound a few turns around a stout pillar or post, one man can quite easily control a great force or load on the other end of it simply because of the friction generated between the rope and the pillar when he keeps the rope taut. When he relaxes his grip slightly, the rope can be paid out slowly and smoothly, but its forward movement can easily be checked again if he tightens his grip, which in turn increases the friction between the rope and the pillar. I believe that a heavy wooden beam would have been used here but it would have been set up in the horizontal position, not the vertical. This would have been a heavy square section beam which would have been both bolstered and supported by limestone blocks on the platform. You will see from the drawing (Fig. 5) on the next page that a section of the beam would have been turned to create a cylindrical section near the centre of the beam and the ends of the rope would have been looped over and around this section of the beam before they were pulled taut by the team of men entrusted with the job. (A completely cylindrical wooden beam would have been of no use as it would simply have turned like a roller, providing little or no braking effect.) But these were huge limestone monoliths; two ropes, no matter how strong, were never going to be enough to ensure that this operation was undertaken in a safe and controlled manner. If the bottom end of a beam or the ridge in the channel on which it was supported had begun to crumble on one side, there would have been nothing to prevent this huge beam from crashing sideways down into the gulley. It is therefore possible that the builders also had anchor ropes on either side of the beam to ensure that there was no sideways movement when the beam was being hauled up through the vertical position and then lowered down onto the top of the lower gable. That is how I believe the builders would have set up and executed this manoeuvre.

Now that our first limestone beam has been lowered into position on top of the lower gable, the bottom corner of our beam is in the gully and now held in check by the angled face on the side of the ridge nearest the gables (Fig.4). This will prevent the bottom end of the beam from slipping outwards. With our limestone beam now lying on top of the lower gable, but in a much lower position than we need it to be, we can now proceed to the next and final part of the operation knowing that the most difficult stage is behind us. Using

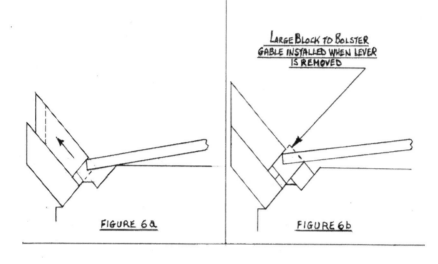

LARGE BLOCK TO BOLSTER
GABLE INSTALLED WHEN LEVER
IS REMOVED

FIGURE 6a   FIGURE 6b

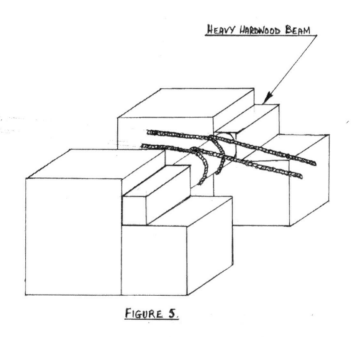

HEAVY HARDWOOD BEAM

FIGURE 5.

water as a lubricant again, we now have to push the heavy beam up the slope of the lower gable until its apex is positioned directly above the apex of the lower gable. This operation would only have been executed after the limestone beam that would form the opposite half of the upper gable, had been lowered into position on top of the lower gable on the other side of the channel. The weight of this beam countered the weight of the beam we are about to push up into position and this will keep the lower gable stable when this operation is underway. Indeed, the builders may in fact have opted to lever both of these limestone beams – that make up any of the upper gables – up and into position directly above the lower gables simultaneously. By choosing this option, the stresses exerted on both sides of the lower gable would have been kept in balance when the upper gable was being installed.

In the drawing on the previous page (Figs. 6a & 6b) you will see that heavy wooden beams would have been used as levers to jack up the huge limestone beams. If these beams had been long enough, a few men would have been able to pull the high end of the beam downward, which in turn would push the limestone beam up into position directly above the lower gable. (It is also possible that the builders used a counterweight on the high end of the beam to push the wooden beam down and push the limestone beam up into position.) This operation to jack up these limestone beams would have been a two or three stage operation. After a beam had been levered up a short distance, a small block would have been slid underneath to support it until it could be levered up to the next stage (most probably a small granite block as this was a much stronger material than limestone). At the final stage, the beam would have been jacked up until the apex of the upper gable was directly above the apex of the lower gable and a final small supporting block would then have been installed under the leg of the gable (Fig.6b). These granite blocks were less than half as deep as the limestone beams they supported but they were just as wide. These smaller blocks supported the full weight of the limestone beams until they could be bolstered by much deeper limestone blocks. These larger blocks / beams were later lowered down the slope from the platform and rammed under the bottom of the limestone beams behind the shallower supporting blocks; each of these beams would probably have bolstered the legs of two or three of the upper gables and this would have ensured that they could not slip out of position before the platforms on either side of the gables were built up further.

If you take a look at the photograph of the grand doorway in the Great Pyramid on the guardians.net website, you can just see two of the shallow supporting blocks under the right leg of the upper gable at the grand doorway if you zoom in. These small blocks were installed as the beams were jacked up and used temporarily to support the limestone beams until the much deeper blocks / beams behind them could be put in place to bolster these legs of the upper gables. The small blocks that we see here confirm that this was a two stage operation.

Looking at the deeper limestone block behind the shallow supporting blocks, we can see that it projects out from under the limestone beam towards the front of the pyramid (the north side). I suspect that these deeper supporting blocks were much longer than the width of the limestone beams that formed the gables and the joints between these supporting beams would most probably have been staggered to ensure that they were not aligned with the joints between the gables. Clearly, a few of these upper gables would have been installed before the heavy beams that bolstered them could have been installed if these bolstering blocks were longer than the width of the limestone beams that formed the gables. This being the case, the first leg of the gable to be installed on each side of the gabled roof would only have been bolstered by the deeper blocks when the next limestone beam (gable leg) and possibly a third, had been put in place and supported by the small, shallow, granite blocks also. The large, horizontal limestone beams that bolster the legs of the upper gables were possibly as long as the width of three limestone beams that formed the gables but we have no way of knowing if this was the case as it is only the double gables at the grand doorway that are exposed.

When the heavy wooden beams that had been used as levers had been removed, the bottom ends of the gables would have been bolstered by the large horizontal limestone beams which were installed in the gap between the bottom of the gable legs and the sloping face on the edge of the platform on both sides of the channel. The masonry that was eventually installed on subsequent levels of the structure then ensured that these blocks and the gable legs were firmly locked into place for all eternity.

The installation of the next and subsequent gables wasn't just as straightforward as that of the first double gable, but it didn't present any great problems either. One of the ropes that had been attached to the beam to prevent any lateral movement when it was being hauled up and over into position on top of the lower gable would have been used here to pull the limestone beam slightly away from the adjacent beam as it was lowered into position. The top of the beam was pulled over slightly to the left or right side, away from the adjoining gable, to provide clearance between the limestone beams for the ropes that were used to lower the beams into position. When all the ropes had then been removed, the top end of the limestone beams would then have been nudged or pulled over against the adjoining gable before these beams were levered up into their final positions directly above their corresponding lower gables.

Work on the platforms would have slowed considerably when work on the gabled roof of the tunnel was taking place as this would have disrupted the movement of barges into and out of the structure. But when all of the lower gables had been installed, the builders would have been able to get back to the task of building up the perimeter platforms, unhindered by any operations in the inlet tunnel. There should in fact have been no interruption to the normal rhythm of the construction again until they had constructed the 49th course of the inner platform, the one just below the floor level of the upper chamber floor. But we still have a way to go with our reconstruction before we reach the 49th level.

More than 500 miles away at Aswan, the huge blocks of granite that would be used to construct the upper chamber were probably being quarried around the time that the pyramid builders were constructing the roof of the inlet tunnel. When these blocks eventually arrived on site, they would have been transported through the entrance tunnel right into the heart of the pyramid. However, we have still to put the gabled roof on top of the lower chamber and build up the limestone levels of the inner area to the 49th level before we can begin to install the upper chamber.

Distinguished companions

Before we continue with our reconstruction we need to take a look at our structure as it now stands. The construction of the tunnel roof was a slow, laborious job but there was nothing to present the builders with such difficulties again for such a prolonged period until they reached the level of the upper chamber. The gabled roof of the lower chamber had still to be constructed but this was much shorter than the roof of the inlet tunnel and would have presented the builders with few difficulties. By the time the inner platform had been built up to the floor level of the upper chamber, a sizeable portion of the grand gallery had been constructed. This did not present the builders with anything like the difficulties or dangers they faced when building the gabled roof of the entrance tunnel as there were no massive limestone beams installed in the gallery. The sidewalls and corbelling of the grand gallery were certainly constructed at the same 26 degree angle as the slope of its floor but any technical difficulties here were in its design, not in its construction, and for the most part, it was simply a matter of laying one block on top of another.

Leaving the construction of the grand gallery aside for now, there were no new internal features to construct until the inner platform reached the 49th course, the course below the granite floor of the upper chamber. As you are now aware, the distribution hub was located at the centre of the structure when the earliest perimeter platforms were being built up but much of the inner area at that stage of the construction could not be built up at this time. It was only after this operation came to an end that the builders could then turn their attention to the lower chamber and the inner area.

Until I discovered otherwise, I had always assumed that each platform of the Great Pyramid had been almost completed – minus the outer casing blocks – before the builders moved on to complete the next course. This, after all, is how it has been portrayed in countless reconstructions in books, on film and on television. Perhaps you too concluded that this was how it had been constructed. However, as we have now discovered, all of the internal features that we have reconstructed so far have been reconstructed purely to accommodate the next, and / or later phases of the construction. It has been a logical progression from one stage to the next since we discovered why the original builders excavated the very first features of the hydraulic system out of the bedrock beneath the plateau. We have also discovered why the outer casing blocks had to be installed first on each level and how the building materials had to be transported into the distribution hub at the heart of the structure in order to build up the outer levels of the structure, the perimeter levels. We simply had no option but to continue to install the outer casing blocks first on each level of the structure before we built up the core of the structure. Although our perimeter platform has now been pushed much higher since we completed the roof of the tunnel however, we have a great empty space in the centre of our pyramid, just as the original builders had at this stage of the construction. In fact, the floor of the lower chamber still stands open to the sky for its gabled roof has yet to be installed. To all intents and purposes, it looks like we have just been pushing the construction forward wherever and whenever the opportunity presented itself. Nothing could be further from the truth.

Theorists have nearly always assumed that the Great Pyramid was constructed using external ramps of one sort or another. Some of them also believe that some sort of lifting device like the shadouf, or some modified version of it, was used to raise the building materials up through the stepped levels to the highest point of the structure. What nearly all these theories have in common is the belief that the stepped platforms were constructed one after the other, with each one being completed, minus its polished exterior casing, before work moved on to the next. This would have made perfect sense if external ramps had been used to construct the pyramid, but only up to a point. We have known for a very long time now that it was not possible to construct the Great Pyramid and its nearest neighbour using such ramps. Nor would it have been possible to install the exterior casing blocks after the core of the structure was complete.

If on the other hand, you create a channel and then convert that channel into an entrance tunnel as a way to take building materials into the heart of the structure, you can get around most of the difficulties that present themselves when you try to construct a smooth-sided pyramid. In fact, as we have only now discovered, this is the only way to construct a smooth-sided pyramid of the size and dimensions of the Great Pyramid. Had we realised this earlier, we may have suspected that the grand doorway was in fact the entrance to a supply tunnel used during the construction of this magnificent structure.

There is also another factor to be considered with this type of pyramid construction and that is the methods that were employed to transport the building blocks all the way to their final destinations. Each method had its limitations and its requirements. Of all the methods employed by the builders, it was water power that was way ahead of all the others when it came to raising and transporting heavy building blocks and slabs. When they had no choice but to resort to brute strength, it was obviously much easier to haul a limestone block weighing several tons up a lubricated ramp than it was to hoist it up vertically as a dead weight. When the designers of the Great Pyramid created a tunnel into the structure on the sixteenth level, it was these considerations that ultimately determined the layout of its internal structure from that point onward.

I realise that some of you may be thinking here that I am on the wrong track as the internal features of the Middle Pyramid at Giza are completely different from those of the Great Pyramid; it was built using a different design. That is not entirely true however. It is true that the inlet and outlet tunnels are configured differently to those of the Great Pyramid but it was its proximity to the feeder canal on the north side of the Middle Pyramid that led to the inlet tunnel being created on the same side of this pyramid as its outlet. The feeder canal supplied water to the north side of the middle pyramid but this same canal also supplied water to the underground feeder pipe of the Great Pyramid. This pipe / tunnel led directly to the subterranean chamber in the Great Pyramid.

The only practical option with the middle pyramid was to have its inlet tunnel on the same side of the structure as its outlet tunnel; it was much simpler to have the inlet and outlet tunnels on opposite sides of the Great Pyramid because the feeder canal was on the south side of this structure and the supply canal on its north side. The inlet and outlet tunnels of these two pyramids though are only a small part of the inner structure of both of these edifices. The pump, the upper chamber, the antechamber, the grand gallery and most of the connecting corridors (pipes) within the Middle Pyramid have yet to be discovered. All of these features are undoubtedly there, as it would have been impossible to construct the Middle Pyramid using such large blocks of limestone without them.

All of the aforementioned features are intrinsic parts of this pyramid design and it was only with this internal structure that it was possible to build these two magnificent pyramids. The different configuration of the inlet and outlet tunnels in the Middle Pyramid, and the creation of its lower chamber at ground level, simply indicates that there was a certain amount of flexibility with the positioning of some of the components of the structure. But each and every one of these components are vital parts of the design – vital parts of the whole – and it was simply impossible to build a large, smooth-sided pyramid from such large blocks of limestone without most or all of the internal components of the Great Pyramid being present in the Middle Pyramid.

You can't build a machine and expect it to work if you leave out a vital component. The Great Pyramid, while it was under construction, functioned like one enormous machine with water as its power source. When it was completed, the machine became inoperable and the builders then removed all of the materials that could be recycled, traded, or sold before sealing it up. Each and every component part of the two largest structures on the Giza Plateau played its part in the construction of these buildings. That has been the case so far with our reconstruction of the Great Pyramid, and, as you will soon discover, it continues to be the case until we no longer need to haul any more limestone into the structure.

Although the canal and the entrance tunnels had eliminated the need for external ramps when these structures were under construction, ramps still had a major role to play in the construction process. After the builders created the entrance tunnel in the Great Pyramid in order to transport masonry into the structure in bulk, ramps had to be created within the structure on the north and south sides of the central distribution chamber in order to push the perimeter platform much higher from this central location. It was this method of transporting the limestone blocks up to the platforms, coupled with the need to complete the outer casing of each platform first that led to the development of the rather odd internal shape of the structure at this stage of the construction. As we have clearly seen so far in our reconstruction of the Great Pyramid, each of the features that we have recreated had originally been created to accommodate the various methods of transportation. A number of methods of transportation had to be employed in order to construct the Great Pyramid and each method of transportation also had to support the delivery of the smooth limestone casing blocks, first and foremost, to the outer edges of each platform.

I sincerely doubt that anyone envisaged the pyramid taking on a shape such as this during its construction, where the smooth outer faces have been constructed up to the perimeter platform somewhere between the 70th and 80th course of the structure, and where the inner stepped levels plunge down towards the floor of the lower chamber from all sides of the perimeter platform. As the perimeter platform on the north side of the structure was built up, the lower section of the grand gallery began to take shape. So before we proceed with our reconstruction, we should familiarise ourselves with the layout of the inner structure at this stage of the construction.

The channel that we created within the structure of the Great Pyramid on the sixteenth level was a dual width channel that extended from the locks at the doorway almost to the inner end of what has now become a grand entrance tunnel. The supply canal on the north side of the Great Pyramid was a dual channel canal that had been constructed specifically for the construction of the two largest pyramids on the plateau. When this canal was in use, there would have been a constant stream of barges entering and exiting the entrance tunnel on the north side of the Great Pyramid (this was not the case with the Middle Pyramid). At the inner end of the entrance tunnel the channel narrowed to a single width channel and it was here that the lower courses of the walls of the grand gallery began to take shape as the platforms were built up on the north side of the structure. A lock was installed here, at the inner end of the entrance tunnel, and the water level could be increased in the inner channel (between the walls of the Grand Gallery) and the inner area as the top opening of the ascending corridor was beyond this lock. The water level could be increased in the inner area without it spilling out into the entrance tunnel when the lock gate was closed. The channel between the walls of the grand gallery, at this stage of the construction, extends as far as the partially constructed lower chamber at the centre of the structure. This is just a recess in the floor of the inner platform at this stage. The floor level of the inner channel at present is just above the level of the horizontal passageway and it will be built up further as we build up the inner area around the upper chamber.

As I mentioned earlier, water flowed freely up the ascending corridor and into the inner lock here and the supply canal, and the water level in this inner area could be increased by closing the lock gate at the inner end of the entrance tunnel. However, water will only flow freely up and into the inner lock at the bottom of the grand gallery and the inner area, up to a level that is determined by the head of water at the opening on the inlet pipe, somewhere south and west of the Great Pyramid. The only way that it can exceed this level is if a pump is used to pump large volumes of water into the lock and the inner area. Clearly, if we hope to continue to use barges to transport masonry into the structure in bulk for some time to come, and raise it up to elevations well beyond the natural limit determined by the head of water on the inlet pipe, we will soon have to make use of the pump. I'm not sure at exactly what point the builders began to pump water up into the inner area but they were probably pumping water into this inner area when they came to install the beams that form the gabled roof in the lower chamber. By making use of a pump and locks, the pyramid builders found that they could greatly increase the water level in the inner area and make further use of hydraulic power when they began to build up this inner area, including the floor of the grand gallery.

Now that we know that we have the ability to pump water up the ascending corridor and into the bottom of the grand gallery, the water level in the lower chamber and the inner channel (between the walls of the grand gallery) can be controlled at the inner lock gate. The pump was also controlled from this area and the builders could communicate with the pump operators via the access shaft to the grotto, the opening to which was on the end of the west wall of the gallery. This opening was just inside the dual channel inlet tunnel and very near to the lock gate. The opening to this shaft would have been much higher than the opening to this shaft in the gallery today as it would have been positioned above the maximum water level mark in the entrance tunnel. (Although the opening to the access shaft is to be found at the lower end of the grand gallery today, this is not the original access to the shaft as this opening is located within the inner lock and water would have poured down the shaft into the pump room (the grotto) and flooded this chamber. This access to the pump room and the 'well shaft' was created in the 1830s by Captain G. B. Caviglia when he smashed his way through the lower sidewall of the gallery here and gained access to the pump room access shaft.)

I have to admit that I found it very difficult to visualise the inner layout of the Great Pyramid as it would have looked at this stage of the construction and the only sectional drawing of the pyramid that I was familiar with, prior to this reconstruction, was a vertical cross section through the pyramid bisecting its main chambers and corridors. When we go on to reconstruct the grand gallery and the chambers above, the structure will become more recognisable as the one we are familiar with. For the moment though, you can see from the drawing (Fig. 7) on the next page the section of the structure that we have reconstructed so far.

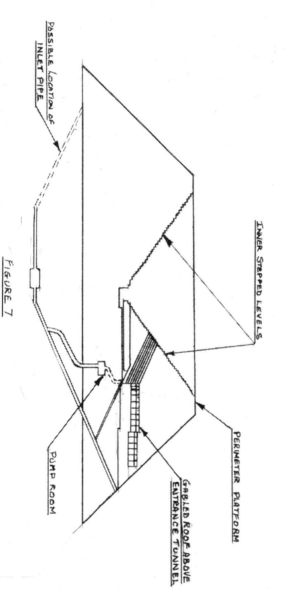

DRAWING NOT TO SCALE

POSSIBLE LOCATION OF
INLET PIPE

INNER STEPPED LEVELS

FIGURE 7

PUMP ROOM

PERIMETER PLATFORM

GABLED ROOF ABOVE
ENTRANCE TUNNEL

The completion of the lower chamber

The gables that we can see today in the roof of the lower chamber were installed in the same manner as the lower gables in the roof of the inlet tunnel. The barges transporting the limestone beams that formed each gable would have entered the inner lock and after the water level in the inner channel had been increased, the barges would have made their way (one after the other, for the channel here was only wide enough for one barge) to the lower chamber. When the two barges were within the sidewalls of the chamber, the barges would have been brought alongside one another with the lower ends of the limestone beams (when they are in the vertical position) at the west end of the chamber. The water level in the inner area would then have been decreased until the undersides of these beams were just slightly above the level of the ledges on top of the sidewalls of the chamber. Once again, the builders would have formed the 'A' shape of the gable while these beams were still in the horizontal position, ensuring that the bottom ends of the legs were up against the west end wall of the chamber as this wall acted as the buffer when the gables were being hoisted up into the vertical position. (The wall and the stepped levels at the west end of the chamber would have been built up by two or three courses and a good landing would have been created on this level. The gables would have been hauled up into the vertical position from this landing.)

The procedure here would have been no different to the procedure we employed in the inlet channel when we installed the lower gables there; two barges were brought into the chamber and the barges were brought alongside one another; the 'A' shape of the gable was formed while the beams were still in the horizontal position on the decks of the barges; the bottom ends of each leg of the gable would have been positioned above the ledges on either side of the chamber and up against the west wall of the chamber. The first gable would then have been hauled up into the vertical position, assisted initially by hydraulic power as the water level in the inner area was increased. These gables were hauled up into the vertical position in exactly the same manner as the lower gables in the inlet channel and although some of the west end wall had been built up prior to the installation of the first gable, the inner platform and the west wall on the west side of the chamber would not have been built up by more than a few courses above the height of the sidewalls as a good clear landing (working area) would have been needed here in order to haul the gables up into the vertical position.

Most of the gables in the lower chamber roof would have been installed using this same method. Yet at some point, the builders would have been unable to take the barges into the chamber as the gap would have become too small at the east end of the gabled roof if the platform here had been built up. Therefore, in order to facilitate the installation of the last two gables, the inner platform at the east end of the chamber would have been constructed no higher than the course below the level of the ledges in the chamber. The barges that transported the limestone beams that formed the last two gables into the inner area would then have been brought around to the east end of the chamber and the water level reduced until the legs of the gables were just above the ledges on the sidewalls of the chamber. In this way, the last two gables would have been installed in exactly the same manner as the others, with the inner platform and the east wall of the chamber then being built up until the chamber was complete.

As far as I am aware, the area above the lower chamber gables has not been tunnelled into or explored in order to determine the nature of the structure directly above the chamber. However, if the builders thought that they needed double gables to support the weight of the structure above the entrance tunnel, then it is almost certainly the case that they installed double gables in the roof of the lower chamber. This chamber is in the centre of the pyramid and it therefore it had a much greater load bearing down upon it than any section of the entrance tunnel. Logic therefore dictates that the builders would have installed double gables here also.

The installation of the upper gables above the lower chamber was a much simpler operation than the one to install the upper gables above the entrance tunnel. The big difference here was that the builders could transport the limestone beams right into the area around the gabled roof of the lower chamber on barges. You will no doubt remember that when we installed the legs of the upper gables on the roof of the entrance tunnel, it was a multi stage operation. Each leg had to be lowered down into a gulley, hauled up and through the vertical position and then lowered onto the top of the lower gables. The beams were then jacked up until they were directly above the beams of the lower gables. Only then were the beams bolstered by large limestone blocks / beams and locked into position directly above the lower gables. The initial procedure here was very different.

The builders had another option when they came to install the upper gables due to the fact that they could transport the limestone beams into the area around the gabled roof of the chamber on barges. This made all the difference, since the bolster blocks on one side of the lower gables could be installed prior to the limestone beams being lowered into position on this side of the gabled roof. As water could be pumped up into the inner area around the gabled roof, the barges could be raised until their decks were just above the peak of the lower gables. You will see from the drawing (Fig. 8) on the next page that this gave the builders the opportunity to discharge the limestone beams from the decks of the barges directly onto the lower gables on one side of the roof. The limestone beams would have been hauled from the barge until they reached the pivot point when they would have tilted and began to slide down the slope of the roof before coming to rest against the bolster beam at the bottom of the slope. The angle was a fairly shallow one and the water in the pond in the inner area would have slowed the passage of these limestone beams as they slid down the slope of the lower gable.

There would have been little stress placed on the lower gables during this operation, other than the fact that they had now to support the weight of the upper gables. There would have been a very low probability that the lower gables could have been damaged during the operation to install the first bank of limestone beams on top of the roof of the chamber in this manner. The limestone beams on the other side of the gabled roof, however, could not have been installed in this manner. The beams on this side of the roof would have been installed in the same manner as the limestone beams that comprise the upper gables in the entrance tunnel.

When the roof of the chamber was complete, the end walls of the chamber were built up and all of the joints sealed with mortar. The lower chamber was now watertight, complete and more or less how we see it today. Unfortunately, since its inner chambers and corridors were discovered in the 9th century, some excavations have been undertaken within the lower chamber with the floor of the chamber and the back wall of the niche incurring some damage. In 1872, the English engineer Waynman Dixon cut through the limestone slabs in the sidewalls of the chamber to reveal the shafts in the north and south walls after he suspected that it may have had

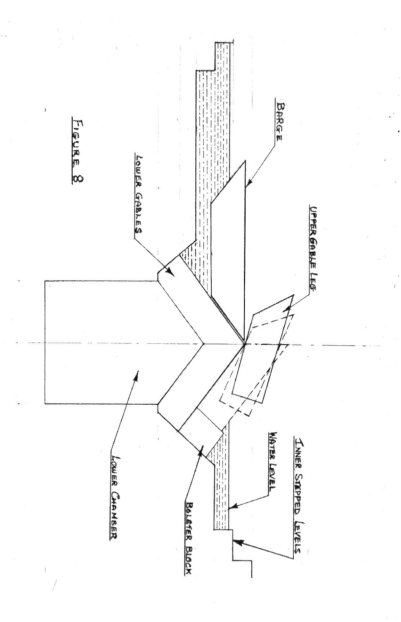

FIGURE 8

BARGE

LOWER GABLES

UPPER GABLE LEG

LOWER CHAMBER

BOLSTER BLOCK

WATER LEVEL

INNER STEPPED LEVELS

shafts similar to those in the upper chamber. Despite this damage, its walls, floor and roof are not much different today than they were four and a half thousand years ago (most probably longer) when the builders completed it.

The grand gallery

Now that we have completed the lower chamber, we have to build up the inner platform within the tiered inner structure. Although we can't reconstruct the inner platform up to the height of the perimeter platform just yet, we can certainly construct it up to the 49th course where we will begin to reconstruct the granite walls of the upper chamber and the antechamber. As we push the inner platform higher, we will also extend the floor of the grand gallery up to the 49th level. Fortunately, the grand gallery is the only internal feature of the Great Pyramid that we have to extend further at this stage of the construction.

The grand gallery is quite staggering in its proportions. Most visitors to the Great Pyramid find it breath-taking to exit the top of the ascending corridor and gaze up at it for the first time. Stretching into the gloomy distance, it is inclined at 26 degrees to the horizontal, as is the ascending corridor through which the visitor enters this inner area. Standing in the horizontal passageway looking up to the top of the gallery, the 60 cm deep slot in the floor between the ramps seems to extend all the way to infinity. In fact, it extends all the way up to the 1 metre deep granite step stone at the top of the gallery, as do the ramps on either side of this channel.

The ramps today are used as walkways at the bottom of the gallery, with the opening to the horizontal passageway lying between them. As today's visitors walk up the ramps past the point where the horizontal passageway disappears into a vertical face between the ramps, the handrails guide the visitors from the ramps on either side of the gallery onto the wooden walkway that now runs up the channel between the ramps. This walkway extends all the way up to the top of the grand gallery and the dizzy heights of the antechamber and the upper chamber some fifty courses up from ground level.

Earlier, when we reconstructed the pyramid up to the 25th course, one course above the sidewalls in the lower chamber, we began to build up the ramps on the floor of the gallery. We will now take a look at how the inner platform and the floor and walls of the gallery were built up from this level until our inner platform has reached the 49th level – the foundation level of the upper chamber.

When we had reached the roof level of the lower chamber, we had installed a good few courses of the floor and the ramps at the bottom of the grand gallery. As we built up the inner platform from here, the slot up the middle of the floor in the gallery was created. The sidewalls at the bottom end of the gallery had been constructed up to their full height on either side of the ramps as each course of the pyramid had been stepped upwards and outwards from the lower chamber during our reconstruction of the perimeter platforms. The limestone blocks / beams that spanned across the gap at the top of the corbelled walls of the gallery had been put in place over about a third of its length as these perimeter levels were built up.

Behind the sidewall on the right hand side of the gallery, as you would enter it from the ascending corridor, the vertical shaft that went down to the chamber known as the grotto exited the end wall of the gallery (at the inner end of the entrance tunnel and not now accessible) some distance above the high water mark in the entrance tunnel. The channel in the entrance tunnel was much wider (it was twice as wide) than the channel in the grand gallery, so this shaft would have been accessed here on the inner end wall of the entrance tunnel. The pump operators would have gained access to the pump room from here and the builders would have been able to communicate with the operators in the pump room via this opening. This access remained open for as long as the canal and locks within the structure were in use and it was only blocked up later when the inlet tunnel was sealed up (the access shaft was only discovered in fairly recent times).

After the roof of the tunnel had been put in place, there was a long period of uninterrupted construction work. All of the masonry came through the tunnel, along the horizontal passageway to the lower chamber and from there it was hoisted up the ramps to the perimeter platforms as they were built up. The sidewalls of the grand gallery began to take shape during this build-up of the perimeter platforms; as each course was put in place above the 4.5 metre high sidewalls, its walls were stepped outwards 7.5 centimetres at a time to create the corbelling we see in the walls of the gallery today.

Construction of the gallery sidewalls was not a straightforward matter however, as the courses of the walls follow the same 26 degree slope of its floor (ramps). The builders had constructed them in this way so that the corbelling followed the same slope as the floor of the gallery and therefore ran parallel with it. The corbelling of the sidewalls in the grand gallery was a necessary feature as it reduced the gap at the top of the walls. The beams or blocks that were placed across this gap to complete the roof of the gallery could not be too long, as long beams would be weak and prone to cracking under the massive weight of the structure above. Constructing the walls of the gallery in this way reduced the gap between the walls at the top to the same width as that of the slot running up the centre of the floor. The corbelled arch that was created when the walls were constructed in this manner gave the roof of this large chamber tremendous strength.

The blocks in the sidewalls of the gallery are rectangular blocks with their end faces perpendicular to their base. In order to have the corbelling parallel with the ramps on the floor of the gallery, these blocks were set down on a sloping base. The blocks in the top course of the sidewalls however, vary from all the others in that their top faces were not parallel to the lower faces, as the top faces of these blocks were cut at an angle to create a series of notches along the top of the walls on either side of the chamber. The beams that bridged across the gap at the top of the gallery to form the roof were checked into these notches in its sidewalls over the full length of the chamber. Had the top faces of the blocks in the sidewalls not been cut at a steeper angle to form this series of notches, the combined weight of these limestone beams would have put tremendous pressure on the double gables that bolstered the bottom end of the gallery. Constructing the roof in this way ensured that much of the load acting on the roof beams was directed down through the sidewalls of the gallery and that the lesser loads acting on the 26 degree slope of the roof were checked at each section of the roof and buffered by the great mass of each horizontal course of the structure. In other words, the mass of the structure on the north side of the pyramid was used to bolster much of the load that would otherwise have put a great deal of pressure on the double gables at the inner end of the entrance tunnel (it was these inner gables that bolstered the lower end of the gallery).

This is yet another example of the builders' phenomenal understanding of structural mechanics. This is knowledge that can only be gained through many years of experience and experiment and by learning from their mistakes. However, we have not even reached the half way stage of our reconstruction and the best is yet to come. If you think the difficulties that the builders have overcome so far were really challenging, they were nothing compared to the difficulties that lay ahead of them at this stage of the construction. The construction of the inner platform up to the 49th course, the course below the granite floor of the upper chamber, did not present the builders with any difficulties as there were no significant features, other than those I have already mentioned, between the roof of the lower chamber and this course. The grand gallery was the only significant feature that had to be extended up through the courses of the structure at this stage of the construction.

Looking up to the top of the ramps in the gallery today, you will notice that the ramps only extend as far as the step-stone but they would have ended on the same elevation as the 49th course of the structure originally. This is one course below the level of the floor in the antechamber and the upper chamber, and one course below the top of the step-stone at the top end of the gallery. Later, we will have to install this granite step-stone at the top end of our grand gallery but that operation has to be put on hold for some time until we reconstruct the upper chamber.

When our inner platform reached the 49th level, we had reached a major milestone with the reconstruction of our Great Pyramid with the surface area at this level now exactly half that of the base. At least it would have been if the pyramid had been constructed course by course and each course completed before we moved on to the next. Fortunately, the original builders did not construct the pyramid by finishing one complete course at a time, so we are now well past the halfway stage in volume terms if not in elevation. As we have now discovered, the builders pushed the outer (perimeter) platform of the structure, and the external faces of the pyramid, up to the optimum level before they completed the lower chamber and began to build the inner platform up to the floor level of the upper chamber. In the next chapter, we will see the extraordinary lengths they had to go to in order to construct the upper chamber and its layered roof. We will discover how they transported the materials for its construction up to this inner area.

If we could have stood at the bottom of the grand gallery at this stage of the construction, we would have been unable to see the horizontal passageway or the floor of the gallery. Find out why this was so in the next chapter.

Chapter Three

Stairway to eternity

The grand gallery is an awesome sight but when I first realised why it had been created, and what they did with it, I was absolutely blown away. I had begun by then to believe that nothing was impossible for the builders of the Giza pyramids but it now looked as if they were out to prove it conclusively. Every time I thought they'd pushed themselves to the absolute limit, they'd go that little bit further and come up with another astonishing feat. With the grand gallery, they totally excelled themselves.

Sooner or later we will have to raise the granite blocks of the upper chamber up to the top of the grand gallery and then raise the massive granite roofing slabs up and onto the structure known today as the 'King's chamber', the upper chamber. (The term 'King's chamber' is grossly misleading so I will refer to it as the upper chamber from now on.) We will also have to install those granite slabs and blocks in the stack above the upper chamber at a height in excess of 60 metres above the base of the pyramid. (The stack is the term I prefer to use for the granite slabs and blocks commonly known as the relieving chambers above the upper chamber.)

The largest of the granite blocks that make up the walls of the upper chamber are estimated to weigh around 70 tons with some of the roofing slabs thought to weigh around 50 tons. I have absolutely no doubts about how these blocks and slabs were raised up to the inner area of the Great Pyramid at the top of the grand gallery. I believe that it would have been impossible for men to haul blocks of this size and weight up to such an elevation on even the very slightest of gradients and utterly impossible on the 26 degree slope of the gallery. We do know that it was possible to get all of this granite up to the inner platform at the top of the grand gallery because that is where it is today and the gallery was the only possible route up to the inner platform at this stage of the construction. We just had to figure out how they did it.

Time after time, the builders of the Great Pyramid have shown that they applied brain over brawn, their approach to this little difficulty being no different to that of any other difficulty they encountered. In fact, they approached the problem of transporting the granite up to the inner platform in the same way that they had approached the transportation of the standard limestone blocks that make up the bulk of the structure. They applied their intellect and their engineering knowledge and prowess to the problem before employing the phenomenal power of water (hydraulic power) to transport these massive blocks of granite up to the top of the grand gallery. Although this may sound preposterous to you at first, and it certainly did to me when I first considered the possibility, I ask you to bear in mind that this has been their modus operandi so far. Why would they change it when faced with their greatest challenge?

Water was to those ancient builders what diesel or electricity is to modern man. It was the fuel that powered their ingenious contraptions. These people, whoever they were, must have realized long before the time of the 4th Dynastic Period that if they could tap into a pre-existing water source, or create a reservoir at an elevation above the level of their intended operations, they could exploit this most abundant resource and use it to power their machines and to transport goods. They undoubtedly used it for both transportation and lifting operations here at Giza, employing it to such great effect that their achievements here would not be equalled for millennia. It is very difficult to determine exactly when the pyramids at Giza were actually constructed and with so much misinformation published over many decades, it is now very difficult to separate fact from fiction. John Anthony West and others believe that the Sphinx and the pyramids at Giza are much older than Egyptologists believe them to be. Their beliefs are based on water weathering on the Sphinx and the Sphinx Enclosure. But one thing is for certain, vast quantities of water were needed to build the pyramids and most of the other structures on the Giza plateau. It was only by harnessing the phenomenal power of water – hydraulic power – that the pyramid builders were able to transport and raise such enormous blocks and slabs up to the level of the upper chamber and beyond. Hydraulic power was, quite simply, the only force on the planet capable of moving such enormous blocks of granite and vast quantities of water were needed in order to move these blocks.

It was not only the granite upper chamber and its multi-layered roof that had still to be constructed at this stage, as the builders had still to construct another very large part of the pyramid on top of all of this. They had almost 100 metres of the pyramid still to construct when they reached the floor level of the upper chamber.

In order to transport this vast amount of building material up to the level of the upper chamber and beyond, they constructed the grand gallery. This, the longest of the internal chambers, housed the escalator that was used to transport the building material coming into the pyramid up to the 49th level of the structure. This was undoubtedly the most inspired feature of their wonderful pyramid design (so far) and it effectively extended the supply canal all the way up to the top of the grand gallery when the inner platform had been completed up to the 49th course. This was why they had installed a pump in the Great Pyramid, because without a pump, it would have been impossible to extend these hydraulic operations beyond the level of the lower chamber.

When the builders had made all possible use of the hub down in the lower chamber, they needed to create a new hub at a higher elevation within the pyramid to extend the perimeter platform higher still. It was their intention to make use of the largest limestone blocks for as long as it was possible to do so in this construction, but sooner or later they would have to reduce the block size. However, the longer they could continue to use the larger blocks in the construction, the less time it would take to complete the structure. What they now needed was an escalator to transport the building materials up to the new hub that they would create on the 50th level of the inner platform (the floor level of the upper chamber). They created one in the grand gallery by constructing a flight of canal locks all the way up to the 50th level. The grand gallery was the vessel within which they constructed this flight of locks to transport the building materials up to the new hub, and somehow, they found a way to pump water up to the top of the gallery and into the top lock.

I've made this all sound so simple but it didn't all come to me as easily as that. I spent an awful lot of time going down blind alleys trying to discover how they got materials up to the top of the gallery. When I first suspected this as a possibility, I almost dismissed it immediately. Surely it was preposterous! Impossible! That was my first reaction as I'm sure it is yours at this moment. Believe me when I say that I tried to figure out an alternative method for months on end without success, for I truly thought that it was impossible to achieve such a feat.

When I could find no other possible explanations as to how they transported such enormous blocks of granite up to the top of the gallery, I began to wonder if there could be more passageways or chambers within the structure that we had not yet found; or could they have had another method of raising this material up to the top of the gallery – a mechanical contraption? These were my thoughts at the time but as time went by, I could make no progress with any of these ideas as they just didn't fit into the bigger picture. Everything pointed to the canal being extended up to the top of the gallery. Eventually, I realised that it was unlikely that the builders would have gone to all the trouble of constructing a tunnel and taking the canal all the way into the Great Pyramid if they'd had another means of lifting and moving such heavy blocks of granite – such as a mechanical device. We almost certainly would not see the internal features we see today within the Great Pyramid if this had been the case. They could have designed a much simpler internal structure if there had been no need to take the canal into the pyramid. In fact, there would have been no need for most of the chambers and passageways that they created within the structure. But they had gone to extreme lengths to ensure that water was available at each and every location within the structure where masonry had to be moved or lifted up to higher levels, and they had installed a pump. In the end, I could only conclude that they had constructed a series of locks up through the grand gallery and extended the canal all the way up to the inner platform on the 50th level of the structure. It was the only possibility left to explore, no matter how preposterous it seemed.

Everything pointed to this being the mode of transportation of the huge granite blocks in the upper chamber and it was certainly in keeping with the methods they had employed up to this stage of the construction. In truth, I'd come to realize that it was only hydraulic power that could possibly account for the transportation of these massive loads up to such an elevation. After all, they had used this resource to raise the barges and their loads up to the plateau. If this had been the only way to get these massive slabs and blocks onto the plateau, then I was certain that it would have been the only way to get these loads up to the top of the grand gallery. I then set about trying to find out how it had been done.

The main problem I had with this idea of a flight of locks within the gallery was the water supply. How was it possible to get water up to the top of the gallery to feed the locks? My reconstruction of the Great Pyramid was in serious danger of coming to an abrupt end at this stage of my quest, since no supply pipe that could possibly fit the bill had ever been discovered within the structure. There simply was no evidence to indicate that such a pipe existed. Even assuming that there was such a pipe, concealed and not yet discovered, where could it possibly be? Where in the hydraulic system was its inlet and outlet?

I realized that if there truly was a concealed pipe within the structure that had still to be discovered, I could not progress beyond this point as I could no longer provide the hard evidence to show how each and every operation had been executed. I needed to be able to prove conclusively that the Great Pyramid had been constructed from the inside, as I have been able to do up to this stage of our reconstruction. I simply had to prove that the builders were capable of transporting the massive granite blocks through the tunnel and up to the top of the grand gallery for it was the only possible route to the inner platform at this stage of the construction. But if the pyramid builder's greatest achievement so far could not be explained, my quest would have come to an end for I would never have considered publishing an incomplete account of how the Great Pyramid had been constructed. I felt both deflated and defeated. I began to think that I might have to wait until the water supply pipe was discovered before I could continue with my project and goodness knows how long that would be... if ever. It certainly didn't look as if it would be any time soon.

This was a difficult time for me and although my quest had come to a dead end, I could not get this problem out of my head when I knew for certain that this was the route the builders had taken. The possibility that they could have pumped the water to supply the locks up to the top of the gallery by the same route seemed so ridiculous that I hadn't given it a second thought. But I was desperate now. My whole project hung in the balance and I simply had to explore each and every possibility no matter how ridiculous it might at first seem. When I did finally discover how they'd managed to pump water up to the top of the grand gallery, I walked around for days afterwards with a great big grin on my face every time I thought of it. I had completely underestimated their ingenuity. They truly were master builders and designers of the highest order. They *had* achieved the impossible!

This was my eureka moment; not because I'd discovered how they'd pumped water up to the top of the gallery, although I was delighted I had done so, no, the instant I realized how they'd achieved the impossible and created the escalator in the grand gallery it confirmed that they had gone all the way to the top of the Great Pyramid by this very same route. There simply was no other route to the top.

I know, it sounds crazy. It sounded crazy to me. But I'm sure you'll have realized by now that if it were possible to complete the pyramid by this route, these extraordinary builders would have worked out how to do it. In theory it was possible. However, at this point in time I was having great difficulty trying to understand how many of the features constructed on the 49th level at the top of the gallery had been put together, and more importantly, the order of their construction, for this was not at all clear. Eventually, I'd have to work out how they pulled off this amazing feat but I had still to work out the finer details of how the builders got the granite blocks for the upper chamber and the antechamber up to the top of the gallery and the order of their installation. That was all that was on my mind at that point. As to how the builders completed the pyramid that would have to wait until later.

The corbelling in the grand gallery of the Great Pyramid, set at the same angle as its floor, provided the overhangs or step-outs that bolstered the wooden uprights of the locks constructed in the gallery. By setting these outward steps in the sidewalls of the gallery at the same angle as its floor (the ramp), the timber uprights of the locks could be wedged under, and bolstered by, the overhanging limestone blocks. When each timber upright was inserted into its socket on the edge of the ramp with one side of the upright against the sidewall, the top end of the hardwood upright would have been wedged under the overhang (the step out of the corbelling). The pressure of the water pushing against the lock gates on the upside when the lock was in use would only have served to wedge the uprights tighter against the 26 degree slope of the corbelling that bolstered them. The lower ends of the uprights were anchored in the sockets on the outer edges of the ramps at the base of the sidewalls and the uprights would also have been bolstered by the wooden beams that were laid across the ramps and made up the floor of each lock. But the top ends of the uprights could not be fitted into a socket, so the builders opted for the next best option and used the angled corbelling to bolster them.

The builders had to create a very robust flight of locks within the gallery to transport such heavy granite blocks and slabs up to the level of the upper chamber. Space was at a premium, for there was very little clearance on either side of the barges as they passed through these locks. A heavy timber structure was therefore out of the question. They could, of course, have made the gallery itself a bit wider to accommodate heavy timber uprights but that could have compromised the stability of the structure as a whole. They didn't have the option of blocking up this inner space when it was no longer required as they did with the entrance tunnel therefore the only solution here was to keep the width of the gallery to an absolute minimum. By setting the corbelling at the same angle as the floor, they could keep the width of the gallery to a minimum by wedging the uprights of the locks under the overhangs of the corbelling to bolster them. This enabled them to create a lightweight but strong framework to support the lock gates in the gallery.

If you take a look at the photograph of the walls of the grand gallery on the guardians website (www.guardians.net), you can clearly see that the corbelling in the walls has sustained some damage (as have other parts of the internal structure). Nearly all of the damage here was sustained during the construction of the pyramid and it was most likely caused by the application of extreme pressure on the uprights of the locks and failure of the corbelling. Almost all of this damage can be attributed to the great pressure exerted on the corbelling by the great weight of water in the locks acting on the lock gates as the massive granite monoliths were transported up through the gallery to the inner platform. That is the only logical conclusion that can be drawn now that we know the true purpose of the grand gallery.

The grand gallery had been constructed in such a way that it would contain both the locks and the water supply pipe to deliver the head of water to the top lock in the series at each and every stage of their construction. And the elusive water supply pipe? Well, that was the slot up the middle of the floor in the gallery between the ramps. When the wooden floor was installed in each lock as the flight of locks was extended up through the gallery, this water pipe was extended also. The water pipe was incorporated into the floor of the grand gallery and when the pump was operated, water was pumped up the descending corridor, then on up through the ascending corridor and finally, on up through the channel under the wooden floor in the gallery until it spilled out into the top lock. That is why the ascending corridor was aligned with the slot in the floor of the gallery, as the slot was converted to a pipe by the installation of the wooden floor in the gallery. The slot simply became an extension of the existing supply pipe (the ascending corridor) at that stage of the construction. In the drawing below (Fig. 9) we can see how the structure would have looked at this stage of the construction.

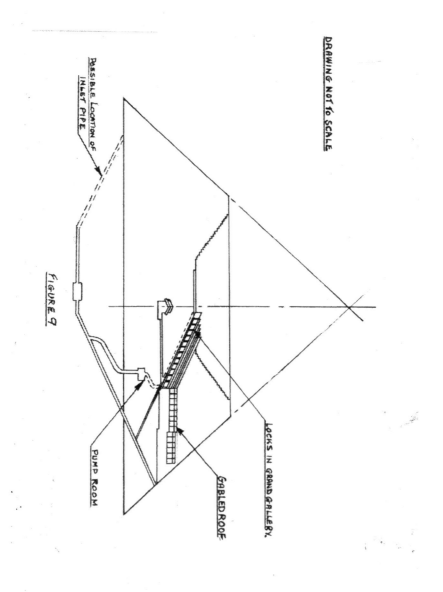

We are all familiar with the most prominent features of the grand gallery, the corbelling, the ramps and the slot in the floor and the step-stone at the top end of the gallery. Yet there are other, more obscure, features within this chamber that also had a role to play when the locks in the gallery were in use. Indeed, I was totally unaware of some of these features until I read *The Great Pyramid Decoded,* by Peter Lemesurier. I'm glad that I came across this book for two features mentioned in it explain more than any other how the locks in the gallery were operated and how they functioned.

The lock gates in the gallery would have consisted of a number of heavy wooden planks laid horizontally which were probably fixed to two or three vertical battens. The lock gates would have been lowered into position against the topside of the uprights along the sides of the gallery. Only two lock gates were required in the gallery and these gates were first moved up the slope behind the load carrying barges, and then moved down through the gallery again ahead of the empty barges as they made their way back down through the flight of locks.

A number of pulleys and ropes were also needed for the lifting mechanism that was installed in the gallery. These ropes were used to both raise and lower the lock gates, and to move the gates from station to station as each barge progressed up and down the flight of locks in the gallery. The lock gates were moved only one station at a time, there are 28 in all, with the leading gate being moved forward by one station as soon as the water levels had equalized, followed by the trailing gate being moved by one station. This was the case no matter which direction the barges were progressing.

There were no manually operated sluices in these locks but there was a constant trickle of water from the locks into the canal system to ensure that the water level in the system was maintained when the lock gates in the gallery were closed for a period of time. As I discovered in *The Great Pyramid Decoded,* the builders had ensured that there was always a constant flow of water bypassing the locks as they had cut relieves in the walls of the gallery behind the lock uprights. A small but steady flow of water was continually released from the locks through these relieves.

The other feature of the gallery that had a major role to play when the locks were in use were the 15cm wide channels that run the full length of the gallery just above the third step-out in the sidewalls. I hadn't been aware of either of these features in the grand gallery until I read *The Great Pyramid Decoded,* and it was only when I came across these 15cm wide channels in Peter Lemesurier's book that I fully realized how the lock gates had been operated. I discovered the true purpose of these channels (sorry Peter, they did not support a sliding floor). Each lock gate in the gallery was in fact suspended from a carriage (Fig. 10d) and both of these carriages travelled the length of the gallery, most probably on rollers, although it is possible that the carriages may just have been slotted into these channels. The carriages were cranked up and down these channels as the lock gates were moved from station to station in the gallery. The winding mechanisms would have been installed at the inner end of the entrance tunnel just beyond the lower end of the gallery, which was open-ended when the locks in the gallery were in use. Two other winding mechanisms were also installed at this location and these would have been used to raise and lower the lock gates.

The smallest and lightest blocks to be transported up to the top of the gallery were the limestone blocks that comprised the great bulk of the material transported by this route. It's likely that a number of these blocks would have been loaded onto each barge, I have therefore shown a barge loaded with these blocks making its way up through the gallery in the drawing (Fig. 10) on the next page. I have produced three drawings to indicate the sequence of events as barges made their way up to the top end of the gallery. You will see from the first drawing (Fig. 10a) that the upper lock gate has been raised slightly so that water can flow into the lower lock. The water levels have equalised here at the maximum level and the load carrying barge has been manoeuvred forward until its trailing end is beyond the next station. The upper lock gate can now be raised and moved to the next station.

In the second drawing (Fig. 10b), the upper lock gate has been lowered into position two stations beyond the lower gate and the lower gate has now been raised slightly, releasing the water from this lock. In the next drawing (Fig. 10c) the lower lock gate has been moved forward one station and lowered into position. With this lock gate in position, the upper lock gate is then raised slightly to let the water levels in the locks equalise and water is then pumped up into the upper lock to increase the water level. When the water level has been increased to the point where the barge can be manoeuvred forward, well beyond the next station, the upper lock gate can be

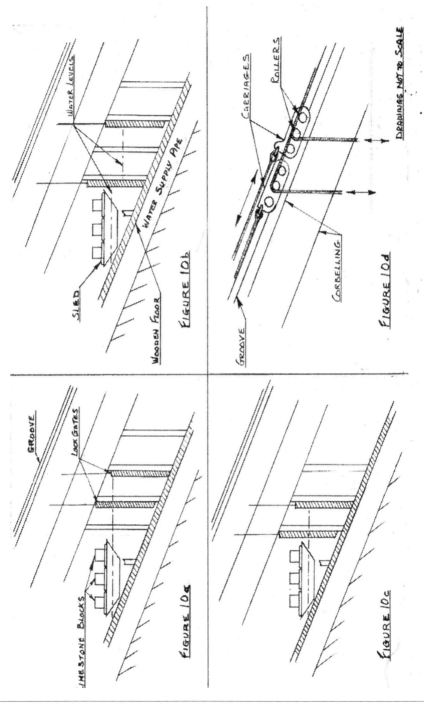

WATER LEVELS

SLED

WOODEN FLOOR

WATER SUPPLY PIPE

FIGURE 10b

CARRIAGES

ROLLERS

DRAWINGS NOT TO SCALE

CORBELLING

GROOVE

FIGURE 10d

GROOVE

LOCK GATES

LIMESTONE BLOCKS

FIGURE 10a

FIGURE 10c

fully raised and the whole sequence repeated again and again until the barge finally reaches the top end of the gallery.

Earlier, I mentioned the carriages from which the lock gates were suspended. These carriages could be moved longitudinally up and down the slope of the gallery. The gates were also lowered and raised from the carriages and this vertical movement was controlled by winding mechanisms. However, as the width of the gallery becomes narrower due to the corbelling in its walls, the lock gates would never have been raised until their undersides were above the tops of the lock uprights on the sidewalls, as the corbelling would almost certainly have prevented the gates from being hoisted up far enough to clear the top of the uprights. But the gates did not need to be hauled up such a distance as they had only to be hauled up far enough to be moved to the next station. Once the bottom of the lock gate had been hauled up beyond the floor level of the next station, its carriage would have been cranked slowly forward. The lock gate, however, would have been pulled towards the barge at one end as the carriage was being slowly cranked forward, until the leading edge of the gate was well beyond the uprights of the next station (it was pulled through the gap at an angle to the uprights). Having got the leading edge of the gate beyond the uprights, the trailing end of the lock gate would then have been pulled towards the barge until the gate was beyond both uprights. When the bargees then released their grip on the ropes, the lock gate would have settled back against the upside of the uprights at the forward station, it would then have been lowered until it bottomed on the (wooden) floor of the lock / gallery. More water would then have been pumped up into the top lock and the barge manoeuvred forward to the next station.

As I have previously mentioned, the corbelling in the lower levels of the grand gallery has sustained considerable damage; this damage is entirely consistent with the limestone overhangs (corbels) failing due to too much pressure being exerted on them by the uprights of the locks (the greatest damage has occurred directly above some of the sockets for the uprights). It is probable that the builders would have foreseen that a certain amount of damage was likely to be incurred here over the period when most of the granite masonry was being transported up to the top of the gallery. They may have tried to limit this damage by placing long wooden beams under the step-outs and wedged the lock uprights under these beams. This would have spread the load and afforded some protection to the limestone step-out just above the lock uprights. When the corbelling above one of the sockets failed, the lock uprights at that station could have been bolstered by heavy wooden struts placed against the lower end of the uprights in the station just below the failed lock. These struts would have been checked into the back of the lock uprights at the failed station to bolster them.

It is patently obvious that some of the corbelling in the gallery did fail, but equally obvious that the builders went on to complete the upper chamber and the upper sections of the Great Pyramid. This confirms that the builders designed a system of locks here that was extremely fit for purpose and more than capable of enduring the tremendous pressures placed on it when granite monoliths weighing up to seventy tons were being transported up to the inner area beyond the gallery.

Visitors who venture inside the Great Pyramid today and ascend the grand gallery will notice the series of vertical slots cut down into the side ramps; there are 28 pairs of slots in all. These slots are the sockets that the timber uprights of the locks were placed in. When the uprights were put in place, the top ends of the uprights would have been wedged under the overhang of the corbelling in the walls of the gallery. After the first pair of these uprights had been installed, broad timber beams were laid across the floor of the gallery (the ramps) creating a wooden floor in the lock. This floor was installed one lock at a time as the inner platform and the floor of the gallery was gradually built up. The timber beams of the wooden floor would also have bolstered the lower ends of the wooden uprights.

As each lock was completed, water was pumped up the channel underneath the wooden floor of the lock and into the top lock and the inner area where the platforms in the centre of the structure were being built up. This was a continuation of the method they had used earlier to flood the ponds and feed the canal and its locks at the earliest stages of the construction. Once again, masonry was being delivered by barge directly to the location where it was to be installed within the structure. The only difference at this stage of the construction was that the canal itself was being pushed higher within the structure now, and it was extended up to each new level as it was created. As the elevation of the inner platform increased and the ramps of the grand gallery were extended, another lock was created. It was only when the inner platform had reached the 49th

level and the last of the locks had been installed at the top of the escalator, that the builders were (almost) ready to begin the construction of the upper chamber. Before we move on to the construction of the upper chamber, let us take a look at the cut-away drawing again (Fig. 9) showing the construction as it now stands.

The topmost levels that form the perimeter platform around the top of the pyramid as it stands have not been extended any farther since we last looked at the reconstruction. We have been unable to build the perimeter platform any higher during this last phase of the construction when we were building up the inner platform to the 49th level. The perimeter platform will be extended farther from the hub that we will set up in the upper chamber, but that won't be for some time yet, as we have a lot more work to do in this area at the top of the gallery before we can set up the hub in this chamber.

We have been using the pump to pump water up the pipe under the gallery floor to the top lock in the gallery and into the inner area in order to continue with the transportation of the limestone blocks to all sectors of this inner platform. However, water could only be pumped up into the locks and the inner area under the right conditions. Earlier we discovered that the shafts in the sidewalls of the lower chamber had been sealed in order to make the chamber air and watertight. If these shafts hadn't been sealed, then the pump would have been unable to pump very much water up the pipe in the gallery floor, as each time the pump was operated, some of the water being pumped up the ascending corridor would have been pumped along the horizontal passageway and into the lower chamber, then into the shafts in the chamber walls. With a sealed chamber however, the air pressure in the chamber would have been greatly increased as water was forced into the chamber on the downward stroke of the piston. But as the piston in the pump reached the end of its stroke, and the pressure pushing the water along the horizontal passageway suddenly dropped, the increased air pressure in the lower chamber would have reacted to this sudden drop in pressure. The sudden decrease in the water pressure would have generated a pressure wave in the opposite direction as the increased air pressure in the chamber pushed the water in the chamber back down to its mean level. Work on the inner platform would not have progressed very far if the shafts in the lower chamber had not been sealed up, as the chamber had to be air and watertight so that the water pressure was maintained in the pipes that supplied the water to the locks in the gallery. This secondary pressure wave that was generated in the lower chamber as the water level was suddenly and violently pushed back down to the mean level, greatly improved the efficiency of the pumping operation. This secondary pressure wave would have travelled up the water pipe under the floor of the gallery and more water would have been pumped up into the locks in the gallery with each stroke of the pump as a result. The volume of water being pumped up to the top lock with each stroke of the pump was therefore greatly increased by the action of the secondary pressure wave that was generated in the lower chamber. This pressure wave delayed the closure of the non-return valve in the water supply pipe and made the pump much more efficient as a result.

The installation of the 49th course of limestone on the inner platform brought about a change in the pattern of the construction because it was on this level that the builders began the construction of the granite upper chamber (the 49th course is the course immediately below the granite floor of the upper chamber). The builders had created a square sided bowl in the centre of the pyramid with the sidewalls of this bowl stepping upwards and outwards from the 49th level, all the way up to the perimeter platform of the structure above the 70th course of masonry. The grand gallery was almost complete now and the locks within it had been extended up to the top of the gallery as the inner platform and the walls of the gallery had been built up. However, it is in fact only fair to say that most of the inner platform had been constructed up to the 49th level at this stage, since, as you can see from the drawing (Fig. 9) the area directly below where the granite floor of the upper chamber and the antechamber would be installed had not been completed on this level; it ended on the 48th course of the structure. We will discover why this was so when we begin to transport the large granite blocks that form the walls of the upper chamber up to the top of the gallery.

The upper chamber

The upper chamber of the Great Pyramid is constructed entirely of granite and the antechamber is almost completely made of granite. The granite blocks in the walls of the upper chamber are around twice the height of the limestone blocks in the courses that surround it. The builders would therefore have had to raise the surrounding inner platform by two courses each time they installed one course of the walls of the upper chamber. This would have provided the builders with a working platform around most of the granite structure when they came to install the next course of the chamber's walls. I should point out here that although most of the limestone blocks used in the construction of the lower sections of the Great Pyramid were generally much larger than most of those blocks used in the construction of the upper section of the structure, blocks of differing sizes were used to build up the platforms of the structure throughout the construction in order to accommodate some internal features of the structure. In general, the average size of the blocks used to construct the bulk of the structure below the one hundredth course was much larger than the average size of the blocks used in the construction of the courses above this level.

When I first began to reconstruct the walls of the upper chamber and the antechamber, I got into all sorts of difficulties before I realized that I had not given nearly enough thought as to the difficulties the builders faced at this stage of the construction. We have so far discovered how the construction of the Great Pyramid was far removed from the simple method of putting one course on top of another until it was complete. Indeed, the construction process was just as complex as the inner structure of the pyramid itself. But I had grossly underestimated just how complex the building process became at this stage, accepting that the reason for this was that I didn't understand the order of construction of the chambers and features – I didn't know in what order they had been utilized. I knew what purpose each of these chambers had served but I hadn't figured out *when* they had been used for their intended purpose. This became abundantly clear to me when I realized that the antechamber could not have been constructed in conjunction with the upper chamber, as I'd previously assumed. Rather than go into the reason for this now, let us get on with the reconstruction of the upper chamber, as it will soon become clear why the antechamber could not be installed at this stage as we build up this structure.

Looking back, it should have been obvious to us a very long time ago that the heavier granite slabs and blocks used within the Great Pyramid could only have been transported by this means. After all, if the idea that the bulk of the limestone was transported up to the top of the pyramids using earth ramps seemed ridiculous, how could we possibly accept that the much heavier granite blocks and slabs (some more than twenty five times heavier than the average limestone blocks) were transported by this same method. But when we had no idea how the Giza pyramids had been constructed, it was the views of those who professed to know how the pyramids had been constructed that was promoted by the media of the day.

The granite blocks that make up the walls of the upper chamber are all the same height and depth (with one exception). If you take a look at the photographs of the upper chamber in the Great Pyramid on the guardians.net website, you will see that the lowest blocks in the walls appear shorter than those in the four courses above. This is simply because the granite walls of the upper chamber were built up from the 49th course of limestone masonry, then the granite floor was installed within the chamber walls on that same limestone base. It is the raised floor that makes the lower course of granite blocks in the chamber walls appear to be shorter.

This floor could not have been installed before the lower courses of the walls had been put in place as this would have made it impossible to install the walls of the chamber. I eventually realized that I had gone wrong with my first attempt to reconstruct the upper chamber as I had completed the 49th level of the inner platform all the way out to the top of the gallery. I had failed to realize that the builders would have ensured that these very large blocks of granite were offloaded from the barges as close as possible to their respective final positions within the structure. It would have taken an almighty effort by the workforce to move the largest of these blocks the smallest distance. Therefore, I am 100% certain that the builders would have brought the barges alongside the ledges on which the granite blocks for the walls of the chamber were to be installed before the blocks were transferred onto the limestone foundation course on the 49th level. In order to do this, they could not have completed the 49th level of limestone beneath the floor of the chamber and the antechamber until the first course of the upper chamber walls had been installed.

The other reason why they installed the granite floor in the chamber after most of the walls of the upper chamber were complete was all to do with levels. The builders hoisted a large quantity of limestone masonry up onto the lower sidewalls of the upper chamber after it was almost complete (just as they had done in the lower chamber) and this masonry was then hoisted up ramps on either side of this chamber to build up the stepped inner levels and extend the perimeter platform. The upper chamber that we are now in the process of reconstructing will therefore become our next hub and from here the existing perimeter platform and the inner stepped levels will be extended farther. The builders used the same lifting mechanism in the upper chamber to hoist the masonry up onto its sidewalls as they had used previously in the lower chamber. This device could not lift the limestone blocks much higher than the height of three average courses of limestone masonry in the chamber below (1.5 courses of granite masonry). The courses of granite used in the walls of the upper chamber are on average twice as high as the limestone blocks used to construct the walls of the lower chamber. So the builders installed the granite slabs that make up the floor of the upper chamber on the same limestone base as the walls of the chamber and this reduced the distance from the floor to the landings in the sidewalls to approximately one and one half courses of granite, approximately the same height as three courses of the average sized limestone blocks. The distance from the floor to the ledges on the sidewalls of the upper chamber then corresponded to the approximate distance from the floor of the lower chamber to the ledges on its sidewalls, just under the maximum height the lifting mechanism could handle. We will take a good look at this lifting mechanism when we press it into service later.

It all gets extremely complicated now. As we build up the walls of the upper chamber, we have to bring much, but not all, of the inner platform around the chamber up another ten courses to the 59th level. These will provide the working platforms around the chamber as the granite courses are built up, five in total. We also have to complete the walls and roof of the grand gallery as we build up the inner area around the upper chamber. As we build up the inner area on the north and south sides of the upper chamber we will also need to create two ramps, one on either side of the chamber. We will use these ramps to build up the inner stepped levels and extend them further as we push the perimeter platform up to a much greater elevation from the upper chamber.

The order of construction

When I first began to reconstruct the upper chamber and the antechamber, I tried to do it the simple way by placing one block on top of the other and working from the south wall of the upper chamber back towards the top end of the grand gallery. I soon realized that it could not have been done that way originally as I discovered that there were many more factors that I should have considered before I began my reconstruction of the upper chamber. The enormous weight of many of the granite blocks and the roof slabs made this by far the most difficult part of the whole construction. The complexity of this granite structure also greatly increased the degree of difficulty as a way had to be found to get all the granite blocks and slabs to their final locations with the minimum of physical effort. No small task. It required such a tremendous effort on the part of the builders to move some of these enormous granite blocks and slabs the smallest distance that every effort would have been made to keep those distances to an absolute minimum. In most instances, so far, the builders had used water power to eliminate or reduce the amount of physical effort required. We have extended the canal system as far as the top of the grand gallery now and logic tells us that there has to be a limit as to how far we can extend the canal. In short, we have now reached the stage of our reconstruction where we have to transport and install the largest and heaviest blocks and slabs in the structure, and yet this has come at the point where the main driver of the project so far – water power – looks as if it is going to be of very limited use from here on in. So how did the ancient pyramid builders construct this granite edifice?

It's odd how things pan out sometimes. As I was wrestling with the problem of how to reconstruct this seemingly overcomplicated structure (the upper chamber) I suddenly realized the true reason for its construction and, needless to say, why it was so ridiculously complicated. My initial theory about it being constructed to push the next stage of the construction forward at a greater pace was only partially true, as I now realized that this whole pyramid design and all of its internal corridors, chambers and passageways that we have reconstructed so far, had been configured in the way that they were, in order to enable the builders to construct this very complex granite structure at the top of the grand gallery.

I realize that this statement may sound somewhat ridiculous at this stage of our reconstruction but it had suddenly become clear to me that the canal system was the only possible way to raise the monstrous granite blocks and slabs of the upper chamber and the stack up to such a tremendous elevation within the Great Pyramid. Having accepted that almost all of the internal features of the pyramid had been designed to extend the canal system up to the top of the grand gallery in order to transport these huge blocks and slabs up to the inner area, I also realized that this was not the sole reason for the extension of the canal up to this level. We must therefore not overlook the true reason for the existence of the upper chamber at this elevation. This complex structure evolved purely because of the need to transport a much greater proportion of the largest limestone blocks, those that we have used to reconstruct the bulk of the pyramid so far, into the largest pyramid that had ever been constructed using blocks of this size. The extension of the canal up to the top of the grand gallery not only enabled the builders to construct the upper chamber, it also enabled them to transport many more of the large limestone blocks up and into the upper chamber when it functioned as a hub. The lifting device in the chamber raised this limestone masonry up onto the ledges on either side of the chamber, and from there they were hauled up to the inner stepped levels and the perimeter platforms to extend the perimeter platform to the greatest elevation possible using these large limestone blocks. The greater the elevation that these blocks could be hauled up to, the more stable the structure was likely to be and the more robust its outer casing would be. But the greatest benefit of all would come from the time saved. By creating the upper chamber, the builders were not only able to push the perimeter platforms higher using large limestone blocks, it also enabled them to construct much of the inner area around the upper chamber using these large limestone blocks. However, in order to be able to do this, they had to postpone the installation of the gabled roof that had to go on top of the upper chamber until a much later stage of the construction; hence the reason for the stack above the upper chamber.

This was a very different situation to what we had encountered down in the lower chamber. There, we had begun to haul masonry up ramps from the chamber when only a few courses of its walls had been completed; the chamber itself was not completed until this central distribution hub had ceased to function as such. But this was not the case with the upper chamber as this structure and the tiered stack above it was almost complete before it was used as a distribution hub. This granite structure was a free-standing structure constructed on the 49th level of the inner platform before it was used as a central distribution hub and the reasons for this will become clear as we make further progress.

Anyone standing on the plateau today at a suitable distance, can't help but notice that the topmost section of both large pyramids are constructed of smaller blocks than those in their lower sections. This is particularly obvious in the middle pyramid as it has managed to retain much of its smooth outer facing blocks at these higher levels. This boundary marks the point where the builders could push the perimeter platform no higher from the hub in the upper chamber using the large blocks of limestone used to construct the bulk of the lower sections of the structure; or, if you prefer, the point at which the builders had to revert to using much smaller limestone blocks to complete the pyramid for reasons that will become clear later.

The design of the granite structure at the heart of the Great Pyramid could only have come about after a tremendous effort on behalf of the architects to devise a structure that would enable them to build such a large pyramid within a given timeframe. It was born out of a desire to revolutionize pyramid design to the point where it was possible to build monsters like the Great Pyramid – and its immediate neighbour – by employing all of the technology at their disposal to reduce the time it took to construct them. The upper chamber was the last great feature to be designed that finally made it possible to push these limestone structures much higher by utilising the canal system to transport more material into these pyramids than had ever been done before, and raising those very large blocks of masonry up to a much greater elevation than had ever been achieved before. The stack above the chamber came into being because at some point the designers realized that they could not install a gabled roof on the upper chamber as there was simply nothing to support it over some of its length. They solved this problem by postponing the installation of the gabled roof until it was possible to put it in place at a much higher level; the stack was born.

Granite was the only material strong enough to span across the width of the upper chamber although it wasn't strong enough to support any great weight, certainly not the weight of the structure above. That is why the roof is extended upwards in the manner that it is, since the tremendous weight above the flat roof of the chamber is supported by the walls of the chamber and the spacing blocks in the stack, not the granite roofing slabs. But in using granite for the roof and the stack, they greatly increased the weight that the walls of the chamber had to bear; limestone wasn't robust enough to support this tremendous load. In the end, the whole of the structure that comprised the upper chamber and the stack had to be constructed entirely of granite for it was the only material robust enough for the purpose. This was another phenomenal achievement as I'm sure you will agree when you discover just what they had to do to make it happen.

Something that is most noticeable about the upper chamber is that it has a much larger internal space than the lower chamber. The width of the upper chamber is the same as that of the lower chamber at 5.45 metres, but the length of the upper chamber is almost double the length of the lower chamber, at 11.5 metres. This puzzled me for a long time until I discovered that, unlike the lower chamber, the upper chamber was almost complete when the builders began to use it as a distribution hub. In fact, there was no lower chamber when a distribution hub had first been set up; it was just a depression in the floor at the centre of the pyramid when limestone was first routed through it. The upper chamber, on the other hand, was a free-standing, granite edifice constructed in the heart of the structure on the 49th course of limestone. When limestone was being routed through this chamber, its walls were almost complete except for a few small granite blocks in its north and south walls, the gaps through which the limestone masonry was hauled. These blocks could only be installed after the chamber had ceased to be a distribution hub and there was only one place to store these granite blocks until it came time to install them. Yes, you've guessed it; they had to be temporarily stored within the chamber when the lifting mechanism was in operation. This was the reason why the upper chamber was longer than the lower chamber; space had to be found for these blocks as well as the lifting mechanism within the upper chamber when it functioned as a distribution hub. The granite blocks stored within the chamber at this time were to be slotted into the openings in the sidewalls of the chamber when the builders ceased to use the chamber as a distribution hub and when the ramps were no longer needed. However, as these blocks had to be installed from inside the chamber, space was also needed for the storage of the barge that was used to raise these blocks up to the required level within the chamber before their installation. This is the reason why the upper chamber is much longer than the lower chamber.

The two horizontal shafts in the north and south walls of the upper chamber were extended back into the limestone blocks behind the granite walls as the inner platform was built up around the chamber. These shafts were then extended up through the courses of limestone when the inner stepped levels and the ramps were later built up. The shafts (water pipes) in the upper chamber were extended up to a much greater elevation than the shafts of the lower chamber simply because they were part of the infrastructure that supported the extension of the perimeter platform to its maximum elevation. The angles at which the shafts and ramps were extended up through the pyramid here differ from those of the lower chamber and from each other. There has been much speculation regarding these shafts, but I now find it difficult to believe they were designed for any purpose other than the practical one to which they were put. We now know that all four of these shafts were used to supply water to the ramps and platforms on either side of the lower and upper chambers when the perimeter platforms were under construction. This water was used as a lubricant on the ramps and on the platforms of the upper structure. The two shafts in the lower chamber are at an almost identical angle to one another, simply because the lower chamber is situated right slap bang on the east-west axis of the structure (see Fig. 9). The upper chamber is situated much further south of the east-west axis and therefore the angles of the shafts, if they had been calculated to reach the outside edge of the pyramid on the same course as one another, had to differ, simply because the upper chamber did not straddle the east-west axis of the pyramid. This I believe to be the only determining factor in calculating the degree of incline of the shafts and the ramps.

There was good reason as to why the upper chamber was set much farther south of the east-west axis than the lower chamber. If the builders had wanted to place the upper chamber directly under the centre of the pyramid, as they had done with the lower chamber, they could easily have done so, but it would have been at a much lower elevation, since the grand gallery could not have been extended nearly as far if its 26 degree angle had been maintained. The gallery would therefore have been much shorter. (The slot in the floor of the grand gallery was an extension of the ascending corridor and it was set at 26 degrees to the horizontal.) This statement probably doesn't make much sense until you realize that the antechamber had to be positioned between the gallery and the upper chamber near the east-west axis, with the antechamber having to be constructed at the greatest elevation possible. The reason for this will become clear when we begin to construct the antechamber. There is some distance between the north wall of the upper chamber and the south wall of the antechamber as these chambers were not simply constructed on either side of a dividing wall. The upper chamber was positioned a bit farther south than the south wall of the antechamber, and once again, there was good reason for this and we will soon discover why.

The granite blocks used in the construction of the lowest course of the upper chamber were transported up to the top of the gallery, then through the channel where the 49th level had yet to be completed. The whole area of the 49th level below the granite floor in the upper chamber had yet to be completed at this stage and the barges would therefore have gone through the channel and into the canal basin created on the 48th level of the structure. The barges would then have been manoeuvred right up to the edge of the limestone platform.

The builders created a canal basin where the floor of the chamber would later be installed, the barges could therefore be brought alongside the ledges of the 49th limestone level and their cargo discharged directly onto the limestone foundation. The whole point of the grand gallery was to extend the canal system up to the greatest possible elevation within the structure. The more masonry that could be transported into the structure in bulk shipments, the less time it would take to construct the pyramid. But it was not just the speed at which these blocks were transported into the pyramid that was responsible for the great reduction in the time it took to construct such a pyramid, the great size of most of the limestone and granite blocks transported in this way also contributed greatly to the reduction in the construction time. As we have now also discovered, the builders took the canal system beyond the limits of the grand gallery when they established the lower course of the walls of the upper chamber. This was only made possible because they had not completed the 49th course of limestone on the inner platform when they transported these first granite blocks into this area. There are however, five courses of granite blocks, one hundred in all that make up the walls of this chamber. Was it possible that they could have extended the canal up to an even greater elevation?

The construction of the upper chamber

The first course of the upper chamber walls would have been the most difficult to put in place. At first I had assumed that the granite blocks had been hauled from the barges in the top lock directly onto the 49th level (the one metre deep granite step at the top of the grand gallery hadn't been installed at that stage of the construction). It would have taken a tremendous effort to get each of those granite blocks from the landing at the top of the gallery to their final locations within the structure as the upper chamber was some distance from the opening at the top of the grand gallery. It was while I was pondering this problem that I realized I'd made a mistake in completing the 49th course of limestone all the way out to the top of the gallery. I realized that the section of the 49th level beneath the floor of the upper chamber and beneath the antechamber could only have been completed after the installation of the first course of granite blocks (that form the walls of the upper chamber) had been installed. By postponing the installation of this section of the 49th level and leaving a channel on this level open, it made it possible for the builders to manoeuvre the barges from the top lock in the gallery through into the area where the upper chamber was to be constructed. These barges would have been brought alongside the limestone ledges on the far side of the chamber from the gallery and the granite blocks would then have been transferred from the decks of the barges on to the limestone foundation level. The absolute minimum of physical effort would have been needed to put each of these granite blocks of the first course of the upper chamber in place, as each block would have been transferred from the barge as near as possible to its final position on the ledge.

When the first course of the south wall was complete, the builders would then have established the lower course of the west wall and established both of its corners before working their way back along the north wall to the end nearest the channel and the top of the gallery. The lower course of the east wall would then have been established.

Almost all of the granite blocks in the lower course of the north wall were installed on the ledges at this time, but not all. The reason for this will soon become clear. The walls of the antechamber could not be established at this time as a clear passage through to the area within and around the walls of the upper chamber had to be maintained for now, at least until they had constructed much more of this free-standing granite structure. In fact, a great many operations were undertaken in this area just beyond the top end of the gallery and the north wall of the upper chamber before the antechamber was established. The granite blocks that comprise the upper chamber walls, one hundred in all, are not all the same length; some of them are quite short while others are as long as half the length of the chamber. However, they are all the same height and depth with the exception of one massive block, the granite block above the entrance to the chamber, the lintel, which is in fact twice as high as all the others. The position and size of this double depth block speaks volumes as to how the walls of the upper chamber were constructed. This block could not be put in place at this stage of the construction for the simple reason that a gap was needed in the north wall of the chamber for the transportation of masonry into the chamber. Most of the granite blocks that make up the walls of the upper chamber were transported through this gap and into the area within the chamber walls before being transferred from the barges onto the top of the granite blocks already in place.

If we just take a few minutes to familiarize ourselves with the layout of this area at the top of the grand gallery, it should give us a better idea as to how we will proceed from here. You will see from the drawing of the upper chamber on the page opposite (Fig. 11) that it seems to stand quite far back from the top end of the gallery (the drawing does not clearly indicate the true distance) but the antechamber has still to be constructed in the space between the top of the gallery and the upper chamber. When we put the walls of the antechamber in place, the passageway through this chamber will link the top end of the gallery with the upper chamber. However, it is only this gap between the top of the gallery and the upper chamber that provides access to the inner area for the barges, so it will be some time before we can block this route to the inner area and the upper chamber by constructing the antechamber in this space.

You will see that I have drawn dotted lines indicating where the position of the entry passageway into the upper chamber will be when we have completed the chamber. You can clearly see from the drawing that the east wall of the passageway (the east wall of the antechamber) is aligned with the inner east wall of the upper chamber. Looking at the drawing we can also get a much better idea of how the limestone blocks to complete the 49th level of the inner platform, and the granite slabs to complete the floor of the upper chamber, were transported into the chamber and installed. In fact, by

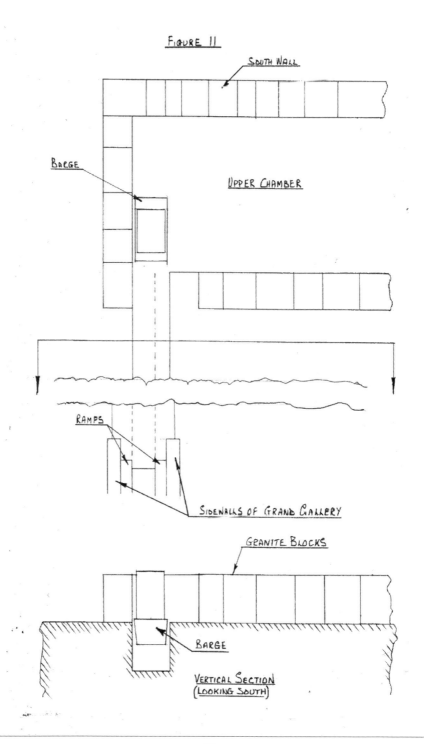

FIGURE 11

SOUTH WALL

BARGE

UPPER CHAMBER

RAMPS

SIDEWALKS OF GRAND GALLERY

GRANITE BLOCKS

BARGE

VERTICAL SECTION
(LOOKING SOUTH)

postponing the installation of the double depth block above the passageway, the lintel, until the very last moment you can see that we can take most of the barges with the limestone blocks and granite flooring slabs forward, from the lock at the top of the gallery, right into the chamber. By postponing the installation of the double depth lintel block, the builders were able to complete most of the 49th limestone level within the walls of the upper chamber and install most, but not all, of its granite floor.

I'm sure you'll have realized by now that the granite blocks that comprise the next four courses of the walls of the upper chamber could not be installed using only the top lock in the gallery, because we simply cannot raise the barges much beyond the level of the inner platform using this lock. Somehow, the builders of the Great Pyramid managed to install all five courses of the upper chamber as well as all five courses of granite slabs that make up the stack above the chamber (the so called relieving chambers). We therefore now need to take a close look at the area of the limestone platform immediately beyond the top end of the grand gallery for it was here that the builders extended the canal locks beyond the gallery and onto the 49th level of the inner platform. The completion of the upper chamber and the construction of the stack would have been impossible if the canal locks had not been extended beyond the gallery, as it would have been impossible to raise barges up to such levels.

When the builders installed the first course of blocks in the upper chamber, the water level in the inner area was controlled at the top lock in the gallery. However, they clearly could not have installed a further four courses of the walls here using only this lock. In order to raise the barges up to these levels, the water level in the inner area must have been increased considerably, and the only way to do that was to create a lock at the top end of the grand gallery, a lock gate that butted up against the top end walls of the gallery. To extend the locks beyond the top end of the gallery, the water supply pipe for the locks had to be extended into the inner area beyond the gallery. However, we cannot do that at present for we have a channel extending through the 49th course of limestone from the top end of the gallery to just beyond the north wall of the upper chamber.

As we have just discovered, after the builders had established the lower course of the upper chamber walls, they would have begun to transport limestone up to the inner area again. With the lower course of the chamber walls established, however, there was no need for the canal basin they had created on the inner levels so they would then have built up the limestone in this basin area to the 49th level. It was on this level that the builders installed the granite floor of the upper chamber and this floor would almost certainly have been installed in conjunction with the installation of the limestone blocks on the 49th level in the course below. In this way, the granite flooring slabs would have been transported right up to each of the limestone ledges as the limestone floor was gradually built up. The builders would have begun to install the limestone blocks on the 48th level at the far end (west end) of the upper chamber and then installed the granite flooring slabs on top of these limestone blocks before they began to install the next bank of limestone blocks. Although the limestone floor was built up to the 49th level in what had been the basin area, the granite floor could not be extended out to the top of the gallery at this stage of the construction. The granite floor in the passageway could not have been installed until much later and certainly not before the double depth lintel block had been installed above the passageway.

As previously mentioned, the limestone levels beyond the top end of the gallery simply had to be built up at this stage of the construction in order to extend the slot in the floor of the gallery beyond the end of the gallery. This was the water supply pipe for the canal system and the locks in the gallery. It was through this pipe that water would have been pumped up into the lock installed on the inner platform beyond the end of the gallery. In addition, the wooden floor in the gallery would also have been extended from the top lock in the gallery to the top end of the gallery in order to form the topside of the water supply pipe here.

The channel (the pipe) up the centre of the grand gallery floor had to have been extended into the area beyond the top end of the gallery, the inner platform, as it was through this pipe that water would have been pumped up into the lock that the builders established on this limestone level – the inner lock beyond the gallery. With the extension of the water pipe into this inner area, the builders set up a lock beyond the grand gallery by placing a heavy wooden door (lock gate) across the end walls of the gallery and sealing off the inner area. Having complete control over the water levels within this inner lock, the builders would have had no difficulty in raising the barges up to each level of the chamber walls as they installed the next four courses of granite blocks. But now we need to take a closer look at how the water level was controlled in the locks in the gallery, and in the lock beyond the grand gallery, to see how they achieved this amazing feat.

You are now aware that the lock gates in the grand gallery consisted of heavy wooden doors lowered into place between its lower sidewalls and against the topside of two vertical wooden uprights, one on either side of the gallery. The water pumped into these locks would simply have drained away instantly on the upstroke of the pump if a valve had not been installed in the water supply pipe. The water could only be retained in the top lock by means of a non-return valve, which had been placed in the slot (water supply pipe) in the centre of the floor in the gallery shortly after the builders first began to pump water up into the locks created here. The non-return valve was probably a block of limestone that could easily slide up and down the slot in the floor of the gallery. It was this sliding valve that sealed the top end of the water supply pipe when the piston of the pump reached the end of its stroke and the water pressure in the pipe instantly dropped to a negative pressure. The valve then slammed shut and prevented the water in the top lock from draining away down the supply pipe.

Sometime after the first pair of uprights had been installed in the gallery, heavy wooden beams were placed across the ramps running up either side of the gallery to extend the floor in the gallery as far as these uprights. This floor effectively converted the slot running up the centre of the gallery floor into a pipe – the water supply pipe. In order to prevent the water in this lock from flowing back down the supply pipe on the return stroke of the pump, a non-return valve was incorporated into the hydraulic system. This sliding valve had to be installed in the supply pipe at this stage of construction as the pump would have been required to pump water up to ever greater elevations as the locks were extended up through the gallery. The non-return valve was a very simple device, consisting only of a close fitting, stone block placed in the slot in the floor of the gallery. Although the block was ever so slightly narrower than the slot itself, it was much deeper than the slot at one end, the top end. In fact, it was as deep as the distance from the topside of the wooden floor in the locks to the bottom of the slot for around a third of its length, as the wooden floor of the locks acted as the buffer stop for the sliding valve on its return stroke, as can be seen in the drawing (Fig.12) on the next page.

The stone block (the non-return valve) completely sealed the top end of the pipe and retained the water in the top lock when there was no pressure in the supply pipe. When the pump was operated, the limestone block was pushed up the slot by the force of the water coming up the pipe, and water was pumped up into the top lock. When the pump reached the end of its stroke, the water pressure in the pipe suddenly dropped and the flow of water began to reverse. As it did so, the weight of water in the top lock pushed the sliding valve back down the slot until it hit the buffer stop, the wooden floor in the gallery. The top end of the pipe was now sealed and the water level in the lock maintained until such times as the pump was operated again or the lock gate was opened. Although just a simple device, it was incredibly effective and served its purpose well. Our reconstruction of the upper chamber and the stack would simply not be possible without the inner lock beyond the grand gallery and the non-return valve in the water supply pipe. However, it would have been utterly impossible to construct a lock here at all if the arrangement of the floor at the top of the gallery was as we see it today. If the builders hadn't extended the slot in the floor of the gallery slightly beyond the top end of the gallery, then they couldn't have extended the locks up and into the inner area. Fortunately, there was no need to install the granite step stone at the top of the gallery at this stage of the construction.

There would have been a tremendous amount of pressure put on this topmost lock in the system when it was in use, as it had to hold such a huge volume of water. The builders would have ensured that the open space within this inner area was always kept to a minimum as the walls of the upper chamber were slowly built up. They would have built up as much of the limestone levels around the upper chamber as possible after each course of the upper chamber walls had been completed to keep the cubic area of the inner space (the inner lock) around the upper chamber to a minimum. But nonetheless, a great volume of water would have been pumped up into this area when many of the operations were being undertaken here. The inner lock definitely needed something more substantial to brace it than two wooden uprights and the step-outs of the corbelling in the gallery, and by placing this lock gate against the top end of the

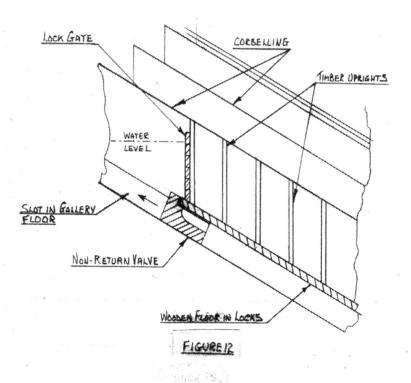

Labels: Lock Gate · Corbelling · Timber Uprights · Water Level · Slot in Gallery Floor · Non-Return Valve · Wooden Floor in Locks

FIGURE 12

SECTION THRU' FLOOR OF UPPER CHAMBER
(LOOKING NORTH)

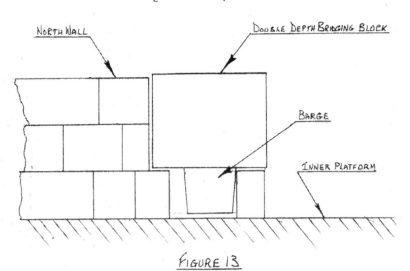

Labels: North Wall · Double Depth Bridging Block · Barge · Inner Platform

FIGURE 13

gallery walls a tremendously robust inner lock was created on the inner platform beyond the gallery.

Now that the inner lock could be pressed into service, the builders would have pushed ahead with the construction of the upper chamber and built up of some of the inner stepped levels around the chamber without any diversions. The channel through the limestone platform on the 49th level and the canal basin within the walls of the upper chamber had now been built up, but the massive double depth lintel, and a granite block on the lowest course of the north wall of the chamber beneath this lintel, had not yet been installed at the entrance to the upper chamber. Barges therefore, could enter and exit the area within the walls of the chamber from this northeast corner of the structure through a clear channel from the top of the gallery to the chamber, albeit at a slightly higher elevation than before. There is nothing to stop us now from taking our barges through into the chamber here again and transferring the granite blocks for the second course of the upper chamber walls onto the top of the granite blocks we installed here earlier. We can simply take the barges up into the lock on the inner platform and then manoeuvre them forward from here until they are within the walls of the chamber. When the water level is adjusted so as to bring the undersides of the granite blocks on the decks of the barges to just slightly above the top of the lower course of granite blocks, we can then transfer the blocks for the next course of the chamber walls from the barges onto the top of the lower course of granite.

Before we press on with our reconstruction of the upper chamber, we should bear in mind that the roof at the top end of the gallery at this stage of the construction is unfinished. As the water level was increased in the inner area and work continued on the stepped inner levels here, the sidewalls and roof at the top end of the gallery would have been built up also, since it was only after the inner lock had been installed that the walls and roof at the top end of the gallery could be completed. We will soon have to increase the height of the lock gate in order to raise barges up to the top of the upper chamber and the five levels of the stack above; therefore the sidewalls and roof of the gallery would have been built up as work progressed on the upper chamber. Only when the walls and roof of the gallery had been completed could the upper chamber and the stack have been completed.

It was not just the position of the entry passageway at the extreme east end of the upper chamber that made the early construction work on the upper chamber straightforward, for the size and the layout of the granite blocks in its walls also contributed greatly to the success of this operation. If you take a look at the drawing (Fig.13) showing the east end of the north wall (viewing it from inside the chamber), you will see that the only double depth block in the chamber walls was positioned at the extreme east end of this wall, above the entrance to the chamber. What is interesting here is that when this block was finally installed, so that the two courses above it could be put in place, the granite block in the lowest course of the north wall directly under the double depth block had not been installed. The installation of this block could not take place prior to the installation of the lintel for the only way to install this massive double depth block above the entrance passageway was to float it in on a barge until it was positioned directly above its final position. When the water level in the inner area was then reduced, the lintel came to rest on the granite supporting blocks at either end of it (one of these was in the east wall of the chamber). Only then, could the granite block that sits directly beneath the double depth block have been installed in the lowest level of the north wall (this is the granite block on the left side of the passageway looking from inside the chamber).

Once again, I have made it all sound so easy but getting this massive block of granite into a position where it could be lowered onto its supporting blocks was no easy matter. If this block could have been brought up to the top of the gallery sitting astride its transportation barge, it would have been as simple an operation as I have just described. However, this was simply not possible as this block was much too long to be transported up to the top of the gallery in this manner. At some point after the barge transporting this massive block reached the top of the gallery, the water level in the inner lock must have been reduced until the barge bottomed on the inner platform between the gallery and the upper chamber. The block then had to be turned through 90 degrees in order to have it sitting astride the barge, since it was only when its ends extended beyond the sides of the barge that it could be moved into position and lowered into its final resting place. It would have taken a great deal of effort to nudge or lever this massive block around until it sat astride the barge but with men working on it at both ends with rams or levers, possibly both, the men would have slowly turned the block through ninety degrees until it was in the ideal position on the barge to enable them to install the massive lintel above the passageway.

Having turned this massive block through ninety degrees on the horizontal, it was not just a simple matter of increasing the water level again and floating this massive block into position. As you can see from the drawing (Fig. 13) that we looked at earlier, the barge would have been extremely unstable with this massive block sitting astride it. Precautions would have been necessary to ensure that the barge did not begin to roll as it was manoeuvred forward to bring the lintel into alignment with the other blocks in the north wall of the structure. The first problem that had to be addressed though was the position of the block on the deck of the barge after it had been turned through ninety degrees for it is highly unlikely that the block would have been sitting dead centre on the deck after this operation. However, this block was far too massive to be bumped lengthways using a ram so another means of moving the block had to be employed in order to position it dead centre on the barge; the only force capable of doing this was hydraulic power.

After the lintel block had been turned until it was sitting astride the barge, limestone piers would have been built up under the ends of the granite monolith on either side of the barge. The water level would then have been increased until the barge began to float free of the inner platform. If one end of the lintel block had been heavier than the other, the lighter (shorter) end of the block would have been raised higher than the other end of this block. At this point the space underneath the higher end of the lintel block would have been built up with hardwood blocks, or one of the limestone blocks here could have been replaced with a deeper block. Either way, when the water level had been reduced again, the barge would have been manoeuvred nearer to the heavy end of the lintel block before the water level was increased again. Eventually, in one or more similar moves, the builders would have succeeded in positioning the lintel block dead centre on the barge.

Even after the lintel block was centred on the barge, the barge would still have been fairly unstable with such a massive load sitting astride it. In order to ensure that the load did not come crashing down onto the limestone platform when the water level was increased sufficiently to float the barge, a row of limestone blocks would probably have been placed on either side of the barge, with these walls extending all the way to the north side of the granite blocks in the lower course of the north wall (it was only a few metres at most) of the upper chamber where the granite lintel was to be installed. The undersides of the lintel block would have come to rest on top of these limestone blocks if the barge had begun to roll ever so slightly and this would have ensured the stability of the barge during its short journey. Only then, when both ends of the lintel were supported by blocks should the lintel tilt to either side, would the water level have been increased and the barge have been manoeuvred forward until the lintel was positioned directly above its final resting place. However, we cannot install our lintel just yet, for we need to keep the channel open until we have constructed more of our upper chamber.

The blocks for the second course of the upper chamber would have been transferred from the barges directly onto the top of the lower course of the wall from inside the chamber. After each course of granite was (almost) complete most of the limestone levels behind the south, the west and the north walls would have been built up to around the same level as the granite blocks to provide working platforms, where possible, for the installation of the next and subsequent courses of granite, and also to reduce the inner space here, the cubic area of the inner lock. The limestone levels on the east side of the upper chamber could not however have been built up to the same extent as access to this end of the chamber was needed at the next stage of the construction.

The same was also true for a small section of the east end of the platform behind the south wall of the chamber, the area between the ramps and the limestone stepped levels east of the upper chamber. The area between the top end of the gallery and the north wall of the upper chamber and a small area on either side of this cannot be built up beyond the 49th level at this time either as this is our inner lock. We will have to construct the antechamber here later, so some space will be needed on either side of this area beyond the gallery to construct the antechamber. But by building up most of the surrounding limestone levels after each course of the walls had been installed, the builders were able to complete most of the chamber walls working from both sides of the walls by pushing and pulling the granite blocks outward onto the courses below. A ram would undoubtedly have been used to bump (nudge) the granite blocks into position, and to accurately align them with the other blocks in the wall, an operation made much easier by the application of wet lime mortar on the adjoining faces of the blocks (both the vertical and horizontal faces). By building up the inner stepped levels in conjunction with the construction of the upper chamber, the builders kept the cubic area of the inner lock to a minimum. Even so, it's more than likely that a number of barges were taken into the inner area before the water level in the inner lock was increased. In this way, the builders would have made the most efficient use of the water resources at their disposal.

If the builders had brought two barges alongside one another in the chamber when the walls were under construction, this would have provided a good working platform on the inside of the chamber when the blocks were being transferred onto the lower courses and aligned with the other blocks in the wall. By bringing more than one barge into the inner area before they increased the water level in the inner lock, the builders would have made more economical use of the water resources and almost certainly have made savings in the time it took to construct the chamber walls.

The channels cut into the top of the two granite blocks in the lower course of the upper chamber walls, one each in the north and south walls, were capped when the granite blocks in the second course were installed, the channels becoming shafts (pipes) in the process. These shafts were then extended back into the limestone levels behind the granite walls as the inner limestone levels were built up around the chamber. These shafts were then angled upwards and extended up through each course of the inner platform as it was built up to the 59th level, the level at the top of the upper chamber walls. (They were later extended all the way up to the perimeter platform when the builders began to build up the stepped inner levels and push the perimeter platform much higher from the hub in the upper chamber.)

The ramps on either side of the upper chamber began to take shape after the granite blocks in the second course of the chamber walls had been installed. The ramps were one course above the shafts and these were also extended up through the stepped limestone levels from the level of the second course of granite in the chamber walls. When we have completed our reconstruction of the upper chamber and the stack above it, we will set up the lifting mechanism in the upper chamber. Eventually, we will haul limestone blocks up these ramps to build up the inner stepped levels and push the perimeter platform up to a much greater elevation than it is at present. However, that won't be for some time yet as we have still much to do in the upper chamber.

Apart from the double depth block that forms the lintel above the passageway into the upper chamber, there were also some very long, single depth, granite blocks / beams that would have been too difficult to haul from the barges onto the walls of the chamber. Fortunately, all of these very long blocks of granite are in the top, the fifth, course of the upper chamber walls. If you take a look at the drawing (Fig.14) on the next page showing the configuration of the blocks, slabs and beams in the walls, floor and roof of the upper chamber, you can clearly see that the top course of the north wall is comprised of only two blocks of granite, very long blocks of granite. In fact, almost the whole of the fifth course of the upper chamber walls is comprised of very long blocks / beams of granite. These blocks could not, or would not, have been hauled into position from the decks of the barges that transported them into the inner area. We can clearly determine when we look at the configuration of the granite blocks in the fourth course of the north wall how these very long granite blocks / beams were installed. They were undoubtedly lowered into position in the same manner as the double depth lintel above the passageway. They would have come up through the locks in the gallery lengthways and then been turned through 90 degrees after the barges had been grounded on the inner platform. When the water level was then increased again, they would have been floated into position above their final positions on the top course of the upper chamber. The water level would then have been decreased and these beams would have been lowered onto the three granite blocks previously installed in the 4th course of the north wall (the blocks indicated by the cross-hatching in the drawing) (Fig. 14). It was only after these two beams had been installed in the top course of the north wall that most of the much smaller blocks in the course below would have been nudged into place to complete the 4th course of the north wall.

You will see from the drawing that I have indicated where the three granite blocks were installed in the 4th course of the north wall (cross-hatched) prior to the installation of the two granite beams in the 5th course of this wall. These three blocks would most likely have been transferred onto the top of the 3rd course of the north wall from the outside of the chamber walls after the double depth lintel

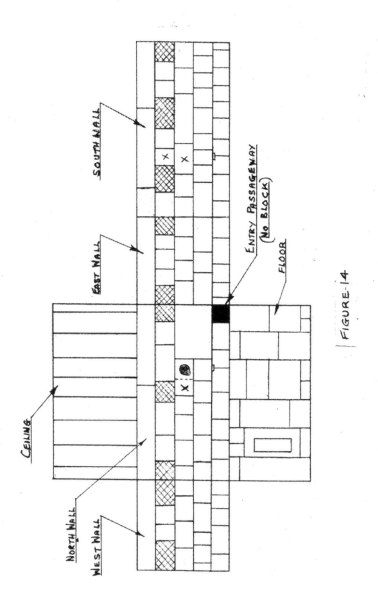

FIGURE-14

block had been installed. As you see from the drawing, two similar granite beams were installed in the 5th course of the south wall and another granite beam was installed in the top course of both the west and the east wall of the chamber. The 4th and 5th courses of both the east and the west wall of the chamber could not be installed at this stage of the construction however. These two end walls remained unfinished for some time after the two sidewalls of the structure had been completed; the reason for this will soon become clear.

If anyone doubts that water power was used to good effect here, they only need take a look at the configuration of the granite blocks in the fourth and fifth courses of the upper chamber walls. Here is all the proof that we need to confirm that hydraulic power was used to lower the granite beams in the fifth course of the wall onto two or more smaller blocks in the course below. Having then installed these massive beams at this elevation, the builders went on to achieve even greater feats using hydraulic power.

Before we move on, I would just like to draw your attention to the block marked with an X on the drawing of the north wall (Fig.14). This block was not installed in the north wall as it was built up, at least not in its final position. A gap was needed in both the north and south walls one course above the shafts, as most of the large limestone blocks used to build up the perimeter platform to an even greater elevation at a later stage of the construction were hauled through these gaps in the sidewalls. These blocks were first hoisted up onto temporary landings on either side of the chamber, just in front of, and below, where the blocks marked with an X in the third course of the structure had been omitted. The lifting mechanism that the builders had put to good use down in the lower chamber was again used here to hoist the limestone blocks up onto the landings on either side of the chamber. However, we will have to come back to this later when the time comes for us to build up our perimeter platform as we must push on with our reconstruction of the free-standing upper chamber. I only raised this matter now as something very unique may have occurred here when the builders were constructing the north wall of the chamber.

The builders had to create a gap in the 3rd course in the north wall, one course up from the shaft in the chamber wall. Due to the length of this block (marked with an X), they simply could not have omitted this block in the north wall at this early stage of the construction as it supported a much shorter block in the 4th course of the wall. This block in the 4th course of the wall, in turn, supported one end of each of the granite beams in the top course of the north wall. These beams simply could not have been installed without this short supporting block having been installed near the centre of the 4th

course of the north wall prior to their installation. There were two ways around this problem. Given the configuration of the granite blocks in the north wall of the chamber, one option was to place the block marked with an X in the 3rd course of the north wall in a temporary position – offset 90 degrees from its eventual position in the wall – and place it across the wall, instead of along the wall. The granite block, which was longer than it was wide, could have been pushed over to the left side of the gap (viewed from inside the chamber) to support the granite blocks in the courses above. By turning this block through 90 degrees and then installing it in this temporary position, it would have provided a temporary support for the granite blocks in the course above, which in turn supported one end of the two granite beams in the course above. By placing it in this temporary position a gap would have been created in the north wall of the chamber between this block and the double depth block (the lintel). It was through this gap that the limestone blocks were hauled through to the ramp on the other side of the north wall before being hauled up the ramps to the perimeter platform (at a later stage of the construction). (The builders did not have this problem with the south wall of the chamber they simply didn't install one block in both the 3rd and 4th courses to create the necessary gap in the wall.) These granite blocks were eventually installed in the positions that we see them in today at a later stage of the construction.

The other option here, of course, was to install a much shorter block in the gap in the north wall to support the masonry above until the full length block could be installed. I suspect that this would have been the option favoured by the builders because if they had gone for the first option, a shorter block would have had to be installed in the opening before the longer granite block was removed, turned through 90 degrees, and then re-installed in the gap later. The builders could not have risked removing the longer granite block without providing a temporary support for the masonry above because if the masonry in the two courses above had begun to sag, it would have been impossible to install the longer granite block in the opening. No matter which option the builders chose here, it would have been a rather unique situation as the block that was installed here, prior to the hub being set up, would have been the only granite block installed in a temporary position in the walls of the upper chamber when they were under construction.

With the completion of most of the upper chamber walls and some of the inner stepped levels around the chamber, the builders were then ready to move on to the next operation, the installation of the granite roof of the chamber. Although some of the limestone platform on the south side and the north side of the upper chamber would have been built up to the same level as the top of the chamber walls at this stage of the construction, this was not the case on the east and west sides of the chamber. We cannot build up the stepped levels immediately east of the east wall of the chamber just yet, as we have not installed the top two courses of the east wall (the area of the inner platform east of the ramps on the north and south side of the upper chamber could not be built up yet either). We have not completed the east wall of the chamber for it was from this end of the chamber, the one nearest the top end of the gallery, that the barges transporting the roofing slabs entered the chamber. The limestone levels behind the 4th and 5th courses of the west wall would not have been built up at this stage of the construction either and the reason for this will soon become clear.

The barges that transported the granite roofing slabs up to the inner platform had to be traversed eastwards after they had entered the inner lock beyond the top end of the gallery. You will see from the drawing (Fig.15) on the next page that the barges were traversed here until they were just beyond the east wall of the chamber, then the barges were manoeuvred forwards (southwards) until they were broadside on to the east wall of the chamber. The east wall of the upper chamber is only three courses high at this stage of our reconstruction as it can't be completed until we have installed the roof of the chamber. The gap between the east end of the upper chamber and the limestone stepped levels on the east side of the chamber would have been wide enough to allow the barge to be manoeuvred forward until it was positioned directly east of the chamber, since most of the stepped levels on this side of the upper chamber couldn't be built up at this stage of the construction. Before we begin the reconstruction of the roof, (I have shown the roof of the chamber partially completed in the drawing) we need to take a look inside the chamber, as we have overlooked something that probably occurred before the builders installed the double depth block in the north wall of the chamber and completed it.

As I mentioned earlier, the granite blocks that the builders were unable to install in the sidewalls of the upper chamber at this

FIGURE 15

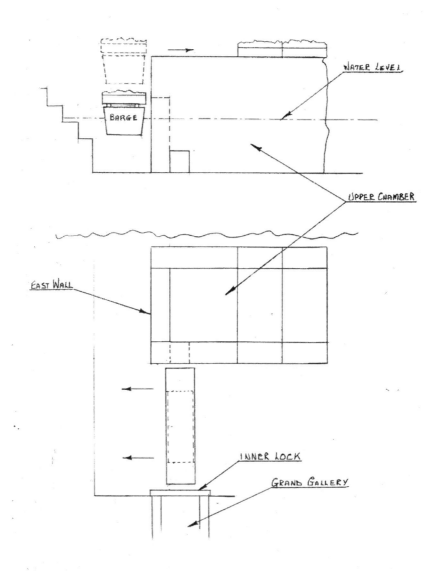

stage of the construction were almost certainly stored at the far end (west end) of the chamber until they were needed. The blocks that were installed in the gaps in the sidewalls at a later stage of the construction were almost certainly installed in these gaps in the sidewalls from inside the chamber. These blocks had to be flush with the other granite blocks in the sidewalls and the best way to ensure that they were flush within the chamber was to install them from inside the chamber. I believe that this is the sole reason why this chamber is much longer than the lower chamber; space was needed at the west end of the chamber to store these granite blocks that were later used to plug the gaps in the sidewalls. The blocks had to be stored for a period of time within the upper chamber after its walls and roof were almost complete – for as long as the ramps on either side of the chamber were in use – as it was only when the builders had no more use for the ramps that these blocks could have been installed and the sidewalls of the chamber completed.

But it was not only the blocks themselves that had to be stored here. The barge, the means to raise these blocks up to the required level within the chamber, would also have been stored in this chamber. Although the granite blocks could have been transported into the chamber through the gap in the unfinished east wall, it's more than likely that these granite blocks would have been transported into the chamber before the double depth lintel block had been installed above the passageway in the north wall of the chamber. The blocks would most likely have been transferred onto a plinth on the floor of the chamber until such times as they could be transferred back onto the deck of the barge, prior to their installation in the sidewalls of the chamber.

I have to say that I was initially uncertain as to how many blocks remained to be installed in the sidewalls of the chamber at the later stage. Fortunately, and completely by accident, I came across a drawing of the walls, floor and roof of the upper chamber that was originally published in *Charles Piazzi Smyth, Our Inheritance in the Great Pyramid* (2nd Edition 1877) showing all the blocks and slabs that make up the chamber walls, ceiling and floor. I then produced my own drawing (Fig. 14) that we looked at earlier, based on this drawing by Piazzi Smyth.

When I first viewed Piazzi Smyth's drawing I realized, when I could plainly see for myself the configuration of the blocks in the sidewalls of the chamber, that at least one block in the third course of the south wall and one block in the fourth course of the wall could not have been installed when the chamber was initially constructed. Although the builders could not install these blocks in their final positions at this stage of the construction however, it was possibly only two granite blocks that had to be temporarily stored in the chamber until later, for, as we discovered earlier, one of the three granite blocks that could not have been placed in its final position when the north wall was constructed, could have been temporarily installed in the north wall of the chamber side on to the adjoining block on the west side of it (turned through 90 degrees). However, I think this was unlikely and a much shorter temporary block was probably installed in the third course of the north wall of the chamber for the reason I mentioned earlier. These three granite blocks that had to be temporarily stored within the chamber would almost certainly have been unloaded from the barge when they were put into the chamber. We can therefore state that before they completed the walls of the chamber, the builders manoeuvred the barge carrying these granite blocks – that were later used to close the gaps in the sidewalls of the chamber – into the upper chamber and then placed them on a plinth at the west end of the chamber. Sometime after these three granite blocks had been transported into the upper chamber, some of the components of the lifting mechanism would also have been transported into the chamber. However, most of the components of this mechanism would not have been placed in the chamber until the builders were ready to complete the end walls of the chamber as these components were made of wood. These components would have floated freely within the chamber and obstructed the barges transporting the roofing slabs along the chamber, had they been transported into the chamber prior to the installation of the roofing slabs.

Evidence suggests that much of the granite and some of the limestone blocks (the casing blocks) in the Great Pyramid had been cut with machine precision, the granite blocks used to construct the upper chamber being a case in point. It is impossible to cut granite by hand and achieve the degree of accuracy that we see in the blocks used to construct the walls of the upper chamber. If we accept that this was indeed the case, it is therefore inconceivable that the builders would have taken the risk of leaving gaps in the sidewalls of the chamber only to find, when they came to install the remaining blocks in those gaps, that they were not a good fit. This would not have been a great problem if the blocks were slightly undersize as the builders could have put a bit more mortar in the joints. However, if any of the blocks were oversize, the masons would have had to cut them down to size in the chamber before they could be installed in the gaps in the sidewalls. It is entirely possible that these blocks would have had to be cut to size by the masons using hand tools only, and no doubt the masons would have done a good job of reducing the size of the blocks so that they would fit into the gaps. But this would have taken some time and the end result would not have been nearly as good had these blocks been machine cut like all the others.

The way in which the builders probably got around this little difficulty was simply to install these blocks in the sidewalls when the walls were being constructed and then knock them out again after all of the adjoining blocks had been installed, and before the mortar had set. That way, the builders would have known for certain that they would not encounter any difficulties when they came to install these blocks in the gaps in the sidewalls later. If this had indeed been the case, then the builders had only to ensure that the lifting mechanism and a barge were placed in the chamber before its walls were complete. The gaps in the sidewalls would then have been created when these blocks were knocked through into the chamber and onto the deck of the barge, before being stored at the west end of the chamber well clear of the lifting mechanism.

Chapter Four

The roof

Before we begin to install the granite roofing slabs in the upper chamber, I should point out that these slabs would have been transported up to the top of the gallery on the largest (longest) of the barges used by the builders if they had used barges of varying lengths. When these slabs were being transported up through the flight of locks in the grand gallery they would have been manoeuvred forward from one station to the next each time the water level was increased. The architects of the structure had in fact provided the builders with many stations (twenty eight in all) in the gallery where the uprights of the locks were installed against the sidewalls. The barges would simply have been manoeuvred forward a short distance from one station to the next, and as each lock gate was lowered into position behind the barges and the trailing lock gate then moved forward to the station behind the leading lock gate, the water level would have been increased again in the top lock. As we discovered earlier, the builders would then have simply repeated each of these actions again and again until the barge and its load was at the top of the gallery. When the barges reached the top of the gallery they would then have been manoeuvred forward into the inner lock beyond the gallery.

The progress of these barges up through the flight of locks in the gallery would have been very slow due to the fact that they had to take so many small steps before they reached the top of the gallery and the lock beyond. It was simply because these barges had to be so long that there were so many stations created within the gallery. The water level in the locks could only be increased by a relatively small amount before each barge was manoeuvred forward as the trailing edge of the loads (the granite roofing slabs) could have fouled the corbelling in the walls of the gallery if the water level was increased too far. There was also a tremendous pressure on the uprights that bolstered the lock gates at each stage of the process when such massive loads were being transported up through the gallery, but as we discovered earlier, these uprights could have been bolstered by heavy struts as well as the corbelling in the walls of the gallery.

When each of these barges reached the inner lock in the area beyond the grand gallery, they would have been traversed to the east end of the upper chamber before being manoeuvred forward again until they were broadside on to the end of the chamber. After the inner lock gate had been lowered into place and the water level in the lock increased, each barge would have been raised until the underside of each roofing slab was just above the level of the top of the chamber walls. The top two courses of the upper chamber's east wall had still to be installed at this stage and it was from here that the barge transporting the first roofing slab was traversed between the walls of the chamber to its far end (the west end) where the first of these slabs was to be installed.

You may find it easier to visualize this whole operation if you bear in mind that the passageway through the antechamber and into the upper chamber is at the extreme east end of the upper chamber. This passageway is centred on, and dead ahead of, the slot running up the centre of the floor in the grand gallery. If we could remove the antechamber from the Great Pyramid today we would see that the outside face of the east wall of the upper chamber is almost aligned with the inner east wall of the grand gallery. The barges transporting the roofing slabs were inherently unstable, especially when they were being manoeuvred sideways (traversed) but with the east end of the upper chamber being so near to the opening at the top of the grand gallery, the barges had to be traversed little more than the width of a barge at this stage of the construction until they were beyond the east wall of the chamber.

The installation of the nine granite roofing slabs would have been a fairly straightforward operation and although the barges displayed some instability when being traversed in the inner lock, when they were being traversed within the walls of the chamber, the overhanging ends of the granite roofing slabs would have guaranteed their safe passage. The very small clearance between the top of the upper chamber walls and the lower faces of the overhanging slabs when the barges were being traversed would have ensured that movement was very limited if the barges had begun to roll.

The first roofing slab to be installed would have been the one at the far end of the chamber, the west end. The builders had used a wet lime mortar in every joint of the chamber walls as the granite blocks were manoeuvred into position. The same mortar would also have been applied to the top of the walls of the chamber before the roofing slabs were set down on these granite blocks. This would have provided a good seal between the slabs and the walls of the chamber. Lime mortar would also have been applied to one side of each granite roofing slab before another roofing slab was butted up against it. This would have sealed the joints between the granite slabs and ensured that the roof of the chamber was watertight and airtight when the mortar dried.

The roofing slabs at both ends of the chamber are supported by the end walls as well as the north and south walls; therefore roughly half the area of the underside of these slabs rests on top of the end walls of the chamber. In order to install the roofing slab at the west end of the chamber so that it would be supported by the end wall, the builders would not have installed the 3rd and 4th courses of the west wall of the chamber prior to the installation of this first roofing slab. I eventually realized that if the builders had installed all five courses of the west wall, it would have been impossible to haul such a massive slab towards the west end of the chamber until its leading edge was above the outside face of the west wall. However, I had by then figured out how they had installed the roofing slab at the east end of the chamber and came to the conclusion that the slab at the west end of the chamber would have been installed in exactly the same manner. Using this method, it was possible for the builders to install the roofing slabs at both ends of the chamber and have them completely cover the blocks in the end walls without the need to move any of the roofing slabs after they had been lowered onto the top of the structure. This granite roof, when it was complete, provided a base for the stack which was as long as the chamber itself and this would undoubtedly have been a very stable free-standing structure. Eventually, of course, the stack was buttressed on all sides when the limestone levels in the inner area were built up, but much of the area around the stack could not have been built up until a much later stage of the construction. We will soon discover why this was so.

Earlier, I mentioned the drawing by Charles Piazzi Smyth (Fig.15) that shows all of the blocks and slabs that comprise the floor, the walls and the ceiling of the upper chamber. When I discovered this drawing, I was delighted to see that it confirmed my suspicions, as the drawing clearly indicates that the granite slabs at each end of the chamber did indeed extend to the outer edges of the east and west end walls. I have to say that I would have expected no less of the builders as this undoubtedly was the best way to ensure the long term stability of the stack and the whole pyramid structure above the upper chamber. After looking at the options of the builders, I eventually realized that all of the roofing slabs had been installed from the east end of the chamber (this was why the passageways, including the grand gallery, were at the extreme east end of the upper chamber in the Great Pyramid) but in order to do so the builders could not have installed the top two courses of the east end wall. I then realized that the top two courses of the west wall had not been installed prior to the installation of the roofing slab at the west end of the chamber. This was how the builders had managed to install the roofing slabs at either end of the chamber with the far edge of these slabs directly above the outside edge of the east and west walls of the chamber, since these roofing slabs were far too heavy to be hauled into position after they had been lowered onto the top of the chamber walls. Just as the builders had lowered the double depth lintel block and the granite beams that comprise the 5th course of the walls in the upper chamber into position, so it was now with the granite roofing slabs.

As you can see from the drawing (Fig15) it is one single granite block / beam that comprises the 5th course of the east and the west walls of the upper chamber. Sometime after the first roofing slab had been installed at the west end of the upper chamber, the builders would have installed the end blocks of the 4th course of the west wall, leaving a gap in the middle. There was good reason as to why the other two blocks were not installed at this stage of the construction of the west wall because this gap in the wall was necessary for the granite beam to be installed in the 5th course of the west wall. As we now know, there was only one way to install these very long and very heavy beams and that was to float them into position using barges. In this instance, the granite beam that comprised the 5th course of the west wall would have been slotted into position between the two supporting blocks installed in the 4th course of the wall and the granite roofing slab above. This was the only way that these very large granite blocks could have been installed as they were much too heavy to be hauled into position. But although logic tells us that this was the only way to install these very large granite beams, it is the configuration of the smaller blocks in the courses below all of these very long beams that comprise the 5th course of the upper chamber that ultimately confirms that this was indeed the case. When the granite beam in the 5th course of the west wall had been installed, the two smaller granite blocks would have been installed in the course below and the west wall of the chamber would have been complete. All of these blocks and beams would have been nudged into their final positions by the use of rams wielded by a number of men.

The installation of the eight remaining roofing slabs would have been a very straightforward operation and when the roof was complete, the 4th and 5th courses of the east wall of the chamber would have been installed in exactly the same manner as those in the west wall. I have no way of proving to you that the original builders of the Great Pyramid installed the roof of the upper chamber in exactly the way I have described. I have simply deduced that this was the most logical and safest way of transporting the blocks to their intended destination and installing them, based on what I have discovered so far about the builders of the Great Pyramid. But like so many of the limestone and granite monoliths used in the construction of the many structures at Giza, hydraulic power is simply the only means by which these monoliths could have been transported to their destinations and lowered into their respective positions within these structures. There is simply no doubt that hydraulic power was used for these operations and the configuration of the blocks in the courses below all of these great monoliths confirm that this was indeed the case. The configuration of the blocks and beams that comprise the walls of the upper chamber of the Great Pyramid should convince even the most hardened sceptics that the builders of this structure and many others on the west bank harnessed the power of water to create these marvels of a once great, technologically advanced, people.

The roof of the chamber was now complete and its walls were complete, except for the few blocks stored within the chamber. These blocks could not be put in place at this stage of the construction but the upper chamber, to all intents and purposes, was now effectively complete and one could easily conclude that the distribution hub could in fact have been set up in this chamber at this stage of the construction. But that was not the case.

By this stage of the construction the shaft (channel) in the south wall of the chamber had been extended back into the limestone behind the granite wall and extended up through the ten courses of the inner platform that we have put in place behind the south wall to bring it up to the level of the top of the chamber walls. This shaft will be extended up through the courses of limestone at an angle of

45 degrees as we extend the inner platform up to, and beyond, the existing perimeter platform when the new hub in the upper chamber becomes operational.

Above the shaft that has been extended up through the limestone on the south side of the chamber, a ramp has also been created. This ramp extends up from the level of the ledge we created in the south wall of the chamber when we omitted to put the granite block in place in the third course of the wall directly above the shaft (or removed it). This ramp, and the one created on the north side of the chamber, were used by the builders to haul all of the limestone up to the inner stepped levels and the existing perimeter platform to extend them. But the hub could not be brought into use at this stage of the construction, as the stack had still to be constructed and this could not happen without the use of the inner lock at the top end of the gallery or without the use of hydraulic power. There were still many granite blocks and slabs to be transported up into the inner area at this stage and the lock at the top end of the gallery was the only way to get the barges up to the levels where these blocks and slabs had to be installed. The step-stone could not be installed at the top end of the grand gallery yet as the inner lock could not have functioned if the step-stone had been put in place at this time. The granite step-stone was the landing where the limestone blocks were later unloaded from the barges and then hauled from here into the upper chamber – the new distribution hub – *en route* to the inner stepped levels and the perimeter platforms. But as the builders could not install the step-stone at this stage of the construction and the hub could not have become operational at this stage of the construction either.

Aswan granite

Each granite block of the upper chamber is cut very precisely. Its faces are very flat and square and the dimensions of all the blocks are extremely accurate. A mortar was applied to the top faces of each course of the upper chamber walls before the next block was placed on top and one of each of the adjoining faces had a thin layer of mortar applied to it as well before the blocks were butted up against one another. The weight of these massive blocks made them difficult to transport but the most difficult operation was getting them onto the barges.

When the smaller granite blocks were first loaded onto the barges at the quarry, it is most likely that the barges were grounded on a ledge within a dry dock. These granite quarries would have been set up as dry docks, huge locks that were continually being extended as more and more masonry was removed from the stepped levels of the quarry. The barges used to transport the smaller granite blocks would have been floated off of the stepped levels after the granite blocks had been loaded and centred on their decks and the lock / dry dock had been flooded again. Although it is possible that draught animals were used to haul the granite blocks from the quarry faces to the decks of the barges, the quarry would have been set up in such a way that the barges could be floated right up to the ledges where the granite blocks were being removed from the rock faces above and cut to size. The distance they had to be moved from the ledges where they were cut out of the bedrock would have been kept to an absolute minimum. Granite blocks would have been quarried from a series of stepped levels within the quarry boundaries – within the dry dock – and the water level would simply have been increased after the granite blocks had been hauled onto the barges ready to be removed from the quarry / dry dock.

It is possible that the water source for the dry dock / lock within the quarry was the River Nile. A channel could have been extended from the higher reaches of the Nile to the quarry, where a sluice gate would have been installed to control the water flow into the quarry / dry dock. However, I am not familiar with the topography of this area and cannot say if this would have been possible. Had this not been possible, then a water reservoir would have been created at a higher elevation than the quarry to provide the dry dock with water when it had to be flooded.

When the lock gate was opened at the entrance to the dry dock, a number of barges would have entered the dock and taken up their positions above the ledges before the water level was decreased. The granite blocks would have been hauled from the quarry ledges onto the decks of the barges now grounded below these ledges. By setting up the quarry in this manner, they did not have to haul the granite blocks and slabs any great distance to the grounded barges on the edge of each level. When all of the barges within the dock had been loaded, the water level in the lock would have been increased again until all the barges could be floated off the ledges and the masonry transported out of the quarry, then on down through a series of locks to the canal that linked the quarry with the River Nile.

Each of the granite blocks quarried here would most probably have been loaded from the side of the barge onto two or more hardwood beams laid across the deck. However, it's also possible that metal rails could have been fixed to the deck of the barges as these would have presented a much smaller surface area and greatly reduced the drag due to friction when the granite blocks had to be hauled on and off the decks of the barges. These beams or rails would not have been very deep as the centre of gravity of the blocks had to be as near as possible to the deck for stability. Once again, water would have been used as a lubricant on the beams / rails to further reduce the drag due to friction.

A canal basin would have been created at Aswan, near to where the canal entered the river, and it was here that the barges would have been made ready for their journey down the Nile to Giza. A good number of barges would most probably have been lashed together to create a much larger, more stable craft for the long journey ahead. It is around 800 kilometres from the granite quarries at Aswan to the canal basin at Giza and a number of difficult stretches of the river had to be negotiated on the journey north. A larger craft consisting of a raft of small barges lashed together would have been much more stable on the more turbulent stretches of the river than the smaller barges. Nonetheless, it is unlikely that so much granite was transported north to Giza without incident and possibly even the loss of some of the masonry. When the barges / rafts finally reached the safety of the canal basin below the escarpment at Giza however, these rafts would then have been broken back down into their component parts.

But that was only one option and it is entirely possible that many of the smaller blocks of granite were transported down the river on much larger barges than those used to transport the masonry up to the plateau and into the Great Pyramid. If this had been the case, then this masonry would have been transferred from the larger craft to the smaller barges within the canal basin below the escarpment at Giza before it was transported up to the plateau. If the builders had chosen this option, then another dry dock where these barges could be grounded may possibly have been constructed next to the canal basin at Giza to facilitate the transfer operations. However, it is possible that this may not have been necessary.

The long granite beams and roofing slabs used in the construction of the upper chamber would have been almost impossible to move even the slightest distance manually and these would undoubtedly have been transported all the way from Aswan on the barges that eventually transported them all the way up to the top of the grand gallery. These barges would almost certainly have been stabilized by lashing a number of them together to create a much larger, more stable craft and it's also probable that outriggers were attached to these larger craft, with pontoons having been installed on both sides of the raft, prior to its journey down the Nile.

We discovered earlier that the largest granite blocks and slabs installed within the Great Pyramid were floated into position on barges and then lowered onto the supporting blocks of masonry. These monoliths were simply too large to be hauled into position. This was also the case in reverse when these monoliths were removed from the quarry. The small blocks of granite used in the construction of the upper chamber would have been removed from the stepped levels in the quarry below the levels where these large beams and slabs were quarried. The upper levels would have been undercut when the smaller blocks were removed, leaving the granite beams and slabs supported by columns at either end. These granite beams would only have been cut free from their supporting columns after a barge had been manoeuvred under the slab or beam to support it. When the beam or slab had been cut free from its supporting columns and transported away from the quarry face, the barge would then have been grounded on the stepped levels within the quarry. Here the excess material on the undersides of the beams would have been removed and the areas at the ends of the beams dressed and finished.

As regards the nine roofing slabs that form the ceiling of the upper chamber, the underside of these beams would have been dressed and finished over their whole length, prior to them being transported north to Giza. The underside of these roofing slabs would almost certainly have been vertical faces when these slabs were being quarried, and these faces would have been machine cut until they were perfectly flat. It was only after this operation had been completed that these slabs would have been lifted up and out of the quarry. There were a number of different ways in which these slabs could have been turned through ninety degrees and lowered onto their smooth undersides ready for transportation to Giza.

However, it is unlikely that these huge slabs could have been raised or moved other than by the use of hydraulic power, therefore it is for this reason that I suspect that a specially constructed barge would have been used to lift these slabs up and out of the quarry. The slabs would have been tilted slightly as they were lifted and they would have come to rest against a rigid wooden structure that had been constructed across the full width of the barge. Once the slabs had been tilted five or ten degrees from the vertical onto the sloping face of this rigid structure it would then have been a fairly simple matter to lower these slabs down onto supporting columns that had a buffer stop at one end. After all of the edges of the slab had been machined smooth and square, not forgetting, of course, the areas at either end on the top surface, the slab would then have been lifted up and out of the quarry and transported to the holding basin ready for transportation to Giza.

The method I have just described here of lifting these slabs up out of the quarry and tilting them over until their smooth undersides were horizontal, is just one of the methods that the builders may have used but we have simply no way of determining what technology – over and above hydraulic power – the builders may have had at their disposal. However, we do know that they exploited hydraulic power to a phenomenal degree when they constructed these large, stone block pyramids. Indeed, these pyramids could not have been constructed had the builders not become absolute masters of this technology. The example that I have described above is just another example of how the builders could have exploited this power source in order to manipulate these huge granite slabs into the desired position for transportation to Giza after the undersides of the slabs had been machined.

When the smallest of the granite blocks had to be transferred from the barges onto the limestone platform and the walls of the upper chamber, it is likely that these blocks were both pulled and pushed onto the ledges. It is possible that draught animals could have been used here on the inner platforms to haul these blocks from the barges on to the next three courses of the walls, but it may be that manpower was all the force that was needed to manoeuvre the smaller blocks onto the walls. Once there, and with the wet mortar acting as a lubricant on the top surfaces of the platform and the walls themselves, these blocks would have been nudged into their final positions by the use of heavy rams. Pulling a heavy block into position is not always an option but these granite blocks would almost certainly have been nudged into their final positions by a few skilled men wielding these rams. The accuracy of the upper chamber's individual components was paramount if the chamber itself was to be built to a very high degree of accuracy, and it certainly was. Great care had also to be taken to ensure that each block was aligned with those below it and those on either side of it, no easy task when confronted with 70 ton blocks of granite. Fortunately, most of the granite blocks in the walls of the upper chamber are much smaller than these monoliths and all of these monoliths would simply have been lowered into their final positions very slowly. These monoliths would have been impossible to move by any means other than hydraulic power after they came to rest on their supports.

We will probably never know for certain all of the methods the builders employed when they constructed the upper chamber but regardless of the methods they used, they certainly did a good job of it as the upper chamber has been constructed with great precision. But although the mortar under each of the blocks would have acted as a lubricant, greatly reducing the friction between the contact surfaces, a considerable force would still have been required to move each block. A heavy ram was the most effective way to move these large granite blocks by small incremental steps, to both nudge them up against neighbouring blocks, or to align them with others in the walls of the chamber.

We can't say for certain that the builders definitely employed a heavy ram to nudge the granite blocks into their final positions but a heavy ram wielded by a few skilled men is a very effective instrument for this purpose. This instrument could quickly and easily be deployed on either side of the blocks or at either end of them. It is an instrument that can be wielded with great accuracy by skilled operators and I believe that the builders of the Great Pyramid would have chosen to slowly and accurately nudge the granite blocks into their final positions using such an instrument. The only other force that could have been employed was leverage and it's entirely possible that both levers and rams were used to nudge some of these granite blocks into position when the upper chamber was under construction. But rams were the more flexible of these two instruments as they could be used in almost all circumstances, whereas levers can only be used where there is a solid body to use as a pivot for the lever.

The construction of the upper chamber and the stack above was a slow and complex operation; the construction of the antechamber could not begin until the five courses of granite slabs and the granite spacing blocks of the stack above the chamber had all been put in place. The antechamber could not be constructed at this stage since the area at the top of the grand gallery, the inner lock, was where the barges carrying the granite blocks and slabs for the construction of the stack were traversed to the east end of the chamber. It was only possible to construct the free-standing upper chamber and the stack on the 49th level because the builders had extended the hydraulic system into the inner area. To do that, they had to construct a lock on the inner platform at the top end of the grand gallery. It was not humanly possible to construct this free-standing granite edifice on the inner platform of the Great Pyramid without the use of hydraulic power. The configuration of the blocks below the largest blocks, beams and slabs in this structure leave us in no doubt that this was indeed the case.

After the barges transporting the roofing slabs had entered the inner lock, they would have been traversed to the east end of the upper chamber and then manoeuvred forwards until they were end on to the chamber. The barges were then raised up until the undersides of the roofing slabs were slightly above the level of the top of the walls. They were then traversed along between the walls of the chamber to where each slab had to be installed. All of this could only have been accomplished by making use of the inner lock beyond the top end of the grand gallery; for the lock to function, the slot (pipe) up the middle of the floor of the gallery had to have been extended beyond the top end of the gallery (Fig. 16).

The stack

As you are aware by now, the stack is the term I use for the layered roof above the upper chamber, the so called 'relieving chambers'. For as long as I can remember, I had been puzzled as to why the area above the upper chamber was constructed in this manner as I could see no logical reason as to why this should be. When I eventually discovered that the grand gallery housed a series of locks for the transportation of barges and their loads up to the level of the upper chamber, I then realized that the hydraulic system must have been

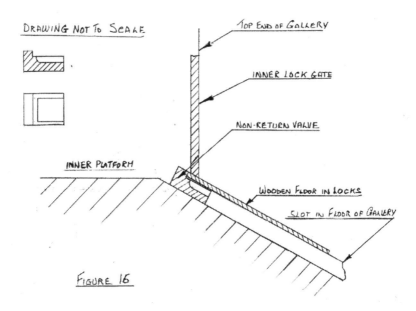

DRAWING NOT TO SCALE

TOP END OF GALLERY

INNER LOCK GATE

NON-RETURN VALVE

INNER PLATFORM

WOODEN FLOOR IN LOCKS

SLOT IN FLOOR OF GALLERY

FIGURE 16

extended as far as the inner area beyond the grand gallery and utilized during the construction of the walls of the chamber and the stack. However, I didn't know at that time how the builders had accomplished this feat since I hadn't figured out how the chamber and the stack had been constructed.

There had been one thing about the upper chamber that had intrigued me for a very long time. Why, if the upper chamber was not constructed as a tomb or for ceremonial purposes, was it constructed of red granite? What was the significance of this? I didn't begin to get a handle on it until I began to mentally reconstruct the upper chamber, and began to compare the differences between the construction of the upper chamber and that of the lower chamber. I also went down many blind alleys before I discovered how the upper chamber had been established on the inner platform. I saw that it was not at all clear how the work had progressed when the construction reached the 49th level. In time, however, as you now know, I began to make progress and eventually I managed to mentally reconstruct the upper chamber in more or less the same order and manner as the original builders of the Great Pyramid. But we still have a long way to go so we'd better push on with our reconstruction of the stack. It will all become clear when we discover why this free-standing granite structure was created; when we discover its true purpose.

We have now installed the nine granite roofing slabs on top of the upper chamber and, to be frank, the construction of the stack was no more complex an operation than the construction of the upper chamber had been. In fact, it is much more straightforward, because here, we are simply extending the walls of the chamber up beyond the roof of the chamber and then installing another roof on top of these low walls... and so on and so forth until we have completed our stack. When we have completed this first section of the extended roof, we will then repeat this operation another three times until the stack is complete. But you are now fully familiar with the various methods used to transport and install the granite blocks and slabs in the upper chamber. There is nothing to be gained by going back over these operations here, for the blocks and slabs of the stack would have been installed in exactly the same manner as those in the upper chamber itself, although there are no really enormous blocks installed between each roof section here, just smaller, more easily handled blocks.

It was simply the need to forestall the installation of the gabled roof above the upper chamber that this feature of the Great Pyramid was created. This was the simplest and quickest way to extend the roof of the upper chamber up to an elevation where it would later be possible to install a gabled roof. The gabled roof could not be installed directly above the chamber itself when the chamber walls were complete as there was no way to bolster some of the gables at the east end of the chamber. The inner limestone levels could not be built up in this area around the east end of the chamber for the ramps were here and the antechamber had still to be constructed. So there was nothing to bolster the beams of a gabled roof at this end of the chamber when the chamber itself had been, to all intents and purposes, complete. The only way to get around this difficulty was to postpone the installation of the gabled roof.

We also have to remember that the limestone beams that form these gables are massive and these could only be transported into the inner area, and then up to the limestone levels where they would later be installed, when the inner lock at the top end of the gallery was still operational. Just like the gables in the tunnel and those above the lower chamber, I am certain that the builders would have installed double gables here also. However, although these gables could be transported up to the inner stepped levels and temporarily stored there, they could not be installed until the limestone levels on the inner platform had been built up around the chamber and the stack. That could not be done until after the perimeter platform had been pushed up to a much greater elevation and that could only have happened after the distribution hub had been set up in the upper chamber. So all we can do with the limestone beams at this stage is to ensure that they are placed on the stepped limestone levels at the elevation where they will later be installed. These beams would almost certainly have been placed on hardwood or metal rollers before they were loaded onto the barges and these would also have been used when the beams were being hauled onto the inner stepped levels prior to their installation. Chocks would have been placed against the rollers at either end of the beams before they were transported, to ensure that they did not move during transit.

Although the architects had designed a very complex, free-standing, granite structure that would have taken a great deal of time to construct on the 49th level, the benefits gained far outweighed the time and effort that was needed to create this structure. By extending the canal system beyond the gallery to the inner area, it enabled the builders to transport a phenomenal quantity of large granite and limestone blocks into this inner area to construct many of the features here and build up much of this inner space.

In addition to the many granite monoliths used in the construction of the upper chamber and the stack, there was the massive limestone beams that comprised the gabled roof of the chamber. The granite blocks that were used to construct the antechamber and other large limestone beams that were used to construct the wall at the top end of the gallery were also transported into this area on barges. There was also a vast quantity of limestone blocks used to build up the inner space transported into the area around the stack in bulk when the upper chamber and the stack were under construction. Apart from the fact that the upper chamber and the stack would not have existed, almost none of this masonry could have been transported up beyond the 49th level if the canal had not been extended beyond the gallery and into the inner area. Without the inner lock, the structure from the 49th level up would have been constructed using the smaller limestone blocks that were used to construct the uppermost section of the Great Pyramid, the section above the extended perimeter platform. This is what the upper chamber and the stack are all about. Had the builders not extended the hydraulic system beyond the top end of the gallery, the upper chamber and the stack would not exist. Having devised a way to extend the hydraulic system into this area, a way then had to be found to exploit this resource to the maximum. The free-standing granite upper chamber and the stack were the means to that end.

Due to their amazing ingenuity, their great skill and their phenomenal technical knowledge, the builders of the Great Pyramid and its immediate companion produced very stable structures. The blocks used in the construction of these two great structures at Giza were much larger than the blocks used to construct any of the earlier pyramids at Dashur. It was all about taking the greatest quantity of the largest blocks of masonry possible into these structures and transporting them up to the greatest elevation, as it was the much larger block sizes and the speed at which these could be transported that made it possible to construct these monsters within a very short timeframe. The designs for these Super Pyramids (as I like to refer to them) drastically reduced the time it took to construct pyramids on this scale.

The development of the Super Pyramid began with the Bent Pyramid at Dashur; the Great Pyramid and its immediate neighbour are the finest examples of these structures. Although bulk deliveries and larger block sizes drastically reduced the construction time of these large, stone built pyramids; it was hydraulic engineering that made it all possible. If the canal system had not been extended beyond the top end of the grand gallery, all of the masonry from that point onward would have to have been hoisted up to the inner stepped levels from the 49th level. The limestone blocks used to build up the remaining levels would have been much smaller and it would therefore have taken much longer to complete these magnificent structures.

Although it took an incredible degree of ingenuity to design the upper chamber and the stack, and a great deal of physical exertion to cut and dress the much harder granite masonry used in their construction, the builders were rewarded for all their efforts by a great reduction in the overall construction time for the project. The quarrying of the granite blocks and slabs would not in any way have hindered the project as these would have been quarried and prepared at Aswan when work on the pyramid was at the early stages. They would have been ready for use when they were required. We now know that ramps were constructed on either side of both the lower and upper chambers for the hauling of large blocks of limestone up to the perimeter platforms, but the key to understanding what happened and when it happened after the construction had reached the 49th level of the inner platform, was in understanding that the canal system had been extended into this area beyond the gallery. I then had to fully understand what the builders needed to achieve when hydraulic power was made available in this inner area. Although the ramps on either side of the upper chamber originated on the level of the second course of granite blocks in the upper chamber walls, (one course above the level of the shafts), I discovered that these ramps could not have been pressed into service until it was no longer possible to bring any more limestone into the inner area on barges.

By completing the upper chamber and the stack before they made use of the ramps at this location, the builders were able to make use of the inner lock for a very long period of time. They certainly needed to, for having constructed an upper chamber with the stack placed on top it was only with the aid of hydraulic power that they were able to transport the massive limestone beams that formed the gabled roof above the stack up to the inner stepped levels. For the builders to have made use of the ramps on either side of the upper chamber earlier, by installing the step stone at the top of the gallery and putting the granite floor in place, it would have been impossible to make any further use of the inner lock beyond the gallery. That is why they created this free-standing granite structure, and why they had not yet begun to install the antechamber and the step-stone at the top of the gallery at this stage of the construction.

One point I would like to make before we move on, is that there simply would have been no reason to construct an upper chamber in the Great Pyramid (or in its immediate neighbour) at all if it had been used as a distribution hub after only two courses of its sidewalls were complete. Unlike the lower chamber, the upper chamber would not have had a secondary role to play after it had been used as a hub. The builders would simply have used limestone to construct the low walls of a central hub and then built up solid courses of limestone from the floor level of this hub when it was no longer required. The upper chamber and the stack would not have existed.

The builders of the Great Pyramid lowered a lock gate into position at the top end of the grand gallery each time they had to raise barges in the inner area. There must have been a limit as to how much water they could pump up into this area (inner lock) before the pump ceased to function. The weight, and therefore the volume of water pushing down on the non-return valve, increased as water was pumped up into the inner lock; the volume of water being pumped up into the inner lock with each stroke of the pump would therefore have slowly diminished the greater this volume of water became, with the pump having to fight against the ever increasing back pressure acting on the valve. Sooner or later, the back pressure would have become too great and the weight of the piston dropping into the cylinder of the pump would not have been enough to push open the non-return valve. If the builders had simply relied on the pressure generated by the piston dropping into the cylinder of the pump to pump water up into this lock, they would never have been able to raise barges up to the levels that they did. But they fully understood the limitations of such a pump and that is why they created an expansion chamber (the lower chamber) to generate a secondary pulse. This improved the efficiency of the pump many times over.

The pulse generator

After the builders had constructed the first few locks within the grand gallery, they then had to install the non-return valve in the water supply pipe, which was created when the wooden floor was installed in the locks. The weight of the water in the topmost lock in the system maintained an external pressure on the non-return valve, but it was the way in which this valve was opened that was ingenious and it fully explains why the builders went to all the trouble of making the lower chamber air and watertight. The lower chamber was the expansion chamber where a secondary pulse (a pressure wave) was generated when the piston of the pump plunged down into the cylinder.

When the pump was operated and water was pumped up the supply pipe (the ascending corridor, which had in effect been extended all the way up to the top of the gallery when all the locks had been installed here), a good volume of that water was pushed along the horizontal passageway and into the lower chamber, increasing the water level in the chamber in the process. As the water level in the lower chamber increased, it pushed up against the pocket of air trapped beneath the gabled roof of the chamber and for as long as the piston of the pump maintained its downward stroke, the pressure of the air trapped under the gables continued to increase. However, when the piston bottomed and then began its return stroke, the highly pressurized pocket of air in the lower chamber reacted suddenly and violently, pushing the water level in the chamber back down to its mean level. In doing so, a pulse, a pressure wave, was generated by the compressed air in the chamber reacting to the sudden drop in water pressure when the piston of the pump bottomed. This increased air pressure pushed the water in the chamber back down to its mean level. The pulse that was generated by this rapid reaction travelled back along the horizontal passageway and up the water supply pipe where it pushed the non-return valve open again just as it was about to close. This secondary pressure wave had much more force behind it than the pressure wave generated by the downward action of the piston, and not only did this secondary pulse extend the time that the valve remained open each time the piston was operated, it was purely as a result of the generation of this pulse in the lower chamber that the builders were able to pump such a great volume of water up to such phenomenal levels within the inner lock. In short, the builders of the Great Pyramid managed to raise such massive volumes of granite masonry up to such a great elevation within the structure simply because they had discovered an ingenious way to greatly improve the efficiency of their water pump. Or put another way, the upper chamber could not have been constructed if the builders had never created the lower chamber (the expansion chamber).

The lower chamber itself served no other purpose for the builders had no need to create, or complete, this chamber when the recess they had created in the centre of the platform at this level ceased to be used as a hub. The space created for the operation of the lifting mechanism could simply have been filled in and the area above built up with limestone masonry after it ceased to function as a hub. The builders could easily have built up the centre of each platform with solid limestone masonry all the way from its foundation to the 49th level but for one single reason, they needed to create an expansion chamber to generate this secondary pulse in order to transport great volumes of masonry into the inner area on barges and construct the upper chamber. There has been much speculation over the years as to why the openings in the shafts in the lower chamber were concealed but this was certainly not an attempt by the builders to hide these shafts. The shafts in the lower chamber were only concealed behind slabs of limestone because the builders needed to create an expansion chamber in this central location after it had functioned as a distribution hub. For the chamber to function as such, it had to be made air and watertight.

The designers of the hydraulic system in the Great Pyramid, and undoubtedly in the Middle Pyramid also, had incorporated an expansion chamber into the system long before they came to construct the upper chamber. The pressure wave generated by this powerful secondary pulse would have easily overcome the tremendous pressure acting on the top side of the non-return valve, enabling the builders to pump great volumes of water up into the lock on the inner platform. It pumped water in sufficient quantities into this inner lock to enable the builders to complete the upper chamber and the stack using this ingenious hydraulic system. This free-standing granite structure on the 49th level of the Great Pyramid simply could not have been constructed without it.

The complexity of the upper chamber and the stack must have presented the designers and builders of the Great Pyramid with many difficulties that no doubt took a long time to resolve, but they were greatly rewarded for their perseverance as it enabled them to construct the largest pyramids it was possible to construct on this site. The design of the upper chamber became so complex simply because it could not serve its primary function until the granite floor of the chamber had been extended as far as the step-stone (the docking station) at the top of the gallery. This in turn could not be installed until the builders had completed the upper chamber and the stack as the hydraulic system had to be utilized to transport the granite up to these elevations within the inner area.

As you now know, it took me a very long time to get a handle on how and when the chambers and features in this part of the pyramid were constructed, but it was undoubtedly here that the older, simpler, pyramid designs evolved into something completely revolutionary in pyramid design and construction. I am certain that it was this breakthrough that led to the construction of the two large pyramids at Giza on such a massive scale, for never before had such large blocks of masonry been transported up to such an elevation. This feat was never to be repeated after the Great Pyramid had been completed and it was this fact alone that led me to believe that all of the experimentation that occurred with the earlier pyramids of this type was simply attempts by the architects to design and configure an internal structure that would enable them to construct the largest, most stable, smooth sided pyramids at Giza in the shortest possible time. The fact that the limitations of the site meant that they could not have made the two large pyramids at Giza any bigger – and kept the same configuration – only reinforces my belief that the earlier pyramids at Dashur were experimental prototypes. In other words, the super pyramids of the west bank were all about the most sacred site of all – Giza. That is not to say that there was no other reason for their construction, but primarily, it was in the construction of these pyramids that the ancient builders perfected their designs and honed their skills prior to the construction of the pyramids at Giza.

As I mentioned earlier, apart from the enormous limestone beams used to construct the gabled roof of the upper chamber, there were also other, very large limestone beams that had to be transported into the inner area and temporarily parked on some of the inner stepped levels. These were the limestone beams that form the top end wall of the gallery (and the north wall of the antechamber). These limestone beams were simply too heavy to hoist up into the inner area. So, like the limestone beams used to construct the gables, they had to be transported into the inner area on barges before the inner lock was decommissioned. These beams would have been placed on rollers and parked on their respective stepped levels of the inner area. Before these inner levels were later built up, these beams were manoeuvred across the inner platforms and installed on their respective levels at the top end of the gallery. However, most of these beams could not have been installed until after the antechamber had been constructed.

Before the builders dismantled the inner lock gate, there was probably one other very important piece of masonry that would have been temporarily parked on the stepped levels of the inner platform at this time. It would be some time before this piece of masonry would be installed but I think it would most likely have been transported into the inner area before the inner lock was disabled. I will leave you to speculate for the time being as to the role this piece of masonry played in the overall scheme of things.

With all of the very heavy components too large to be hauled up on to the inner stepped levels having been transported into the inner area on barges, the builders would have gone on to build up as much of the inner area as possible using the large limestone blocks used to construct most of the structure so far. The granite floor of the antechamber and the step-stone had to be installed before the builders could begin to haul limestone blocks into the upper chamber to push the perimeter platform higher (these were the last of the large limestone blocks used in the construction of the Great Pyramid). That will be our next task.

After the inner lock had been decommissioned, the antechamber (partially) constructed, and the perimeter platform extended as far as it was possible to extend it from the central distribution hub in the upper chamber, it would have been impossible to use the large limestone blocks used so far in the construction to construct any further sections of the Great Pyramid. We will soon discover why.

The dock and the passageway

We are now at another of those clearly defined stages where the focus of the construction changes; all activity ceases at one location and emerges in another. The inner lock had been the hub where all the building materials had been raised up to the inner levels after the grand gallery had been completed and work had begun on the upper chamber, but it was the upper chamber itself that became the next distribution hub. It was only when the upper chamber was complete and all the larger than standard blocks and beams had been transported up and into the inner area, that the ramps on either side of the upper chamber could have been pressed into service. All of the limestone used to further build up the inner stepped levels and the perimeter platform now was discharged from the barges docked at the step-stone at the top of the grand gallery, hauled through the passageway and into the upper chamber, before being hoisted up onto the landings in front of the openings in the sidewalls of the chamber. However, I have got a bit ahead of myself again as we have still to recreate the dock where all of this activity took place and create a clear pathway from the docking station to the chamber.

If there was one feature of the Great Pyramid that I had to single out as having had to endure the greatest amount of wear and tear, it is the step-stone at the top of the gallery. This block of Aswan granite played a major role in all of the operations within the pyramid from the moment it was installed. As we discovered earlier, if it had been installed when the gallery was first completed, it would have blocked the pipe (slot) under the gallery floor. As I also mentioned earlier, I eventually realized that this pipe had to have been extended bcyond the gallery to serve an inner lock as the builders could not have pumped water up into this inner lock beyond the gallery if the step-stone had been installed at this time. This granite block is located at the top end of the gallery but not beyond it, for the ends of the gallery walls are flush with the far side of this block (looking from the gallery).

I now know that the builders constructed the top lock beyond the gallery to transport the granite blocks, beams and slabs into the inner area. But for the inner lock to function, the wooden floor in the locks in the grand gallery had to have been extended all the way up to the inner lock gate, since it was only with the installation of the wooden floor in the locks that the supply pipe was extended up to the top of the gallery (the wooden floor itself forming the topside of this supply pipe). But the ramps on either side of the gallery do not extend all the way to the top end of the gallery; they stop at the granite step-stone; at least they do now. We can therefore deduce from this that the builders also extended the ramps to the top end of the gallery originally, for had they not done so, there would have been nothing to support the wooden floor in the top lock in the gallery. They had to have extended the wooden floor as far as the inner lock gate in order to extend the pipe beyond the top end of the gallery and pump water up into the inner area.

This is how we find the layout of our imaginary structure when we bring our barges with the granite blocks that will form the sidewalls of the antechamber into the top lock in thc gallery. The ramps on either side of the gallery extend all the way to the top end of the gallery at the moment and end where they meet the 49th course of limestone, the foundation upon which we will reconstruct the antechamber. However, as I eventually discovered, the builders merely laid the foundation course of the antechamber at this stage and installed the granite floor and the step-stone; they did not build up the walls of the antechamber beyond the first course at this time. A tremendous amount of activity took place in this area after the lower course of the antechamber and its granite floor had been installed. All of the limestone used to build up the inner stepped levels, and to extend the perimeter platform, had to be discharged from the barges at the step-stone, the docking station, and hauled into the upper chamber from here. So this is as far as we can take our reconstruction of the antechamber at this stage of our reconstruction.

Before we can transport any limestone into the upper chamber, we have to install the first course of granite blocks that form the sidewalls of the antechamber and complete the granite floor of the passageway all the way out to the top of the gallery. When we installed the granite floor in the upper chamber, we only completed it as far as the entrance to the chamber. When we install the granite floor in the antechamber, we will extend the floor of the upper chamber all the way out to the top of the gallery and create a clear pathway from the dock, all the way to the upper chamber. Before we can begin to install the lower course of the antechamber walls however, we will have to install the granite step-stone at the top end of the grand gallery.

When we put this granite block in place, its top face will be flush with the granite floor in the passageway. The granite floor however is built upon the same course (49th) of limestone as the sidewalls of the antechamber and this is at a lower elevation than the top of the step-stone (the 49th course of limestone is approximately half the height of the granite blocks in the sidewalls of the antechamber below the top of the step-stone). We are therefore left with no option here but to transport the granite blocks for the first course of the antechamber sidewalls, and the blocks / slabs that make up the floor of the passageway into this area beyond the gallery before we install the step-stone. We will then need to push and, or, haul the granite blocks that comprise the lower course of the sidewalls of the antechamber out beyond the sides of the gallery or back towards the upper chamber to create some space. We will need space in this area when we bring the large step stone up onto the 49th level, as it has to be hauled onto the inner limestone platform before it can be installed; it cannot be installed from the gallery.

You will no doubt remember the difficulty I had trying to figure out how the first course of granite blocks in the upper chamber had been installed on the 49th level. I had assumed that the builders had hauled the blocks from the barges (docked at the top of the grand gallery) onto the 49th level, and then hauled them from there to their respective locations. However, moving these massive blocks even a small distance required a gargantuan effort, and I soon realized that the builders would have devised a way to install these blocks and keep the physical effort required to an absolute minimum. It was then that I realized that the builders had not completed the 49th level back out to the top of the gallery but had instead transported the granite blocks as near to their respective locations as possible using the barges. It was only when the lower course of the upper chamber was almost complete that the limestone platform on the 49th level was built up until it was complete all the way out to the top of the gallery. We do not have the option here of floating the barges right up to the edge of the limestone platform now that we have come to install the first course of granite blocks that form the sidewalls of the antechamber, as the 49th limestone level is complete (it had to be completed earlier to extend the slot / water supply pipe into the inner area beyond the gallery). Fortunately, the granite blocks used to construct the lower course of the walls in the antechamber, although they are the same height as those in the upper chamber, are much shorter in length, so they would have been much easier to manoeuvre into position.

We begin this operation with the 49th limestone level complete. If you take a look at the drawing (Fig.16) that we looked at earlier, you will clearly see how the builders extended the water supply pipe into the inner area and created the lock beyond the grand gallery. However, now that we have no further use for the inner lock, one of our tasks will be to cut a channel across the ramps at the top end of the gallery as the step-stone has to be installed in this channel. But as we cannot install this very heavy granite block from the north side of the channel (the gallery side), it will have to be hauled from the barge onto the limestone inner platform on the 49th level before it can be installed. This being the case, we therefore cannot cut the channel across the gallery to accept this granite block until we have hauled it onto the inner platform. After the heavy wooden beams that comprised the inner lock gate are removed from the area at the top of the gallery and the lifting mechanism for this lock has been dismantled and removed, we can begin our operations by removing the wooden beams that form the floor in the top lock in the gallery. The wooden floor in the gallery only needs to extend as far as the upper lock gate position (or the one below) within the gallery now, for it is in this lock that the loads will be discharged from the barges onto the dock. Once we have removed this floor section, we also need to release the non-return valve. This valve would have been wedged in place at the top of the gallery until the builders had removed the floor in the top lock, then the wedges would have been removed and the valve released. It would have slid down the channel until it came up against the new buffer stop just below the top lock gate in the gallery (now one or two stations before the top end of the gallery). As I mentioned earlier, the granite blocks that form the lower course of the sidewalls in the antechamber cannot actually be installed at this time, but we have no option but to transfer these blocks onto the platform before we install the step-stone as this is the simplest, most logical way to do it. These granite blocks would probably have been hauled and pushed from the deck of the barge, docked in the top lock of the gallery, directly onto the limestone platform. The blocks would then have been hauled as far back from the top end of the gallery as possible as the step-stone had to have been hauled onto the 49th level here prior to its installation.

The barges used to transport all of the building materials during the construction of the Great Pyramid – and most probably the Giza complex as a whole – would undoubtedly have had square ends and, most probably, steeply angled faces at both the leading and trailing ends (the bow and the stern). I know that there are depictions of ceremonial barques / boats with pointed prows and sterns with what looks like blocks of limestone on their decks in existence. These paintings or carvings were produced at a much later period and are certainly not an accurate depiction of the barges used during the construction of the many structures at Giza. If the boats in these much later depictions were meant to represent the barges used in the construction of the super pyramids, then they are extremely naive depictions created by people who simply had no idea what the barges used in the construction of the pyramids looked like. However, as these are depictions of ceremonial barques, it is very unlikely that the rectangular object sitting amidships was a representation of a block of limestone masonry; it more than likely depicts a canopy of some sort used to provide shade for the pharaoh.

The step-stone is a very large block of granite. It is around a metre deep and it is as long as the width of the floor in the grand gallery. It sits in a channel that is cut across the floor of the gallery at its very top end and the step-stone is contained entirely within the gallery walls (its rear face is flush with the ends of the gallery walls). The channel was cut down into the limestone vertically as far as the bottom of the slot running up the centre of the floor in the gallery. However, as we discovered earlier, this channel across the top end of the gallery could not have been there when the inner lock was in use as the floor in the top lock in the gallery had to have been supported here.

The granite step-stone lay on its back on the deck of the barge as it was transported up to the inner platform on the 49th level. It would have been placed on the deck of the barge lengthways for it would have been too long to have been placed astride the barge (it was as long as the gallery was wide). The block was hauled from the barge onto the same limestone level that the granite blocks of the antechamber walls had been transferred onto prior to this operation. The builders may have put two hardwood battens or metal rails down on the top surface of the platform before they began to transfer the granite block from the barge, but it's more likely to have been rollers that were used here. This would have greatly reduced the drag (due to friction) of such a large piece of granite and made it much easier to haul the block onto the platform. Although ropes would have been used to haul the block from the barge to the landing, it is also possible that levers were used to move this hulking piece of granite from the deck of the barge onto the limestone landing.

The granite block had to have been hauled well back from the area where it was to be installed as the channel across the top end of the gallery, where we will install the step-stone, could not have been created until the step-stone had been hauled away from the edge of the platform. The step-stone also needed to be turned through 90 degrees on the horizontal plane before it could be installed, as it bridges across the top end of the gallery floor to provide a full width dock at the top end of the gallery when installed. This operation to turn the block through 90 degrees would not have been too difficult with the granite block propped up on hardwood battens, metal rails or rollers.

The channel that is cut across the width of the gallery at its top end is cut down vertically as far as the bottom of the slot between the ramps on the gallery side. The step-stone is much deeper than the depth of the slot and the ramps on either side of the gallery butt up against its face at the top of the gallery, creating a step up to the landing and the level of the floor in the antechamber. Our granite block now has to be hauled back in the direction of the gallery in order to install it in its transverse channel, however, the limestone platform on the south side of the channel (the far side looking from the gallery) would have been cut down at an angle towards the bottom of the far side of this channel, creating a ramp on the edge of the platform to facilitate the installation of this great stone. As can been seen in the drawing (Fig.17) on the next page, the builders would have cut away much of the limestone on the edge of the platform to create an angled face down to the bottom of the transverse channel. When the step-stone was then hauled and levered back in the direction of the gallery, it would eventually have reached a tipping point where it would have tilted onto the angled face on the edge of the limestone platform. It would then have slid down the slope until it came to rest in the bottom of the channel. The water level in the top lock would have been almost up to the level of the limestone platform when the granite step-stone was tilted onto the sloping face and the water would have acted as a buffer and slowed the descent of the granite step-stone as it slid down the slope to the bottom of the channel. Having got it into this position, it would then have been a fairly simple task to lever it up into the vertical position with its front face hard up against the vertical faces of the transverse channel that had been cut down through the ramps on either side of the gallery floor.

This was the only way to install the step-stone and that is why the walls of the antechamber and the floor of the passageway could not have been installed until after the operation I have just described had been completed. After the builders had levered the step-stone up and into its final position, they would then have built up the angled slope behind the step-stone to the level of the limestone platform again, before they began to install the lower course of the antechamber walls and install its granite floor.

The area on either side of the top end of the gallery had not been completed above the 49th level at this stage of the construction and this provided the builders with the space that was needed to manoeuvre into position the granite blocks that comprise the antechamber sidewalls and the granite slabs that form the floor of the passageway. The builders would have installed the lower course of the granite wall on the west side of the chamber only – on the right, looking from the gallery – before they went on to install the granite floor in the passageway. Only then would they have installed the sidewall on the east side of the passageway to complete the lower course of the antechamber. With the granite floor of the upper chamber and the passageway now complete all the way out to the

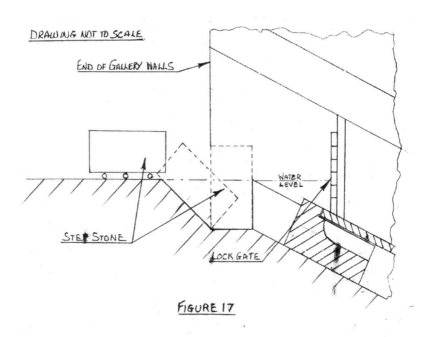

FIGURE 17

docking station at the top of the gallery, the next phase of the construction would have begun.

When we look at the various features and structures within the Great Pyramid, we tend to view them in their entirety. It is only when we try to understand how those structures and features were created or pieced together, that we have to try to visualise the various stages of their construction / creation. However, as you are aware by now, some of the structures in the Great Pyramid remained in a partial state of construction for a considerable length of time before they were completed and the lower chamber was one such feature. This normally occurred because the completion of a structure would hinder or make it impossible to execute another operation (this was the case with both the lower and upper chambers).

We now have a similar situation here at the top of the gallery. If we were to go on and complete the walls of the antechamber, it would not make the execution of the next operation impossible, but it would certainly hinder it greatly and make it very difficult to execute. We have reached another of those stages where the bulk of the material coming into the structure is directed towards a central distribution hub (the upper chamber) and then redirected to the inner stepped levels and the perimeter platforms. Since the completion of the first stage of the perimeter platform, all of the masonry coming up to the top of the grand gallery has been routed to some part or other of the inner levels and the structures built upon and within them. Now that we have established a clear channel through to the upper chamber however, all of the limestone masonry transported up to the top of the gallery will now be routed through the upper chamber, *en route* to the inner stepped levels and the perimeter platform for some time to come. This platform and the inner stepped levels can now be built up until we can push them no higher from the hub in our upper chamber.

As I mentioned earlier, this landing at the top of the grand gallery, the step-stone, was in constant use from almost the moment it was installed until the builders finally put the capstone on the Great Pyramid. It took a great deal of physical exertion to transfer much of that masonry from the barges in the gallery into the upper chamber, and if anything could be done to make that task easier it had to be given serious consideration by the designers and builders. Completing the antechamber walls before this operation got underway, would have made the task of hauling the limestone blocks from the barges into the upper chamber a much more difficult task. If the antechamber walls had been put in place before this operation had begun, then the men working at the top of the gallery would have had little room to manoeuvre as they hauled and pushed the limestone blocks from the barges onto the landing. But it was the next stage of the operation that would have been so much more difficult if the antechamber walls had been completed at this time. The workmen would have had no choice here but to push the blocks through the narrow passageway in the antechamber, as workmen in the upper chamber hauled the sleds or trolleys through the passageway from the other end. It was for these reasons that the construction of the antechamber walls ceased after the first course of its walls and its granite floor had been installed.

As well as creating more space for the workmen, the lower course of the antechamber's sidewalls provided excellent walkways on either side of the passageway for the men employed in the transfer of the limestone blocks from the landing to the upper chamber. Not only did the workmen have more space in which to operate, it also gave them the opportunity to haul the blocks toward the upper chamber rather than push them from behind. This would undoubtedly have reduced the effort required by each team member when transferring the limestone blocks from the barges to the upper chamber; it would have preserved their stamina, enabling them to work for much longer periods than if they'd had to push and pull the blocks through a narrow passageway. With the remaining courses of the antechamber walls still to be installed, the sleds and their loads could be hauled all the way up to the opening on the north wall of the upper chamber. The pulling force exerted from inside the chamber and the momentum of the sleds at this point would probably have ensured that the sleds or trolleys reached their destination in the chamber without the men on the walkways having to push the blocks through the opening into the chamber.

The lifting mechanism

To build up the stepped levels and extend the perimeter platform to a much greater elevation, we have to raise the limestone blocks coming into the upper chamber up and onto the landings next to the openings in its sidewalls, just as we had done previously in the lower chamber. (The procedure here is no different to the one we deployed in the lower chamber.) We will use the same modified shadouf that we used in the lower chamber to carry out this task, having transported some of its components up and into the upper chamber before we completed the north wall of the chamber above the passageway (other components of the shadouf were placed in the chamber before we completed its east wall). Along with this mechanism, we also transported its mystery component up and into the chamber at this time. It was this mystery component that made it possible for the builders of the Great Pyramid to raise such large blocks of masonry up and onto the landings on the sidewalls of both chambers. In fact, it was this mystery component that enabled the builders to operate a shadouf in these very confined spaces, for without it, the beam would have been much longer. However, the sidewalls of these chambers would have to have been farther apart in order for such a shadouf to operate and I doubt very much that the builders would have been able to construct a gabled roof over such chambers. Even if it had been possible, it is very unlikely that such gables would have supported the enormous weight of the structure above when the span was much greater. The mystery component therefore played a major role in the construction process and contributed immensely to the success of this project.

But it wasn't just the modified shadouf that made it possible to hoist large limestone blocks up onto the sidewalls of the upper chamber (and the lower chamber), as the builders had also to create the right environmental conditions within these chambers in order that the modified shadouf could function as intended. That, however, presented no great difficulty as the builders had been manipulating the environment within the structure since they'd first laid down its foundation course.

The mystery object is one that is known to anyone who knows anything at all about the Great Pyramid. It is as well-known as the upper or lower chambers or the grand gallery. I refer, of course, to the granite coffer – sometimes referred to as a sarcophagus – that is still to be found within the upper chamber. Since we began to reconstruct the Great Pyramid, we have discovered that the builders of the structure had developed various strategies and technologies to speed up the construction process from those of its earlier counterparts. The transportation of vast quantities of masonry up and into the structure by canal barge undoubtedly made the greatest impact on the overall construction time of a pyramid of this size, but there is no point in transporting this masonry into the pyramid if you don't have the systems in place to handle such large blocks of limestone. A lifting device had already existed that could be used to lift the largest of the limestone blocks used in the construction of the two largest pyramids at Giza, but it couldn't handle these loads in the very confined spaces of the upper and lower chambers in its existing form. Under normal operating conditions, a very long beam was needed to lift such weights, but it was not possible to employ a shadouf with a long beam within the confines of the upper and lower chambers. So a more a more compact version of this simple device was needed.

Fortunately, the ingenuity of the builders won through again. They found a way around this problem and designed a new modified version of the traditional shadouf with a much shorter beam, a shadouf that could lift a much greater weight than the standard machine with a beam of the same length. The development of this machine however, would not have been possible without the great technological advances that these people had made prior to the inception of the Giza project, as both the canal lock and the modified shadouf only came into being after the builders of these very early pyramids had discovered how to harness and manipulate the power of water on a grand scale. Hydraulic engineering was the secret weapon of the Super Pyramid builders and it was their mastery of this resource that transformed pyramid construction and set them on the road to Giza. The Super Pyramids simply would not exist if the pyramid builders had not learned how to manipulate the power of water on a grand scale. And just as hydraulic power had transformed the transportation system, it was also hydraulic power that the builders turned to in order to transform a primitive lifting device and turn it into an efficient, hydraulically operated crane capable of lifting very heavy loads, yet small enough to be operated in a very confined space. Indeed, this new modified version of the traditional shadouf could only operate in a confined or controlled space for the environment in which it operated had to be carefully managed.

For those not familiar with this device, a shadouf is simply a lever mounted on a column. It has a counterweight at one end of the beam (lever) and the beam pivots and swivels on the central column. The operators of such simple machines pull the end of the beam without the counterweight downward and a load is then attached to the lifting beam – or a bucket is filled with water. When the operator releases the tether, the load is hoisted upward as the counterweight at the other end of the beam is slightly heavier than the load on the lifting end. It works because the operator uses his body weight and gravity to haul a load, the counterweight, upward by means of a lever and this load is then used to haul the actual load up to a landing or platform by means of the same lever. If you want to lift a heavier load, you use a longer lever and a heavier counterweight. However, if you need this simple device to operate in a very confined space, then using a longer beam is not always an option. If you simply increase the weight of the counterweight without lengthening the beam, the shadouf soon becomes inoperable as the operator(s) cannot raise the counterweight when they pull on the tether at the other end of the beam.

The builders of the Great Pyramid needed a machine that could function within the confines of the lower and upper chambers – with a beam that had to be shorter than the width of both of these chambers – and the way to get around this little difficulty was to employ a hydraulically assisted shadouf. At each and every stage of the construction, water had to be pumped up and into the topmost lock on each level in order to raise the barges up to those levels. In fact, when the Great Pyramid was under construction, the water level in the locks was in an almost constant state of flux. The water level was either being increased, or it was being decreased, therefore it made good sense to exploit the constantly changing water levels and use this powerful hydraulic force to assist in the operation of the shadouf. That is exactly what the pyramid builders did within the confines of the upper and lower chambers in the Great Pyramid.

The builders of the pyramids at Giza came up with an absolutely ingenious way of exploiting the ever changing water levels within the two main chambers of the structure. They designed a counterweight for the shadouf where its weight was heavier on the down stroke (as it raised the limestone blocks) and lighter on the up stroke, where they had to rely upon the strength of the operators to haul the beam down at the lifting end. In actual fact, the weight of the counterweight did not vary they simply used hydraulic power to assist with the raising of the counterweight on the upstroke by using a granite counterweight that was hollow.

The granite coffer that we can still see today in the upper chamber was the counterweight on the shadouf – the mystery component. This coffer, it originally had a sealed lid, had buoyancy when the water level in the chamber was increased, yet became a dead weight when the water level was decreased. This was the true purpose of the granite coffer and that is why we find it in the upper chamber and not in the lower chamber as this is where it was deployed for the very last time. (Its original lid has long since been prized off and is no longer to be found within the structure.)

This was truly inspired problem solving. They couldn't increase the width of the upper and lower chambers to accommodate a longer beam on the shadouf, so they did the next best thing and created a power assisted shadouf. The confined space of the chambers had precluded the use of a longer beam but it worked in their favour when they opted for a hollow counterweight, as the water levels could be easily and quickly increased and decreased within these confined spaces to accommodate the operation of the newly modified, hydraulic shadouf. (The water level in the chamber was controlled at the top lock gate in the gallery.) I don't mind admitting that I had a great deal of difficulty accepting this staggering discovery but no matter which way I looked at it, the fact remained that the ancient pyramid builders of Egypt were using a hydraulic crane at Giza (probably) more than five thousand years ago. I know it sounds ridiculous, but when you weigh up all of the evidence, that is the only conclusion that can be drawn.

When the water level was increased within the confines of the upper chamber, the beam would have been pushed up due to the buoyancy in the hollow counterweight. This would have lowered the other end of the beam, the lifting end. When the limestone block had been attached to the lifting end of the beam, the water level in the chamber was then decreased and the full dead weight of the counterweight then hoisted the limestone block up to the level of the landings on the sidewalls of the chamber. Although the idea of a hydraulic crane this early in the historical period may seem difficult to accept, when we take a step back and look at the bigger picture, we can see that the builders were simply applying the exact same principles to raise and lower the hollow counterweight as they were applying in the grand gallery when they raised and lowered the barges that transported the limestone blocks up to the upper chamber. In fact, hydraulic power was responsible for the transportation of the limestone blocks all the way from the River Nile to the landings on the sidewalls of the upper chamber in the Great Pyramid. It was only when these limestone blocks reached this level, that the builders had finally to resort to hauling limestone up and onto the platforms using manpower and probably some other mechanical contraption such as a windlass.

The lifting device that was put to work in both the lower and upper chambers was a hydraulically assisted shadouf; it was a natural development from, and an extension of, the ingenious hydraulic system that had been designed within each of these large pyramids. The great advances made by the ancients in this field stemmed from their understanding that water, if it could be contained, could be controlled and manipulated and used to raise tremendous tonnages up to great heights within a structure. The internal structure of the Great Pyramid and its nearest companion was designed to give its builders the greatest opportunity to exploit the power of water at each and every stage of its construction. This layout enabled them to gain the maximum benefit from the advances they had made during the construction of both large pyramids at Dashur. Hydraulic power was their truly great secret. It was their mastery of hydraulics and their great hydrological works that revolutionised pyramid building in the very early Dynastic Period –

possibly pre-dynastic period – and this led directly to the construction of the greatest stone block pyramids ever to be built anywhere on the planet.

When the builders had no more use for the lifting device in the upper chamber, they had by that time pushed the perimeter platform as high as it could possibly go. They literally ran out of space on the landings as the inner stepped structure drew closer to the smooth outer faces of the pyramid with the installation of each course. The hub in the upper chamber had served its purpose by this time and was no longer of any use to the builders. It is certainly true to say that the flow of masonry up to the top end of the grand gallery continued for a very long time after the hub in the upper chamber was decommissioned, but this masonry was not routed through the upper chamber. It was probably around this time that most of the components of the lifting device were removed from the upper chamber. It may be that the only component of the lifting device that was not removed from the chamber was, of course, the granite counterweight, the coffer that has remained in the upper chamber to this day – minus its lid. (The lid was most likely smashed or prized off by Caliph Al Ma'mun's workmen more than three thousand years after it had been fitted.)

The granite blocks that were used to fill the gaps and complete the sidewalls of the upper chamber were not very large blocks, relatively speaking. When the water level in the chamber had been increased and they had been raised up to their respective levels, they would easily have been nudged into the gaps in the sidewalls of the chamber using a hand held battering ram wielded by a few workmen. When this task was complete, the barge used to transport and raise these blocks up to the apertures in each sidewall could possibly have been dismantled and removed from the chamber, but again, we cannot say for certain that this was the case. I suspect that all of the metal would have been recovered from the chamber before the builders sealed the entrance tunnel and the ascending corridor, but any wooden artefacts left behind would probably have dried out and deteriorated to the point where they would possibly have been unrecognisable by the ninth century when Al Ma'mun entered the upper chamber. We know that over the years, pieces of old wood and debris have been cleared from many of the inner chambers and passageways but it's unlikely that anyone showed the least interest in such items at the time. It's therefore entirely possible that the builders left the barge behind and parts of the lifting mechanism also. But unlike the granite coffer, these wooden artefacts would not have stood the test of time nearly so well.

Before we move on, I would just like to say that I realize just how fantastical the idea of the ancient pyramid builders deploying a hydraulic crane in the upper chamber is. I found it very difficult to believe that a hydraulic crane was in use in Ancient Egypt five thousand years before the industrial revolution in Europe. However, if we accept that the ancient pyramid builders did create a complex hydraulic system within the Great Pyramid to transport masonry into the structure, and they certainly did, for that is the only way that it was possible to transport the massive granite blocks and slabs up to the top of the gallery, then making use of a buoyant counterweight (a granite barge) in the upper chamber was simply an extension of this transportation system. There is more evidence to indicate that just such a machine existed than there is evidence to corroborate the fact that the builders constructed a flight of locks in the grand gallery for instance. We can plainly see the damage that the gallery walls incurred during the construction of the pyramid but there is no physical evidence to prove conclusively that a flight of locks was constructed within this chamber. On the other hand, in the upper chamber there is what remains of the counterweight from the hydraulic crane that once operated within this space. Although it is no longer a sealed coffer, it is clear that it did at some time in the remote past have a lid as the holes for the locating pins can still be seen. Once this machine had been set up in the upper chamber, the only other requirement for its successful operation was a means to increase and decrease the water level within the chamber. The water level within the chamber was easily increased by means of the pump in the grotto, and decreased by raising the lock gate at the top lock in the grand gallery. With a major component of the hydraulic crane still to be found in the chamber today, and given the builders' undoubted ability to manipulate the water levels within this chamber, I find it impossible to believe that they somehow devised some other method of lifting a dead weight up vertically from the floor of the upper chamber.

As you will soon discover, the builders of the Great Pyramid did in fact have another means of lifting a dead weight up vertically. However, when you realize just what this entailed, and the limitations of this system, you will realize that such a system could not have been put into operation in the upper chamber. The builders simply had no option but to devise another lifting mechanism after their work in the upper chamber was complete, as hydraulic power could not be used beyond the level of the top lock in the gallery by this stage of the construction. As you are about to discover, it was only a mechanical contraption and manpower that the builders had at their disposal from here on in, and this contraption, just like the hydraulic shadouf, had its limitations. Nonetheless, as you will soon discover, it was no less ingenious than the hydraulic crane used in the upper chamber.

As you have now discovered, every feature of the Great Pyramid had a role to play when this structure was under construction as all of its chambers, pipes and shafts were all component parts of the whole. The granite coffer in the upper chamber was one such component and that is the only reason that it is still to be found in this chamber. I will offer further evidence to this effect in my summing up.

Chapter Five

The antechamber

The antechamber is undoubtedly the most enigmatic of all the confined spaces within the Great Pyramid. It is certainly the chamber that has intrigued me most for longer than I care to remember. When I first began to write this account of my reconstruction of the Great Pyramid, I still had more than a few unanswered questions with regard to this small chamber, but little did I realize that those questions would still be unanswered when I was about to begin the actual reconstruction of the chamber. I'd made little progress with the problems posed by the construction of the upper chamber and it was those problems that had occupied my mind as I mentally reconstructed the grand gallery and its locks. By the time I'd reached the top of the gallery ready to begin the reconstruction of the upper chamber, I'd made little progress trying to decipher the secrets of both of these chambers and my writing came to an abrupt standstill.

When I'd set out to mentally reconstruct the Great Pyramid, I had the key to how it was originally constructed. The key confirmed some of my earlier conclusions (and disproved others) regarding the possible function of some of the internal chambers of the Great Pyramid, but even with confirmation that a feature performed a specific function it can be of very little help when trying to determine how, and when, it was constructed. That was the problem I came up against when I reached the top of the gallery since there were very few clues as to how and when the two chambers on this level had been created – very few clues as to how I should proceed.

When you have tried to think of every possible way that a particular feature could have been constructed and still not discovered the answer, there is really only one course of action left; you simply have to begin to reconstruct it the way you think it was most likely done and continue on this path until you encounter difficulties. This process focuses the mind on the physical difficulties that its original builders would have encountered putting each and every piece of a chamber in place during its construction. By figuring out how the builders of these features overcame each of these difficulties, I'd hoped to get some idea of the techniques and the technology that may have been employed in order to create these features. Needless to say, that if a technique or technology had been introduced at some stage of the process that had not been used previously to construct a chamber or feature, this further complicates the picture and we then have to try to discover what new technology or technique could have been introduced here. With a structure as complex as the upper chamber and the stack above it, there were so many possible paths to take when my reconstruction reached the top end of the grand gallery that I didn't know where to begin.

But you have to start somewhere and follow each path as far as it takes you. You know from the beginning that each path most likely leads nowhere but unless you follow it to the very end, you don't know if you are on the right track or not. After many attempts, and many dead ends later, I began to believe that I would never discover the way forward with the construction of the chambers at the top end of the gallery. As doubt crept in, I began to think that maybe I had been on the right track earlier and didn't see that I had not exhausted all of the possibilities in that direction. It is at that point that you have to walk away and leave it until another day; you know that there is only one thread that will lead to the answer you are looking for and you just have to have the patience to wait until you discover it.

That was how it was for me with the reconstruction of the chambers at the top end of the gallery. Fortunately, when I eventually got over the first hurdle, it pointed in a direction that I'd not even considered. The way forward, as it turned out, involved the construction of the upper chamber and the stack above it prior to the construction of the antechamber, which I had earlier assumed was constructed in combination with the upper chamber. However, having shifted my focus to the reconstruction of the upper chamber and the stack, I then had to put all of the unanswered questions I had about the antechamber to the back of mind, at least until I had solved most of the problems associated with the reconstruction of the upper chamber. Only when I had overcome all of the many difficulties faced by the ancient builders when they constructed the upper chamber, could I then begin to ponder the difficulties faced by the builders when they constructed the antechamber.

As you are now aware, the reconstruction of the upper chamber, the stack and the areas of the inner platform around it, proved to be an infinitely more complex procedure than I had ever envisaged. I got bogged down and confused on so many occasions when faced with too many possibilities as to how I could proceed. Each wrong turning that I took only confused the bigger picture to the point where I oftcn had to give up my search for a solution and put it all to one side until another day. I found it much more difficult to envisage the structural landscape of the inner area at the top of the grand gallery than I had when I was reconstructing the lower chamber and the grand gallery. This was by far the most difficult area of the Great Pyramid to reconstruct and I had grossly underestimated the complexity of the construction process when I set out to reconstruct the chambers beyond the gallery. Eventually, I realized that the upper chamber and the stack could only have been constructed if the canal had been extended into the inner area beyond the top end of the grand gallery; thcrefore the antechamber could not have been constructed until after the upper chamber and the stack were complete.

Now that I fully realized just how complex the reconstruction of this part of the structure was going to be, I had to put all of my energies into the reconstruction of the much larger chamber behind the antechamber and the layered structure above it. I knew it would be a long time before I got back to the reconstruction of the antechamber at that stage, as I was finding it very difficult to hold all of the threads of my reconstruction together and was making very slow progress. I found it so disheartening every time I made a wrong move and expended precious energy trying to make a supposed solution work, only to discover at a later stage that it didn't. I began to despair that I would ever discover how they'd put it all together as there seemed to be so many different ways the builders could have built up this area beyond the gallery at the outset.

When I did finally overcome all of the difficulties associated with the reconstruction of the upper chamber and the stack, I realized that I would have to approach the reconstruction of the antechamber, and the area above and around it, in the same manner that I had approached the reconstruction of the upper chamber. With the antechamber itself, it was not the reconstruction of the chamber that presented me with any great difficulty, it was the component parts of the system the builders had employed here and the configuration of those components that presented the difficulty. It was not that I had no idea of how the system installed here functioned because I knew how it was utilized, but I had still to work out what form its component parts took and how they were interconnected. However, I doubted that I had the mental stamina for a long drawn out process of elimination again after my experiences with the upper chamber and the stack, so I needed to get some lucky breaks here early on. I'd come close to throwing in the towel with the reconstruction of the upper chamber and the stack and I simply couldn't risk getting so bogged down again. It was only the fact that I had invested so much time and energy in the project by that stage of the reconstruction that had kept me going. But there was a limit to my endurance and I couldn't have gone through such a long painstaking process again.

There was something else troubling me at this time. I had pushed it to the back of my mind after I'd discovered the key, for it was something that I wouldn't have to deal with for a very long time. I also hoped that I would have solved it by the time I reached that particular stage of the reconstruction. But that stage was fast approaching and I hadn't figured it out. The problem was that I knew that the antechamber was the last hub – the last portal on our journey to the top of the Great Pyramid – but I still had no idea how the builders had managed to complete the Great Pyramid. I was mentally drained after my great difficulties with the upper chamber and the stack, with my thinking processes not as they should have been. I really hoped at that moment in time that I had not used up my quota of lucky breaks for there would be some daunting tasks ahead and I knew that I would need all the luck I could get on this the last leg of the journey. Surely lady luck wouldn't desert me now!

As visitors to the Great Pyramid today enter the antechamber, the first thing they notice is how small it is. The next thing they usually notice is the amount of damage its walls have sustained. Some of the damage inflicted upon the Great Pyramid – other than the damage possibly incurred during the earthquake in 1301AD – has been inflicted by various adventurers and explorers all the way back to the days of Caliph Al-Ma'mun and beyond. However, this was not the case with the grand gallery, nor was it the case with the antechamber as most of the damage that can be seen in these chambers today is damage that was sustained during the actual construction of the pyramid. Most of the damage that can been seen in the grand gallery was caused by the tremendous stresses and strains put on the corbelling by the timber uprights of the locks and the tremendous pressures placed upon the lock gates during their long period of use. However, after the operations in the upper chamber had come to an end, it was the antechamber that then played the pivotal role in the construction of the upper portion of the Great Pyramid, with a tremendous amount of limestone having been routed through this small chamber *en route* to the levels above. After the sidewalls of the upper chamber had been completed, all of the limestone to complete the pyramid was transported up to the docking station (the step-stone) at the top of the gallery, and then each limestone block was hauled into the antechamber. The antechamber is in fact the bottom end of a lift shaft and it was from here that all of the smaller blocks of limestone needed to complete the pyramid were hoisted up to the inner stepped levels and the platforms beyond when they were under construction. There was no other route to the top now and the area within and around this small chamber would have been a great hive of activity for a tremendously long time, as you can no doubt imagine. This is the true reason for the existence of this small chamber and for the damage that it incurred so let's take a look now at how this little chamber was constructed and then utilized.

Like most of the other chambers and pipes in the Great Pyramid, the antechamber is a very misleading name for this small chamber but it will have to do for now as to rename it at this stage of our reconstruction will only confuse matters. The barges that had previously come up into the inner lock here have only been able to come as far as the step-stone (the dock) at the top end of the gallery since we installed this granite landing, established the lower course of the antechamber walls and installed its floor. We have yet to complete our antechamber walls and construct the wall at the top end of the gallery so that is our first task here.

The granite blocks to complete the second course of the walls of the antechamber would most probably have been hauled from the barges directly onto the top of the first course of granite blocks that we installed earlier. The top surface of the lower course of blocks in the sidewalls of the antechamber is a good deal higher than the top of the step-stone (over half the height of the granite blocks in the lower course of the sidewalls was above the level of the step-stone) so it would probably have been possible to bring the leading edge of the barges right up to the granite blocks at the ends of the lower course of the antechamber walls. Had this not been possible, a simple solution would have been to build up some smaller blocks on top of the step-stone until they were flush with the top of the granite walls. These temporary plinths would have bridged the gap between the barge and the north ends of the lower course of the antechamber walls when the granite blocks for the second course were being hauled from the barges. The plinths would then have been removed when all of the granite blocks to complete the second course of the walls had been unloaded. But having said that, I do think it's more than likely that the granite blocks for the second course of the antechamber walls could have been discharged directly onto the top of the lower course. Had this not been possible then the granite blocks that comprise both the second and third courses of the walls here would have been transported into the inner area earlier before the inner lock had been decommissioned.

The inner platform on either side of the lower course of the antechamber walls would have been built up with limestone prior to the installation of the second course of blocks in the walls. This would have provided a good platform from which to work as the second course of the antechamber walls were built up (there was not much space on the west side of the antechamber as the sidewall of the chamber here was fairly close to the ramp on the north side of the upper chamber).

Although the roof in the upper chamber is almost 7 metres high, the ceiling in the antechamber is just a little over 3.5 metres high, with the granite walls in the antechamber giving way to limestone 0.3 metres or so below its ceiling. Unlike the upper chamber, where they had four more courses to go on top of the first at this stage of its construction, the walls of the antechamber had only two more courses of granite to be put in place after the first course had been installed. In addition, the north wall of the chamber, between the antechamber and the gallery, was constructed of limestone as it did not have to endure any of the wear and tear that the sidewalls of the chamber were subjected to after the chamber was complete and the hoist had been set up. This dividing wall was constructed of limestone beams and these beams also form the wall at the top end of the grand gallery and extend beyond its sidewalls (the first of these beams bridges across the passageway into the antechamber). We parked these beams on their respective levels on the inner platform earlier as they could not have been hauled from the barges in the gallery at this stage of the construction.

The construction of the antechamber and the construction of the top end wall of the grand gallery was a simultaneous operation.

However, the limestone beam that formed the north wall of the antechamber, and the top end wall of the gallery, had to have been manoeuvred onto the top of the first course of the granite sidewalls before the granite blocks that comprise the second course of the walls in the chamber could have been installed in their final positions. These were huge beams and a lot of space was needed when the beams were being levered and hauled into position. The beams had in fact been brought up onto the inner stepped levels on the east side of the antechamber before the inner lock had been dismantled as this was the only way to get these huge beams up to these levels (it would have been impossible to increase the water level in the top lock in the gallery to discharge these beams directly onto the granite walls). Just as we did earlier with the granite blocks that made up the lower course of the sidewalls in the antechamber, we again have to manoeuvre some of the granite blocks that make up the second course of its sidewalls onto the limestone platform on either side of the antechamber, away from the working area on the north side of the antechamber. Once we have installed the limestone beam across the top end of the gallery on this level, we can then install these blocks in the sidewalls of the chamber.

The first limestone beam to be installed across the top end of the gallery also forms the roof of the passageway into the antechamber, as it bridges across the granite blocks in the lowest course of the antechamber walls. This lower course of granite extends all the way from the north wall of the upper chamber out to the back of the step-stone and it forms the sides of the passageway through to the upper chamber from the top of the gallery. The second course of granite blocks in the sidewalls of the antechamber only extends from the south wall of the antechamber to the back of the limestone beam that we are about to install across the top end of the gallery. As the limestone inner platform would have been built up on either side of the antechamber to the same height as the lower course of its sidewalls prior to the installation of this beam, there are good working areas on both sides of the chamber here. Earlier we parked this beam on this level of the inner platform (and parked all the others that form the wall at the top end of the gallery on their respective levels) as it could not be installed at that time, but now it has to be manoeuvred into position at the top end of the gallery. This is the lowest beam in the wall at the top end of the gallery and you have to duck under this crossbeam in order to enter the antechamber.

Unlike many of the huge beams that make up the walls of the upper chamber, these limestone beams could not be floated into their final positions using the barges and the inner lock, as this was no longer possible after the step-stone had been installed. But apart from these limestone beams, a lot of smaller limestone blocks had also been brought up into the inner area on the east side of the antechamber after the limestone beams had been parked on the stepped levels here. These small limestone blocks were easily manoeuvred and the builders would almost certainly have positioned some of these smaller blocks behind the limestone beams that make up the end wall of the gallery here, as the beams were levered over to the top opening of the gallery to close the gap. The limestone beams would have been set down on rollers when they were placed on the stepped levels so the builders would have had no difficulty manoeuvring the beams into their final positions. However, when the leading end of the beam had bridged the gap (passageway) between the lower course of the walls of the antechamber and been levered forward from here, it would have tilted slightly when most of the weight of the beam was beyond the fulcrum point – the roller nearest the centre of the beam – and come to rest on top of the granite wall on the west side of the chamber (on the right looking from the gallery). With the limestone beam now closing the gap on this level at the top end of the gallery, the trailing end of the beam may have been levered up and the few remaining rollers removed from under the beam. When the beam was lowered again, it would have been levered into its final position and the first course of the north wall of the antechamber and the top end wall of the gallery, was now in place.

This was the most likely method used to manoeuvre these beams into their final positions and the builders certainly had plenty of small blocks of limestone to put in place behind these beams to use as fulcrums when they slowly levered the beams across the top end of the gallery. The pyramid builders were very resourceful and more than capable of manoeuvring these beams into position at the top end of the gallery using large hardwood beams as levers, but they may not have used levers to raise the trailing end of the beam in order to remove the last of the rollers. They may have used wedges to raise the trailing end of the beam to remove this roller and then have pushed the trailing end of the beam off the wedges when they levered the limestone beam the short distance to its final position. This may have been the simpler of the two options.

The inner limestone levels would have been built up by two courses on the east side of the antechamber after the first of the limestone beams had been installed, as the next limestone beam to be hauled and levered into position at the top end of the gallery would have been installed on this level. As they levered this beam into position, the platform behind it also had to be built up here, with the limestone blocks installed on this level providing the pivots for the levers at each stage of the operation. Lime mortar would have been applied to the top surface of the limestone beam on the lower level as the second limestone beam was levered into position. This beam, and all subsequent beams that comprise the north wall of the antechamber, had to have been levered a greater distance than the beams that preceded them as the inner stepped levels would have been stepped upward and outward and therefore farther away from the top end of the gallery on each level.

Before we move on, I would just like to mention the south wall of the antechamber; this is the wall facing you as you enter the antechamber and it has four vertical rope grooves cut into its face. The granite blocks that you see here are not the blocks that form the north wall of the upper chamber as the passageway between the antechamber and the upper chamber is much longer than the depth of these blocks. This granite mass above the passageway into the upper chamber was built up after the upper chamber and the stack had been completed. It may seem odd that there is such a long passageway between these two chambers but there were very good operational reasons as to why the builders chose to construct the upper chamber and the antechamber in the spaces that they occupy. As you will no doubt remember, the north wall of the upper chamber had to be a far enough distance from the top end of the grand gallery so that the barges transporting the granite slabs for the roof and the stack could be accommodated within the inner lock. It was the length of the longest loads that determined the distance from the inner lock at the top end of the gallery to the north wall of the upper chamber. However, after the upper chamber and the stack were complete, it was then imperative that the antechamber was placed as near to the top of the grand gallery as possible for two reasons: the antechamber was placed in this position as it had to be as near as possible to the east-west axis of the structure, and it was also advantageous to have the antechamber as near as possible to the top end of the gallery and the docking station, as the limestone blocks to be hauled up the lift shaft had only to be hauled a short distance from the barges to the bottom of this shaft. When the plans for the Great Pyramid were drawn up, the architect positioned the grand gallery within the structure so that it would come to an end near to the east-west axis. The reason for this will become clear as our reconstruction nears the top of the structure.

The opening on the north wall of the upper chamber was extended out towards the south wall of the antechamber after the upper chamber and the stack were complete this created the passageway between these two chambers. Most of the structure above the passageway into the upper chamber would have been built up as the antechamber walls were built up and most of the granite blocks for these constructions would have been transported into the inner area before the inner lock had been decommissioned. These blocks would have been parked on the inner levels on the east side of the antechamber and the upper chamber until they were needed.

The next task for the builders after the first limestone beam had been positioned at the top end of the gallery, was the installation of the second course of granite blocks in the sidewalls of the antechamber. All of these blocks have vertical channels cut into them and there are four channels in all, one more than in the granite blocks that formed the first course of the walls. As those familiar with this chamber are aware, there are four pairs of vertical channels cut into the sidewalls of the antechamber, three of those pairs of channels extend all the way to the floor of the chamber but the first pair of channels (as you enter the chamber from the gallery) only extend from the top of the granite walls down to the first course of the walls (the top of the passageway); they do not extend as far as the floor here.

There is no sign of any portcullis slabs in the three pairs of channels in the antechamber but there are two granite slabs in the first pair of channels that do not extend below the level of the roof of the passageway into the chamber. Anyone entering the antechamber today has to duck under these granite slabs before they can stand up in the chamber; failure to do so can result in a knock on the head. Contrary to popular belief, these slabs are not portcullis slabs, nor were there ever any portcullis slabs installed in the antechamber.

Even though Egyptologists often refer to the portcullis slabs that they presume to have been installed in this chamber, the regularity with which these slabs are mentioned does not make this a fact; it is a belief. There never were any portcullis slabs in this chamber. This is a complete myth. Having said that, I can understand how Egyptologists came to believe that three portcullis slabs had at one time been installed here, for it is almost certainly the case that three such slabs had once been installed in one of the passageways (pipes) in the smallest of the three principal pyramids at Giza. But that was certainly not the case in the Great Pyramid, as the three pairs of channels that extend all the way to the floor of the antechamber served a completely different purpose. After we complete the chamber, we will discover the true reason as to why the builders cut these three pairs of channels into its sidewalls. (We will also take a look at the small pyramid later to see why the builders needed to install portcullis slabs in one of its corridors.)

Just like the limestone beams that were used to construct the wall at the top end of the gallery, the granite blocks that formed the walls of the antechamber had also been transported up into the area beyond the gallery, prior to this end wall of the gallery being constructed. These granite blocks would also have been placed on their corresponding inner levels and propped up on rollers or sleds – probably both. When the limestone blocks on either side of the antechamber (behind the granite walls) had been put in place to bring the limestone platform up level with the top of the granite blocks in the first course of the sidewalls, the granite blocks that formed the second course of the sidewalls would then have been hauled over towards the antechamber prior to their installation. Earlier we installed the first of the crossbeams across the top end of the gallery and before we install the second and third course of the antechamber walls, I have to say that I believe that the builders would have installed the second and third crossbeams here at the top end of the gallery before they completed the sidewalls of the antechamber. This would have completed the north wall of the antechamber up to the level at the top of the third course of the granite sidewalls. I believe that the builders would have built up the north wall of the antechamber to this level first, as I think that they would have installed all the granite blocks of both the second and the third courses of the antechamber walls on the west side of the chamber next. The reason that I believe this to have been the case, is

163

that the two granite slabs that we can see in the first pair of channels in the antechamber today had to have been installed as the sidewalls were being constructed; they could not have been lowered into these channels later for they were just too heavy. These slabs were probably put in place after the granite blocks on the second and third courses on the far side (the west side) of the chamber had been installed. The slabs would have been transported up to the inner levels earlier on sleds, along with the granite blocks that make up the sidewalls of the antechamber.

The granite slabs in the first pair of channels in the antechamber straddle the passageway and the lower of the two slabs rests on the top surface of the lower course of granite blocks in the sidewalls of the chamber – on the same surface as the first crossbeam that we installed earlier at the top end of the gallery. Before we install the granite slabs we need to install the granite blocks that comprise the second and third courses of the west wall of the antechamber. This would have been a straightforward operation as these blocks would have been hauled over to the west side of the chamber from the stepped levels on the east side of the antechamber. A limestone block on a sled would have been placed in the passageway and a wooden block would have been placed on top of the limestone block to bring it flush with the top of the granite blocks in the lower course on the walls here. Each of the blocks that make up the second course of the west wall of the antechamber would have been hauled across to the west side of the chamber and installed. The builders would have installed the block nearest the north end of the chamber first and then worked their way back towards the south end of the chamber. They would then have installed the granite blocks that form the lower course of the south wall here next (the one above the passageway into the upper chamber) as well as all of the blocks on this level between the south wall of the antechamber and the north wall of the upper chamber. After this level had been completed the blocks that form the third course of the walls in the antechamber would have been hauled over to the area at the south end of the chamber and these blocks would then have been installed in the west wall in the same manner as those we have just installed in the second course of the west wall here.

Now that we have installed all of the granite blocks on the west side of the chamber, we can begin to install the granite slabs in the first pair of channels at the north end of the chamber. The vertical channel that is cut into the inner face of the two blocks nearest the north end of the antechamber on its west side is the channel into which we have to insert our two granite slabs. These slabs had to have been inserted into this vertical channel in the west wall of the chamber before the builders put the two granite blocks in the east wall at the north end of the chamber in place. The easiest way to install the lower slab in the two vertical channels was to position the limestone block on the sled we had used earlier in the passageway, below the channel in the west wall where we will install our granite slabs, and then place a wooden block on top of the limestone block to provide a temporary support for the lower slab as it was nudged across the gap (the passageway). The granite slab would almost certainly have been placed on a wooden sled before it had been transported up to the inner platform and this would have made it fairly easy to haul the slab back across the inner platform to the east side of the antechamber prior to its installation. It's most likely that the granite slab would have been levered up into the vertical position very near to its final location, then nudged or levered across the passageway until the far side of the slab was located in the vertical channel on the west side of the chamber.

With the first slab located in its channel in the west wall, the builders had then to install the second (upper) of these two slabs before they could place the granite blocks in the east wall here. These two slabs were once fastened together; therefore one large granite slab would have served the same purpose. However, one large granite slab would have been much heavier and I suspect that two slabs were used as a single granite slab would have been much too difficult to manoeuvre and install in the guide channels due to its much greater weight. More care would have been taken with the installation of the upper slab, as the top face of the lower slab only provided a narrow landing when the slab was nudged into position. A few blocks of limestone would most probably have been temporarily installed on the east side of the slab we have already installed, to bring the level of the platform up to the required height for the installation of the upper slab. After the slab had been hauled over to the east side of the chamber, it would then have been levered up into the upright position, just as we had done with the lower of the two slabs. It would then have been aligned with the slab already installed here. It would have been nudged on to the top of the lower slab and carefully nudged across the passageway until its leading edge was firmly located in the vertical channel on the west side of the chamber.

As I mentioned earlier, the builders simply had to install both of these granite slabs in the pair of channels at the north end of the chamber before they put the two granite blocks on the east side of these slabs in place. It would have been almost impossible to install these granite slabs after the sidewalls of the chamber had been completed for they were simply far too heavy to be hoisted up vertically and then lowered into the channels here.

When the two granite slabs had been installed at the north end of the chamber and the two granite blocks on the east side of these slabs had been installed in the sidewalls, the builders would then have completed the second course of the sidewalls on this side of the chamber, then built up the limestone platform on this side of the chamber also before proceeding to install the remaining granite blocks in the third course of the sidewalls to complete the walls of the antechamber. You have to bear in mind, of course, that the builders were not bringing any more limestone blocks up to the inner platform at this stage of the construction; they were simply shuffling limestone blocks from one section of the inner levels to the areas on either side of the antechamber as its walls were being built up at this stage of the construction.

This would have been a very physically demanding stage of the construction for the men working on the inner platform. Up until now, almost all of the limestone and granite used in the construction had been transported up and onto the inner levels with the minimum of physical effort on the part of the workmen. These granite blocks and slabs were brought right alongside the ledges where they were to be installed and it was only a matter of hauling the blocks from the decks of the barges on to the adjacent ledges. But the beams, blocks and slabs being installed at this stage of the construction had been brought up onto the inner stepped levels before work on the antechamber began; in order to construct the antechamber, the inner lock had to be decommissioned and the step-stone installed. Every piece of this masonry therefore had to be hauled or levered over to where it was to be installed from where it had been parked on the inner stepped levels on the east side of the antechamber, prior to the installation of the step-stone. In fact, the installation of the step-stone had been a major transition point for the builders, for they were never again able to transport masonry on barges, from its point of origin, to where it was to be installed. Most of the masonry from that point onward had to be hauled a considerable distance to its final destination as the barges could go no further than the dock (the step-stone) at the top end of the grand gallery by this stage of the construction. But the large limestone beams used to construct the wall at the top end of the gallery, and the granite blocks used to construct the antechamber, would have proved the most difficult to install on the inner levels for these were much heavier than the standard limestone blocks used to build up the inner levels after the antechamber was complete (the limestone beams are twice as high as the average limestone blocks). I will not bore you with the details of how the granite blocks in the second and third course of the sidewalls were installed for it was a very straightforward operation. Suffice to say that the walls of the antechamber were built up in conjunction with the south wall of the chamber, and the area above the passageway into the upper chamber.

Now that we have completed the sections of the antechamber constructed of hard wearing granite, and installed the two granite slabs in the channels at its north end, we need to continue with the construction of this chamber until it is complete. Before we move on, I should mention that the four pairs of vertical channels in the granite sidewalls of the antechamber do not extend beyond the top of the granite sidewalls; the limestone blocks that form the sidewalls of the antechamber above this level are set well back from the edge of the granite walls.

There are four pairs of vertical channels in all in the sidewalls of the antechamber and the aforementioned slabs sit in the first pair of channels as we enter the antechamber from the grand gallery. There are no slabs in the other three pairs of channels that extend all the way to the floor. If we are to believe most accounts of the inner workings and passageways of the Great Pyramid, then these three empty pairs of slots at one time held three "portcullis slabs" that once sealed the so called "King's Chamber" (upper chamber). There is absolutely no evidence to indicate that this was the case and when we come to build up the inner stepped levels later you will discover why there were never any portcullis slabs in the three empty pairs of channels in this chamber... and the true reason for their existence. As Graham Hancock pointed out in *Fingerprints of the Gods,* the roof of the antechamber is much too low to accommodate such slabs if they were to be pulled up clear of the passageway. But the slabs would not have sealed the upper chamber if they had been shorter, as anyone could simply have gained access to the upper chamber by climbing over the top of them. The fact that the only slabs still to be found in the antechamber cannot be lowered all the way to floor level, is totally at odds with this theory also. This in itself is a very good indication that something else must have taken place here.

This myth goes hand in hand with the other myth that the upper chamber was a "King's Chamber" but these are simply theories conjured up by others in the past as they tried to make sense of these chambers and the artefacts found within them. These myths have only existed for so long because no one had been able to disprove them. However, that was before the Great Pyramid began to give up its secrets.

The true reason why we don't find any evidence that portcullis slabs had once been installed in the antechamber is because they never existed. This little room wasn't constructed as an antechamber for the much grander "King's Chamber" next door because the "King's Chamber" didn't exist either. These are simply figments of an over fertile imagination somewhere in the distant past – myths that have endured until the present day simply because we did not discover the true purpose of these chambers. The myths have been kept alive by those who couldn't see what it took to put this structure on the plateau, or how ridiculous such notions were. The upper chamber, on the other hand, does exist and its features – like all the other chambers, shafts and passageways within the great pyramid – are all fully explained by the role they played in the construction of this magnificent structure. But although the very imposing upper chamber played a crucial role in the construction process, it is the little room next door, the one we are in the process of reconstructing, that played a much greater part in the construction of the Great Pyramid than its tiny size would otherwise indicate. The term "antechamber" does it no justice whatsoever.

When the antechamber was complete and the wall at the top of the grand gallery had been built up, all of the limestone to complete the pyramid had to be offloaded from the barges at the granite step-stone at the top of the grand gallery, the docking station. The masonry that was discharged from the decks of the barges was then hauled through the short passageway and into the antechamber. There was only one route to the limestone levels and the partially constructed structure above now, and all of the limestone to complete the structure came through this little chamber. Every block of limestone needed to complete the pyramid was hauled into the antechamber then hoisted up to the levels above. That was the true purpose of the antechamber.

Before the builders had decommissioned the inner lock beyond the gallery, they transported all of the limestone and granite blocks that were too heavy or too large to be hoisted up vertically from the antechamber up to the inner stepped levels on barges. Along with this masonry, they also transported the components of a hoist onto the inner stepped levels before they decommissioned the inner lock. This was the hoist that they positioned above the antechamber at this stage of the construction and it was up through the roof of this chamber that the great mass of limestone needed to complete the pyramid was hauled up and onto each of the unfinished levels above.

After the antechamber was complete, it would have been impossible to haul the largest of the outer casing blocks that had been used in the earlier part of the construction up to the unfinished levels. Smaller limestone blocks had to be used from this stage of the construction until the structure was complete as these had all to be routed through the small antechamber and hauled up to the platforms from this level. When the builders closed off the top end of the grand gallery, it was only these smaller sized blocks that could be hauled up to the inner stepped levels and the upper courses of the structure since all of these blocks had to be hauled through the narrow passageway into the antechamber, before being hauled up vertically to each of the limestone levels. These limestone blocks were considerably smaller than the standard limestone blocks used to construct the bulk of the structure up to the current level of our perimeter platform, but they had to be much smaller as they had to be hauled up vertically as a dead weight from that point onward. No ramps or hydraulically assisted lifting devices could be employed after the step-stone (docking stone) at the top end of the grand gallery had been installed.

Before we move on, I would like to mention another feature of the antechamber, its roof. The roof of the chamber consists of three slabs of limestone. I have only mentioned the roof at this time simply because this is one feature of the Great Pyramid where the potential exists to prove easily and quickly that what I am about to tell you is the truth. These are not limestone beams that we see above the antechamber; they are limestone slabs that were lowered into position to form a ceiling in the chamber when the structure was almost complete. They were lowered into position above the antechamber when the builders had hoisted all the limestone needed to complete the pyramid up to the platforms above, for above those three slabs in the roof of the antechamber there is a lift shaft that extends to very near the top of the pyramid. It was up through this shaft that all of the limestone to complete the Great Pyramid was hauled up to the platforms of the structure as this was the only route up to the upper levels after the builders of the Great Pyramid sealed the sidewalls of the upper chamber and constructed the antechamber just beyond the gallery.

The three slabs that form the roof of the antechamber were not installed in the position that they are to be found in today when the walls of the antechamber were completed, as the shaft above the chamber remained open for a very long time after operations first began here. When these slabs were first installed above the chamber they stood on edge, most probably two at one end of the shaft and one at the opposite end. They were only lowered into the horizontal position and slid along the ledges to close the lower end of the shaft when the builders made their retreat from the inner chambers and passageways after the completion of the pyramid. If Egyptologists have any doubts about the existence of this shaft they can easily verify that it exists, simply by driving wedges into the gaps between two of these slabs to create an opening here. This will not only verify the existence of the lift shaft, it will prove conclusively that the ancient builders constructed the Great Pyramid from the inside for it couldn't have been done any other way.

Before the builders exited the inner passageways of the Great Pyramid and sealed it, any materials that could be recycled were removed from the structure –commodities like wood, metal and rope were much too valuable to leave behind. The removal of the temporary wooden structures and machinery used during the construction of the Great Pyramid however, robbed us of the opportunity to see this inner structure for what it truly was. But for more than a thousand years, it has been possible to gain access to the inner chambers, corridors and shafts of the Great Pyramid and had all or most of the hydraulic and mechanical machinery survived intact until modern times, there would have been no great mystery to solve, as it would have been plain for all to see why all of its chambers, corridors and shafts had been constructed in the manner they had been. However, this was not to be, and since the time of Herodotus, probably much longer, man could only speculate as to the purpose of this structure and how it had been constructed.

Over a thousand years after the time of Herodotus (c. 484 – c. 425 B.C.E.), Caliph Al Ma'mun (786 – 833 C.E.) cut a passage into what would later become known as the ascending corridor and gained access to the greater part of its inner chambers and shafts. The only artefact that we know for sure was there when he first gained access was the granite coffer in the upper chamber. The Caliph was certainly not on an archaeological expedition and it's more than likely that there would have been other artefacts that may have given us a clue as to what had taken place here when the Caliph first entered the inner chambers and passageways (pipes) of this structure. If there was, they have long since disappeared.

But artefacts are only one aspect of the bigger picture for, as we have discovered on this journey, the Great Pyramid is full of clues as to how it was constructed; we just needed the key to open the door. Once that door was opened and we realized that each and every feature of the Great Pyramid held clues as to how it was constructed, it was only a matter of time before the Great Pyramid gave up most of its secrets. Some of these features have provided us with many clues and others with few but the antechamber, despite its small size, turned out to be an Aladdin's cave when it came to clues. It took me a long time to recognize and understand what all of its features represented – and even longer to piece it all together – but I eventually discovered that all of its features played their part in a highly mechanized and efficient operation that was centred on this small chamber.

To read the clues – to decipher the language of the structure – we first have to understand what the builders needed to achieve here. I had long since rejected most of what Egyptologists had told us about the pyramids and the supposedly primitive level of technology available to the builders of these magnificent monuments for it has been plain to many for decades that these structures were built by a technologically advanced people. I had by this time reconstructed two thirds of my own pyramid mentally and I now understood much of what it took to put the Great Pyramid on the Giza plateau. It was now plain to see that its builders had harnessed a great natural resource for the purposes of transportation and for lifting, but they had also developed the technology to take full advantage of this great power source within the structure. Without this power source and the technology they developed to take advantage of it, the pyramids in their present form would never have existed. It was only the power of water (hydraulic power) that made it all possible.

The only route to the inner levels and the perimeter platform now is through this little room at the top of the grand gallery and all of the building materials now have to be hauled up to the platforms under construction from the floor of this chamber. Countless generations of pyramid builders and mastaba builders had probably been raising loads up to the platforms of these structures through shafts like this for centuries. It's an absolute certainty that the builders would have used all of their accumulated knowledge and ingenuity to create the most technologically advanced lifting mechanism for the construction of the Great Pyramid and its near neighbour. After all, hadn't that been the one defining attribute of these builders throughout this project – their ability to push themselves, and their technology, to the absolute limit? The hoist they devised for this operation was used to transport the largest limestone blocks ever (by this method) up to platforms more than 140 metres from ground level. It was the final piece of technological innovation deployed on the project.

I have to admit though, that although I'd realized what the function of the antechamber was long before I came to rebuild it, when I did come to rebuild it I still hadn't figured out how the builders had managed to complete the pyramid. It still seemed almost impossible to me that they had completed the Great Pyramid by this route. But the fact remained that the builders had made it very clear when they created the entrance tunnel on the 16th level what route they were taking to the top, and when they created the grand gallery and its flight of locks they were clearly stating that they were fully committed to this route. I kept telling myself that this was the only route to the top so they had to have managed it somehow; it was only a matter of figuring it out. I'd been giving this matter a lot of thought and getting nowhere and I'd begun to believe that this last piece of the puzzle would defeat me. So I did what I'd done earlier when I got into trouble with my reconstruction of the upper chamber; I continued with my mental reconstruction regardless, hoping that I'd get one last break before my reconstruction came to a standstill yet again. I had come too far now and I simply had to put that capstone on top of my reconstructed Great Pyramid just as the builders of the original structure had done so long ago. I had known since I discovered the secret of the Great Pyramid's construction that the builders had completed the pyramid by this route, as there was no other viable alternative for a structure of such massive proportions. But the last clue as to how they achieved this great feat still eluded me.

Fortunately, my last break came while I was trying to put this chapter together, but only after I'd made one of those sweeping statements that you suddenly realize is completely wrong before you get to the end of it (I'd made a few of those). However, I didn't mind that I'd been completely wrong on this occasion, for if I hadn't made the statement, I probably wouldn't have realized that the opposite was true. In fact, it is indeed possible that I may not have discovered the last piece of the puzzle for some time. I'd studied this structure for so many years and if I'd had to wait another few months or even years for the final piece of the puzzle to drop into place, then that is what I would have done. I was determined that I would present a complete account of how the Great Pyramid had been constructed. Too many before me have selected one or other parts of the structure and theorized as to how it was created – or what purpose it served – as if it was some stand-alone feature unrelated to the Great Pyramid. But no one to my knowledge had compiled a complete account of how this structure was constructed. The Great Pyramid deserved more than idle speculation and those who built it deserved to be recognized for the intelligence and skills that they possessed, not as those people who went to an awful lot of trouble just to create a mausoleum for an ancient king and his queen. I will come back to this subject later, but we have to push on with the project for we still have more than 60 metres and one hundred courses to go before we get to the top.

Before we move on to the next stage of the construction, I would like to mention again the item I referred to earlier that had to be taken up onto the inner platform before the wall at the top end of the grand gallery was completed. We certainly won't need this component for a long time to come and it will have to make the journey with us all the way to the top of the pyramid before it is required, as it was an essential feature of the structure. I'm referring here, of course, to the capstone – the pyramidion – that had to be installed right at the very top of the Great Pyramid. This piece of limestone, granite or basalt was in all probability much too large to go through the passageway into the antechamber so it would most likely have been taken onto the inner stepped levels on a sled or wooden frame before the walls of the antechamber were installed. We may have a long way still to go before we get the opportunity to put this piece of our jigsaw puzzle in place, but we can at least say now that the end is within sight with the capstone in such close proximity to our lift shaft. (I should of course have mentioned earlier that the three slabs used to create the ceiling of the antechamber would also have been transported onto the inner stepped levels on the east side of the chamber prior to the decommissioning of the inner lock.)

The hoist

The builders of the Great Pyramid had to find a fast and efficient way of raising the limestone blocks up to the platforms. They needed a lift – an elevator. If a modern day lift engineer could have seen the lift system the builders created in the Great Pyramid, he would instantly recognize it. The ancient builders installed a system of rollers, ropes and weights within the structure that was not so very different from the systems we use today in our modern buildings, for exactly the same principles apply to both. You may be tempted to believe that I have just installed a contemporary system in our reconstruction simply because I had no idea how they rigged their hoist, but once again, the evidence speaks for itself. I discovered how they had set up and rigged their hoist the hard way – by a process of elimination. We should not, however, be too surprised that the system they created here was so similar to the systems we use today, as it had to perform the exact same function; the principles are the same for both systems. But in order for us to fully understand what the builders had to accomplish here, let us first take a look at a very primitive system.

The builders of the Great Pyramid could not use a shadouf to hoist the limestone blocks up to the stepped inner levels above the antechamber, as the distance from the floor of the antechamber to the inner stepped levels was just too great. This distance also increased as each course of the structure was completed and the hoist was raised up to the next level. But I wanted to mention the shadouf here for although they didn't use this particular device, they did in fact use a counterweight to hoist the limestone blocks up to the working platforms from the antechamber. I can well imagine that when man first began to hoist loads, using a rope slung over a branch, for instance, he must have realized that the weight, or size, of the loads he could raise using this method was limited to, more or less, the weight or size of the load he could physically lift. If he could enlist the help of others, collectively, they could lift a much greater load, but it would not always have been possible to enlist the help of others. At some stage along the way, man realized that he could use multiples of these small loads to raise a much greater load (larger block size) up to a platform or landing by breaking the much larger load down into smaller units. He realized that, if he raised two, three, or more small loads up to a landing, he could then use these collectively as a counterweight to hoist the much greater load up to the landing. It was precisely this method that was adopted and adapted by the pyramid builders for use in the Great Pyramid to create a very efficient compound lifting device – a hoist.

To put all of this into practice, the builders needed a tree with many branches up on the platform to sling their ropes over in order to hoist, first a counterweight, then a load up to the platforms. The builders first had to construct their own tree with many branches – a rig – and install it on the platform, one that had the complexity to give them complete control over the various components of the hoist. The rig had to be robust enough to withstand the pressure placed upon its structure by the weight suspended from its crossbeams – multiples of the weight of each limestone block – yet lightweight enough that it could be raised up to the next level without the need to dismantle it every time a course was completed. The rig that the builders first set up on the inner platform above the lift shaft formed the principal structure of the lifting apparatus and all the other components of the apparatus were suspended from this rig.

The hoist operators controlled the movement of the smaller fractional weights mentioned earlier but these weights were not used to hoist the load up to the top of the lift shaft directly; they were used here to haul a counterweight up to the top of the lift shaft. It was this counterweight that was then used to hoist the limestone blocks up to the inner stepped levels. The control (fractional) weights controlled the rate of ascent and descent of the counterweight, and the

175

counterweight hoisted the limestone blocks up to the inner stepped levels as it made its descent to the antechamber. Down at the bottom of the lift shaft, some sort of sling, cradle or platform was required before a load could be hoisted up the shaft. However, none of these components could have played their part in the lifting operation without a good number of interconnecting ropes having been used here. Eight (four pairs) ropes in all were needed for the hoist to function as intended, with six of these ropes giving the operators complete control over the movement of the hoist. No load could have been hoisted up to the platform until all of these ropes had been attached to their respective components and the apparatus rigged for operation.

The lift also had to be a very efficient means of transporting limestone blocks up to the platforms from the 50th level of the pyramid because for the very first time since they'd began to construct the Great Pyramid, the builders could only transport one limestone block at a time through a single access point to the platforms above (there were two ramps in use in the lower and the upper chambers when blocks were hauled up to the platforms from these chambers). That access point was, of course, the inappropriately named antechamber.

This was a tall order by any stretch of the imagination but when we consider that, when a limestone block was hauled through into the antechamber on its sled, there was no room in the chamber for any workmen; it would seem to have been an almost impossible task. But we know for certain that the builders somehow managed to get the limestone blocks into the hoist without actually entering the chamber, as this was unquestionably the only route up to the platforms by this stage of the construction. Remarkably, I discovered that there had been not just one, but a number of possible options available to the builders when they came to secure the load to the lifting apparatus. As I had by this time deciphered many of the clues in the antechamber, this had led to me making a breakthrough as to how the hoist was rigged. I now hoped that it would also provide some clue as to what option the builders had chosen as a means of securing the load to the lifting mechanism.

Before they could bring any limestone up to the platform by this route, the builders had first to set up the lifting apparatus. It is impossible to know exactly how the rig was constructed but we can glean a lot of information from what we already know about the antechamber. In fact, the antechamber, once we understand exactly what it is, presents us with more clues as to what took place within its walls than any other chamber within the Great Pyramid. Once I fully understood what was required of the hoist, this chamber proved to be a veritable mine of information as you will soon discover.

As members of the public go through the passageway from the grand gallery into the antechamber, they have to duck under the two granite slabs in the first pair of vertical channels in the sidewalls of the antechamber. Together, these granite slabs formed the counterweight that was used to haul the limestone blocks up to the platform when the hoist was in operation. These slabs, like the granite coffer in the upper chamber, did not need to be removed when the builders had no further use for the hoist and they have remained here ever since.

Two metal hoops or bands would originally have been placed around these granite slabs vertically, one on either side of the boss on the side of the top slab nearest the grand gallery. A metal bar would most likely have formed a bridge between the two hoops on the top of the counterweight and two metal rings would have been attached to this bar. (The marks left by the metal bands on the counterweight can still be clearly seen on the face of the counterweight on the side nearest the grand gallery.) Two ropes would have been attached to the metal rings on top of the counterweight, and after they had been looped over rollers on the rig, the other ends of these ropes would have been attached to the cradle, sling, or platform that was used to hoist the limestone blocks up to the top of the shaft. This counterweight would have been slightly heavier than the combined weight of the largest sized limestone blocks and the cradle or platform used to haul them up to the top of the shaft.

In order to hoist the limestone blocks up to the inner levels that were under construction, the builders first had to hoist the counterweight up to the top of the shaft, for the counterweight countered, or offset, the weight of the limestone block and the cradle that contained this block. The ropes that were attached to the two rings on the metal bands of the counterweight would have hoisted the counterweight up to the top of the shaft as the cradle descended. Likewise, the same two ropes would have hoisted the cradle up to the platform when the counterweight descended.

Once we realize that a particular object or feature performed a specific function, it can alter our perception of all that is around it. When I suddenly realized that the original doorway to the Great Pyramid was the key to its construction, my altered perception of the structure led to one discovery after another in quick succession as I mentally made my way up through the pyramid. When I had reached the level of the upper chamber and the antechamber, I then knew for certain that the builders had created a lift shaft above the antechamber as this was the only possible route up to the levels above. It was far from clear at that time how the builders had managed to hoist all of the limestone needed to complete the pyramid up the lift shaft, but now that I knew for certain that the builders had set up a hoist above the antechamber, I realized that the antechamber itself probably held most of the clues as to how the hoist had been set up. When I discovered that the only way up to the platform was up through the roof of this small chamber, it also confirmed my belief that the three empty pairs of channels in the antechamber must have served some purpose other than that imagined by many Egyptologists – as channels for portcullis slabs. Now that I knew for certain that the limestone blocks to complete the structure had all come this way, and realized that the granite slabs contained within the first pair of channels in the antechamber were almost certainly the counterweight for the lifting mechanism, I was off to a good start.

So what conclusions can we draw from the other features in this small chamber? As I mentioned earlier, the antechamber is a very complex little chamber in that its walls are unlike any of the walls in the other chambers within the Great Pyramid. When we had no idea what purpose this chamber served, it was just another of those enigmatic features that the Great Pyramid had in abundance. When we realize that this small room forms the bottom of a lift shaft however, the complex features within it then work to our advantage for they are clues as to how it was utilized. It is immediately obvious that some kind of cage, cradle or sling must have been used to hoist the building blocks up the shaft to the platforms that were under construction, but the complex structure of the chamber walls also offer us clues as to how the hoist was rigged and operated.

As I mentioned earlier, the granite walls in the antechamber have sustained more damage than any other feature of the Great Pyramid with the possible exception of the grand gallery. Most of the damage that we can see in both of these chambers is damage that was sustained during the actual construction of the pyramid. It is only now, when we fully realize the true purpose of these chambers that it becomes blindingly obvious as to how this damage was incurred. In the case of the antechamber, it is most likely that a metal cage (cradle) would have come down into the antechamber from above as the counterweight was hoisted up to the top of the shaft. A large limestone block would then have been hauled from a barge at the top of the grand gallery, through the passageway, and into the antechamber on a sled. From here, it would have been hoisted up the shaft to a platform high above. These operations would have gone on day after day for a horrendously long period of time, as the builders had still to construct another pyramid over 60 metres high on top of the perimeter platform when they began this operation. But before they could construct this pyramid on top of the existing perimeter platform, they had to build up the inner stepped levels to the level of the perimeter platform, those areas around the east end of the upper chamber and the antechamber that could not be built up earlier. This in itself was a great undertaking as there was still a tremendous amount of limestone to be hauled up to the inner levels to complete them.

We should therefore not be too surprised that the antechamber sustained so much damage and, in all honesty, I find it astonishing that so many of its features have survived when we consider the volume of masonry that was hoisted up the lift shaft from this chamber. The ribs between the channels on its sidewalls, for instance, could so easily have been completely obliterated by the time the builders had hoisted all of the limestone to complete the pyramid up to the levels above. Unlike the walls of the upper chamber, constructed of granite to bear the tremendous weight of the granite structure above it, the walls of the antechamber were constructed of granite for its durability. This chamber was subjected to a tremendous amount of wear and tear simply because of the phenomenal amount of activity that was concentrated in this one small area for such a long time; this is a space not much longer or wider than the limestone blocks that were routed through it. The lift shaft had to be wider than the antechamber because the builders had to create a ledge on either side of the chamber at roof level to support the three slabs that would eventually form the roof of the chamber. The length of the lift shaft was also longer than the chamber below as the three roofing slabs had to be stored out of the way at either end of the shaft until the pyramid was complete; they were then lowered to create the ceiling in the chamber and seal the bottom of the shaft when the builders had no more use for the hoist. The antechamber therefore had to be made as small as possible to keep the lift shaft as small as possible. A much wider and longer shaft could easily have compromised the structural integrity of the pyramid.

The lift shaft, like the grand gallery, could not be blocked up when the builders had no further use for it; the shaft could only be sealed top and bottom. As we are only too well aware, there is no shaft visible at the top of the Great Pyramid today, even though it has lost its smooth outer casing blocks and around 10 metres in height; but at some point the builders managed to close the top end of the shaft. However, they certainly could not raise large limestone beams up to the platform after they began to use the hoist and their only option had been to close the top end of the shaft using the same limestone blocks that they used to complete the inner stepped levels and all the courses of the pyramid above the 102nd course (the perimeter platform). They obviously did a very good job of it for despite the damage that the structure sustained during the earthquake at the beginning of the 14th century, the top of this shaft has still not been exposed (it can't be very far below the topmost level as the pyramid now stands.)

The width of the antechamber was ultimately determined by the width of the cradle or platform that was used to secure the limestone blocks as they were hoisted up to the platforms. At first it appeared that the builders had a few options as to how they secured the limestone blocks to the hoist and we should explore these options in order to discover why the builders chose to use a cradle for this operation, instead of slings, or a suspended platform.

Up on the working platform a wooden framework, a rig, would have been installed directly above the shaft opening. The rig would have had to be tall enough to ensure that the bottom of the limestone blocks cleared the top of the shaft by a good margin, for a wooden sled had to be placed across the top of the shaft after the blocks had been raised well clear of its opening. These were the platforms onto which the blocks were unloaded and then transported to their final destinations. If a cradle was used to secure the blocks as they made their ascent then this, in all probability, had to be hoisted up clear of the top of the limestone blocks before they could be hauled away from the top of the shaft. It was these considerations that determined the height of the rig.

The wooden framework of the rig had to be very strong as it had to be able to support the combined weight of the limestone block and the granite counterweight. In addition, it also had to support the weight of the metal cradle (if one was used) and the weight of the control weights, for without them the mechanism could not have functioned. There was also a considerable weight in all of the ropes that were suspended from the rig – eight in all – when it was in operation. The weight of these ropes would have increased each time the rig was raised up onto the next level after the completion of each course, as the length of each rope would have increased by a corresponding amount.

The control weights were the weights used to operate the hoist. Lowering the control weights lowered the cradle or wooden platform and raised the counterweight. When these control weights were hoisted upward again the counterweight descended, hauling the cradle and the limestone block up to the working platform. The combined weight of the control weights was about the same as the weight of the counterweight. I mentioned earlier how man probably discovered that he could hoist a weight much greater than his own body weight up to a landing by breaking the load down into smaller units – fractions of the weight to be raised. He would first haul these smaller units up to the landing one at a time and then use their combined weight to raise the greater load up to the same level as they were lowered to ground level. The control weights used to control the movement of the hoist were fractional weights, smaller weights whose combined weight equalled that of the counterweight in this instance. Each of these smaller weights could be hoisted up to the top of the lift shaft by the operators of the hoist and two men would have hauled each of these weights up to the top of the shaft.

When the builders had almost completed each course, the rig had to be raised up onto the newly completed platform. The rig itself would have been a substantial structure as it had to be very robust to perform the function it was designed for, yet light enough to be easily manoeuvred up and onto each new level by the operators, an operation that would have occurred with increasing regularity as the pyramid was pushed ever higher and the working platforms became much smaller. The simplest way to secure the limestone blocks to the lifting apparatus would have been with rope slings. If each limestone block to be hauled up the lift shaft was raised up off the deck of the sled (Fig.18) that had been used to transfer it from the barge to the antechamber, it would have been a fairly easy task to slip slings under each end of the block. Each sling would have been attached to one of the two ropes at the bottom of the shaft, the other ends of which were attached to the counterweight suspended from the rig at the top of the shaft. As the counterweight was lowered, it would have hoisted the limestone block up the shaft to the working platform. A variation of this method is where the aforementioned slings had loops at the ends. These could have been looped over the ends of the wooden runners of the sleds (Fig.19) or over metal hooks at its four corners, providing a stable platform for the limestone block as it was hoisted up the lift shaft.

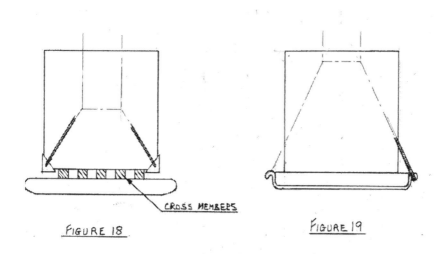

CROSS MEMBERS

FIGURE 18   FIGURE 19

At first glance a simple system like this seems pretty straightforward until you realize that the greatest difficulty with the hoist was in getting the counterweight up to the top of the shaft. If we can't get the counterweight up to the top of our shaft, then we can't get the limestone blocks up to the top of the shaft. Rope slings on their own were no good as the builders needed something solid to push back down to the bottom of the shaft with the control weights in order to raise the counterweight. Some sort of wooden or metal frame or platform therefore had to have been suspended from the lifting ropes of the hoist since this platform had to be pushed down the shaft in order to hoist the counterweight back up to the top of the shaft.

There are two difficulties with a compound apparatus such as the one that was set up in the Great Pyramid. In order to overcome them, the simple frame or platform has to become much more complex. The major difficulty with the idea of a simple platform is the fact that it is impossible to get a limestone block onto the platform after it has been pushed down to the bottom of the lift shaft with the control weights. If we use control weights to push the platform down the shaft, we cannot raise them up off of the platform without the platform itself moving upwards. But even if we could get around this little difficulty, it would make no difference as we cannot get a limestone block onto a platform. I could therefore only conclude that a more complex cradle was used here to overcome these difficulties.

In the end I realized that a cradle was the only possible way to overcome the difficulties the builders faced with this operation. I was not completely certain as to its form yet, but I knew that it had to have been open across most of its width at the bottom. I thought it unlikely that the cradle had been lowered down the shaft after the limestone block had been hauled into the antechamber but I now understood that this cradle had to have been much deeper than the limestone blocks it had to transport if the control weights were to push the cradle down the shaft and raise the counterweight. This is where the clues in the antechamber became invaluable for the information to be found here informs us – almost screams at us – what type of apparatus the builders devised and how it functioned.

If we did not know the dimensions of the limestone blocks used to construct the upper section of the Great Pyramid, we could easily determine what those dimensions were just by looking at the antechamber. The dimension that we most need to determine here is the width of the blocks; we need to know how wide they were if we are to determine what type of cradle the builders devised and how it functioned. We know that the blocks had to be narrower than the width of the passageway into the chamber. We also know that the width of the antechamber between the ribs on either sidewall is the same width as the passageway, therefore the width of the limestone blocks had to be slightly smaller than this at least.

There are three pairs of vertical channels in the antechamber sidewalls and the width of the chamber, if it is measured from the bottom of one of these channels to the bottom of the channel on the opposite side of the chamber, is much wider than the maximum width of the limestone blocks. You certainly don't need to be a rocket scientist, or an Egyptologist, to realize that these channels cut into the sidewalls of the chamber make no difference to our earlier calculations as the limestone blocks had to remain squarely between the ribs of the chamber. Naturally, the cradle the builders devised had to be wider than the limestone blocks it had to lift; therefore the only possible reason for the channels to be cut into the sidewalls of the antechamber was to accommodate the arms of the lifting cradle.

As I stated earlier, when we make a small discovery within a larger feature it alters our perception of that feature. This is how it was when I realized that the granite slabs in the first pair of channels in the antechamber was a counterweight. But now that we know the likely reason for the existence of the other three pairs of channels in the chamber, our perception changes again for we see the chamber in a different light with each new discovery. In this case, we certainly would not be going out on a limb if we concluded that the builders designed a cradle that had three arms on each side. We can also safely conclude that the odds greatly favour a metal structure of some kind that was considerably deeper than the limestone blocks it would haul up the lift shaft.

When we had no idea what the function of this small chamber was, it was just a complex little chamber shrouded in mystery; but as I stated earlier, no other feature of the Great Pyramid provides us with quite so many clues as to what went on inside its walls when the pyramid was under construction. It's unlikely that Caliph Al Ma'mun recognized this chamber for what it was when he first set foot in the inner chambers and corridors (pipes) of the Great Pyramid in 832 C.E. but little did he know that the real treasure of the Great Pyramid was to be found here.

Orthodox Egyptologists have their own opinions about this little chamber but others had long suspected that it held many secrets, as the orthodox theory has never made any sense. In fact, if Egyptologists had been around in the ninth century, the Caliph could have told them that he didn't have to hack his way through any portcullis slabs to enter the upper chamber. When he tunnelled his way into the inner passageways (pipes) of the Great Pyramid, he let us see that the internal layout of the chambers and passageways in the Great Pyramid were much more complex than those parts of the structure observed during the Greek and Roman periods. But despite the fact that we have had access to its inner chambers for more than a thousand years, we failed to find the treasure within the antechamber, as we didn't have the key to how this great structure had been constructed. However, now that we have finally discovered the true reason for the channels in the sidewalls of the antechamber, we can begin to build up a picture of what the cradle would have looked like and how the hoist functioned.

There are many clues within the antechamber that indicate how the hoist and the cradle were utilized, but let us begin by constructing a cradle based on the knowledge that we have at present. As there are three channels on either side of the chamber, we must conclude that there were three arms on either side of the cradle. I am also one hundred per cent convinced that this cradle was made of metal, for only a metal cradle would have been robust enough to stand up to the stresses and strains it was subjected to, day after day, for such a tremendously long period of time.

In order for the cradle to lift the limestone blocks however, the arms of the cradle had to have been extended out under the blocks a short distance on either side. From this, we can therefore conclude that the limestone blocks were unlikely to have been positioned within the chamber before the cradle came to rest here at the end of its stroke. I say unlikely, for it is by no means certain that this was the case; there was the possibility that the arms of the cradle could have had articulated fingers on the end of each arm and if this had been the case then it was indeed possible that the blocks could have been hauled into the chamber before the cradle descended to the bottom of the shaft. Although this was a possibility, I suspect that the builders would have chosen the simplest option (not a cradle with articulated lifting fingers) as there was very little to be gained by hauling the limestone blocks into the chamber before the cradle reached the bottom of the shaft.

Irrespective of what option the ancient builders actually chose, we can now conclude that the limestone blocks had to be hauled through into the antechamber on sleds that were much narrower than the blocks, for the sled had to fit comfortably in the gap between the fingers on the ends of the arms on each side of the cradle (both types of cradle would have needed fingers that extended out into the passageway below the blocks). As can be seen in the drawing below (Fig.20) these fingers would have extended beyond the ribs on either side of the chamber. We now have a cradle to hoist our blocks up to the inner stepped levels and the platforms that we will have to construct beyond the existing perimeter platform. Now that we know for certain that we can put our limestone blocks into that cradle, let's take a look at what was required when the cradle reached the top of the lift shaft.

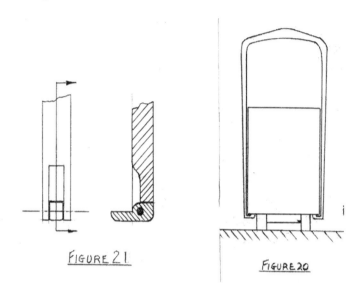

FIGURE 21

FIGURE 20

When our limestone blocks reach the top of the shaft, they have to be loaded onto a sled before they can be hauled off to their final destination. The sled has to be placed across the lift shaft after the block has been hoisted up beyond the top of the shaft opening. The lift shaft is longer than it is wide so, logically, they would have brought the sled in from one side or the other of the shaft and not from either end, as this is the shortest span. If we do place the sleds across the opening of the lift shaft however, the limestone blocks will be positioned across the sleds when they are lowered onto their decks. However, despite the fact that the limestone block has to be positioned across the runners of the sleds, we will still need to use a much longer sled here than those used to haul the limestone blocks into the antechamber (the reason for this will soon become clear).

At the moment our limestone block is suspended above the sled. It is supported by the six extensions (fingers) on the end of each arm of the cradle. In order to load the block onto the sled, the cradle has to be lowered until the block comes to rest on a deck placed across the runners of the sled. However, the arms of the cradle extend below the bottom of the limestone block; therefore the distance between the two runners of the sleds used by the builders must correspond to the distance between the gaps on either side of the middle arm of the cradle, otherwise the runners of the sled will obstruct the downward path of the cradle as we lower the block onto its deck. In order to release the block, the fingers on the arms of the cradle must travel down beyond the point where the limestone block comes to rest on the sled. Now that our limestone block has been loaded onto the sled we are almost ready to transport it to its final destination... we just have one more problem to solve before that can happen.

When we hauled our block into the passageway in the antechamber, we also hauled it into the cradle (the cradle was already in the loading position within the antechamber). Now, with our limestone block on the sled at the top of the lift shaft, we need to haul our block off to one side of the cradle and that is utterly impossible at the moment. Somehow, we need to find a way to extract our block from the cradle or, vice versa, we need to remove the cradle from its present position around the limestone block. This is where I got into all sorts of difficulties and it took me a long time to realize how the builders got around this problem. I had to keep in mind the fact that the builders needed a quick turnaround at both the bottom and the top of the lift shaft because anything complicated would only have slowed down the whole operation. The builders had to have the fastest turnaround possible at both ends of the shaft as they could only transport one limestone block up to the platforms at a time, so a simple solution was called for.

Can we glean anything from the features of the antechamber itself that might help us to better understand how the blocks could have been extracted from the cradle at the top of the shaft? Well, that is where it becomes very interesting. But before we take a look at what clues are to be found there, we need to take a look at what the features of the antechamber tell us about the setup of the rig, and how the various weights and counterweights were employed in the hoist. When we have a better understanding of the interconnection between the component parts of this apparatus, it should offer us some clues as to how the limestone blocks were released from the cradle when it reached the top of the shaft.

We begin by taking a look at one of those features that there seems to be no logical explanation for, the three semi-circular depressions above the channels in each of the sidewalls of the antechamber. Earlier, I indicated that the builders of the Great Pyramid had used smaller fractional weights to raise the much larger loads up to a platform. In the hoist that they set up in the Great Pyramid, this was done indirectly by a compound lifting device. Instead of using these fractional weights to lift the actual load, they used these smaller weights to raise the counterweight; it was the counterweight that then hoisted the cradle and its load up to the top of the lift shaft as it descended into the antechamber. In the lifting mechanism in the Great Pyramid, the smaller fractional weights - the control weights - were fractions of the weight of the counterweight and not of the actual load itself. The weight of the counterweight is slightly heavier than the combined weight of the limestone block and the cradle, so that when it is free to descend, it can easily haul the combined weight of the cradle and the limestone block up to the top of the shaft.

How many control weights? Well, this is where it gets very interesting. Obviously, the more control weights that are used the lighter those weights will be; however, the more control weights there are the more ropes there are and the more operators that are required. We also have to consider that there is not a lot of space in the antechamber and the lift shaft, so the more weights there are the more congested this space becomes. It was therefore in the builder's best interests to use as few fractional control weights as possible.

There had to have been a minimum of two control weights but these would have been very heavy weights indeed and it would have taken many men to haul each of these weights up to the top of the lift shaft. However, there was not a lot of space around the rig when it was first set up and there certainly wasn't a lot of space up on the much smaller platforms near the top of the pyramid; so on balance, I believe that the builders would have opted for three control weights. The stamina of the operators would have been preserved for longer with a three weight system as each of these control weights would have been much lighter than the control weights in a two weight system (there simply wasn't enough space in the antechamber for more than three control weights). Let's take a look now at what we have established so far.

We have a cradle made of metal, possibly iron, and we have established that both meteoritic, wrought iron and possibly smelted iron was available to the builders of the Great Pyramid. This cradle was suspended from two ropes and these were (possibly) attached to the central rib that ran lengthways along the top of the cradle – attached approximately one third of the length in from each end of the cradle along the mid line. The cradle had three arms with extension fingers on their ends that may, or may not, have been articulated. These extensions were at right angles to the arms and pointed inwards towards the passageway; it was these fingers that supported the limestone block as it was hauled up the lift shaft. We have also established that it was most likely that three control weights would have been used to operate the hoist. Is it a coincidence therefore that we have three arms on each side of the cradle, three control weights, and three pairs of semi-circular depressions above the channels in the sidewalls of the chamber? Let us consider now how those weights were used to control the movement of the hoist; it may just explain why this was no coincidence.

Each control weight was suspended from the rig by two ropes slung over a roller (each control weight had its own dedicated roller). In order to push the cradle down the lift shaft, these three weights were lowered onto the top of the cradle after its load had been discharged at the top of the shaft. When the cradle reached the bottom of the shaft, the three control weights had to remain in position on top of the cradle until the next limestone block had been loaded. When the next limestone block had been loaded into the cradle, the control weights were then hauled up off the top of the cradle and hauled back up to the top of the lift shaft. When the combined weight of the three control weights was hauled up off of the top of the cradle the counterweight began its descent to the antechamber, and in the process, the cradle and its load were hauled up to the top of the shaft. (The cradle would in fact have followed just behind the control weights as they were hauled up to the top of the shaft.) The cradle would have come to a halt when the counterweight bottomed in the antechamber but it's more than likely that the ascent of the cradle was arrested before the counterweight bottomed in the antechamber when it came up against the control weights suspended from the rig at the top of the shaft. When the cradle had to be lowered to set the limestone block down onto the sled, the three control weights were once again lowered onto the top of the cradle to push it downward until the limestone block bottomed on the sled. As I just mentioned, they were most probably already on top of the cradle as the upward movement of the cradle would almost certainly have been arrested when the top of the cradle came up against the underside of the control weights suspended just below the crossbeams of the rig. The weights would then have been lowered slowly until the limestone block came to rest on the sled bridging the top opening of the lift shaft.

Let us leave the issue of how the limestone block was freed from the clutches of the cradle aside for now, and take a look at what happened on the downward stroke of the cradle. As I mentioned earlier, the combined weight of the control weights was about the same weight as the counterweight. In addition, there was the weight of the cradle itself to be considered, for the combined weight of the cradle and the three control weights ensured that there was more than enough weight on the lifting end of the hoist to haul the counterweight back up to the top of the shaft when the control weights were lowered onto the top of the cradle. That is how the lifting apparatus in the Great Pyramid functioned.

When we consider that there are three semi-circular depressions in the sidewalls of the antechamber directly above the three vertical channels in the sidewalls – and consider where the control weights would have made contact with the top of the cradle – we can surely only conclude that the builders used three granite cylinders as control weights. I do not believe that coincidence played any part in the configuration of the antechamber walls, as I am certain that the three pairs of semi-circular depressions above the channels in the sidewalls were where these three cylindrical control weights came to rest just before the cradle would have bottomed in the antechamber. In other words, these semi-circular depressions were the three pairs of mounts for the control weights and the downward path of these weights was arrested here, on the ledges at the top of the channels, just before the cradle would have bottomed on the floor of the antechamber. As long as these control weights remained in these mounts, the cradle would have remained in the loading position.

The two semi-circular depressions nearest to the south wall of the antechamber – the wall with the four vertical grooves cut into its surface – are right at the end of the ledges on the sidewalls; if square section control weights had been used here the diagonals across the squared section of the control weight could have been no greater than the diameter of the cylindrical spigots at the end of the control weights (that would have come to rest in the semi-circular depressions). If, on the other hand, the diagonals had been greater than the diameter of the cylinders, the control weights would have fouled on the south face of the chamber. But surely no one would have gone to the trouble of producing three square section control weights with turned cylindrical spigots at either end anyhow, for wouldn't it have been much easier just to have used square section weights and let them come to rest on ledges on either side of the chamber? I can therefore only conclude that the pyramid builders created the three pairs of semicircular depressions on the ledges as they had used three cylindrical granite control weights to control the movement of the hoist.

We need to remind ourselves now why we decided to take another look at the sidewalls of the antechamber earlier. If you remember, we had just hoisted our limestone block up to the top of the shaft. We had then placed a wooden sled across the mouth of the shaft and lowered our limestone block down onto that sled; it was no longer being supported by the fingers of the cradle. The limestone block was still positioned within the confines of the cradle for we could not remove it from the cradle. However, we know that the sled has to be hauled off to one side or other of the shaft, so somehow or other, we have to find a way to hoist our cradle up clear of the block on the sled in order to move the block away from the top end of the shaft. It was at this point that we went back to the antechamber to see if there were any clues there as to how the builders overcame this difficulty. But before we try to determine how the builders could haul the cradle up beyond the top of the limestone block and haul the block away from the top of the shaft, it is important to understand the reasons why the sled had to be placed across the shaft in the first place.

The rig that we set up above the antechamber would have consisted of two A-frames and these would have been linked to each other by a number of crossbeams. Each A-frame would have had at least two horizontal crossbeams and these would have supported the six rollers that spanned the width of the rig. Each control weight had a corresponding roller and another three rollers were needed to suspend the cradle and the counterweight from the rig also (one above the counterweight and one for each of the ropes attached to the cradle). In all, at least six rollers were supported by the crossbeams on the sides of the rig on at least two levels, possibly three. We also know that the counterweight was suspended from the rig on the north side as this counterweight is still to be found at the north end of the antechamber. This ruled out any possibility of the sled being hauled off to the north side of the rig as the ropes attached to the counterweight would have obstructed the path of the sled here.

But we also have to take a look at the bigger picture. The antechamber in the Great Pyramid is situated between the top end of the grand gallery and the north side of the upper chamber. Therefore, when we first set up our rig above the antechamber to haul the first limestone blocks up to the inner area, our rig is sandwiched between the top end wall of the grand gallery and the north wall of the upper chamber. Although there was some distance between the rig and the north wall of the upper chamber, it's unlikely that the sleds would have been hauled off to this end of the rig as this was more than likely the landing where the hoist operators were positioned. In fact, placing the sleds across the opening at the top of the lift shaft longitudinally was a non-starter anyhow, for the runners or skids on such a sled would have been much longer than those on the standard sled; they would also have needed to be of much stronger construction to support the weight of the limestone block over such a span when it was lowered onto the deck of this sled. The only practical solution therefore was to bring the sleds in from one side or the other at the top of the shaft and haul the blocks away to one side or the other of the lift shaft. However, as we discovered earlier, we cannot haul the limestone blocks off to the east or west side of the cradle until we find a way to hoist the cradle up beyond the top of our limestone block.

When we hauled our first limestone block into the antechamber, the sled had been on a solid granite base. The sleds used at the top of the shaft had to be positioned across the opening at the top of the lift shaft before the limestone block could be lowered down onto it. Naturally, the runners on the sled would have been long enough to span across the width of the shaft opening for the block to be loaded safely onto the sled. However, the runners on these sleds had to have been much longer than the width of the shaft since the builders had to have hauled the sled and the block safely away from this precarious position before the trailing ends of the runners cleared the far side of the lift shaft. In fact, in order to safely haul the limestone block away from the opening at the top of the lift shaft, around two thirds of the weight of the limestone block had to have been beyond the edge of the lift shaft (the bulk of its weight) before the ends of the runners on the sled cleared the platform on the far side of the shaft. In other words, the centre of gravity of the block had to have been well beyond the edge of the lift shaft before the ends of the runners on the sled cleared the platform on the far side of the shaft.

So how did they manage to haul the cradle up clear of the top of the limestone blocks in order to haul these blocks away to their final destinations? Once again there is no definitive proof that the method I fully believe they implemented here was the method chosen by the builders. But given the fact that they had to haul the limestone blocks off to one side or other of the shaft, they did not have a lot of options available to them. Although we have no definitive proof however, there are some indications that the method I am about to describe was the method most likely adopted by the builders of the Great Pyramid.

The cradle

We have already established the basic form of the cradle based on information we gleaned from some of the features in the antechamber and what was required of the hoist. I am certain that it was not dissimilar to the one I have described. However, the cradle I described earlier had a rigid structure and as we now know it would have been impossible to remove the limestone blocks from such a cradle at the top of the lift shaft. Earlier, we discovered that we could only haul the limestone blocks off to the sides of the lift shaft as they could not be hauled off to either end of the shaft. Given these constraints, there was only one way for the cradle to go when the limestone block had been lowered onto the sled at the top of the shaft, and that was up. A rigid cradle was therefore out of the question.

The cradle used by the builders of the Great Pyramid had to have been articulated (hinged) in one of two ways. The cradle could only have been hauled up clear of the limestone blocks if the fingers on the ends of the lifting arms could be swung up out of the way to open up the bottom end of the cradle. Either the fingers themselves were articulated in this way or the sides of the cradle itself were articulated. This is the only logical conclusion that can be drawn here, as the limestone blocks simply cannot be hauled off to one side or the other of the shaft if the cradle cannot be hauled up clear of the blocks on the sleds.

As can be seen in the drawing (Fig. 21) that we looked at earlier, the fingers of the cradle could easily have been articulated in such a way that they could be hinged upwards, but buffered so that they could not drop beyond the horizontal position when released. It would then have been possible to flip the three fingers on each side of the cradle back against its arms until the cradle was hauled up clear of the limestone block sitting on the sled at the top of the lift shaft. I mentioned earlier that it may have been possible to haul a limestone block into the antechamber before the cradle descended into the chamber. If the builders had constructed a cradle with hinged fingers on the ends of the lifting arms that could be flipped upwards, then the limestone blocks may indeed have been hauled into the antechamber before the cradle bottomed here. As the cradle descended, the fingers on the ends of the lifting arms would have swung upwards as the lower end of the cradle passed the top end of the limestone block – and the fingers made contact with the top edges of the block. When the cradle bottomed, the fingers would have dropped back down into the horizontal position as they cleared the underside of the block. They were then ready to support the limestone block as the cradle was hauled back up the lift shaft again.

This type of cradle would undoubtedly have resulted in a quicker turnaround when the cradle reached the bottom of the shaft. Using a cradle such as this, the builders may not have had to wait until the cradle had bottomed before they hauled the limestone blocks into the antechamber. The cradle could therefore have been hauled back up the shaft as soon as it bottomed in the chamber and the fingers on either side of the cradle had dropped into the horizontal position. A quick turnaround indeed!

Articulated fingers were certainly a distinct possibility and the simpler of the two methods that could have been employed here. All six fingers would have been down near the level of the platform when the block was lowered onto the sled at the top of the lift shaft and all of these fingers had to be flipped up into the vertical position before the cradle could be hoisted up again. However, someone would have had to physically flip these fingers up into the vertical position on either side of the cradle before the cradle could have been hauled upwards to free the limestone block therefore this was not such a simple solution to this problem. But there was another way to achieve the same result at the top of the shaft and have the lower end of the cradle opening almost instantly when the limestone block was released from its grip. I had got the impression by this time that the features in the antechamber, and the set-up of the rig and its components, was pointing to an altogether more sophisticated operation here using a more complex cradle than the rigid sided one I have just described. They were pointing to an articulated cradle that could be opened by the hoist operators to release the limestone blocks after they had been lowered onto the sled at the top of the lift shaft. As I mentioned earlier, I believe that there are a number of clues to indicate that such a cradle could have been used here and we shall take a look at these clues shortly. But for now, I'd like you to take a look at the drawings I have included to get some idea of how such a cradle could have been fabricated and how it would have functioned.

The first example on the next page (Fig. 22) shows a cradle with a central hinge between the two halves of the cradle; the brackets on top of the lifting arms would have supported the control weights as they pushed the cradle down the lift shaft. The two ropes that the cradle is suspended from would have been fixed to metal rings on the centrally hinged spine of this cradle. The lower ends of the cradle arms on a cradle such as this could have been pulled open after the limestone block came to rest on the sled at the top of the lift shaft; the cradle would then have been hauled up clear of the limestone block.

In the second example (Fig. 23) you will see that the two ropes that the cradle is suspended from are not attached to the centrally hinged spine. Instead of two metal fixing rings on the central spine of the cradle that we have just looked at, this cradle has four fixing rings, two on either side of the central spine. The lifting ropes here have two ends and each end is attached to a metal ring on top of the cradle; the metal rings are not attached to the central hinged spine but are in fact offset some distance on either side of this central spine. The fixing rings here have been moved out towards the shoulders of the lifting arms at either end of the cradle. (I have not shown the fixing rings or the ropes in this drawing as it would be too cluttered I have simply indicated where the ropes would have been attached to the top of the cradle.)

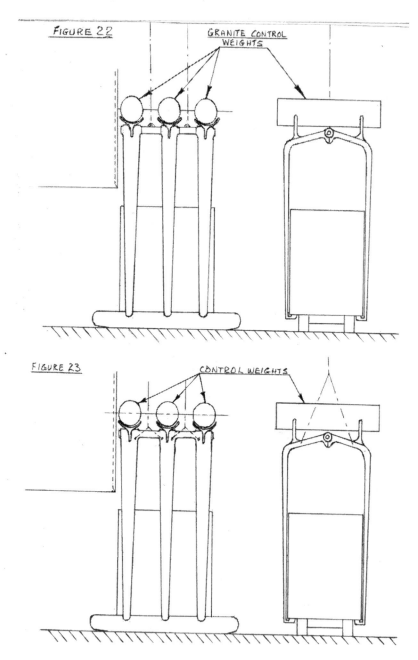

FIGURE 22

GRANITE CONTROL WEIGHTS

FIGURE 23

CONTROL WEIGHTS

When we look at what the builders had achieved by the time they had reached this stage of the construction and look at the complex layout of the antechamber, it is clear that they employed a fairly complex hoist system within the Great Pyramid. As we have now discovered, they could not have used a rigid cradle to hoist the limestone blocks up to the upper levels for the cradle had to have been hauled up beyond the top of the limestone block after the block had been lowered onto the sled at the top of the shaft. It was obvious to me that some degree of articulation was required, but it was the fact that the builders used cylindrical control weights, and that the downward movement of those control weights was arrested when the weights came to rest in the semi-circular depressions on the ledges on either side of the chamber, that was the first indication that something other than a rigid cradle had been used here. We know that the cradle was held at the bottom of the shaft by the combined weight of the three control weights and that those three control weights could descend no further than their mounts on the ledges on the sidewalls of the antechamber. But the ledges on the sidewalls of the antechamber are much higher than the roof of the passageway into the antechamber, much higher than the top of the limestone blocks. It's therefore obvious that the cradle must have been much deeper than the limestone blocks that it had to haul up to the top of the lift shaft. Why? Surely it would have made much more sense to have the ledges and the semi-circular depressions lower down; in that way a much shorter cradle could have been used. Knowing that the downward movement of the three control weights was arrested when they came to rest in their mounts on the ledges, it's plainly obvious that if a much shorter cradle had been used in the antechamber as we see it today it would have stopped far short of the bottom of the shaft when the control weights came to rest in these mounts. But we know that the fingers at the bottom of the lifting arms of the cradle had to have been below the level of the underside of the limestone blocks when they were hauled through into the antechamber on their sleds; therefore the cradle itself had to have been almost as tall as the height of the ledges on the sidewalls of the antechamber when it bottomed in the chamber. The only conclusion I could come to here was that the builders must have had good reason to construct such a deep cradle. After all, hadn't there been a very good reason for everything they had done so far?

When I reached the stage where I had to mentally set up my hoist and began to hoist the first block up to the inner platform, I found that I could not extract the limestone block from my cradle. I then wondered if the cradle could have been made so deep because this extra depth may have been needed when the cradle reached the top of the shaft. It certainly didn't need to be nearly so deep to accommodate the limestone block and this extra depth served no purpose, as far as I could see, when the cradle was at the bottom of the lift shaft. Was that it? Was the extra depth needed when the cradle reached the top of the shaft? That was the conclusion I came to.

The sleds used on the platforms were wider than those used to haul the limestone blocks from the barges into the antechamber. These sleds could only be hauled off to one side or other of the lift shaft; therefore the blocks had to be placed across the runners of the sleds as opposed to lengthways on when they had been hauled into the antechamber. It was, however, only the narrow deck of these sleds that was much wider as the distance between the two runners of the sled had to be much shorter than the length of the deck. As we discovered earlier, the spacing of the runners had to correspond with the spacing of the two gaps in the sides of the cradle between the three lifting arms. When the block came to rest on the deck of the sled, the outer lifting arms would have come down on either side of the runners. However, the middle lifting arms came down between the runners of the sled. As the cradle was lowered and the block came to rest on the deck of the sled, the long arms of the cradle could travel farther, well below the level of the sled. So why should this be?

I had earlier rejected the possibility of the cradle having articulated fingers and had concluded that the builders would have opted for an articulated cradle, where the sides of the cradle would have been splayed open at its lower end before it was hauled up clear of the limestone block. Having come to this conclusion, I had to consider how the sides of the cradle were splayed outward before it was hauled up clear of the block. With an articulated cradle the sides of the cradle, or more accurately, the bottom ends of those sides, could be pulled open and away from the sides of the block. It would probably only have required one man on either side of the shaft to pull the sides of an articulated cradle open at its lower end after the block had been released from the cradle. But there was also another, more intriguing, possibility. If the points where the ropes were attached to the cradle were configured differently, it is possible that the hoist operators, the men operating the control weights, could have opened and closed the cradle without the need for intervention by others.

If you take a look at the second example of how the cradle was suspended from the rig (Fig. 23), you will see that the ropes are attached to the top of the cradle at four points instead of two. They are attached to fixing rings offset either side of the central hinged spine. In the first example (Fig. 22) when the three control weights were quickly hoisted up out of their mountings on top of the cradle, the sides of the cradle would have remained in the vertical position until they were physically pulled apart at the lower end. But the same is only true of the second configuration (Fig. 23) up to a point. The sides of this cradle would certainly have been held in the vertical position when the limestone block was released, but only as long as the three control weights remained in their mountings on top of the cradle. As we are now fully aware however, if we raise all three control weights up out of their mountings simultaneously the cradle will travel upwards until it comes up against the underside of the control weights again. But the big difference with this type of cradle, with four fixing points offset from its central spine, is that it is only the combined weight of the control weights that prevent the bottom ends of the lifting arms from springing open after the block had been released. That is exactly what would have happened if the three control weights had suddenly been hauled up out of their mountings at this stage of the operation.

In this type of cradle, the fixing points of the ropes are strategically placed well away from the central hinge and the control weight supports are positioned beyond those rope fixing points. When there are no control weights in the mounts on top of a cradle configured in this way, the top of the cradle would sag in the middle. If the top of this cradle sagged in the middle, the sides of the cradle would splay out at their lower ends. In other words, it took the combined weight of all three control weights to hold the sides of the cradle vertical if the fixing points of the ropes were offset from the central spine of the cradle. When the three control weights were suddenly hauled up and away from the top of the cradle however, the cradle would have splayed open at its lower end as its top end sagged in the middle with the rope fixings configured in this manner when there was no weight on top of the cradle to hold the sides in the vertical position.

When a cradle such as this was at the bottom end of the shaft, the sides of the cradle were held in the vertical position by the walls of the antechamber. When the control weights were hauled up out of their mountings on top of the cradle and the cradle began to move upward, it was the walls of the chamber that held the arms of the cradle in check until the fingers at the bottom of the arms made contact with the underside of the limestone blocks. As the cradle cleared the top end of the antechamber, it was the weight of the limestone blocks that ensured that the sides of the cradle could not splay open at their lower end. It was only after the cradle had released its load at the top of the shaft that the sides of the cradle could splay open again when the three control weights were suddenly hauled up out of their mountings on top of the lifting arms. There was nothing to restrain them here – nothing to prevent the top of the cradle from sagging in the middle – other than the combined weight of the three control weights.

Now we can clearly see why such a cradle would have to have been much deeper than the blocks of limestone that it hauled up to the platforms, for when a limestone block reached the top of the shaft and a sled had been positioned underneath it, the control weights would have been lowered until the block came to rest on the sled. But the hoist operators would have pushed the cradle down much farther until the fingers on the lifting arms were well below the bottom of the limestone block. The operators would then have arrested the downward path of the control weights and quickly reversed their direction, hauling them back up towards the rig again. Naturally, the cradle would have begun to move upwards as soon as the control weights were hauled up out of their mountings for the counterweight would instantly haul the cradle upwards. But as it did so, the sides of the cradle would have splayed outwards at their lower ends and the fingers at the ends of the lifting arms would have been well clear of the sides of the limestone block here as the cradle moved upwards. The cradle would only have come to rest again when it came up against the three control weights suspended from the rig, and as the cradle made contact with the control weights, its sides would have been pushed inward at their lower ends until they were in the vertical position again. The cradle was now ready to be lowered back down the shaft as soon as the limestone block was hauled away from the top of the lift shaft.

Was this the true reason why the cradle was so much deeper than the limestone blocks it hauled up to the working platforms of the Great Pyramid? I certainly think so, as I have been unable to find any other explanation as to why the cradle should have been so deep. This type of cradle had to be pushed down much farther than was necessary just to release the limestone block. The fingers on the lower ends of the lifting arms had to be pushed down a considerable distance from the underside of the limestone block before the control weights could be hauled upward. This gave the sides of the cradle the necessary distance (time) to splay open before the fingers came back up to the level of the underside of the block sitting on the sled as the cradle ascended. The cradle would have immediately and rapidly begun to travel upward when the control weights were hauled up out of their mountings; the arms of the cradle therefore had to be long enough to give the lower end of the cradle time to splay fully open before the fingers came up to, and moved beyond, the sides of the limestone block sitting on the sled. The opening at the top end of the lift shaft was wider than the walls in the antechamber leaving plenty of clearance for the sides of the cradle to spring open.

When all of the clues in the antechamber are considered, I believe that the features here strongly indicate that a cradle not dissimilar to one of those I have just described was employed in the lift shaft in the Great Pyramid. The operators of the control weights would have had complete control over the movement and actions of a fully articulated lifting cradle. I believe that the configuration of the sidewalls in the antechamber indicate most strongly that a fully articulated cradle was in use here during the construction of the upper levels of the Great Pyramid and, as we discovered earlier, it would have been impossible to remove the limestone blocks from a rigid cradle when it reached the top of the lift shaft. Even if it had been possible to remove the limestone blocks from a rigid cradle, it would have been more complex, and therefore a very slow operation. Everything at the bottom of the lift shaft however, indicates that the hoist was designed for a fast turnaround and it stands to reason that the builders would have designed a system to give them as fast a turnaround as possible.

We have now established that when a fully articulated cradle did not have the weight of a limestone block, or the combined weight of the control weights, to keep the sides of the cradle in the vertical (closed) position, the sides of the cradle would splay open at their lower ends if the fixings for the ropes had been offset from the central spine of the cradle. There was only one situation where that was not the case and that was when the sides of the cradle were constrained by the sidewalls of the antechamber. There had to be some clearance between the tops of the fingers on the lower ends of the arms and the underside of the limestone block when the block was hauled through the passageway into antechamber, but although the cradle only had to travel a small distance for the fingers to make contact with the underside of the limestone blocks, when the control weights were hauled up out of their mountings the arms of the cradle could not splay open when the cradle began its ascent as the chamber was much narrower than the lift shaft. The weight of the limestone block then held the sides of the cradle in the vertical position as it exited the top of the antechamber and entered the lift shaft on its ascent to the upper levels.

There are two main themes that run through the construction of the Great Pyramid from start to finish; the builders set out to build the Great Pyramid using the largest blocks and slabs of masonry ever used in the construction of a smooth-sided pyramid; they also set out to build it in the shortest possible time. If we were ever in any doubt about this, we only have to take a look at the many ingenious ways and contraptions that they devised to turn this once impossible dream into reality. At almost every location, and certainly at every hub within the Great Pyramid, it is plain to see that the system was designed to move the greatest volume of masonry in the fastest manner possible. The lifting mechanism that I have just described was the only logical option here if the builders wanted to move the greatest volume of masonry in the shortest possible time up to the platforms, and if ever there was a time to do so, it was when this hoist was first pressed into service. It was at this stage of the construction that the average block size became smaller and it was also at this stage of the construction that the limestone blocks could only be transported up to the platforms one at a time, through one portal. The pace of construction would have been greatly reduced at this stage and therefore it was imperative that the builders had a hoist that could give them the fastest possible turnaround.

Everything that we have discovered about these remarkable people since we set out on this journey of discovery, indicates most strongly that they would have chosen no other way to raise this masonry up to the upper levels of the Great Pyramid if it had been at all possible to do it in the manner I have just described. They certainly needed to transport these limestone blocks to their final locations as quickly as possible at this stage of the construction, for the barges could go no farther than the docking station at the top end of the gallery. I am therefore utterly convinced that the builders would have used a fully articulated cradle in order to keep the masonry moving at the fastest rate possible for they still had such a long way to go when they first set up the hoist above the antechamber. I think it very unlikely that we will ever discover the configuration of the rope fixings on the cradle, so we are never likely to know if the hoist operators had complete control over the cradle or if its sides were pulled open manually. But it really doesn't matter if the rope fixings for the articulated cradle had been on the hinged spine of the cradle; it just means that two more men would have been required for the operation of the hoist.

When we didn't know how the builders transported all of the masonry up to the upper levels of the Great Pyramid, all we could do was speculate as to the methods they could have used. However, when we discovered the true purpose of all of its pipes and chambers and then realized, that eventually, the only route to the top of the pyramid was through the opening in the roof of the antechamber and the shaft above it, there was no longer any need for speculation; it was obvious that they had to have employed a hoist at this stage of the construction. By understanding what was required of that hoist and interpreting the physical evidence in the antechamber, we have built up a picture of what the hoist mechanism would most probably have looked like. But so far we have only focussed our attention on the components of the hoist and paid little attention as to how the hoist was rigged. We also need to consider what was involved when the rig had to be raised up onto a new level when a platform had been almost completed before we move on to the next stage of our reconstruction, so let us take a look at these issues now before we begin to make full use of our hoist.

Now that we have established what the major components of the hoist were, and the most likely form that they took, we must not forget that a considerable number of ropes were also needed before the hoist was ready for operation. I have already mentioned that the metal bands that girded the counterweight had rings attached to the top of them. The two ropes that were attached to the top of the lifting cradle went up over rollers on the rig before being attached to these two metal rings on the top of the counterweight. One of these ropes would have been slightly longer than the other as it had to go over a roller on the rig that was farther away from the north end of the rig where the counterweight was also suspended from a roller. The two ropes that the cradle was suspended from were positioned in the gaps between the control weights, one on either side of the central control weight. The other ends of these ropes were attached to metal fixing rings on the top of the counterweight.

At every stage of the construction of the upper levels, there was a fixed length of rope between the cradle and the counterweight. When the cradle was at the bottom of the shaft, the counterweight was at the top of the shaft, and vice versa. However, the length of rope between the cradle and the counterweight had to be increased each time the rig was moved up to the next level, as the stroke of the apparatus was increased each time the rig was raised up and onto each newly completed platform. The three control weights pushed the cradle down the shaft and the counterweight hauled it back up the shaft. The counterweight could only haul the cradle up the shaft if, and when, the three control weights were hoisted up the shaft ahead of the cradle – if the combined weight of the control weights was removed from the top of the cradle.

As we discovered earlier, the control weights would have been cylindrical and most probably made of granite. Two ropes would have been attached to each of the control weights and it's almost certainly the case that rope grooves would have been cut around the circumference of the cylinders some distance in from each end. One end of each rope would have been looped around the cylinder and then fixed (whipped) to the main body of the rope. The cylindrical control weights were used to control the movement of the cradle, not the movement of the counterweight, although they did control the movement of the counterweight indirectly. Each control weight would have been suspended from its own dedicated roller on the rig. Eight ropes in total would therefore have been required for the rig to function, two on each control weight and two attached to the cradle / counterweight.

Although there was a fixed length of rope between the cradle and the counterweight on each level, this fixed length changed each time the rig was hoisted up onto the next level; therefore these two ropes had to have been very much longer at the outset than the fixed distance between the cradle and the counterweight. The same was also true for the control ropes as the control weights had to travel a longer distance each time the rig was hoisted up onto a new level in order to push the cradle down into the antechamber. In fact, it is true to say that there was a tremendous quantity of excess rope to be stowed somewhere when the builders first began to hoist limestone up the lift shaft to the upper levels.

Chapter Six

Raising the rig

The rig used by the builders had to be very robust to support the great load that was suspended from its framework (a weight greater than three limestone blocks) but it had also to be light enough to be easily manoeuvred when it came time to raise it up to the next level. When that time came, the builder's first job would have been to detach the two ropes that connected the cradle to the counterweight. These ropes had been looped through the metal rings on top of the metal bands around the counterweight and whipped (tied off) with cord to secure them to the counterweight; this whipping had to be undone and some slack drawn through the metal rings prior to the rig being raised. Good access to the counterweight was a requirement here therefore the simplest, most logical thing to do was to arrest and prop up the counterweight when it was at the top of the shaft.

When the counterweight was at the top of the lift shaft, the other four components of the lifting gear, the control weights and the cradle, were at the bottom of the shaft. Only the ropes that connected the cradle with the counterweight had to be detached from the fixing rings on top of the counterweight before the rig could be raised, as it was only these ropes that had a load on each end. The length of rope between the cradle and the counterweight had to be increased each time the rig was raised up to the newly created level to take account of the increased length of the stroke.

You will see from the drawing (Fig. 24) on the next page that the counterweight was most probably propped up on a heavy wooden beam that spanned the opening at the top of the shaft prior to the ropes being unfastened. When the cradle was at the bottom of the shaft, the counterweight would have been suspended a good distance above the almost completed new level; after all, the cradle had to be hoisted up clear of the limestone block when it was at the top of the shaft, therefore the counterweight had to have been suspended well above the platform when the cradle had been pushed back down to the bottom of the shaft. The wooden beam(s) used to support the counterweight, would have been placed on the new level that was almost complete, the level we are about to hoist our rig up to.

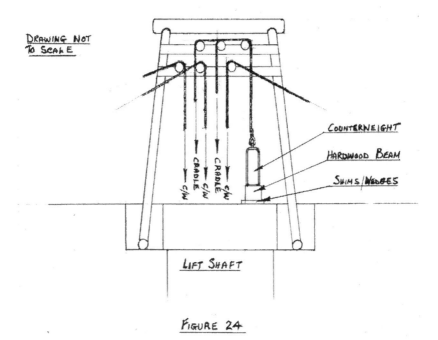

COUNTERWEIGHT

HARDWOOD BEAM

SHIMS/WEDGES

CRADLE C/W
CRADLE C/W
C/W CRADLE

LIFT SHAFT

FIGURE 24

The wooden beam would have been placed across the north end of the shaft on top of two limestone blocks that had been positioned right on the edge of the lift shaft (all of the blocks around the lift shaft cannot be installed until we hoist the rig up to the next level). The gap between the bottom of the counterweight and the top of the wooden beam would have been packed up with wooden shims until the gap between the top of the block and the bottom of the counterweight was almost closed. Wooden wedges would then have been driven under the wooden beam from either end until the counterweight was fully supported.

With the cradle and the three control weights down at the bottom of the lift shaft and the counterweight propped up, the bindings on the two ropes on the counterweight were unfastened. Some rope would then have been pulled through the metal rings on top of the counterweight to provide some slack as the rig was being raised. With all of the hoist components on solid footings and no load on any of the ropes, the rig was ready to be manoeuvred up and onto the next level. But although the rig was being raised up to a new level, that course was not complete; it could not be completed until all four legs of the rig were clear of the existing level on which it was positioned. The builders therefore had to raise one end of the rig at a time and manoeuvre two limestone blocks on that level until they were directly below the legs of the rig; they then repeated this procedure at the other end of the rig until the rig was positioned above the newly extended lift shaft on the newly completed platform.

With all of the ropes still suspended from the rig it would not have been difficult to manoeuvre the rig up onto the next level and the simplest way to get the rig onto the new level was simply to tilt it to raise two of its legs up off the platform, then repeat the operation with the other two legs being raised up onto the new level. Ropes would most likely have been attached to the cross member at the top of the rig for this purpose and as the top of the rig was hauled over to one side the legs on the opposite side would have been raised up off the platform. This would have been the simplest and most logical way to raise the legs of the rig. Before the builders reattached the ropes to the counterweight, and manoeuvred the rig until it was perfectly aligned with the antechamber below, the platform around the lift shaft would have been completed. Limestone blocks would have been levered over to the edge of the lift shaft from the platform behind to extend the shaft up to the new course. Once the rig had been set up and it was in operation again, the gaps thus created in the platform, well back from the edge of the lift shaft, would then have been built up with some of the first blocks of limestone to be hauled up to the new level. Some of these blocks may have been cut into two or four smaller blocks in order to fill in the last of these gaps.

When the rig was accurately positioned on the new level and aligned with the antechamber below, the first task of the rig operators was to reconnect the ropes to the counterweight. The stroke of the hoist was longer now, so they couldn't just reconnect the two ropes to the counterweight here as they would not have been able to haul the cradle up beyond the top of the limestone blocks on the sled if they did so. With our cradle bottomed in the antechamber and the counterweight positioned on top of the temporary support, these components are in exactly the same positions as they were prior to us hoisting the rig up onto the new level. We therefore need to move one of these components to take account of the longer stroke; we cannot move the counterweight as it is much too heavy, but fortunately, we can use the two ropes that the cradle is suspended from to hoist the cradle up off the floor of the antechamber.

That is exactly what the builders would have done. The rig operators would have hauled the three control weights up out of their mountings and secured the ropes; the cradle would then have been hauled up off the floor of the antechamber and some wooden props then placed under the cradle to support it in the temporary position until the ropes could be reattached to the counterweight (the length of these props would have corresponded to the height of the limestone blocks on the newly completed platform). When the rig operators then took up the slack on the ropes on the counterweight, pulled them until taut, then doubled them back to form loops, they would then have bound (whipped) the rope with cord again to secure it. The two largest components of the rig were now set to the new longer stroke. However, had we not propped up the cradle before we tied off the ropes again, the cradle would not have cleared the top of the limestone block at the top of the lift shaft when the counterweight bottomed in the antechamber. By always releasing the connecting ropes when the counterweight was at the top of its stroke and then propping up the cradle before reconnecting the ropes to the counterweight after the rig had been raised up on to the newly completed level, the cradle and the counterweight were always set to the new stroke length when the ropes were pulled taut and reattached to the counterweight.

Now that we are familiar with the components of the lifting mechanism and know how the rig was hoisted up onto the next level, we need to take a look at the ropes that were an integral part of this apparatus. We are not concerned here with the material itself, as it is evident that they had a strong enough material with which to produce ropes that would endure the rigors of this particular task. (Hemp has been in use since 8,000 B.C.E. and it is possible that this was the material used for the ropes in the construction of the Great Pyramid, but it's just as likely that other fibres, such as cotton, were used to produce ropes as this material would almost certainly have been available at the time. Ropes produced using Egyptian cotton fibres are the strongest ropes produced today from natural fibres.) It is also possible that the builders may have had to replace some, or possibly all, of the ropes used in the hoist over the lifetime of the project. However, it is the sheer quantity of rope that is of concern to us here, since all of this rope had to be carefully stowed and looked after for a very long time while the builders got on with the business of the construction. Great care had to have been taken to ensure that this huge quantity of rope did not get damaged during the long periods each day when the hoist was operating.

The height of the Great Pyramid today is approximately 137 metres from ground level. In spite of the fact that it has lost around 10metres from its original height, the top of the lift shaft has not yet been exposed. The top of the shaft could theoretically be within one or two metres of the current top of the pyramid, but let's assume that it is 7 metres below the top of the pyramid as it now stands. That gives us a nice round figure of 130 metres from ground level to the top of the lift shaft. The floor of the antechamber and the upper chamber are approximately 50 metres up from ground level; when we subtract this figure from the other to determine the approximate height of the lift shaft we can therefore say that within the structure of the Great Pyramid there is a lift shaft approximately 80 metres in height. This of course is the approximate completed height of the lift shaft, but if the builders had used the same ropes from start to finish the ropes would have to have been long enough to take account of the final height of the lift shaft. The height of the topmost rollers on the rig though could have been another three or four metres above the platform so the length of most of the ropes could easily have exceeded 85 to 90 metres. This however would have been the minimum length of rope required for the two ropes that linked the cradle with the counterweight, assuming that they did not replace the original ropes at any time when the hoist was in operation. (When the counterweight was at the top of the shaft, the cradle was at the bottom of the shaft; at no time could the cradle and the counterweight both be at the bottom of the shaft.) Likewise, the two ropes on each of the control weights needed to extend from the platform, up and over the rollers on the rig, and down to the control weights when they were at the bottom of the shaft; therefore these ropes would have been of a similar length to those used on the cradle / counterweight. The two ropes attached to the counterweight were looped through the rings on its metal hoops and tied off, but as the counterweight descended to the antechamber, it also hauled two lengths of excess rope (rope not currently being used) down with it. This excess rope would have looped down into the space between the back of the counterweight and the north wall of the lift shaft as the counterweight was hauled back up to the top of the shaft. Apart from this length of rope however, there had to have been a considerable amount of excess rope attached to the counterweight when the rig was first set up and it had to have been stored somewhere.

There would also have been a great deal of excess rope on the control weights as well when the rig was first set up and it's possible that the excess rope on the control weight at the north end of the rig (the control weight nearest to the counterweight) could have been stored on the working platform. The excess rope at the early stages of the hoist operations had to have been stored well away from the working area at the top of the lift shaft as there would have been a considerable quantity of it. The excess rope attached to the counterweight and the control weight on the north side of the rig could have been coiled up on wooden sleds positioned on the working platform on the north side of the rig somewhere, most probably on the east side of the gallery walls at the early stages. Although the excess rope was slowly reduced each time a platform was completed and the rig hoisted up to the next level, for the most part, there was a great quantity of excess rope not being put to any use that needed to be stored somewhere. If some of this excess rope had been stored on the working platforms on sleds, then these sleds would also have to have been hauled up onto each new level as it neared completion. On the face of it, we wouldn't expect to find many clues at this late stage as to where or how the great quantity of excess rope was stored when the hoist was first rigged; but once again, the antechamber walls provide a clue as to where some of the excess rope was stowed during the early stages of this operation, as it was not all stored on the working platforms.

If we were to stand in the antechamber and face its south wall (looking towards the Upper Chamber), we would see that there are four deep vertical grooves cut into this wall. These grooves extend from the roof level of the passageway into the upper chamber, up to the top of the granite wall. These are, without doubt, rope grooves. However, there are only four rope grooves in the south wall of the antechamber and these were undoubtedly the rope grooves for the four ropes used on the two control weights nearest the south side of the rig. At the early stages of the construction of the inner stepped levels, when the rig was first put into operation, there was not a great deal of distance between the south side of the rig and the north side of the upper chamber and the stack. There was no convenient place on the working platform here to store the excess rope for the two control weights on this side of the rig, but there was a chamber on the south side of the antechamber, the upper chamber, with plenty of space to store a large amount of excess rope. It was in this chamber that the excess rope was stored for these two control weights.

The four vertical grooves in the granite face of the south wall of the antechamber were cut into this wall in order to ensure that these ropes did not become entangled or get damaged as the cradle descended into the chamber. If you take a look at my cut-away drawing of the antechamber (Fig. 25) on the next page you will clearly see the reason as to why these four rope grooves were cut into the south wall of the antechamber. The channels on the sidewalls of the antechamber nearest its south wall are right at the end of the sidewalls and the mountings for the control weight at this end of the chamber are directly above these channels. Clearly, if the rope grooves had not been cut into the south wall of the chamber, the ropes could have fouled or been damaged by the cradle as it descended into the chamber. By cutting these rope grooves into the south wall of the antechamber, the builders ensured that the ropes were safely out of the way of the cradle when the hoist was operating. When we didn't know the true purpose of this small chamber, it seemed strange that the builders didn't cut these rope grooves all the way down to the very bottom of the south wall, as the grooves end just short of it. Although I was a bit puzzled by this, I realized that the control weight at this end of the rig would have ensured that these four ropes remained in the grooves at this end of the chamber. A problem would only have occurred if the ropes had not been recessed into this wall and had somehow become crossed or entangled when the hoist was in operation. By ensuring that these ropes were contained within dedicated channels, there was little chance that the ropes would have become crossed or entangled. However, we have to remember that it was only the top end of the cradle that could have damaged these ropes as the cradle descended into the antechamber. It was therefore not necessary for these grooves to extend all the way to the bottom end of this face.

What about the north side of the rig though? Could the builders have stored the excess rope on this side of the rig on the north side of the antechamber, not up on the working platforms as I had supposed? Well, on the north side of the antechamber is the grand gallery and this was in continuous use until this phase of the

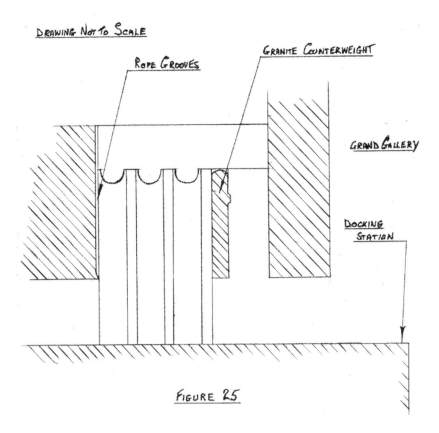

FIGURE 25

construction was complete, until the pyramid was capped, in fact. At first I had thought it very unlikely that the excess rope on this side of the rig could have been stored anywhere other than on the working platforms, and there are certainly no clues to be found in the antechamber to indicate whether or not any excess rope was also stored off the working platform. But then again, rope grooves would not have been required on the north wall of the chamber if this had been the case, as there was plenty of clearance between the north wall of the antechamber and the counterweight.

The north end of the antechamber (nearest the grand gallery) is where we find the counterweight sitting in the first pair of channels in the antechamber. You will see from the drawing (Fig. 25) that these channels are much farther away from the north wall of the chamber than the channels at the other end of the antechamber are from its south wall. There is in fact a 50 cm gap between the north face of the chamber and the back of the granite counterweight.

And as I mentioned earlier, when the counterweight travelled up to the top of the lift shaft, the free length of rope on the counterweight would have looped down into the space between the counterweight and the north wall of the lift shaft. But the builders could have made much more use of this space; they could have looped all of the excess rope that was attached to the counterweight and the control weight at this end of the rig over a crossbar on the rig, and suspended it in the gap between the north wall of the chamber and the counterweight; there was certainly plenty of space here to do so. I believe that this would have been the best option here and the one chosen by the builders of the Great Pyramid, so there would probably have been no need for any excess rope to be cluttering up the working platforms at all.

Going up!

So how did it all function? How did they hoist so much limestone up to the inner stepped levels and the upper platforms to complete the pyramid?

When the three control weights were hoisted up off the top of the cradle and hoisted up the shaft, the counterweight, which was slightly heavier than the combined weight of the limestone block and the cradle, began to descend. The counterweight hoisted the cradle all the way up to the top of the shaft. When the cradle arrived at the top of the shaft, a sled was placed across the top of the shaft under the limestone block. The three control weights were then lowered onto the top of the mountings on top of the three pairs of arms on the cradle, pushing the cradle downwards until the block bottomed on the sled. The cradle, as we discovered earlier, was much deeper than the limestone block so it continued on its downward path until the top of the cradle had almost reached the top of the limestone block; the fingers on the ends of the arms of the cradle were now well below the level of the sled. When the three control weights were quickly hoisted up off the top of the cradle in unison at this point, the two halves of the cradle would have sprung open – or been pulled open – at the bottom end, and with the weight removed from the top of the cradle, it would immediately have begun to move upwards again as its sides sprung open. After the arms of the cradle had finally cleared the top of the limestone block, the top of the cradle would have come up against the three control weights suspended from the rig and this would have arrested the upward movement of the cradle, simultaneously pushing the sides of the cradle inward again until they were vertical. The workmen on the platform would then have hauled the limestone block away from the top of the lift shaft and the cradle would have been pushed back down the shaft to the antechamber again by the combined weight of the three control weights.

This type of cradle was hinged at the top and each lifting rope could have been attached to two rings offset from the central hinged spine of the cradle (Fig.23). Both rings were placed well away from the central hinged rib, out towards the sides of the cradle. The top of the cradle would have naturally sagged in the middle – and its arms splayed out at the bottom – when it was suspended from the ropes with no weight acting on the cradle to hold the arms of the cradle in the vertical position (the control weights, or a limestone block). When the three control weights were lowered onto the top of the mountings on top of the three pairs of arms of the cradle however, their combined weight pushed the sides (arms) of the cradle inward again, their mounts being further away from the central hinge than the fixing points for the ropes. The control weights were then used to push the cradle back down to the bottom of the shaft and it would only have come to a halt when the cylindrical control weights came to rest in their semi-circular mountings in the sidewalls of the antechamber (or earlier if the downward path of the control weights had been arrested by the operators). By then, of course, the three pairs of arms were restrained by the sidewalls of the antechamber and they could not splay out again until the cradle cleared the top of the antechamber on its next ascent, by which time, of course, the weight of the limestone block ensured that the arms of the cradle could not spring open again until the block was lowered onto the sled at the top of the shaft. (The fingers on the ends of the arms would have been turned upwards and probably spiked so that they bit into the underside of each limestone block.)

The combined weight of the control weights was around the same weight as the counterweight. The control weights pushed the cradle down the shaft and hoisted the counterweight back up to the top of the shaft because the combined weight of the three control weights, plus the weight of the cradle, was heavier than the counterweight. It is no coincidence that the semi-circular mountings for the control weights in the antechamber are at the top of the channels in the antechamber walls as the mountings for the control weights on the top of the cradle would have been positioned directly on top of these three pairs of arms. By setting up the mechanism in the manner that they did, using three control weights to raise and lower the counterweight, it gave the operators complete control over the direction and function of the apparatus. With the three control weights accommodated in the area above the cradle in the antechamber, it was only the counterweight that had to be positioned at one end of the chamber. This enabled the builders to keep the length of the antechamber, and the lift shaft, to an absolute minimum, lowering the chances of a collapse of the shaft if the structure was subjected to the violent shaking effects of an earthquake sometime in the future.

We know that the builders of the Great Pyramid lived long before the time of Herodotus – and probably much further back in time than the fourth dynasty – but even after all of the discoveries I have made at Giza and further afield in my quest to discover how these magnificent structures had been constructed, I had no doubt at this stage of my reconstruction that the ancient builders of these structures had probably more surprises in store. I now know that there are one or two more surprises ahead of us as we move into the final stages of the construction, but my research and earlier discoveries also revealed that there are more chambers and pipes yet to be discovered in all three of the principal pyramids at Giza. I now know that they exist because they were essential components of the hydraulic systems used in the construction of these structures; we can therefore only hope that in the fullness of time, Egyptologists will gain access to these hidden features to expand our knowledge of these complex structures.

Even by today's standards, the construction of the Great Pyramid would have been a massive undertaking. I have the utmost admiration for the men who achieved this almost impossible feat; the men who provided us with our only remaining wonder of the ancient world and in the process, created one of the world's most enduring mysteries. Can we even begin to imagine what went through the minds of those men who stood on the barges in the top lock of the grand gallery and pushed those limestone blocks through the passageway into the antechamber? No sooner had a block been positioned within the chamber than it miraculously took off skyward as if grabbed by some huge unseen hand. I'm sure it must have spawned some fantastic tales and legends in the centuries following the construction of the pyramids. To those in the know up on the working platforms however, the unseen hand that plucked the limestone block from the sled in the antechamber was nothing more than a puppet on a string; a puppet they had complete control over using the compound hoist mechanism they had constructed for the purpose. This hoist enabled the pyramid builders to construct more than 100 courses of the Great Pyramid and to hoist all of the masonry necessary to complete the pyramid up and onto the inner stepped levels initially, and then onto the levels beyond the perimeter platform.

When the hoist became operational and the inner stepped levels had been built up to the same elevation as the perimeter platform, work continued in a very similar pattern to the one established at the outset of the construction, with the smooth limestone casing blocks being put in position on the outer fringes of each level first, before the core masonry was put in place. The vast bulk of the limestone that came up to the platforms after the elevator became operational was of a standard height, width and length, but there were some exceptions. The blocks used to construct some courses were slightly higher than the average limestone blocks and the outer casing blocks which had one angular face, occasionally two (on the cornerstones), had all to be hauled up to the working platforms from the antechamber. When all of these outer facing blocks on each side of a platform had been installed, the builders slowly worked their way back across the platform, creating ever smaller rectangles, until the course was almost complete. The rig, which was by then sitting in a rectangular pit one course below the level of this platform, had then to be raised up to the higher level.

Whatever type of cradle they put to work in the lift shaft, it obviously fulfilled the job it had been designed for; not only did the builders extend the lift shaft to something approaching eighty metres in height, they also managed to cap it and go on to complete the pyramid.

Building up the inner levels

It would have taken the builders a long time to build up the inner levels for it was not just a matter of putting one course of smaller standard blocks on top of another at the early stages of this phase of the construction. As the first courses of the inner stepped levels around the east end of the upper chamber and the antechamber were built up, the wall at the top end of the grand gallery had to be built up also and a good volume of limestone would have been needed just to bring these levels up to the level of the small platform above the antechamber at this stage of the construction. We could not build up our limestone levels on the east side of the upper chamber earlier for this was the area where we traversed our barges to the east end of the upper chamber when we were building up the courses of the upper chamber and the stack. We also parked the limestone beams used to construct the wall at the top end of the gallery on the inner stepped levels here earlier, and the stepped levels could only be built up by two courses at a time after each of these limestone beams were levered into their final positions. The areas above the ramps on either side of the upper chamber had also to be built up as the stepped levels were built up and many of the limestone blocks used to build up these areas would probably have needed to be cut to size on the stepped levels before being installed. The builders would probably have hauled full length blocks with one angled face up to the inner levels for this purpose and then cut them to various lengths to ensure that all the joints were staggered as they built up the areas above the ramps here. It is also likely that they cut steps into these ramps every few courses and checked standard rectangular blocks into these steps to strengthen the bond on these levels.

Earlier, we brought many limestone beams up onto the inner platforms at either end of the stack and most of these beams will be used to create the gabled roof above the stack. It was almost certainly a double gabled roof that the builders constructed above the stack for it makes no sense to construct a double gabled roof above the grand entrance tunnel and not put a double gabled roof above the stack. There is a comparable weight of masonry above the roof of the stack as there is above much of the entrance tunnel and an absolutely tremendous weight of masonry above the lower chamber; it should therefore go without saying that similar double gables would have been installed above both of these chambers.

We are also reminded here, as our inner platform reaches the top of the stack, why we still have a gabled roof to construct at this elevation. We could certainly have constructed a gabled roof directly on top of the upper chamber over most of its length earlier, but not all of it, for we could not support the gables above the ramps and above the area where the antechamber was later constructed. That was why the builders created the stack; they had to postpone the installation of the gabled roof and extend the flat roof of the upper chamber up to an elevation where the gabled roof could be installed over the full length of the chamber. Now, of course, we are long past the stage where the ramps were in use and we have built up the inner platform around the lift shaft and the east end of the upper chamber to the top of this extended roof (the stack). As we build up the next few courses of the inner stepped levels, we will create ledges on either side of the top level of the stack and it will be these ledges that will bolster the lower ends of the double gables when we install them here. The double gables will in turn support the enormous weight of masonry in the top section of the structure that we have yet to construct.

It was only when the builders first pushed the perimeter platform up from the first central distribution chamber (lower chamber) in the first of the two largest pyramids (the Middle Pyramid) to just beyond the level where the gabled roof would be constructed above the stack, that the opportunity to construct a free-standing upper chamber and layered roof (stack) arose. However, the granite chamber and the stack above it in the Middle Pyramid could never have been constructed if the builders had not designed and installed a very high-tech pumping system such as the one they installed in the Great Pyramid. It was only this two stage pumping system where a secondary pulse was generated in an expansion chamber that made it possible to pump water up to such a great elevation within these two structures. (These features have yet to be discovered in the Middle Pyramid at Giza.) As we discovered earlier, the limestone beams that form the gabled roof above the upper chamber in the Great Pyramid simply had to be transported up to the inner stepped levels when the inner lock was operational. These beams were temporarily parked on the inner stepped levels at either end of the stack on the two levels where they would later be installed. If the perimeter platform had not been extended up to this elevation, and a super high-tech pump not been installed in the Great Pyramid, these limestone beams could never have been transported up to these levels and parked here. It was the inner stepped levels that had been built up when masonry was hauled up from the central distribution chambers in the lower and upper chambers that formed the perimeter walls of the inner lock. It was these walls that retained the water in the inner lock when barges were used to transport these huge beams up to the inner stepped levels.

Not all of the limestone beams that were transported up into the inner area were used to construct the gables. I think it is likely that some smaller limestone beams may have been installed in a section of the platform in the first few courses above the level of top of the stack also. It was the limestone masonry on the next two or three levels that bolstered the gables on the north side of the structure at the east end of the upper chamber, between the gables and the lift shaft. When we began to construct the antechamber, I pointed out that the south wall of the antechamber was not in fact the north side of the north wall of the upper chamber for the passageway here is much longer. Unlike the north wall of the antechamber, where this was simply the other side of the wall at the top of the grand gallery, the builders had in fact set the north wall of the upper chamber some distance from the south end of the antechamber (as I mentioned earlier, the passageway from the antechamber into the upper chamber is longer than the passageway from the grand gallery into the antechamber). This was obviously of benefit to the builders when they first began to hoist limestone up the lift shaft to the inner stepped levels as the small platform here (between the rig and the north wall of the upper chamber) would have provided a good working area on the south side of the rig for the operators of the hoist. However, this was not the reason why the builders had originally set the north wall of the upper chamber so far back from the top end of the gallery; they had to create an inner lock in the space between the gallery and the upper chamber. As we discovered earlier, this lock had to be long enough to accommodate the long granite beams and slabs used in the construction of the upper chamber and the stack. But when the builders later built up these inner levels until they were flush with the granite slabs at the top of the stack, they probably installed the aforementioned limestone beams in some of the courses between the north side of the upper chamber and the south wall of the lift shaft to improve the stability of the structure here. They would certainly have staggered the joints in the limestone blocks in this area, but it would surely have been much safer to place a limestone beam on the south side of the lift shaft on the first few levels above the level of the top roofing sheets in the stack, as the gables at this end of the upper chamber were fairly close to the lift shaft. We will only be able to determine if this was indeed the case when the lift shaft in the Great Pyramid is explored.

We have now reached the level where we have to create the first of the ledges on either side of the granite roof of the stack. In effect, all that we have to do here is leave a recess in the middle of the first course of limestone above the level of the granite roof of the stack; we have to take the limestone platform right up to the edge of the granite roof on either side of the stack. It is the granite blocks in the stack and the walls of the upper chamber that bear the weight of the gabled roof here and the masonry above it; however, it is the limestone platforms on either side of the gables that bolsters the gabled roof on these two levels. As a result, there is also a great deal of pressure acting outwardly (horizontally) on the sides of these recesses, hence the reason I believe that the builders may have installed some limestone beams on the south side of the lift shaft on these levels. These limestone beams are almost certainly longer than the width of the lift shaft for the beams themselves had to be bolstered by the limestone blocks on either side of the shaft on these levels. This, in my opinion, is the only way the gables at this end of the stack could have been safely bolstered here without jeopardising the integrity of the structure in this area.

When it came time to install the first of the gables above the stack, the builders would have been greatly disadvantaged here, as hydraulic power was no longer available at this elevation. Although hydraulic power had been used to partially raise the gables above the grand entrance tunnel and those above the lower chamber also, the inner lock at the top end of the grand gallery had long since been decommissioned by the time the builders came to install the gables above the stack.

I think it most likely that the limestone beams that form the legs of the gables would have been parked on the inner platform at either end of the stack on rollers when they had first been transported up to this inner level. These huge beams had to be hauled over onto the granite roof at the top of the stack before they could be hauled up into the vertical position so rollers would have been an absolute necessity here (these beams could not have been hauled along the platform without rollers no matter how much lubrication was applied, for they were just too heavy). We know that these beams were definitely propped up off the surface of the limestone platform because the top ends of these beams had to have been levered up by a considerable distance from the roof of the stack before the gables could be hauled up into the vertical position.

Once again, I believe that the gables would have been hauled up into the vertical position in the same manner as the lower gables in the roof of the lower chamber and in the grand entrance tunnel. I believe the builders would have begun by installing the two gables in the centre of the roof here and then worked their way back out towards the ends of the roof from there. I believe that this was the most logical way to do it as a good number of these limestone beams would have been parked on the limestone levels at either end of the granite roof when they were first transported into this area. By installing the gables in the centre of the granite roof first, each of these heavy beams had only to be hauled the shortest distance prior to their installation. Hydraulic power could have played no part in the operation to raise these gables for the inner lock had long been decommissioned. But there was another difficulty here for these gables had to be raised without putting any pressure on the granite roof; the weight of these limestone beams had to be borne by the granite spacing blocks in the stack and the walls of the upper chamber at all times. It was only those areas of the granite roofing slabs above the supporting spacing blocks in the stack that could withstand the tremendous weight of the gables therefore they had to be installed without putting any pressure on the area of the slabs between the supporting blocks. No simple feat!

The fact that these lower gables had to be levered and hauled up into the vertical position above the granite roof of the stack without putting any undue pressure on the granite roofing slabs themselves, certainly complicated matters here. We know from past experience that the builders brought the two legs of the lower gables together at the apex when they were in the horizontal position, and before they were hauled up into the vertical position in both the lower chamber and the entrance tunnel. This, however, would have been very difficult to do here without putting a tremendous load on the granite roofing slabs. Earlier, we also discovered that the builders had to raise the peak of each gable by a considerable distance before they could haul the gables up into the vertical position, but once again they could not risk putting undue stress on the granite roof when doing so. Therefore if the gables here had been formed before they were hauled up into the vertical position, the load could not have been borne by the granite roof of the chamber.

The way to get around this little difficulty was to ensure that the load was placed above the granite blocks in the stack and the walls of the upper chamber at all times; at every stage of the lifting operation. As I mentioned earlier, the limestone beams that formed one of the first two gables to be raised up into the vertical position would have been hauled along the machined ends of the granite slabs above the granite supporting blocks until they were positioned near the centre of the granite roof. Just before the leading ends of these beams reached the centre of the roof the builders would have refrained from putting any more rollers under the beams as they were pushed forward. As a result, the beams would have tilted when the bulk of the weight of the beams was beyond the rollers, with the lower edge of these two beams coming to rest on the granite surface of the roof. Chocks would then have been placed under the rollers at the trailing ends of these beams to ensure that the beams could not be pushed back in the direction from which they had come. These two limestone beams were not hauled up into the vertical position at this time, as these beams would have served as the buffers up against which the lower ends of the first beams to be hauled up into the vertical position would have been butted up against. It may be that the builders also formed the gable on the horizontal here prior to these beams having acted as buffers, so we will take a look at how that could have been achieved when we raise our first gable.

The next two limestone beams would have been manoeuvred from the limestone platform onto the ends of the granite slabs, one on either side of the stack, and then manoeuvred so that, what would become the lower ends of the beams / gables, were hard up against the buffers – the limestone beams – we placed here earlier. The underside of these beams was already some distance up off the surface of the platform as they were supported by rollers when hauled into position. However, as these beams neared their destination, no more rollers would have been placed underneath the leading ends of these limestone beams, and as a result, the beams would have tilted until the leading ends of the beams were grounded on the granite surface here. As these beams tilted on the rollers nearest the centre of the underside of the beams, the trailing ends of the beams would have tilted upwards, leaving a very good clearance beneath the beams. It was these trailing ends of the two beams that had to be brought together to form the apex of the gable, but the added complication here was that this had to be achieved without the weight of these beams being placed on the unsupported area of the granite roofing slabs.

We have no way of determining the diameter of the rollers the builders used under the limestone beams; if they had used fairly large diameter rollers it is possible that the trailing ends of the limestone gables were a great enough distance from the granite floor here for the next part of the operation to commence. However, if this was not the case, then levers would have been used at this stage of the operation to raise the trailing ends of the beams higher and hardwood blocks would have been placed underneath the beams some distance from the trailing ends to support them at this steeper angle. The reason this may have been necessary was that the builders had to place a long wooden beam under the raised ends of the limestone beams here prior to bringing the tops of these two beams together to form the apex of the gable. This beam would have been raised up off of the granite roofing sheet (floor) at either end slightly and when the limestone legs of the gable were then brought together to form the gable, it was this beam that took the weight of the legs of the gable and not the granite roofing sheet beneath it. When the apex of the gable had been formed, the builders were then ready to haul it up into the vertical position as they had done many times before.

After the first of these gables had been installed in the upright position, it's possible that the builders would have hauled another gable up into the upright position at the same end of the roof as the first gable installed here while the buffer was still in position. Whether they did or not, they would have continued to raise each of the lower gables in turn in the exact same manner as the first gable until the gabled roof was complete.

Although the installation of these gables would have been more physically demanding at the initial stage – when the top end of the gable had to be levered up and propped up until it was high enough to be hauled up into the vertical position –the second part of the process was exactly the same as that used earlier to install the lower gables in the entrance tunnel. We have to remember that there was no platform or landing below the lower gables in the entrance tunnel and the lower chamber when the gables had to be installed there, so the builders never had the option of levering and propping up the top ends of these gables before they could be hauled up into the vertical position. But they had hydraulic power available at these locations and that made life much easier for them when they installed these gables.

As I mentioned earlier, it would be naive of us to believe that the builders installed double gables in the grand entrance tunnel yet did not do the same here, for they undoubtedly did. However, there is no point in going over the same ground again as to how the upper gables were installed above the stack, as these gables would have been installed in more or less the same manner as those we installed above the grand entrance tunnel. The beams for these gables would have been parked on the next level up when they had been transported up and on to the inner platform and it was from this course of the platform, two courses up from the top of the stack, that they were tilted and then hauled up into position on top of the lower gables.

When the gabled roof of the stack had been completed, the only internal feature of the Great Pyramid that the builders had to work around as they pushed the inner platform up to the level of the perimeter platform, was the lift shaft; all of the other internal features of the pyramid had by then been subsumed by the great mass of limestone that had been transported into the structure. When the final few courses of the inner stepped levels had been completed, the builders had for the first time since they had reached the floor level of the lower chamber, a platform that extended from one side of the structure to the other. The outer and inner levels were now one.

I have referred to hubs and junctions on more than a few occasions on our journey up through the Great Pyramid and you will no doubt be pleased to know that this is the last major junction. Our structure has now been completed up to the level where the shafts – that originated in the sidewalls of the upper chamber – had been extended up to (they did not extend all the way to the north and south faces of the structure but stopped just short of these faces). But there was now a slight change to the routines of the men working on the platforms at this stage of the construction; in fact, for the very first time since the hoist had become operational, casing blocks had now to be hauled up to the platforms from the antechamber. Since the builders had first begun to haul limestone blocks up the lift shaft, they had been building up the inner stepped levels and those areas around the upper chamber and the stack that had still to be built up. But now that the inner levels had been built up to the level of the perimeter platform, they had again to begin installing the outer casing blocks on every level from here on up. These casing blocks, however, were much smaller on average than those used earlier to construct the lower courses of the structure for these blocks had now to be hauled up the lift shaft as a dead weight; they could not be winched up ramps like the larger casing blocks used earlier. (You can clearly see where the builders began to use these smaller casing blocks in the Middle Pyramid at Giza as many of its smaller casing blocks are still in place at the top of the structure.) Great care would have been required when these casing blocks were being hauled up to the platforms as the dressed outer faces and edges of these blocks would have been very easily damaged.

The pace of construction would also have slowed here, for not only were the builders installing limestone blocks on full width platforms again, the men had also to install the outer casing blocks on each level and survey the structure before they could go on to complete each course. They had still to construct another substantial pyramid on top of this platform at this stage and this pyramid was comparable in size to the smallest of the three principal pyramids at Giza. Fortunately, this pyramid had no internal features other than the lift shaft, and the length of each side was now less than half the length of the sides when the builders had first set out to build the Great Pyramid. But although they had no complex features to create within this part of the structure, it would still have taken the builders a very long time to complete this upper section of the Great Pyramid, for, unlike the Small Pyramid at Giza, all of the limestone blocks to complete this small pyramid had to be hauled up the lift shaft, one by one, to each of the platforms.

It would probably have taken the builders a number of years to build up this upper section of the Great Pyramid, block by block and course by course, and this would have been the routine for a very long time. But sooner or later their routine would have changed again, for at some point they had to have capped both the lift shaft and the Great Pyramid itself. But when did they do so, and – more intriguingly – how did they complete the pyramid after they capped the shaft? These were questions that I did not yet have the answer to when I reached this stage of my reconstruction but knowing that the builders had completed the structure, I felt certain that I would eventually discover how it had been done. I pressed on.

Standing room only

The pyramidion - how did they put it in position? That is just one of the questions we will have to answer as we attempt to complete the very top section of our very own pyramid, but it is by no means the only one. I must admit that I felt like the fellow who had almost finished painting his floor, only to discover that he had painted himself into a corner when I reached this stage of the construction. With the addition of each course of the pinnacle (my term for the very topmost section of the pyramid), the square area of the platform on top of the pyramid had become smaller and smaller. At some point I knew that I would have to cap the lift shaft... but when? Most obviously, after we cap the lift shaft it will be impossible to haul any more limestone blocks up to the platforms, so how on earth are we to complete our pyramid when we can't haul any more limestone up to these very cramped levels?

I didn't know the answer to that question yet but the builders of the Great Pyramid had found a way to do it; I just had to figure out how it had been done. However, while I was working on this problem, I realized that the construction of this last section must have differed greatly from all those that had gone before in that it must have involved the construction of a temporary landing, or piers, to support the rig at the very highest levels. Up until now we have been hauling limestone up to each platform, the same platform that our rig stands on. But we now have to contemplate raising limestone blocks up to the very top of the pinnacle, up beyond the last platform wide enough to support the rig. The builders would have found it impossible to raise limestone up to the topmost courses without the use of the rig, so we now have to find a way to maintain a minimum width of the platform on the eastern side of the pinnacle to support our rig at these higher levels... and figure out where we are going to get the material to build this temporary structure.

I'm sure by now you have become accustomed to the ways of those ancient builders. I certainly learned very quickly when I first began to understand what amazing abilities they possessed, that although they had taken on the most extraordinary challenges with this project, they had always favoured the simplest solutions to the problems they encountered along the way. But it is only now, when we are here at the very top section of the Great Pyramid, that we discover the answer to one of those puzzling features of the pyramid that we encountered back down on the sixteenth level of the structure. It wasn't the feature itself (although it has not been recognized for what it truly is by Egyptologists) that I had been puzzled by; it was the position of this feature that had puzzled me.

The grand entrance to the Great Pyramid is set some 7 metres or more to the east of centre on the north face of the pyramid and the entrances into both the upper and lower chambers are at the extreme east ends of these chambers; the chambers themselves straddle the north-south axis of the pyramid. From the moment we came through the grand doorway, there has been nothing whatsoever to indicate why the builders needed to construct the grand entrance and the ascending and descending corridors off centre; they could have positioned the doorway and the corridors right slap bang in the middle of the pyramid for all it seemed to matter. After all, the inner chambers were deep within the structure and the integrity of the structure would not have been compromised in any way had they placed the grand entrance on the north-south axis, with these chambers lying to the west of this axis. Having discovered no logical reason for this 7 metre offset east of the north-south axis, I could only conclude that it was important to the builders of the structure to have the lower and upper chambers straddling the north-south axis of the structure for symbolic reasons. As time went by, I began to doubt that this was the reason for the grand entrance having been offset from the north-south axis by 7 metres, for on my journey up through this structure I had discovered that each and every feature of the internal structure of this great edifice was created as a means to an end. Every pipe (corridor and passageway) and chamber was part of the grand design of this structure and each and every feature had played its role in the construction of this magnificent monument. There was no indication whatsoever that any of its features had been created or positioned within the structure for purely symbolic reasons and I was by now convinced that there had to be another reason for this 7 metre offset.

They say that all things come to he who waits. Well, that was certainly true here, but I hadn't expected to have to wait quite so long to discover why the grand doorway and all of the passageways had been offset 7 metres east of centre. For the answer to this riddle, we once again have to take a look at the small chamber of secrets (the antechamber) nestled between the top end of the grand gallery and the granite mass of the upper chamber; it was the position of this small chamber that was the key to the successful completion of the Great Pyramid. In truth, it was the position of the lift shaft that determined whether the builders would be successful or not, for in order to complete the pinnacle and cap the pyramid, the rig had to be positioned off to one side of its peak. The position of the antechamber therefore determined the position of the lift shaft – how far it was offset from the centre of the structure – and this determined the position of the rig on each platform. If the chamber of secrets had been constructed directly under the peak of the structure, its builders would have been unable to use the rig to install the limestone blocks that would complete the topmost courses of the pyramid.

The grand doorway, the grand gallery, the antechamber and the lift shaft were all offset to the east of the north-south axis of the pyramid in order that the topmost courses of this magnificent structure could be installed and the pyramid capped before the lift shaft was capped. The rig simply had to be offset from the centre of the structure if it was to be used to hoist the last few limestone blocks up to the highest levels and the lift shaft had to remain open until that task was complete. It was only by offsetting the lift shaft from the centre of the structure that this could be achieved and that is the sole reason as to why the grand doorway was not placed in the centre of the north face of the Great Pyramid. Now you may be thinking that they could easily have placed the grand doorway in the centre of the north face of the structure and positioned the antechamber 7 metres north of centre, but there are so many reasons as to why this would not have worked that it would take a great deal of time to list all of them. I will however point out the most obvious ones and leave it at that.

If the antechamber had been positioned 7 metres north of centre, then its floor would have been at a much lower elevation, for the grand gallery could not have been extended as far as it was if it had been constructed at the same 26 degree angle from the horizontal. It therefore follows that the floor of the upper chamber would have been at a much lower elevation also. But the whole point of pushing the top end of the grand gallery up to the greatest elevation possible was to ensure that the floor of the upper chamber and the antechamber were at the highest possible elevation within the structure. The greater the elevation here the less time it would take to construct this wonderful monument; the greatest number of large masonry blocks could be used to extend the perimeter platform and build up the inner stepped levels from the hub in the upper chamber. As we discovered earlier, after the upper chamber had been almost complete, a great number of large limestone blocks were used to extend the inner stepped levels and the perimeter platform much higher from this chamber. However, if the floor of the upper chamber and the antechamber had been at a much lower elevation it would have taken the builders a considerably longer time to complete the structure, as they would have had to construct a much greater part of the structure using the smaller limestone blocks that were hauled up the lift shaft and used to construct the upper section of the Great Pyramid.

As you can clearly see, by offsetting the doorway, the corridors, the grand gallery and the antechamber off to the east of centre, the upper chamber could be positioned much nearer to the south side of the structure and therefore placed at the highest elevation possible. Positioning the antechamber 7 metres north of the east-west axis was an option that the builders would never have considered, in my opinion, for by positioning the antechamber (and the lift shaft) to the east or the west of the centre of the structure the upper chamber and the antechamber, not to mention the inner lock, could be placed at a higher elevation within the structure. Their objective was to construct the greatest part of this structure using the largest limestone blocks possible and to transport as many of those blocks into the structure in bulk. When they had no other option but to haul limestone blocks up the lift shaft one at a time, the rate of construction fell dramatically. That was the primary reason why the antechamber and the lift shaft were positioned on the east-west axis of the Great Pyramid and not on the north side of this axis.

As you have no doubt realized by now, there was one other possibility here and that was to put the antechamber 7 metres south of the east-west axis on the central axis of the structure. Had the antechamber been positioned here, the grand gallery would have been even longer and the floor levels of the upper chamber and the antechamber would have been at a much greater elevation. But this was not an option the builders would ever have considered, for this option would have been self-defeating. Although they may have been able to push the perimeter platform up to a greater elevation from here, there was a negative element to this option. By extending the grand gallery farther, it would have taken a slightly longer time for each barge to reach the docking station at the top end of the gallery. When we consider the tremendous volume of limestone that had still to be transported up to this docking station to complete the structure after the step-stone had been installed, this short distance added to the journey of each barge that docked here would have resulted in a considerable increase in the time it took to transport this masonry to the docking station. We not only have to consider the time taken for the barges to reach the docking station we also have to consider the time taken for those barges to return to the bottom of the gallery, for the next barge could not have entered the locks at the bottom end of the gallery until the barge that preceded it had entered the dual channel canal at the inner end of the entrance tunnel. The gain at the earlier stages could have been cancelled out by the increase in the time taken to complete the pyramid with a longer grand gallery (the law of diminishing returns). But there was possibly another reason why this option could not have been chosen; as I mentioned earlier, the pump would have had its limitations also. It simply may not have been possible to pump water up to a greater elevation to complete the stack above the upper chamber if this free-standing structure (the upper chamber) had been placed at a higher elevation.

Now that we know what lengths the builders went to at the earliest stages of the construction to ensure that the rig would be in the optimum position at the very highest levels of the structure, we can hopefully now figure out how the builders pulled off this final amazing feat. Somehow the builders managed to cap the lift shaft and complete the pinnacle of the Great Pyramid, so we know that it can be done; it has been done. And if it has been done before, it can be done again.

So far on this project, their planning had been thorough, the work extremely efficient and the progress steady, and although the structure is very complex it was always the simplest solution to each problem that the builders sought. If it had been possible to raise the rig up to the height required to cap the pyramid without bringing any extra building material up to the platforms, then that is undoubtedly what they would have chosen to do. It may have been technically challenging, but when you have almost achieved the impossible you take technically challenging in your stride.

Before we continue with our reconstruction, I have to say that I am 100% certain that the ancient pyramid builders had successfully executed this operation on the Middle Pyramid at Giza, and possibly on the Small Pyramid at Giza also, before they began to construct the Great Pyramid so any difficulties they had encountered previously they'd overcome long before they came to construct the pinnacle of the Great Pyramid. When they were at the same stage of the construction that we are at now, they knew for certain that they would complete it. But then again, they knew that long before they began to construct any one of these magnificent structures. It was technically possible to complete the pyramid by constructing a temporary landing for the rig using only the masonry needed to complete the structure and I was now certain that they'd set up and planned this final phase of the construction with that intention. But a question still remained to be answered. When did they seal the top end of the lift shaft?

The builders had ensured that the antechamber, and therefore the lift shaft, was offset from the centre of the pyramid, presumably at the optimum distance from the peak of the structure. This being the case, I realized that the deciding factor when it came to laying down the blocks in the temporary arrangement and closing the top of the lift shaft, had to have been the proximity of the edge of the platform on the east side of the pyramid to the lift shaft, remembering, of course, that the edge of the platform takes a step nearer the lift shaft as each course is added to the structure. If the lift shaft had been too near the east face of the structure when it was capped, this could have jeopardized the integrity of the structure, so we can assume that they would have capped the shaft when the top opening of the shaft was still a good distance from the east side of the structure.

However, they couldn't cap the lift shaft until all the masonry to complete the pinnacle of the pyramid had been hauled up onto the pinnacle, and I suspect that that is why we see the antechamber and the shaft situated in the position that it is, as opposed to a greater offset from the centre of the structure. It was close enough to the north- south axis of the pyramid to facilitate the capping of the pyramid, and its proximity to the centre of the pyramid ensured that the minimum of work was required to complete the pinnacle after the shaft was capped. If, on the other hand, the lift shaft had been offset from the centre of the structure by a greater distance then the builders would have had to place many more limestone blocks in temporary positions before they could cap the lift shaft and the pyramid. They would have had to begin the construction of the temporary structure at a lower level, so the lift shaft would have had to be capped at a lower level. That is undoubtedly why it was so important to discover the optimum distance for the offset of the lift shaft from the north-south axis of the structure (no doubt the builders had discovered what had worked best on pyramids they had built prior to those at Giza) and I can therefore only conclude that the optimum distance was 7 metres.

The inaccessible pinnacle

I couldn't resist using this sub-heading for it is a name well known to anyone who has ever climbed in the mountains of the west of Scotland. It is the name given to an extremely steep basalt pinnacle that sits atop a mountain in the Cuillin Range on the Isle of Skye. I decided to use it here simply because it has been suggested by some that the Great Pyramid may not have been capped. I suspect however, that this theory was put forward simply because no one could envisage how it had been possible to cap the pyramid using the very naïve, and impossible, construction methods envisaged by Egyptologists. The pyramidion from the Great Pyramid has never been found; therefore by implying that it had never existed Egyptologists and others didn't need to explain how it had been installed. This negative perspective is one of the difficulties that the serious researcher has to overcome when sifting through the phenomenal amount of published material on the pyramids of Egypt, for there have always been those who go that one step beyond the line, turn the data on its head, and use it to claim that because an artefact wasn't found, it probably never existed. That is no longer imagination at work, it is lunacy.

When the Great Pyramid was complete, its smooth outer casing stones would have ensured that no one could scale its heights. There would simply have been no point in creating a level area on top of the pyramid if this platform could not be accessed. Indeed, as I discovered when I came to reconstruct the pinnacle, the capstone must have been installed before the structure was complete, so not only was the Great Pyramid capped it was capped before it was complete. Let us take a look now at how that was achieved.

When the Great Pyramid had been completed up to the level where the builders would cap the lift shaft, the pattern of the construction changed. Instead of completing each course before they moved onto the next, the builders concentrated their efforts on building up the courses west of the north-south axis and that part of the east side of the structure nearest the centre of the pyramid (the area between the lift shaft and the centre of the structure). As I mentioned earlier, the builders had to raise the rig up to a level where they could use it to complete the courses that would support the capstone. However, the platforms would not have been wide enough to support the rig at the highest levels so much of the masonry on the east side of the pinnacle had to be placed in a temporary arrangement in order to support the rig at the very highest levels. In effect, the builders constructed a box section around the lift shaft with borrowed masonry and extended this box section up to the very highest levels to support the rig at these levels. The limestone used to build this temporary structure had to be borrowed from somewhere and it was borrowed from the stepped levels on the east side of the pinnacle; therefore this side of the pinnacle could not have been completed until the pyramid had been capped. Let me explain it another way.

The Great Pyramid had now been constructed up to the level where the builders would cap the lift shaft at a later stage of the construction. As each course of the pyramid had been installed, the surface area of each completed platform had always been smaller than the platform that preceded it. The sides of the structure also took a step nearer the lift shaft as each course was put in place and it's very likely that there were at least three, possibly four or more, blocks of masonry between the east side of the lift shaft and the eastern edge of the platform on the level where the shaft was capped. The great difficulty, however, was that the builders couldn't cap the lift shaft until all of the masonry to complete the structure had been hauled up to the platforms of the pinnacle. So although the lift shaft would have been capped on this level, it would not have been capped when the construction reached this level as the shaft had to remain open until all of the masonry to complete the topmost section of the structure had been hauled up onto the stepped levels of the pinnacle. From here on up, the builders would have had to complete the remaining levels on the west side of the structure, and borrow many of the blocks from the stepped levels on the east side of the pinnacle in order to construct the temporary support structure for the rig as it was raised ever higher. This temporary structure would have been built up from the level where the lift shaft had to be capped. However, the shaft couldn't have been capped until the top course but one had been installed, as the limestone blocks for this course had to have been hauled up the lift shaft and then hauled up through the temporary structure to this level. It was only after this penultimate course had been installed that the builders could have capped the lift shaft, and only after the shaft had been capped could the limestone blocks in the temporary structure have been reconfigured.

As you will see from the drawing (Fig. 26) on the next page a box section, temporary structure was built up around the opening of the shaft to provide the support structure for the rig at the higher levels, it was only when the builders had no further use for this temporary structure that the lift shaft could have been capped. It was only after the lift shaft had been capped and the rig had been decommissioned, that all of the limestone blocks used in the construction of the temporary supporting structure could have been reconfigured on the stepped levels on the east side of the pinnacle.

Before we move on, I would just like to point out that the builders could not have constructed limestone piers to support the legs of the rig at the higher levels and there were two reasons why this was not possible. Firstly, the sled had to be supported on the east and west sides of the rig, so a wall had to be built on the east side of the platform to support the sled on each level (the stepped levels on the west side of the rig would have been built up to support the sled here). The other difficulty was that the builders had no way of getting limestone blocks on to free-standing piers. The masonry to build the temporary structure had to be hauled onto the walls of the temporary structure from the platforms on the west side of the pyramid as they were being built up. Some of these blocks would then have been slid under the legs of the rig as they were raised up off of the temporary structure, this could only have been done if walls had been constructed around the opening of the lift shaft on all sides on each level for the builders had no way of getting the limestone blocks onto the top of free-standing piers. But the walls of the temporary structure on the east side of the completed platforms would have been a fairly open structure, because the more blocks that had been used to construct this temporary structure, the more

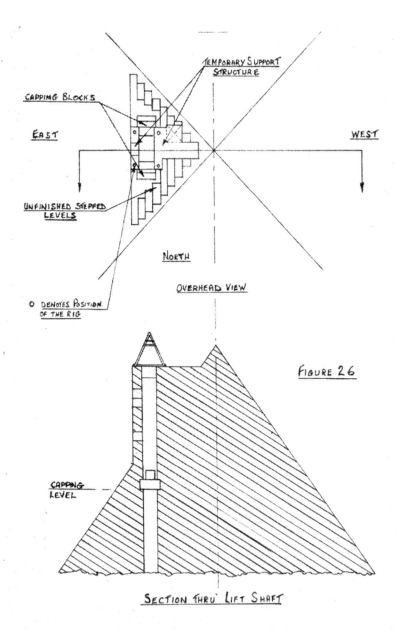

TEMPORARY SUPPORT STRUCTURE

CAPPING BLOCKS

EAST

WEST

UNFINISHED STEPPED LEVELS

NORTH

OVERHEAD VIEW

O DENOTES POSITION OF THE RIG

FIGURE 26

CAPPING LEVEL

SECTION THRU' LIFT SHAFT

blocks that had to be borrowed from the unfinished levels – and the more blocks that had to be hauled back onto these stepped levels to complete the structure after the pyramid had been capped. It is unlikely that the pyramidion would have been hauled up the lift shaft prior to its installation. If the height of this block had been of a similar height to the average sized limestone blocks, then it would have been around 1 metre high. However, a pyramidion 1 metre high would have had a base that was approximately 1.5 metres square. Had the pyramidion been any larger, the builders could not have hauled such a block through the passageway into the antechamber then up the lift shaft to the working platform. It is, of course, possible that the builders reduced the height of the limestone blocks in the last few courses of the structure (including the pyramidion). However I think this would have been unlikely as smaller blocks would have been more susceptible to damage in the event of a lightning strike or an earthquake. In fact, the larger the pyramidion the more stable it would have been (it would have been less likely to be broken into pieces by a lightning strike or shaken loose in an earthquake). Rather than reduce the block sizes here at this final stage of the construction, I believe that the builders would have put the largest pyramidion possible on top of the structure. If they had done so, then this capstone could never have been hauled up the lift shaft.

As I mentioned earlier, the pyramidion would have been taken into the inner lock then taken up and onto the inner stepped levels at the top of the stack when the builders transported the limestone beams up to this level. It would then have been a simple enough matter of levering this limestone block up in a series of steps onto each new level of the structure as it was created. Eventually, the pyramidion would have been levered up onto the level where the lift shaft would later be capped. From here on up, it was only the blocks on the west side of each platform that were installed in their final positions as many of the blocks on the east side of the pinnacle were used to construct the temporary structure here. But the pyramidion would almost certainly have been levered up onto each of the stepped levels on the east side of the pinnacle – just off to one side of the temporary structure – until the limestone blocks of the penultimate course of the pyramid had been installed. The pyramidion had, by that time, only to be moved a short distance until it was installed in its rightful place on top of the greatest man-made structure the world had ever seen.

It is almost certainly the case that the pyramidion (capstone) would have been locked in position when it was finally installed on top of the structure. It would undoubtedly have been set down on a bed of mortar but it would most likely have had a central boss on its underside that would have been located in a recess in the two – possibly four – limestone blocks on the course below when the pinnacle was complete. Rather than prop the pyramidion up on wooden blocks above the limestone blocks it was to be mounted on (so that the underside of the boss cleared the top of these blocks); it's more than likely that two of the blocks in the course below the pyramidion (on the east side of the pinnacle) would not have been butted up against one another initially, so as to leave a gap between them. As the pyramidion was slid over the wet mortar on top of these blocks the boss on the underside of the pyramidion would have passed through this gap. After the capstone had been nudged into its final position, the two blocks below the capstone would then have been nudged towards one another until the gap was closed and the final two courses at the top of the structure were complete.

What an achievement! This was now the tallest structure ever built by man (prior to the capping of the Great Pyramid the tallest structure ever built by man was the Middle Pyramid at Giza – constructed just prior to the Great Pyramid). I doubt that the ancient builders would have believed that it would be more than 4,000 years before another man-made structure exceeded this height (Lincoln Cathedral in 1300 C.E., but the top section of its steeple was a wooden structure with a lead covering and it only survived for 100 years or so when it was blown down in a gale).

Despite the fact that the builders had now capped the greatest structure ever built by man, the Great Pyramid was not yet complete and I'm sure that the celebrations would have been put on hold until these men up on their lofty perch had completed the pinnacle of the Great Pyramid and made their final descent to the plateau below. After all, the builders were now about to embark upon the most dangerous operation since they had begun to haul limestone blocks up the lift shaft to the working platforms; it would have been premature, to say the least, to begin the celebrations before these heroes were safely back on terra firma.

Tensions up on the pinnacle would have been fairly high at this point in time, for the masons had some very difficult manoeuvres ahead of them. They were also about to cut themselves off from their co-workers down below for a time as they could not move on to the final stage of the construction until they had capped the lift shaft. However, before they could seal the top end of the lift shaft, there was some equipment up on the pinnacle that was no longer required and this had to be lowered down the shaft before the shaft could be sealed top and bottom.

Most of the components of the hoist (the sleds would have been lowered back down to the antechamber at various intervals as the platforms became smaller) and some wooden beams and rollers they had no further use for had to be lowered down the shaft now. As I mentioned earlier, all of the masonry to complete the pinnacle had been hauled up onto the stepped levels on the eastern side of the pinnacle by the time the pyramid was capped; all of the blocks to complete each course were on their respective levels, or on a higher level, but they were all there. These blocks, however, could not be manoeuvred into their final positions until the lift shaft was capped and that couldn't be done until the hoist had been decommissioned.

Earlier we looked at how the individual weights of the hoist were grounded in their mountings in the antechamber prior to the raising of the rig up to the next platform. In order to take the weight of the cradle and the counterweight off of the rig, we grounded the counterweight on a heavy wooden beam placed across the north end of the lift shaft up on the working platform. The cradle and the control weights at this point had been grounded in the antechamber and we could therefore unfasten the ropes on top of the counterweight prior to raising the rig up onto the next level. Now, however, we need to get both the cradle and the counterweight back down into the antechamber so we can't simply repeat the action that we have taken each time we raised our rig.

The heaviest of all the components of the hoist was the counterweight. We know that the builders left this component behind when they completed the pyramid and sealed its inner chambers and corridors, as it can still be found in the first pair of channels in the antechamber. After this counterweight had been lowered down to the bottom of the shaft, the cradle would have been secured to the rig at the top of the shaft and the two ropes that had secured the cradle to the counterweight would then have been detached from the securing rings on top of the counterweight. These ropes would then have been used to lower the cradle down the shaft to the antechamber below. The cradle would, no doubt, have been dismantled and removed from the antechamber; in fact, the cradle may have been dismantled up on the temporary structure and its component parts lowered down the shaft to the chamber below, since it may have been impossible to dismantle it in the very confined space of the antechamber. One way or another, it would have been dismantled and removed from the chamber as the metal itself would have been a very valuable commodity even if the builders had no further use for the cradle. The two ropes that had been attached to the top of the cradle would have been retained by the workmen up on the platform, for they still had need of them at that stage of the construction.

I don't know the fate of the three control weights. They would certainly have been lowered down the shaft after the cradle had been dismantled, but they would not have been allowed to come to rest in their mountings on the sidewalls of the antechamber as usual; they would have been turned through ninety degrees as they were lowered into the chamber and lowered all the way to the floor. It is possible that these three control weights were still lying on the floor of the antechamber – or in the upper chamber – when Caliph Al Ma'mun first entered the inner chambers of the structure. However, I have been unable to find any mention of these control weights anywhere and therefore all I can say for certain is that they were removed from the inner structure at some point in the past. The ropes from these three control weights would also have been retained by the masons up on the pinnacle for they would also have been needed later.

Although I don't know what became of the control weights, I can say for certain that these weights would not have been found in their mounts in the antechamber when Caliph Al Ma'mun first entered the antechamber. The builders needed to gain access to the lower end of the lift shaft after the hoist had been dismantled and they certainly could not have gained access to the bottom end of the lift shaft if the control weights had been in their mounts at this time. If you can cast your mind back to when we began to construct the lift shaft on top of the antechamber walls, you will probably remember that we installed three heavy slabs on the ledge above the chamber, possibly two at the south end of the lift shaft and one at the north end. These three slabs were stood on edge and pushed back against the south and north walls of the shaft. (They would most probably have been wedged tightly in place to secure them and ensure that they did not get knocked over during the very long period when the hoist was in use.) These three slabs were now lowered onto their sides one by one, and then levered along the ledges above the antechamber until they formed the ceiling in the chamber, completely sealing the bottom end of the shaft. This ceiling is still intact, as most of the archaeologists who explored the various chambers within the Great Pyramid seemed to attach little significance to this small chamber. Had they known that it contained more secrets than any other chamber in the structure, then they may have paid a little more attention to it and perhaps we would have discovered the lift shaft some time ago. After the limestone slabs had been levered into position to form the ceiling in the antechamber however, the men responsible for their installation were more than likely hauled up the lift shaft after the final slab was levered into position. It would undoubtedly have been much easier to lever these slabs into position from above rather than from below the ceiling. It is also possible that the cradle may have been lowered down the lift shaft and dismantled above the antechamber on the partially completed roof here. When its component parts had then been lowered down into the chamber the final slab would have been tilted over into the horizontal position and levered along the ledges until the ceiling was complete. This may in fact be the sole reason as to why these three slabs were installed here – to provide a platform at this location – as it may have been very difficult to dismantle the cradle up on the pinnacle and impossible to dismantle it in the antechamber itself.

The safety of the workmen up on the pinnacle would have been of paramount importance now, for if one of them had been seriously injured or killed at this stage of the construction, he certainly couldn't have been replaced, not immediately anyway, and the builders would have had no option but to continue their labours with a reduced workforce. (It truly was an inaccessible pinnacle at this stage of the construction.) It is for this reason that I suspect the first operation to be undertaken after most of the components of the hoist had been lowered down into the antechamber would have been the capping of the lift shaft. That, at least, would have removed one of the major hazards at this stage of the construction.

The limestone blocks used to cap the lift shaft were ready to be levered into position from the north and south side of the temporary structure. These were the standard blocks that had been used in the construction of this upper section of the pyramid since the builders had begun to haul them up the lift shaft. The blocks were longer than the width of the shaft opening and a gap, slightly wider than the length of these blocks, had been created between the east wall of the temporary structure – that had been constructed to support the rig and the sled at the higher levels – and the stepped levels on the west side of the lift shaft. Although the lift shaft was much wider than the width of the limestone blocks, not wider than the length of these blocks, it's possible that the builders had reduced the width of the shaft in the few courses just below the level where the shaft had to be capped. This would have been achieved by stepping (corbelling) the blocks on either side of the shaft inward and this would have provided a good landing on the ledges either side of the opening for the blocks that were later slid into place to cap the shaft.

The limestone blocks used to cap the shaft would have been levered along the ledges on either side of the lift shaft until they had all been manoeuvred into their final positions and the top end of the shaft had been completely sealed. These blocks would have been levered into position from the south side of the shaft as well as the north side. Corbelled arches would have been created in the lower courses of the south and north walls of the temporary structure to provide clearance here to enable the capping blocks to be slid into position above the lift shaft.

Although the lift shaft had now been capped, the men working up on the pinnacle at this stage of the construction faced many dangers, more than they had faced at any other stage of the construction. Things got very tricky at this stage, for the temporary limestone block structure that had supported the hoist at the highest levels had now to be dismantled. The masonry used to construct this temporary structure had now to be manoeuvred back onto the stepped levels in order to complete each course on the east side of the pinnacle. With the completion of each course the working area would diminish, until eventually, there would be no ledge or platform to support the builders and their equipment. So how did they overcome this seemingly insurmountable problem?

There was also the other big question that had still to be answered at this stage of our reconstruction. How on earth were these builders to get back down to the plateau when they completed the structure? Fortunately, the builders had the means to resolve both of these problems and the solution was the same in both cases. They created a temporary working platform using the framework of the rig which they lashed to the east side of the pinnacle, just below the temporary structure. This temporary wooden platform also provided the builders with their means of transportation back to terra firma;

when the pinnacle was complete the wooden structure would have been lowered down the east face of the pyramid until it bottomed on the plateau.

We know that the builders had all the materials to hand to construct such a working platform for they had retained most of the ropes and the wooden frame of the rig when they had lowered all the other components of the hoist down the shaft. We also know that they had completed all of the courses on the western side of the pinnacle and installed the capstone, the pyramidion, before they sealed the lift shaft. In order to secure the temporary wooden platform to the east side of the pyramid the builders would have looped one or more of the ropes they had retained when the hoist was dismantled over the peak of the pyramid and around the west side of the pinnacle. It was these ropes that would have been used to lash the temporary platform to the east side of the pyramid. This platform would have been positioned just below the lowest unfinished course of the pinnacle and the men would then have worked their way down towards the wooden platform, installing the last of the limestone blocks on each level of the east face of the pinnacle as they went. The last course of the pinnacle would then have been completed with the men working from this temporary platform.

So what form did the temporary platform take? Well, that is where their great ingenuity and skill came into play again. They already had a structure up on the pinnacle that would provide them with the perfect framework for a platform to complete their task. Long before they had begun to construct the Great Pyramid, they had to design a rig for the hoist that they would need to complete the pyramid after the antechamber had been constructed. As we now know, this wooden structure consisted of two A-frames and a number of crossbeams and spars that tied the A-frames to one another and supported a number of rollers. The legs on the A-frames had to be wide enough apart so as to allow the easy removal of the sleds and the limestone blocks from the top of the lift shaft, and tall enough so that the cradle could be hauled up clear of the limestone blocks when they were positioned on the sleds.

But the builders were looking much farther ahead when they decided on the angle of the A-frames for they realized that, if the angle at the apex of the A-frames was set at 52 degrees, then, when the rig was later tilted over on to its side to provide the supporting frame for a temporary platform, the two legs at the top of the frame would be horizontal. As you are no doubt aware, the four smooth faces of the Great Pyramid were inclined at an angle of 51 degrees 51 minutes from the horizontal (the angle of inclination having been established by W M Flinders-Petrie when he discovered two of the original casing blocks still intact at the base of the Great Pyramid). The wooden structure, the rig, had been constructed to perform when standing on the horizontal plane, but it had also been designed in such a way that, when it was tilted over onto its side, it formed the perfect framework for a platform that could be lashed to the pinnacle of the Great Pyramid, thus providing a horizontal ledge from which to work on the final course of the pinnacle.

Constructing a rig with the same angle at the apex as the angle of the sides of the pyramid provided the perfect support framework for this work platform up on the east face of pyramid after the rig had been tilted over onto its side (Fig 27) and lowered into position on the east face of the structure. All that was needed to complete this platform were a few planks of wood fixed to the topside of the framework and this would have provided the workmen with a deck on which they could stand as they put the finishing touches to the pinnacle... and their means of escape from these lofty heights when it was complete.

I have to say though that this was not immediately apparent to me when I was trying to figure out how they had managed to cap the lift shaft and complete the pinnacle. The builder's ingenuity however, was far greater than my own and I should have realized much earlier that they would have adapted the rig itself for this purpose – as opposed to dismantling it and constructing a temporary structure from its components, which I had earlier assumed. But then again, they had a big advantage over me, for they had a lot of experience under their belts by the time they came to build the Great Pyramid. I, on the other hand, am a novice pyramid builder.

Somehow the builders managed to tilt the rig over onto its side and manoeuvre it over the edge of the temporary structure (they had plenty of rope to give them complete control over the movements of the rig). The ropes that had been looped over the peak of the pyramid and around the western side of the pinnacle prior to this operation, would have been wound around two legs of the rig a couple of turns; the workmen would then have slowly paid out these ropes until the rig had been lowered into position on the east side of the pyramid, just below the temporary limestone structure. When this temporary platform was finally in position below the level of the lowest course of the pinnacle that had still to be completed, the ropes would then have been tied securely to the frame of the structure. The stout wooden planks that would have been fixed to the top of the support structure (rig) to form the working platform would possibly have been hauled up the lift shaft before the shaft had been sealed, as would some other materials or tools needed to continue with the work on the pinnacle (mortar, water, etc). Once the temporary wooden structure had been fixed in position, of course, it would then have been possible to haul planks, mortar and water up the east side of the pyramid to the temporary structure.

In solving this problem, the builders also solved that other great problem; how to get down from these lofty heights when their work was complete, because they had now also provided themselves with their means of transportation back down to the plateau. The apothem, the distance from the top of the Great Pyramid to the middle of one side of the base, was just over 185 metres when the outer casing of the Great Pyramid was complete and intact. It was certainly a long way down but, as you have no doubt realized, our builders had more than enough rope to make their descent to ground level when they had completed the pinnacle. However, I've got a bit ahead of myself again, so we'd best go back and take a closer look at what was required at this very tricky stage of the construction in order to complete the Great Pyramid.

In order to raise the rig up high enough to cap our pyramid, we had to borrow some limestone masonry from the unfinished stepped levels on the east side of the pinnacle to construct our temporary structure. However, now that we have capped the lift shaft and lashed the rig / wooden support structure to the pinnacle and secured it, we can continue with our reconstruction of the east side of the pinnacle. I realize that it is not easy to visualise how this temporary structure was created but if you take a look at the drawings (Figs. 26 - 28), you will clearly see where the masonry had been borrowed from. In Figure 26 that we looked at earlier, I have indicated the temporary position of the capstone prior to its installation but I omitted to show any of the casing blocks in the temporary structure in both Figures 26 & 28 in the interests of clarity. In the drawing on the next page (Fig. 27) however, I have

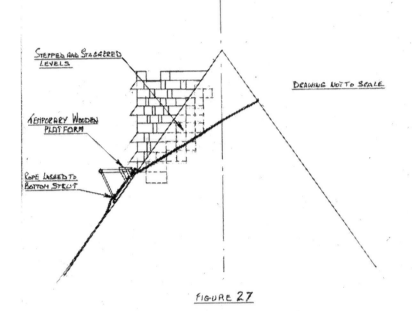

Stepped and Staggered
Levels

Drawing Not To Scale

Temporary Wooden
Platform

Rope Lashed To
Bottom Strut

FIGURE 27

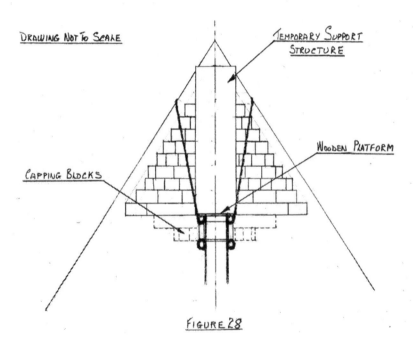

Drawing Not To Scale

Temporary Support
Structure

Wooden Platform

Capping Blocks

FIGURE 28

246

shown the possible positions of some of the casing blocks that would have been incorporated into this temporary structure.

The masonry used to construct the temporary structure was the masonry that was later used to complete the area above the lift shaft after it had been capped, and to complete the east face of the pinnacle. But the stepped levels on both sides of the lift shaft could not be built up beyond the level where the lift shaft had to be capped, as it was on this level that limestone blocks had to have been levered along the ledges within the walls of the temporary structure to cap the shaft after the pyramidion had been installed. It was masonry that was later used to build up the stepped levels and complete the east side of the pinnacle that had been used to construct the temporary structure that supported the rig at the very highest levels until the topmost courses of the structure had been installed. After the pyramid and the lift shaft had been capped, of course, all of the limestone blocks used to construct this temporary structure had to have been hauled from the temporary structure back onto the stepped levels on the east side of the pinnacle to complete the east face of the pyramid. I doubt that the operation to build up and complete the courses on the east side of the pinnacle would have presented the builders with too many difficulties. However, one option that was not available to them was the use of the hoist here, as the hoist had been decommissioned prior to the capping of the lift shaft. Most of the limestone blocks to complete each course would have already been placed on their respective levels as the temporary structure had been built up. Some of the rectangular blocks, however, would have had to be manoeuvred down onto some of the lower courses from the higher levels of the temporary structure as it would not have been possible to borrow enough masonry from the upper stepped levels to complete the temporary structure.

The simplest way to get these blocks of limestone down onto a lower level would have been to create a ramp and there was certainly no shortage of blocks with angular faces on these levels with which to create such a ramp. However, it is just as likely that these blocks were levered over the edge of one level onto some hardwood blocks on a lower level. The wooden blocks would then have been removed one after another as alternate ends of the limestone block was levered up slightly and then lowered. When the last of the wooden blocks had been removed from under the limestone blocks, these blocks would then have been manoeuvred into their final positions. Either way, it would not have been very difficult to manoeuvre some of these blocks onto lower levels as the blocks that make up most of the core of the structure were rectangular in shape and this would have made them much easier to manoeuvre than square blocks. In just a few short steps, each of these limestone blocks would have been manoeuvred down onto the lower levels where they were to be installed.

The building of the temporary structure to support the rig had been carefully planned; it had not just been a matter of building up the structure with the last of the masonry to be hauled up onto the platforms on the east side of the pinnacle. The builders had to ensure that they had enough rectangular blocks and casing blocks installed on each of the upper levels of the temporary structure to ensure that they would have enough of each of type of block to complete each course of the pinnacle when the blocks were reconfigured. It was a simple enough matter to move some of the core rectangular blocks down onto some of the lower levels to build these up after the pyramid had been capped. Indeed, they had no option but to do this as a good number of these blocks were needed at much higher levels on the temporary structure. However, it's unlikely that they would have moved the smooth outer casing blocks from one level to another as these blocks could have so easily been damaged in such an operation. The builders therefore would have ensured that they had placed enough of these casing blocks on each level when they created the temporary structure to ensure that they could complete the outer casing of the structure on each level when the temporary structure was dismantled.

As the temporary structure was slowly dismantled the builders would have completed each course on this unfinished section of the pinnacle working from the top down. All of the limestone blocks had to be repositioned but, as always, a coating of wet lime mortar would have been applied to the surfaces over which the blocks had to be manoeuvred (as well as the adjoining vertical faces) and this lubricant would have made it easier for the builders to manoeuvre these blocks into their final positions. They had earlier completed the core framework of the pinnacle; they now had to slot in the remaining pieces to complete it.

As you can probably imagine, trying to figure out what the builders had done when they brought all of the masonry up onto the stepped levels on the east side of the structure to complete the pinnacle was no easy matter. I struggled with the problem for such a long time that it seemed as if I was never going to figure it out. I can't remember now what it was that set me on the right track but I knew that if I kept going back to the problem and looking at it anew every now and then, I would eventually crack it. It's always a lot easier to hang in there, of course, when you know for certain that there is a solution to the problem and you are not wrestling with an impossible situation. I knew that this problem had been solved before, so it could certainly be solved again. I'd realized when I first began to construct the temporary structure that there would only be one way to complete this last section of the pinnacle; that was to work from the highest unfinished course, down to the lowest course. After all, we couldn't extract the limestone blocks from the lowest courses of the temporary structure on the east side of the pinnacle and then move on up to the next course that was impossible. The builders therefore had no option but to deconstruct the temporary support structure in the reverse order from how they had constructed it. That means, of course, that we have to complete the highest unfinished level first, and then work our way down from here. As ridiculous as this may seem, we can only complete each level on the east side of the pinnacle working from the top of the unfinished section down to the bottom of it. Fortunately, the existing stepped levels on the east side of the pinnacle make it possible to undertake such an operation.

The first of the limestone blocks to be hauled from the top of the temporary structure onto the stepped levels would have been the rectangular core blocks. After these blocks had been manoeuvred down onto the lower stepped levels, the first of the casing blocks would have been hauled onto the topmost ledge. When we built up the west side of the structure earlier in order to install the capstone, all of the corner blocks on each course of the pinnacle were installed at this time, so three full faces of the pinnacle have been completed. Now that we have come to install the casing blocks on the east side of the pinnacle, we therefore have no corner blocks to install; we only have the standard casing blocks to install between the corner blocks on each level. It was likely that all of the casing blocks had been installed on some of the levels below the capstone on the east side of the pyramid as they built up the temporary structure to support the hoist, but sooner or later – probably on the fourth or fifth course below the capstone – the builders would have had to haul the first of the casing blocks from the temporary structure back onto one of the stepped levels.

Although it may seem ridiculous that the casing of the structure could be installed from the top down, due to the stepped nature of the structure and the shape of the casing blocks it was, in fact, a fairly straightforward procedure. The casing blocks could be slotted into position between the ledge on one level and the casing blocks on the level above, for although the casing blocks had not been installed on the levels below, the stepped levels were deep enough to support the casing blocks on each level. The unique shape of the casing blocks made the task of installing them all the easier as the centre of gravity was beyond the mid-line of these blocks and so most of their weight was on the side nearest the core of the pyramid. We also have to remember that the builders would have had a deep landing in the centre of each level on which to turn and manoeuvre these limestone blocks before they were nudged along the ledges to their final positions. This landing had been built up on the west side of the lift shaft and it formed part of the temporary structure (it was this landing that supported the sled on this side of the lift shaft).

If you take a look at the drawing (Fig. 29) on the next page showing the incomplete pinnacle, you will see how it was possible to install the outer casing blocks from the top down. The steps of the core masonry were deep enough to support the casing blocks when they were slotted into the gap between the core blocks on the lower level and the casing blocks on the level above. As I mentioned earlier, the builders would have begun this last phase of the construction by putting any rectangular core blocks in place on each level first, and moved others down onto the lower levels as they dismantled the temporary structure. When the builders had earlier built up the pinnacle from the level of the opening at the top of the lift shaft, they would have completed the south, the west and the north sides of the structure. They would also have put in place all the corner blocks on each side of the pinnacle. They therefore only had to manoeuvre rectangular core blocks and casing blocks – not corner blocks – when they were dismantling the temporary structure and completing each of the levels on the east side of the pinnacle.

As the casing blocks were manoeuvred from the temporary structure back towards the stepped levels, they would have been turned through ninety degrees on the horizontal plane until they were

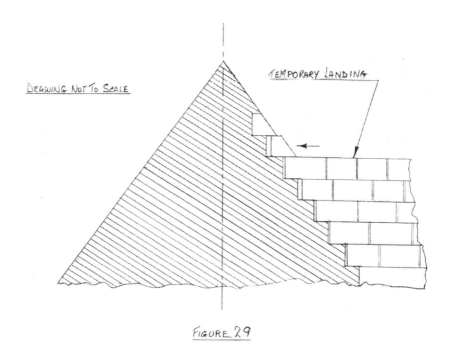

TEMPORARY LANDING

FIGURE 29

lying parallel with the ledge. The casing blocks would then have been pushed back onto the ledge on that level (under the overhang of the casing blocks in the level above) until their sloping outer faces were flush with the sloping face of the casing blocks on the level above (Fig. 29). The first of these blocks would then have been nudged along the ledge until it butted up against one of the corner blocks on that level. These casing blocks would have been supported by the core blocks on the ledges below and slotted under the overhang of the casing blocks on the level above. As the bulk of the weight on the casing blocks was on the side of the blocks nearest the core of the structure, these blocks would have been fairly secure when placed on the ledges formed by the core blocks on the level below. However, it is possible that the builders may have positioned wooden props under the overhangs of these casing blocks until the casing blocks on the level below could be put in place to support them. The last casing blocks to be installed on each level were the blocks nearest the centre of each ledge and these casing blocks would have been trimmed to size and then pushed back into the last gaps on the ledges. These blocks were supported by the deep landings that the temporary structure provided here until they had been trimmed to size and installed. The builders would have employed these methods on each and every course of the pinnacle as they worked their way down towards the temporary wooden platform below the temporary support structure on the east face of the pyramid.

The last course to be completed was the simplest of all, as both the core blocks and the casing blocks had been installed on the course below and the full depth ledge here provided a good landing where the last few casing blocks could be turned and manoeuvred into their final positions. However, the very last casing block to be installed on this level could not be turned through ninety degrees and pushed back into the gap; the gap was not wide enough for this to happen. This block, probably the smallest casing block on the ledge, had to be hauled from the ledge onto the deck of the wooden platform, trimmed to length, then turned through ninety degrees, before it was pushed back into the gap on the ledge to complete the final course of the pinnacle. As this last block to be installed on the final level had to be hauled onto the wooden platform and then turned through 90 degrees and cut to size, it's most likely that the builders would have used a shorter (lighter) block here. This wouldn't have mattered so much on the levels above for the blocks there were solidly supported by the masonry in the temporary limestone structure (landing) at all times. However, the builders wouldn't have hauled a very heavy casing block onto the temporary wooden platform so it's more than likely that this last block was the smallest casing block to be installed on the very last level to be completed. When this final casing block had been pushed into the last gap on the ledge and the face of the casing block was flush with those around it, the excess mortar would have been removed and the east face of the Great Pyramid was now complete. This most dangerous mission was now almost over.

Although we have now completed the pinnacle of our pyramid, we still have a few loose ends to tie up here for our masons are still perched high up on the east side of our pyramid. It's more than likely that the limestone rubble that was trimmed from the casing blocks on each level would have been lowered down to the plateau in leather buckets or some other receptacles, since some of the larger pieces could, in all probability, have damaged the east face of the structure if the masons had simply let them slide down the face of the pyramid. It's also likely that lime mortar and water would have been hauled up to the platform on a regular basis after the rig had been lashed to the east side of the pyramid and until the pinnacle was complete. Likewise, workmen would no longer have been marooned on the pinnacle after the wooden platform had been made secure and they would undoubtedly have come down from their lofty perch before nightfall each evening.

We know that the builders had more than enough rope to lower the platform down the east side of the Great Pyramid for all, or most, of the ropes used in the hoist were retained by the masons working on the pinnacle when the hoist was decommissioned. These ropes would have been secured to the rig when it had first been lowered into position on the east side of the structure to provide the masons with the temporary platform they needed to complete the pinnacle. The anchor ropes would have been wound around two of the legs of the temporary platform and then tied securely. Ropes would also have been suspended from the temporary platform as it was these ropes that the men used to descend to the plateau each night. But when it came time to lower the temporary platform, the anchor ropes were unfastened and the tension taken up. Two men could easily have controlled the rate of descent and the trim of the platform as it was slowly lowered to the plateau, but I suspect that two men would have been used on each of the two ropes as an added safety precaution, an operator and a brake man on each rope. The friction created as the ropes bit into the wooden frame of the rig would have provided the braking effect necessary to ensure that the men had complete control over the platform's rate of descent.

Although most of the workmen's tools and any mortar and limestone debris would have been lowered down to the plateau prior to the release of the platform, there would still have been some buckets of water on the platform at this stage as water would have been used to lubricate the four areas on the underside of the wooden structure where it made contact with the east side of the pyramid. The builders would have ensured that the feet of the rig (at the leading edge as the rig descended) had been chamfered prior to the rig having been removed from the temporary structure; this would have presented a flat smooth surface to the east face of the pyramid. Likewise, two wooden blocks or leather pads could have been placed under the crossbeam at the trailing edge of the structure to ensure that the wooden structure had the minimum contact with the smooth face of the pyramid. Water would have been used as a lubricant to ease the passage of the wooden structure over the polished face of the pyramid to reduce the possibility of damage occurring as the platform made its descent.

We can only imagine the reception the masons received when they finally set foot on the plateau. Although this was possibly the third time that a large pyramid had been capped on the plateau, it had been many years since the last one was capped. But this one was different; this was the culmination of a project that had probably first been explored and planned before many of those who worked on the project had been born. This was the greatest building project that had ever been undertaken by the human race and I'm certain that everyone for miles around would have been able to watch the progress of the work on this, their greatest structure, as the builders slowly completed the last section of the pinnacle. By the time the east side of the pinnacle was almost complete, most of the local population living on the east bank of the Nile would have had a good idea when the builders were likely to complete it and make their final descent. If access to the plateau had not been restricted in any way at this time, then you can be sure that most of the local population would have been up on the plateau that day to see the men who had capped this magnificent structure make their historic descent. They may have been masons and labourers when they first began work on this project, but they would have returned to terra firma as heroes, their great skill and bravery fully acknowledged by all those who had been part of this great project.

This, however, was only the completion of yet another stage of this great building project – albeit a rather significant one – as the Great Pyramid was not yet complete. When the celebrations were over, it would have been business as usual for the workmen who had put their lives at risk to construct this, the first man-made wonder of the ancient world. Work on the grand entrance tunnel, I suspect, would still have been on-going at this time as it had to be completely blocked up all the way from the bottom of the grand gallery back to the entrance on the north side of the structure. The north face of the Great Pyramid, the last face of the pyramid to be completed, could not be completed until this consolidation of the structure was complete. However, for the men who completed the pinnacle of the Great Pyramid, I doubt that anything would ever again have compared to the thrill and excitement of working at the top of the world.

Chapter Seven

Finishing touches

We are now about to embark upon the last stage of our reconstruction of the Great Pyramid but we should bear in mind before we come to the end of our quest that the completion of the Great Pyramid, although it was possibly the last of the principal pyramids to be completed, did not necessarily mean that the project at Giza had come to an end. It's most likely that some of the smaller structures here had still to be built, or completed, and I believe that a perimeter wall surrounded the whole Giza complex when it was complete. The perimeter wall, however, could not have been completed until the canals had been decommissioned and it's most likely that much of the masonry used in the construction of the canals was then used to construct the perimeter wall.

If some of the smaller structures had still to be put in place after the completion of the Great Pyramid, the feeder canal, as we have come to know it, would have been used for the transportation of barges to these sites on the plateau until all the peripheral structures were complete. This was the main supply canal for most of the structures and barges would have been able to enter this canal system from the River Nile from as far away as Dashur. But they would also have been able to enter the single channel system on the east side of the plateau, as very extensive hydraulic operations had been conducted in the area near the Sphinx at a very early stage of the construction here. Water from the locks / dry dock in this area had to be channelled away to the river on the east side of the plateau and it is in this channel that locks would have been incorporated where barges would have entered and exited the single channel canal system. When the masons finally capped the Great Pyramid and completed the pinnacle, the canal infrastructure on the north side of the Great Pyramid was still intact as there was still much work to be done to complete the Great Pyramid at that stage of the construction. Water from the feeder canal still flowed through the bowels of this great structure; the dual channel supply canal was still operational. Although there was no longer any need to transport masonry up to the top of the grand gallery, all the limestone needed to consolidate and complete the structure had still to be transported up to the plateau, and then up and into the entrance tunnel on the north side of the Great Pyramid.

The work still to be undertaken inside the structure at this stage was not like the earlier work; the builders were now engaged in the process of sealing and consolidating the structure now that it was almost complete. The area around the grand doorway had still to be completed on the north face of the structure but this could not be completed until the grand entrance tunnel had been blocked up all the way along its length. The builders had by this time dismantled the temporary infrastructure in the grand gallery (the wooden locks) and they were now about to begin the slow withdrawal from the inner chambers and passageways of the structure.

The first passage to be sealed after the flight of locks had been dismantled in the gallery would have been the ascending corridor. As we discovered earlier, there are many different views as to how and when the granite plugs were installed in this pipe and the wild conclusions drawn by speculators over the years is understandable, to a degree, as they were simply trying to make sense of something without all the relevant facts to hand; no one had any inkling that the grand entrance tunnel even existed at the time these views were expressed. When I discovered the key to how the structure had been put together, however, this was one of the first pieces of the puzzle to fall into place.

Most of the speculation regarding the granite plugs had focussed on two main areas; how the builders exited the structure when they blocked up (what was regarded at the time as) the main access to the inner chambers, and the timing of the installation of the plugs. I believe that one theorist came to the conclusion that the plugs could not have been dropped down the pipe as they would almost certainly have become tightly wedged in the pipe long before they reached the bottom due to friction. However a liberal application of a lubricant was probably all that was required to ensure that the plugs travelled the full distance to the bottom of the pipe. He then concluded that the plugs had been installed in the ascending corridor when the corridor (pipe) was under construction.

How different it is when you have all the facts to hand before you have to come to a conclusion. Knowing what we now know, the builders' egress from the inner corridors is not an issue as they had a very large tunnel that extended from the bottom of the gallery, all the way out to the grand doorway on the sixteenth level of the structure at that stage of the construction... and transportation all the way to the canal basin below the escarpment.

Lubrication wasn't a problem either, as the ascending corridor was full of water when the three granite plugs were aligned with the shaft and lowered into the mouth of it. However, the granite plugs did not rapidly plunge down the shaft, they made a slow descent until they wedged fast at the bottom of the shaft. The water in the shaft acted as a hydraulic brake as there was very little clearance between the sides of the granite plugs and the sides of the shaft (ascending corridor). I believe that a recess was discovered in the floor of the horizontal passageway near to the mouth of the ascending corridor (a limestone slab has been placed over it). This recess would most likely have been created just prior to the installation of the plugs and it would have enabled the builders to get a stout wooden lever under the top end of each of the plugs. Each granite plug in turn would have been levered up until it was almost at 26 degrees to the horizontal. When it was parallel with the ascending corridor it would have begun its very slow descent to the bottom. The area on the far side of the ascending corridor (looking from the horizontal passageway) would have been built up prior to the installation of the granite blocking stones, extending this side of the ascending corridor upward. The granite blocking stones would then have been levered upward with the back of this extended channel acting as a buffer until the stones were parallel with the ascending corridor, at which point they would have begun their descent. Very little water could escape around the sides of the plugs as they made their descent, and it was this that ensured their slow descent to the bottom of the ascending corridor.

When the three granite plugs had been installed, the builders would have moved on to their next task. However, this was not nearly as simple as the task they had just completed and it would have taken them a very long time to complete this one. The blocking up of the grand entrance tunnel and the consolidation of the structure was their next task. It had been a long time since any of the masons had worked on this tunnel. In fact, it was very likely that many of the younger workmen charged with blocking up this tunnel would not have been employed on the project when the tunnel was first created many years earlier. Owing to the cramped conditions in which they would have been working at times, it was probably the youngest, fittest and strongest that would have been chosen for this job.

Before we installed the granite plugs in the ascending corridor, water to feed the canal system had been getting pumped up the ascending corridor for a tremendously long time. But now, before work began in the entrance tunnel, the builders would have had to remove the blocking stones used to seal the top end of the descending corridor after the ascending corridor had been created. This pipe (descending corridor) had been blocked off and sealed at a fairly early stage of the construction in order to divert the water flow up the ascending corridor to feed the supply canal. Now, of course, we have blocked up the ascending corridor so we need to reopen the original water supply pipe in order to supply water to the canal and locks on the north side of the Great Pyramid again. The builders had needed a feeder pipe for the series of canal locks that they constructed in the grand gallery in order to transport the massive granite blocks and slabs used in the construction of the upper chamber and the stack up to the inner lock on the 49th level. But with this pipe now having been plugged, their only option here was to re-open the original feeder pipe – the descending corridor. They'd blocked its outlet up when they created the ascending corridor and began to use it as the main feeder pipe. Now, by removing the limestone blocks that they slid down the basement sheet a long time ago to seal this pipe they reconnected the original feeder pipe (the descending corridor) with the supply canal. (The builders may have unblocked this pipe prior to the installation of the blocking stones in the ascending corridor.)

Before this channel could be reopened however, the builders would have had to stem the flow of water entering the inlet pipe on the south side of the Great Pyramid. The lock gate (valve) on the inlet pipe on the feeder canal had to be closed at this time to ensure that there was little water pressure behind the blocking stones when they were removed. When the water in the lock at the mouth of the entrance tunnel had been drained away and the water removed from the area around the blocking stones, the masons would have set to work to open this channel again. However, they would not have attempted to remove the heavy limestone beams that had been used to block the outlet of the descending corridor; they would have cut a section out of the centre of these blocks / beams to re-open the channel and extend the descending corridor up through this masonry. Prior to the installation of these limestone beams we installed the basement sheet and the upper surface of this sheet was aligned with, and extended, the floor of the descending corridor. After we installed the two limestone beams to block the top end of the descending corridor, we installed a thick limestone slab on top of these beams. The underside of this limestone slab was aligned with, and extended, the roof of the descending corridor. As these slabs form the floor and the roof of the corridor here, when we excavate a channel through the two blocking stones we then only have to widen this channel to extend the sides of the corridor up through these blocking stones... and in the process, extend the descending corridor up to the grand entrance. When the lock gate on the inlet pipe south-west of the Great Pyramid was then reopened after the builders had extended the descending corridor beyond the blocking stones, the flow of water to the supply canal and the entrance tunnel would have been fully restored.

Although the builders restored the water supply to the supply canal at this stage of the construction, the outlet at the top end of the descending corridor was still within the entrance tunnel (it had been extended up to somewhere around the opening of this corridor as it is today). Later, this feeder pipe would have been extended out to the north face of the structure as the entrance tunnel was blocked up, and the stepped levels in front of the doorway built up, prior to the installation of the casing blocks here. However, that is still ahead of us.

I recently came across a drawing of the descending / ascending corridors in Peter Lemesurier's *The Great Pyramid Decoded* that showed "scored lines" near the top end of the descending corridor, just below the first of the double gables. These lines are on either side of the descending corridor and perpendicular to the floor of the corridor. I do not share Peter's belief that these lines were scored into the limestone on either side of this corridor as a date marker however; these lines almost certainly mark the boundary where the descending corridor was blocked up in order to direct the water supply into the ascending corridor. As you will no doubt remember, as the builders extended the descending corridor up through the lower courses of the structure they would have applied mortar to the faces of the limestone blocks as they were installed, and the mortar would have sealed the joints between the limestone blocks. However, when they later slid the blocking stones / slabs down the basement sheet to block the top end of this pipe they would have been unable to enter the pipe to apply mortar to these joints when the blocking stones were slid into position as the pipe was filled with water at this time. This I propose is the true explanation as to why we find scored lines – open joints – at this location within the descending corridor. Just like all the other features within this structure, there is a logical explanation as to their creation.

The masonry used to block and prop up the roof of the grand entrance tunnel would have been transported into the tunnel on barges but the work here would have been very physically demanding, especially on the topmost courses up near the gabled roof of the tunnel. The builders would have begun this operation at the innermost end of the entrance tunnel and the first blocks to be installed here would have sealed the lower end of the grand gallery and barred the access to the inner chambers and passages. (It would be more than three thousand years before anyone set foot in these inner chambers and passageways of the Great Pyramid again.) As they constructed this wall at the bottom of the gallery, it also sealed the access to the pump room (the grotto). The opening to this shaft had been just inside the inner end of the entrance tunnel at the bottom right hand side of the gallery. After the flight of locks in the grand gallery had been dismantled, the builders had no more need of the pump for the head of water at the opening to the inlet pipe was at a great enough elevation to ensure that water would have flowed through the system and up the supply pipe (the descending corridor) to feed the supply canal on the north side of the pyramid again. (The pump had only been pressed into service when the builders began to pump water up to the locks in the grand gallery and the inner area beyond.)

The operation to block up the grand entrance tunnel would have taken a considerable time to complete as it was somewhere between 40 and 45 metres long. Eventually though, the builders would have constructed the wall of limestone that we can see today below the massive double gables above the entrance to the tunnel that they had created so many years earlier. However, their work was not yet done at this stage for the stepped levels in front of this doorway had still to be built up before the final casing blocks could be installed on the north side of the structure. But before we take a look at how the builders completed the north face of the structure, we should give some prior thought to what they had still to achieve as it will help us to better understand what they eventually did here.

We know for certain that the builders would have drained all of the water from the descending corridor and the subterranean chamber after they completed the north face of the structure, as they had still to block up the lower end of, what is commonly termed, the well shaft. They had also to seal the inner end of the inlet pipe, possibly near the bottom of the descending corridor, but it could just as likely have been on the opposite side of the subterranean chamber. In addition, they had to fit the limestone slab in the roof of the descending corridor at the lower end of the ascending corridor after all the water had been drained from the system. These operations could only have been completed after the pyramid was complete and the supply canal was no longer needed.

The subterranean chamber and the descending corridor had been part of the hydraulic system that supplied water to the supply canal on the north side of the Great Pyramid. However, access to the subterranean chamber and the descending corridor could have been gained through the inlet pipe after the water had been drained from the hydraulic system, as the inlet pipe would still have been open at both ends when the north face of the pyramid had just been completed.

Does this mean that the builders could have blocked up the opening to the descending corridor on the north face of the Great Pyramid when they completed the area in front of the grand doorway? Well, they could have done, but there is a great deal of evidence to the contrary, and when we realize what they had to do to complete the north face of the structure it is almost impossible to believe that the builders blocked up this opening to the descending corridor when they completed the structure. They couldn't block up the top end of the descending corridor when they completed the level where the opening to the corridor was located on the north face of the structure, for they had still to complete the levels above this opening to complete this face of the structure. The stepped levels above the opening to the descending corridor up to the top of the double gables had still to be built up and the casing blocks installed here to complete this face of the structure. The supply canal and the lock in front of the grand doorway needed a constant supply of water until this operation was complete; therefore the opening to the descending corridor could not be blocked up until these casing blocks had been installed and the north face of the structure was complete.

So does this mean that the opening at the top end of the descending corridor (pipe) remained open when the builders were installing the last of the casing blocks on the north side of the structure? Well, that statement is only partially true. We can't permanently close the opening to the descending corridor as we need to maintain the water supply to the canal locks on the north side of the structure. But in order to install all of the casing blocks above the opening to the descending corridor, we will have to increase the water level in the lock directly in front of the main doorway. We had to raise barges up to a similar elevation a long time ago when we installed the huge double gables in the inlet channel (as it was then). Can we therefore conclude that the head of water at the inlet pipe on the south side of the Great Pyramid had to have been at a great enough elevation to enable us to increase the water level in the lock in front of the grand doorway up to the level required to install these massive gables in the entrance tunnel?

I very much doubt that it was. In fact, although I did not mention the pump at that stage of our reconstruction, it's very unlikely that the barges in the inlet channel could have been raised up to the levels of the platforms here without the pump having been used to increase the water level in the channel and the outer lock. When we made use of the pump at that stage of the construction, a non-return valve would also have been required. A simple, and temporary, hinged flap could have been installed at the top opening of the ascending corridor at this time to act as a non-return valve. The builders would have had to prevent the water they had pumped up into the entrance channel from flowing back down into the ascending corridor on the upstroke of the piston and a temporary hinged flap would have been the easiest solution. We need to bear this in mind now as we come to the final stage of our construction, for once again, we will have to raise the water level in the lock in front of the doorway beyond the level of the head of water at the inlet pipe. We will need to install another non-return valve in the system somewhere in order to achieve this.

When it came time to complete the north face of the structure, the builders would have begun by installing the rectangular core blocks and the first of the casing blocks on the 17th level – one level above the floor level at the doorway – and then worked their way up from this level, installing the core masonry and the casing blocks on each level as they went. Although I stated earlier that the doorway and the opening to the descending corridor is on the 16th level of the stepped structure (as it is today), when the descending corridor had been extended all the way out to the north face of the completed structure, its opening was probably two courses higher than it is today, on the 18th, possibly the 19th course of the structure. When the stepped levels on either side of the descending corridor had been completed and the casing stones had been installed on these levels, the descending corridor had been extended as far as the north face of the structure. Water may have continued to flow naturally into the lock here from this opening now on the 18th or 19th course of the structure, but it is unlikely that the water level could have been increased from here without the use of a pump.

Now let me take you back to when we installed the gables above the inlet tunnel, for at some point we are going to have to raise the barges in the lock on the north side of our pyramid up to a comparable elevation in order to complete the last of the courses above the opening to the descending corridor. When we raised our barges up to the levels of the platforms on either side of the inlet channel when we installed the gables here earlier we would have had to make use of the pump, and in order to do so, we would have had to install a non-return valve at the top opening of the ascending corridor. (This was just a hinged wooden flap that covered the top opening of the ascending corridor when it was closed. It pivoted on a shaft that bridged across the horizontal passageway and this shaft was supported by trunnion blocks inserted into the recesses on either side of the horizontal passageway, near the opening at the top of the ascending corridor). Likewise, when we pumped water up the pipe in the grand gallery, we had to install a non-return valve in the system to prevent water from flowing back down the pipe on the upstroke of the piston. In fact, such a pump is useless without a non-return valve.

Water was not being pumped up the outlet pipe (descending corridor) into the lock in front of the grand doorway at this stage of the construction though and, as you are now aware, we cannot gain access to the pump room now anyhow. However, if the builders had needed to make use of a pump to increase the water level in the channel to a great enough elevation to install the lower gables – and transport the limestone beams for the upper gables up to the level above – then they would have needed to pump water into the outer lock on the north side of the Great Pyramid also in order to complete the north face of the structure. And if they had to pump water into this lock, then they would have had to install a non-return valve in the system. So where did they install the non-return valve?

There was only one place that the builders could have installed a non-return valve in the hydraulic system at this late stage of the construction. This valve would undoubtedly have been installed at the outlet of the feeder pipe (the descending corridor) to maintain the water level in the lock on the north side of the structure when the last few courses of the structure were being installed in front of the grand doorway. The builders could have rigged up a simple wooden hinged flap here to cover the opening to the descending corridor, just as they had done at the top of the ascending corridor a long time before. Somehow though, I don't believe this is the option the builders would have chosen, as I am certain that the builders would have chosen to install a more permanent hinged flap at this opening. Not only was a non-return valve required at this location at this stage of the construction, a hinged door would also have been more aesthetically pleasing than a gaping hole on the north face of the Great Pyramid when the structure was complete. There is evidence to suggest that just such a hinged flap had been installed on another large, stone built pyramid on the west bank and I have absolutely no doubt that the pyramid builders would have installed such a door on the north face of the Great Pyramid for the reason I have just given. I believe that Strabo (64/63 B.C.E. – c. 24 C.E.), the Greek historian and geographer, was the first to mention that a hinged doorway was installed at the entrance to the descending corridor in the Great Pyramid. However, W.M. Flinders-Petrie FRS (1853 – 1942) was also convinced that just such a hinged doorway had been installed at the opening to the descending corridor in the Bent Pyramid at Dashur, where he discovered circular holes opposite each other just inside the opening to the corridor.

So what is the truth of the matter? Is it even possible to determine the truth of the matter so late in the day? Well, as we discovered earlier, it's patently obvious that Caliph Al Ma'mun knew exactly where the entrance to the descending corridor was prior to his tunnelling operation on the north side of the Great Pyramid. It definitely wasn't a lucky guess on his part when he began to tunnel into the north side of the Great Pyramid at the location he had chosen. He began the tunnel where he believed he had the best chance of breaking through into the ascending corridor above the granite plug(s) that he could see at the bottom of the shaft. This had been his only option here as he would certainly never have considered tunnelling upwards from the very confined space in the descending corridor below the granite plugs. This would have been completely illogical and impractical as the workmen would have been positioned directly below the section of limestone that they had to hack out of the structure in order to bypass the granite plug(s). That is the sole reason as to why the Caliph decided to tunnel horizontally into the north side of the structure. Tunnelling vertically upwards was not an option.

We have seen the great lengths the builders have gone to in order to put the most advanced construction and transportation systems in place to put the greatest structure ever constructed on the Giza Plateau. There is therefore absolutely no doubt in my mind that the builders would have installed a hinged doorway on the north face of the Great Pyramid for the north face of the structure would have been more aesthetically pleasing when the pyramid was complete with such a door installed in the opening of the descending corridor. After all, why would they leave a gaping hole in the north side of the structure after they had gone to such extremes to construct such a magnificent structure?

But we must not forget that the prime function of this door (flap) on the 19th course of the structure at this stage was to act as a non-return valve during the construction of this last section of the north face of the Great Pyramid. The non-return valve would have prevented water from flowing back down the descending corridor when the piston of the pump was on its upstroke and it would have swung open at its lower end when the piston pumped water through the hydraulic system into the outer lock at the grand doorway. The valve would then have slammed shut again as soon as there was a negative pressure behind it (when the piston reached the bottom of its stroke). With the installation of this non-return valve / hinged flap, the water level in the top lock would have stabilised as soon as this valve closed.

The casing blocks of the Great Pyramid have long since been incorporated into many of Cairo's buildings so we have no physical evidence to back up Strabo's account of a hinged doorway in the

Great Pyramid. There is, however, a large block of stone lying just off to the side of the entrance to the descending corridor with two circular holes drilled into it. This block has been broken at some point in time and we don't know what purpose it served, but it is possible that this block is what remains of the hinged door / non-return valve that had once been installed at the entrance to the descending corridor when the pyramid was complete. However, now that we know that a non-return valve had to have been installed at the outlet of the feeder pipe, it's difficult to imagine a stronger case for the existence of a hinged doorway at this location. In my mind at least, Strabo has been vindicated.

So how did they manage to pump water into the lock here when the pump room was no longer accessible? There was only one solution at this stage of the construction and that was to pump water through the hydraulic system within the structure from the opening of the inlet pipe, south and west of the Great Pyramid. I suspect that the opening of the inlet pipe would have been at the top of a vertical shaft beneath a canal lock on a spur from the feeder canal. If so, the builders could easily have set up a pump here to pump water through the hydraulic system. All that would have been required here was a plunger, and a shadouf to raise and lower the piston of the pump; in this way water could have been pumped through the inner pipes of the Great Pyramid all the way to the lock on the north side of the structure. (This pump would have been unsuited to the needs of the builders when they were constructing the bulk of this great structure, for this they needed a pump room close to the theatre of operations. The masons were in almost constant communication with the pump operators during the construction of the Great Pyramid.)

With the installation of a hinged door, a non-return valve, at the opening to the descending corridor (supply pipe), the builders had the means to increase the water levels in the lock on the north side of the structure and to raise barges up to each of the levels here in order to install the last of the core blocks on the stepped levels in front of the double gables. They would then have installed the last of the casing blocks on the final section of the north face of the structure. It would have been a simple matter of building up the stepped levels using the standard core blocks on each level, and then completing each level by installing the outer casing blocks. As work progressed, there would have been a good deal less masonry to be installed on each level, until finally, the very last casing block would have been installed and the double gables would have been completely hidden behind the smooth facade of the structure. (This area in front of the grand doorway, and the east side of the pinnacle, were the only parts of the structure where the casing blocks were installed *after* the core blocks had been installed.)

When the builders were constructing the north face of the structure originally, they installed the casing blocks on each level of the structure, but they could not install the casing blocks in front of the grand doorway as the supply canal entered the structure here. As a result, the casing blocks that were installed on either side of the double gables as the courses were built up, were stepped inward. When the builders came to install the casing blocks on the first course above the peak of the upper gable, they would then have installed all of the casing blocks on this level before they moved on to the next course. In fact, from this level up they could complete the perimeter casing on every face of the structure as each course was installed, as it was only the area in front of the doorway on the north side of the structure where the outer casing could not be completed at this time. This is the section of the structure in front of the entrance tunnel that we have now completed.

Today, however, we can clearly see the massive double gables above the grand doorway for all of the outer casing of the structure has fallen away at some time, possibly during the earthquake right at the beginning of the 14th century. We should however, not be surprised that this masonry has fallen away and exposed the double gables here, for this was undoubtedly the weakest area on the north face of the structure – the weakest area of the complete outer casing of the Great Pyramid. When each course had been built up in front of the doorway the core blocks would have been staggered to key them into the blocks behind. However, when the builders reached the level of the double gables, it was impossible to key the core blocks into the mass of the structure behind. All they could do here was butt the core blocks up against the vertical outer face of the double gables. They would certainly have staggered the joints on the few core blocks on each course they installed here but they could not key those blocks into the structure behind. This area in front of the gables was therefore the most vulnerable external area of the structure and was always at risk of collapse if the structure was subjected to the full force of a major earthquake due to this inbuilt weakness. That is possibly what happened in 1301.

The four faces of our pyramid are now complete but there is still work to be done within the structure for we have some work to do in the descending corridor and in the inlet pipe. The builders would have had to extract the water from the hydraulic system before work could commence in the pipes and we cannot know for sure how they did this. It is, of course, possible that water was drained directly from the subterranean chamber but I think this is unlikely as the drainage pipe would most probably have been discovered at some point in the past when excavation work was undertaken in this chamber. It's more than likely that the water was either pumped out of the system, or hauled out of it, using nothing more than buckets and ropes.

We now know, of course, that the builders of the Great Pyramid were familiar with the principles of the pump as pumps were in use within the Great Pyramid for long periods of time when it was under construction. (Pumps were also installed in the other two large pyramids here also.) As we discovered earlier, the builders had incorporated small shafts into the structure as the perimeter levels were built up; these were the pipes through which water was pumped up to the platforms that were under construction. These pipes were extended up through the masonry on each level as the platforms and the ramps were built up. A pump was used at the lower end of these pipes to pump water up to the upper platform and that is one of the reasons why these shafts were horizontal for a few metres before they turned upwards. The pump would have been a simple ram with a piston on the end of it and this would have been used in conjunction with a non-return valve at the top end of the water pipes. The operators would have pushed the ram into these pipes when the water level in the chambers was above the level of the shafts (pipes) in the sidewalls. When the ram reached the end of its stroke, the pump operator would then have pulled the non-return valve at the top end of the pipe shut to prevent the water in the pipe from draining away as he withdrew the plunger. The "doors" that have been discovered at the top end of these water pipes in the lower chamber are simply the non-return valves used to seal the top end of the pipes when water had been pumped up to the platforms. What Egyptologists have described as the remains of a handle on these doors are simply what remains of the copper cables or wires that were used to pull these valves shut. The pump operator would have held a handle that was attached to the lower end of these cables and

268

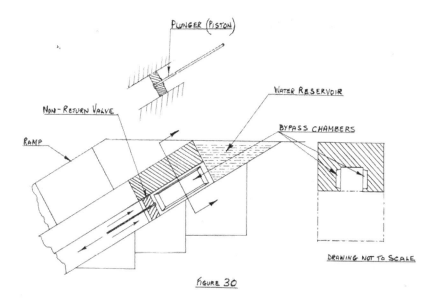

he would have closed the non-return valve just before he removed the piston from the lower end of the shaft. This ensured that most of the water in the shaft remained there until the operator could pump more water up the shaft. Without a non-return valve in the system, the water would simply have been sucked back down the pipes each time the piston was withdrawn. The non-return valve and the block in which it was housed (Fig. 30) would have been moved up one level each time a platform was completed; that is why the sides of these blocks are polished to a smooth finish. The blocks and valves used in the pipes of the lower chamber would have incurred some wear and tear by the time the perimeter platform had been pushed up to its predetermined level and that is why they were left *in situ*. I hate to burst anyone's bubble, but there are no secret chambers to be found behind these supposed "doors"; it is only the solid mass of the structure that is to be found at the end of these shafts.

These pumps required two operators, as a second operator was needed at the top end of the shafts in order to draw the water from the chamber up onto the platform. This operator would also have had a plunger with a piston on the end, and after the non-return valve had been closed by the operator at the lower end of the shaft, the operator on the platform would have slowly pushed the plunger at the top end of the shaft into the pump housing. When he then abruptly pulled this plunger up to the top of the pump chamber, most of the water in the chamber would have been drawn up into a water reservoir on the platform near the top of the ramp (see Fig. 30). These pistons were left *in situ* when they were no longer required as they would have sustained some wear and tear over the period of their use. It is these pistons that can be seen behind the so called "doors" at the top of the lower chamber shafts in the Great Pyramid. These are the "doors" that can be seen behind the "doors" at the top of these pipes that were drilled through by one of the small robots that explored these shafts in the 1990s.

In the drawing of the pump on the preceding page (Fig. 30), I have not shown the plunger in the housing of the pump in the interests of clarity. However, when the piston had been slowly pushed down to the end of its stroke and then abruptly drawn back up to the upper end of the pump chamber, this would have drawn most of the water in the chamber up into the reservoir here (as can be seen in the drawing).

Some artefacts were discovered in one of the water pipes that originate in the lower chamber after these shafts were discovered by Waynman Dixon in 1872. One of these artefacts was a small bronze "hook", as it was referred to at the time (Fig. 31).

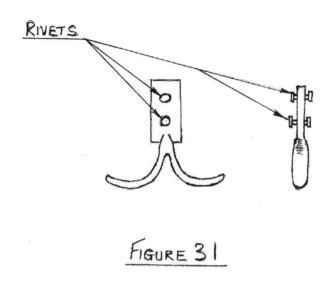

RIVETS

FIGURE 31

I believe that this was the handle that was used to pull the non-return valve into the closed position when the plunger / piston at the bottom end of the shaft had reached the end of its stroke. This valve had to be closed before the plunger of the pump was withdrawn from the horizontal shaft in order to retain the water in the pipe and in the chamber of the pump.

A short length of wooden rod was also discovered in this water pipe but all that remains of the copper wires today are the two small, badly corroded, lengths of wire still attached to the non-return valves at the top of these shafts (these lengths of wire have been mistakenly identified as handles on the non-existent "doors").

It is now plain to see that the builders of the pyramids at Giza knew how to construct and operate pumps and therefore it is possible that suction pumps could have been in use at this time. However, suction pumps have their limitations and water cannot be sucked up to more than a height of nine or ten metres using this type of pump (the height of the column of water is limited to the maximum weight that the atmospheric pressure can support). Such pumps, if they existed, would therefore have been of no use whatsoever in this situation where the water had to be removed from the subterranean chamber one hundred meters below the entrance to the descending corridor.

As I mentioned earlier, it is also possible that the builders created a pipe within the masonry of the structure which could have been used to drain the water from the hydraulic system. However, I don't believe that the builders would have gone to all that trouble just to extract water from the subterranean chamber when the structure was complete, as it's unlikely that there would have been any shortage of labour with the time to do this manually. They had only to drain the system on one occasion; therefore it's unlikely that they would have gone to the trouble of creating a piping system to drain the sump when the structure was complete.

After the exterior of the Great Pyramid had been completed, the builders would have begun to dismantle the lock at the entrance to the descending corridor and in time all traces of the supply canal would have been removed from the plateau on the north side of the Great Pyramid. Although the flight of locks on the escarpment above the canal basin would also have been dismantled after the Great Pyramid had been completed, it is possible that some traces of the considerable engineering work undertaken in this area could still be discovered. However, I am not aware of any excavations that may have been undertaken at this location.

The exterior of the Great Pyramid may have been complete now but there was still some work to be done within the descending corridor. A platform or sled would have been required here in order to support the men and the materials when the cap at the lower end of the ascending corridor was being installed (this was the limestone slab that concealed the granite plugs at the bottom of this pipe). The builders would almost certainly have constructed a wooden sled that would have provided a horizontal platform for the men who had to work in the descending corridor here. The capstone was most likely placed on the sled at the lower end of the descending corridor (the capstone would most likely have been hewn out of the limestone at the west end of the subterranean chamber) and the sled then hauled up the descending corridor from the north side of the structure. When the sled was in the best position for the installation of the capstone, the sled would almost certainly have been secured with wooden wedges on either side to prevent it from slipping back down the corridor.

Before the slab (end cap) could be fitted below the granite plug at the lower end of the ascending corridor though, the recess in the roof of the corridor had to be prepared. This involved the cutting of a slight angle on the inner face of the recess (the lower opening to the ascending corridor) nearest the top opening of the descending corridor. The ascending corridor intersected the descending corridor at an angle of much less than 90 degrees, so there was already an angled face on the one side of this recess. But on the top side of the recess nearest the top end of the descending corridor, a similar angle would have been cut into the limestone to create an opening that became wider at the top end – nearest the granite plugs – and narrower at the bottom, the opening. The slab of limestone that was fitted into this recess to cap the end of the granite plugs would have had corresponding angles on two of its sides, the other two sides having been cut at 90 degrees to the upper and lower faces of the slab. The width of the capping slab would have been ever so slightly smaller than the width of the opening into which it had to be installed – slightly smaller than the width of the descending corridor – but the top side of the slab would have been slightly longer than the opening (the upper face of the slab nearest the granite plugs). Two sides of the slab were angled outwards towards the top face of the slab and when one end of the slab, the lower end, had been pushed up into the recess, the other end would just have gone through the opening. To secure the slab in its socket, it would have been pushed up until its underside was parallel with the roof of the descending corridor. Spacers would then have been inserted into the gaps between the angled faces of the slab and the angled faces of the opening.

As can be seen in the drawing (Fig. 32) below, these spacers would have held the slab securely in place as the opening had effectively been made smaller when the spacers were inserted . The underside of the end cap may have been aligned with the roof of the descending corridor at this stage but it may also have been too low or too high. If it had been too high, some thinner spacers would have been placed in the gaps between the angled faces of the end cap and the opening; this would have lowered the underside of the end cap. On the other hand, if the end cap had been too low when it was first inserted into this opening, thicker spacers would have been placed in the gaps until the underside of the end cap was flush with the roof of the descending corridor. The limestone slab (end cap) could not be dislodged now as the insertion of the spacers had created a smaller opening.

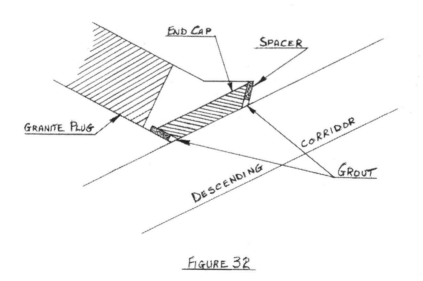

FIGURE 32

The spacers that had been put into the gaps between the slab and the opening would undoubtedly have been pushed up beyond the lower end of the opening to leave a gap below them and the lower face of the end cap. The gaps on all four sides of the end cap would then have been grouted with lime mortar and this would have ensured that the spacers and the end cap were firmly fixed in position. When the mortar dried, this slab would have been almost indistinguishable from all of the other blocks in the roof of the descending corridor.

I've given this slab much thought over the years and I think it's possible, especially if access to the descending corridor had been unrestricted after the Roman conquest of Egypt – possibly even before this time – that this slab had been discovered and removed, or had fallen out and smashed, long before Caliph Al Ma'mun came along in the ninth century. It is believed that all three large pyramids on the plateau sustained some damage as a result of an earthquake in 1301 C.E. but there had been a number of recorded earthquakes prior to this one. Peter Lemesurier, in *The Great Pyramid Decoded* mentioned a quake in 908 C.E. that was reputed to have claimed the lives of 30,000 people (uncorroborated). Although both of these quakes occurred after Caliph Al Ma'mun began tunnelling into the north face of the Great Pyramid, it is unlikely that there would not have been earthquakes of a lesser, and possibly a greater magnitude, over the course of the preceding 3,000 years. The end cap could therefore have been dislodged at any time in the 3,000 – 4,000 year intervening period between the time of its construction and the tunnelling operation of the caliph in the ninth century. But at this late stage, it is simply impossible to determine when it was shaken loose or if it had been prized out of its socket when the caliph first visited the Great Pyramid and entered the descending corridor in the ninth century. (It would, of course, be remiss of me not to mention the fact that the end cap in the ascending corridor in the Middle Pyramid at Giza must still be intact and in its original position as the granite plugs have yet to be discovered in this pyramid.)

It is also possible that some attempt had been made to excavate around the granite plugs prior to the ninth century. Although the caliph understood that there was only one logical way to excavate around these granite plugs, it's possible that some of the excavation that we can see today at the lower end of the plugs had been undertaken by his men earlier, before they discovered that there was more than one plug here and realized the impossibility of their task. Had they excavated as far as the top of the lower blocking stone, they would easily have been discouraged from continuing with their endeavours when they discovered that there was at least one other granite plug in the pipe. If someone had indeed attempted to tunnel upwards from the descending corridor just above its junction with the ascending corridor before they began to tunnel into the structure from the north side, it is now impossible to determine whether or not some of this excavation work had been undertaken prior to the tunnelling work on the north face of the structure. We know that the caliph tunnelled inwards, then upwards at an angle to excavate around the granite plugs, but this tunnel also branches off down toward the descending corridor. If the caliph had already been aware of the opening to the descending corridor before he began to tunnel into the north face of the structure, and he knew where the granite plugs were situated, he would have had no reason to excavate a passage down towards the descending corridor from his tunnel. We therefore have to consider that the tunnel the caliph excavated on the north side of the structure may have intersected an older, short section of tunnel that had been excavated upwards from the descending corridor to just beyond the top end of the lower granite plug. Either way, the caliph was undoubtedly aware of the granite plugs at the lower end of the ascending corridor before he began his tunnelling operation on the north face of the Great Pyramid, because his tunnel certainly did not intersect these plugs purely by chance.

As I mentioned earlier, when the builders installed the limestone end cap at the lower end of the ascending corridor, they secured the slab in the opening with its underside flush with the roof of the descending corridor. They then ensured that there was a gap all around it so that the slab could be grouted in. If you take a look at the drawing (Fig. 32) you will clearly see how the builders managed to secure this end cap in the opening with its underside flush with the roof of the descending corridor.

The builder's next task would have been the sealing off of the lower end of what has become known as the well shaft. The pump had been located in the pump room (grotto) at the top of this pipe and the piston had been removed from the cylinder of the pump (the top section of the well shaft) when the pump was no longer required. (I believe that this granite cylinder is still to be found lying on the floor of the pump room today, but I have been unable to confirm if this is indeed the case. Unfortunately, the public are not allowed into this chamber now so it is unlikely that you will be able to physically confirm that the piston is still there unless you are an archaeologist and can get the necessary permissions to enter this chamber and check this out.)

When Caliph Al Ma'mun tunnelled his way into the north face of the Great Pyramid he was undoubtedly unaware that the well shaft existed, so we must conclude that the builders had done a very good job of sealing off the bottom end of this shaft and disguising the fact that they had done so. (The opening at the lower end of this shaft was only discovered in the early part of the 19th century.) When the work at the lower end of the well shaft had been completed however, the builders would then have turned their attention to the inlet pipe. There is, as you know, a short horizontal corridor of a similar height and width to the descending corridor on the south side of the subterranean chamber and this short corridor can be accessed from the chamber. But it is a blind shaft... a dead end. However, we now know that water entered the subterranean chamber through an inlet pipe that originated somewhere to the south and west of the Great Pyramid. Up until I discovered the equivalent of this chamber in another super pyramid (more on this later), I would have said that the horizontal corridor (pipe) on the south wall of the subterranean chamber most likely formed part of this inlet pipe. However, in this other Super Pyramid, the smallest of the three principal pyramids at Giza – possibly constructed prior to the Great Pyramid – I discovered that the outlet from the inlet pipe was positioned opposite the only opening to the subterranean chamber here, the choke chamber in this pyramid. Water could therefore only have flowed out of this chamber through the same opening that it entered the chamber as there was only one opening.

These features of this smaller structure were configured in this manner as part of the water calming measures taken by the builders to reduce the rate of flow of the water exiting the subterranean chamber, and therefore, by extension, the rate of flow at the opening of the outlet pipe on the north side of this structure (the opening at the top end of the descending corridor). Which begs the question; did they also have the direction of flow from the inlet pipe into the subterranean chamber in the Great Pyramid going counter to the flow of water exiting the subterranean chamber (flowing up the descending corridor)? If this had indeed been the case then we are most likely to discover that the opening from the inlet pipe, its outlet, was almost certainly at the bottom end of the descending corridor.

I am not completely convinced however, that this was the case in the Great Pyramid. For instance, the subterranean chamber in the Great Pyramid differs greatly from its counterpart in the Small Pyramid. In the subterranean chamber in the Small Pyramid, the builders solely relied on baffles and niches as a water calming device. In the Great Pyramid however, the subterranean chamber is much larger, and although it is clear that a number of baffles were created in the niche on the west side of the chamber, the main chamber here is a large rectangular space. This leads me to believe that if the short section of pipe on the south wall of the chamber formed part of the inlet pipe, then the builders had relied on the creation of a vortex in this chamber as a water calming measure, with some disruption to the flow due to the baffles in the niche. But then again, if we consider that the builders had the flow of water in both the small pyramid and the middle pyramid at Giza turning back on itself, then we have to conclude that the opening of the inlet pipe in the Great Pyramid could indeed be on the north side of the subterranean chamber at the bottom of the descending corridor where it intersects the short horizontal section of this pipe. However, if that was indeed the case, then I am puzzled as to the purpose of the short blind corridor in the chamber's south wall, for there seems to be no reason as to why this pipe should exist. I must confess however, that I have little knowledge of fluid mechanics and my conclusions here may be completely wrong. In fact, the short horizontal passage on the south side of the subterranean chamber may be completely unrelated to the flow of water in this chamber, for the subterranean chamber was accessible after the structure was complete. As you will later discover, a feature was created within at least one other pyramid on the plateau after the structure was complete and this feature was unrelated to the construction programme. This may also have been the case here, but if it is, then I have to say that I have no idea as to its purpose. Irrespective of where the inner opening of the inlet pipe is to be found, we can certainly say that the builders did a good job of sealing it up when they had no further use for the hydraulic system, as it has remained hidden for 5,000 years or more.

Before we move on, I would just like to point out that the niche on the west side of the subterranean chamber was not as we see it today when water flowed through this chamber. As I mentioned earlier, the opening at the bottom of the well shaft and the opening at the inner end of the inlet pipe were blocked up after the hydraulic system was drained, with the limestone blocks used to block up these openings having been hewn from the bedrock in the niche here (the west wall). If, however, the blind shaft or corridor (pipe) on the south side of the subterranean chamber formed part of the inlet pipe, then the limestone used to block this pipe would not have been sourced in the subterranean chamber.

Our reconstructed pyramid is now complete and the only access points are the hinged door on the north side of the structure and the opening on the inlet pipe, south and west of the structure, although access to the subterranean chamber cannot now be gained from this pipe / passageway as it has been blocked up and sealed at its inner end. But although the Great Pyramid was the greatest structure of them all and the main focus of my study at Giza, we can also learn a great deal about pyramid construction by studying the other pyramids on the plateau, and by looking at the bigger picture. If anything, the other two principal pyramids at Giza clearly indicate that the architect(s) had a number of options available to them when they designed the internal layouts of these large pyramids. But make no mistake both of these structures were constructed in the same manner as the Great Pyramid. In fact, the layout of the chambers and pipes in these pyramids had to differ from those of the Great Pyramid simply because of where they are situated. However, before we take a look at these structures in more detail, we need to take a look at the bigger picture in order to fully understand how the builders created these structures, and others, on the Giza Plateau.

The peripheral structures

We have no way of knowing for certain how the Giza Project began, how it developed, or when it was completed. I have been able to glean a great deal of information about all three large pyramids on the Giza plateau from my work on the Great Pyramid and I am certain of the order of construction of the two largest structures here. As for the other structures on the plateau though, I do not know if they were constructed prior to the construction of the two largest structures here, or constructed after these structures were complete. I had originally been convinced that the smallest of the three principal pyramids had been constructed before its two larger companions but I have since made some discoveries that lead me to believe that this may not have been the case (We will take a closer look at the Small Pyramid in a later chapter.)

There is also no way for us to determine whether or not work on each of the principal pyramids was complete before work began on some of the satellite structures around these pyramids. In fact, some, most, or all of them, could have been constructed at any time before, during, or after the construction of the three principal pyramids and it is also impossible to determine the order in which most of these peripheral structures were constructed. However, we do know that for the dual channel supply canal and the flight of locks on the face of the escarpment to have been made use of after the Great Pyramid had been completed, a great deal of new infrastructure would have to have been put in place. A new section of canal would have been needed on the plateau to skirt around the Great Pyramid to reconnect the feeder canal with the supply canal again if the builders had intended to make use of this canal at this stage of the construction. But why would the builders go to all the trouble of constructing a new section of canal to reconnect the feeder canal to the dual channel supply canal when they'd had a clear route through to the heart of the complex prior to the construction of the Great Pyramid? The short answer is; they wouldn't, for it just doesn't make sense. All of the evidence points to the Great Pyramid having been the last of the two large pyramids to be constructed on the plateau, with the dual channel supply canal having been constructed solely to provide a two-way transportation system for the construction of the two largest structures here. When the last of these structures was complete – the Great Pyramid – the dual channel canal would have been decommissioned since it was no longer needed. These ancient people were the builders of the greatest structures the world had ever seen... and master planners. There is no doubt they would have encountered problems along the way that were not foreseen when they set out to design and build these magnificent structures. But having planned meticulously how they would construct the myriad structures on this site, and in what order they would be constructed, can we really believe that they then rerouted the supply canal around the west side of the Great Pyramid after it had been completed? No way! This would have been completely out of character for the people we have come to know on this journey. After all, the dual channel supply canal had been extended as far as the north side of the Middle Pyramid prior to construction of this pyramid and the Great Pyramid, so wouldn't they have made use of this canal prior to the construction of the Great Pyramid if it had been needed when the peripheral structures were under construction?

As we discovered earlier, the builders did not need the dual channel supply canal and the great bank of locks they had constructed up the north eastern face of the escarpment after the Great Pyramid was complete. The dual channel supply canal and the basin below the escarpment had been created solely for the construction of the two largest pyramids on the plateau. Masonry used in the construction of the other structures on the plateau would have been transported along the canal that I have referred to up until now as the feeder canal, the canal on the south side of the Great Pyramid. This had been the case before the dual channel supply canal had been constructed and this canal would probably still have been in use long after the Great Pyramid had been completed. In fact, it was the single channel feeder canal that was routed through the Small Pyramid when it was under construction, as the dual channel supply canal was never extended this far. The canal basin and the dual channel supply canal on the north side of the Great Pyramid had been constructed prior to the construction of the Middle Pyramid at Giza; the builders had to have a two-way system in operation in order to construct these enormous structures within an acceptable time frame. Without a two-way transportation system in operation, the rate of construction on the two largest pyramids would have been greatly curtailed due to the constraints of the single channel canal system (what I have so far referred to as the feeder canal). The builders needed an efficient transportation system in order to have a continuous flow of masonry into these structures during daylight hours in order to construct the two greatest Super Pyramids ever constructed in the fastest possible time.

I certainly can't say that work on the temples and the small satellite pyramids on the plateau continued after the completion of the Great Pyramid, but it would have made no difference if it had, for these operations on the plateau were not dependent upon the dual channel supply canal. We know that much of the limestone used to construct these structures was not transported up to the plateau on barges; much of the limestone used to construct many of the satellite structures around the three large pyramids was quarried on the plateau itself (and possibly some in the hills south west of the plateau). Most, or all of this masonry, would have been transported along the feeder canal as a branch of this canal would have extended from a point north-west of the Small Pyramid along past the limestone quarry on the east side of the Middle Pyramid, then along the south side of the Great Pyramid. This canal was routed through the limestone quarry on the east side of the Middle Pyramid and this section of the canal would have been extended as far as the mortuary temple on the east side of the Middle Pyramid. The feeder canal was further extended as far as the Sphinx enclosure. This section of the canal would have extended from the lock constructed around the Mortuary Temple on the east side of the Middle Pyramid, along the course of – what was later to become – the causeway that links the Mortuary Temple and the Valley Temple on the eastern edge of the plateau. (Most of the peripheral structures would have been constructed within huge locks, with the walls of these locks eventually forming the perimeter walls around these structures when their construction was complete.)

I cannot say for certain that barges would have entered and exited the feeder canal system east of the Sphinx enclosure but we certainly cannot rule it out. If the structures on the plateau had not been constructed prior to the construction of the two temples here, then I can only conclude that barges most probably entered and exited the single channel canal system at this location. An enormous walled enclosure would have been constructed around the two temples just east of the Sphinx and very large barges would certainly have entered this lock / dry dock that had been constructed east of the Sphinx Enclosure prior to the construction of the two temples here. These barges were used to transport the massive 200 ton monoliths used in the construction of the two temples constructed within this lock. The Sphinx Temple is situated just east of the Sphinx and the Valley Temple sits alongside this temple on its south side. We know that much of the limestone used in the construction of the Valley Temple and the Sphinx Temple was removed from the Sphinx enclosure (the depression in which the sphinx is located). The two temples here would have been constructed when the masonry was removed from the enclosure which at this time served as a quarry. The limestone blocks used in the construction of the Valley Temple are the heaviest blocks ever quarried and used in the construction of any structure at Giza. The barges used to move these enormous blocks would have been much larger than any of the barges used on the feeder canal or the dual channel supply canal, but they would only have been used in this area around the Sphinx and that part of the lock east of the Sphinx Enclosure. There was never any need for these barges to enter the more extensive, feeder canal system on the plateau, nor could they, for they were much too large for this canal.

The Small Pyramid at Giza has (had) three much smaller pyramids on its south side near the south western corner of the structure, and a Mortuary Temple on its east side that there is little trace of now. Branches of the feeder canal would have been extended as far as these construction sites, as the masonry used in their construction would have been transported along these branches of the canal. However, we also have to bear in mind that the canal system at Giza was only part of a more extensive canal network on the west bank and the canal on the west side of the small pyramid would almost certainly have extended as far south as the locks at Dashur. This canal was constructed prior to work commencing at Giza for without the feeder canal at both Dashur and Giza none of the Super Pyramids on the west bank would exist in their present form. You will see from the drawing (Fig. 33) on the next page that the canal on the west side of the Small Pyramid, that probably extended all the way to Dashur, would have been very near the west side of the smallest of the three small satellite pyramids constructed on the south side of the Small Pyramid. Although I have referred to this canal as the feeder canal on numerous occasions so far, this was simply because it was the feeder canal for the dual channel supply canal. However, this waterway also served as the supply canal on the plateau when the Small Pyramid and all of the peripheral structures on the plateau were under construction. The Small Pyramid itself was constructed using only this single channel (feeder) canal for the transportation of its masonry, and it was only a single channel that was routed into, and through, this pyramid during its construction – as can be seen by the much smaller entrance on the north side of this pyramid. (We will take a much closer look at this pyramid in the next chapter.)

But we must not forget that in addition to the three mortuary temples at Giza and the small satellite pyramids, three valley

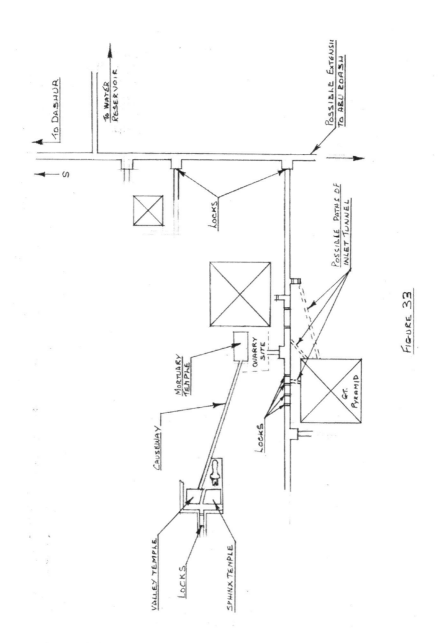

FIGURE 33

temples and the Sphinx Temple were also constructed here, as well as the three covered causeways that linked the valley temples with the mortuary temples on the east side of the three principal pyramids. The feeder canal would have been extended as far as the Sphinx Temple and the Valley Temple alongside it, for these temples, like all the other smaller structures on the plateau, would have been constructed within a very large enclosure, a massive lock. Some of the largest blocks of limestone on the plateau were used to construct the Sphinx and Valley Temples. However, these huge monoliths were not transported very far; they were quarried from the area around the Sphinx, the Sphinx Enclosure. These huge blocks, and many other smaller blocks, would have been cut out of the bedrock here as the enclosure was being created and then used to build the walls of the two temples just east of the Sphinx. The Sphinx Enclosure in other words, was a limestone quarry.

When a block of masonry is too heavy to manoeuvre using brute strength, other ways have to be found to move it, from where it is quarried, to where it has to be installed. These 200 ton monsters were far too heavy to be hauled by men or beasts, but fortunately, the builders had another much greater source of power that they could use to lift these huge monoliths up and out of the quarry. This was, of course, hydraulic power; the only force powerful enough to lift such tonnages and these builders could have been using it to transport masonry and goods on the west bank of the Nile for decades, probably centuries, before they came to construct the Sphinx and Valley Temples, believed to be the earliest structures here. These 200 ton blocks were certainly much heavier than any of the blocks used in the construction of the Great Pyramid, but nonetheless, the builders had at their disposal the most powerful force on the planet and these blocks had only to be transported a very short distance to their final destinations. If hydraulic power hadn't been available to lift these 200 ton monoliths out of the quarry then they simply wouldn't exist for there was no other force powerful enough to transport these huge monoliths from the quarry to the construction site. But they did quarry these monoliths and then they moved them the short distance to the site of the Valley Temple. That is why we can be so certain that these builders had become masters in the use of hydraulic power.

When the builders quarried the smaller blocks of limestone from the Sphinx Enclosure they undercut the bedrock beneath each of the 200 ton monoliths and created a channel wide enough for great barges to enter between the supporting columns at the ends of these monoliths. However, before these monoliths could be lifted up and out of the quarry the supporting columns had to be cut away to free them from the parent rock. This would probably have been a two stage operation, where the builders cut away part of each supporting column, then propped the monoliths up on huge hardwood beams that would have been slotted into the side of each supporting column (Fig. 34). With the monoliths being supported by these hardwood beams the remaining part of these columns would then have been cut away.

A great barge would have been manoeuvred between the supporting columns until its mid-section was directly beneath the limestone monolith. When the water level was then increased, the deck of the barge would have come up against the underside of the monolith, raising it ever so slightly up off the supporting beams. The huge limestone monolith was now free, and after its underside had been dressed – where it had been cut free from the supporting columns – it was ready to be transported the short distance to the construction site of the Valley Temple.

The Sphinx Temple is located just east of and in front of the Sphinx. The Valley Temple is located just south of the Sphinx Temple and the two of them sit side by side with only a small passageway (channel) between them. The largest limestone monoliths used in the constructions here were used to build the Valley Temple walls; therefore we can safely conclude that the Valley Temple here had to have been constructed before the Sphinx Temple. It would have been impossible to manoeuvre the barges from the Sphinx Enclosure to the site of the Valley Temple if the Sphinx Temple had been constructed first. Much larger barges would have been needed to transport the huge 200 ton monoliths used to construct the walls of the Valley Temple than those used on the feeder canal up on the plateau. However, as I mentioned earlier, these barges would have entered the lock / dry dock here from the River Nile on the eastern side of these temples. As long as the locks and the canal on the eastern side of these temples had been wide enough to accommodate these very large barges, that was all that would have been required as these barges would never have gone beyond the massive dry dock that enclosed the Valley and Sphinx Temples and the Sphinx Enclosure. It is also likely that the small barges could enter and exit the single channel canal system via this great lock east of the Sphinx enclosure as this huge lock would have been constructed on the eastern side of the plateau east of the Sphinx Enclosure, before the enclosure was carved out of the bedrock here.

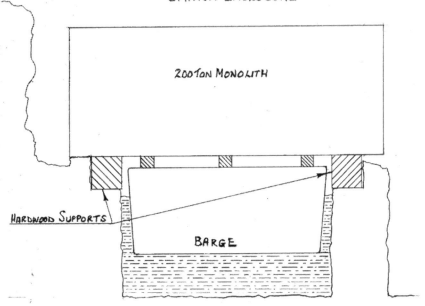

SPHINX ENCLOSURE

200 TON MONOLITH

HARDWOOD SUPPORTS

BARGE

FIGURE 34

The Sphinx Temple and the Valley Temple would have been constructed within this lock, with the limestone that was removed from the Sphinx Enclosure having been used for the greater part of their construction. The quarry here, which was later to become the Sphinx Enclosure, would have been set up in the same manner as the quarries at Aswan, where a series of ledges were cut into the face of the quarry as the masonry was removed. The barges would have been grounded on these ledges when the masonry was being hauled onto their decks from the ledges above. The barges would then have been floated off when the water level in the lock was increased and the limestone blocks would then have been transported to their final destinations within the massive lock.

That system worked well when the smaller blocks were being quarried from the bedrock and hauled onto the barges, but as mentioned earlier, a different method of quarrying, together with huge barges, would have been deployed here in order to get the huge 200 ton blocks of limestone used in the construction of the Valley Temple out of the quarry. These monoliths were far too heavy to be hauled onto, or from, the decks of barges; therefore the barges had to be positioned beneath each of these monoliths before they could be lifted out of the quarry. As previously mentioned, these 200 ton monoliths were used in the construction of the walls of the Valley Temple, just south of the Sphinx Temple. But there were also some spectacularly large blocks of limestone used in the construction of the Sphinx Temple here too and all of these monoliths were almost certainly cut from the upper layers of bedrock in the quarry (Sphinx Enclosure). The extensive, single channel canal system would have been routed through this quarry and the limestone quarry just east of the Middle Pyramid also. When the Sphinx and Valley Temples were complete, it would also have been possible for barges to gain access to the single channel canal system via the massive lock here and the channel that lies between the two temples. This canal would have been in use throughout the period when construction work was being undertaken on the plateau, and the locks, that would have been constructed within the Sphinx enclosure for the single channel canal system after the temples here were complete, would possibly only have been dismantled when all of the structures on the plateau were complete.

I stated earlier that I did not know the order of construction of the peripheral structures, or when these structures were completed. However, although we cannot determine where the construction of these temples fitted into the construction schedule, we can now say for certain that the Valley Temple was constructed prior to, or in conjunction with, the construction of the Sphinx Temple. We can also be certain that these two temples were constructed in conjunction with the creation of the Sphinx enclosure, the source of the masonry used in the construction of these temples. The bigger picture is still very patchy however, but ever so slowly the mists of time are clearing; there is now evidence to suggest that the Sphinx and the temples just east of it, were possibly the very first structures of the Giza Complex to be created. I certainly believe that this may have been the case and I believe that I have uncovered further evidence that points to just such a conclusion. I will present this evidence to you in a later chapter.

I have never been to Egypt or seen any of the structures on the Giza Plateau except in photographs and drawings. I don't know how the blocks in the walls of the Valley Temple are configured but I can tell you for certain that the 200 ton monoliths would not have been hauled from the decks of the barges that had transported them from the Sphinx Enclosure. The builders couldn't have hauled these monoliths onto the decks of the barges and they certainly couldn't have hauled them from the decks of the barges either. These 200 ton monoliths would have been lowered into position on top of supporting columns in the course(s) below them for this was the only way to install these massive blocks of limestone. I have been fortunate enough to discover another ancient structure – not in Egypt – where huge monoliths, much larger than those in the walls of the Valley Temple, were used in its construction. After trawling through many photographs of this structure, I discovered the secret of its construction also. I had known that there had only been one way to install the huge monoliths used to build the walls of this ancient structure, and I realized that the same method would have been employed by the builders at Giza when they constructed the walls of the Valley Temple. In fact, there was no other way of moving and installing monoliths of this size as hydraulic power was the only power source capable of moving such massive blocks of stone. The photographs of this other ancient site had confirmed what I believed was the only way it was possible to install such huge monoliths, and although I have no photographic evidence to confirm that the monoliths used in the construction of the Valley Temple were installed in the same manner, I know for certain that this was the case; it was the only possible means of installing these massive blocks of limestone. There simply was no other way to lift and move such massive tonnages.

The peripheral structures at Giza were all constructed within walled compounds. A lock would have been installed on one side of each compound and it was through this lock that barges entered these small canal basins when these structures were under construction. When all of the structures at Giza were complete and the canal system was no longer required, most of these walls would have been left *in situ* where they would have formed the perimeter walls of these compounds. The masonry used to construct these walls is now long gone as this would have been the most accessible masonry available thousands of years later when masons were looking for building material for the new, stone built constructions in Cairo. Here was a plentiful and easily accessible source of limestone that did not need to be quarried or dressed and it is almost certainly the case that the masonry in the perimeter walls of the compounds would have been hauled away long before the builders began to remove masonry from the much larger structures here. Had some of these walls and parts of the canal infrastructure on the west side of the Giza complex survived, we may have realized a long time ago the part that hydraulic power had played in the construction of these monuments. Alas, it was not to be.

Looking at the bigger picture, it certainly seems reasonable to assume that work on many of the smaller structures and causeways on the plateau could have been on-going when the principal pyramids were under construction, but it is just as likely that the builders put all of their efforts into the construction of the largest structures here before work commenced on many of the peripheral pyramids, temples and walkways. Unless we are fortunate enough to discover documents that clearly indicate the order of construction in the burial chambers beneath the two largest pyramids here, assuming of course that these chambers exist, we are unlikely to be able to determine this by other means.

The middle pyramid

A great quantity of granite was required for the construction of the upper chamber and the stack in the Great Pyramid, but it is almost certainly the case that such a quantity of granite was also required to build a similar structure in the Middle Pyramid at Giza. There are, of course, considerable differences in the layout of the chambers and pipes in the lower section of the two largest pyramids at Giza, but the reason that the internal structure of these two pyramids appears to be so different is due to the fact that the inlet and outlet pipes in the Middle Pyramid are on the same side of this structure. The feeder canal and the supply canal were both on the north side of the Middle Pyramid and that is why its inlet and outlet pipes are on the same side of the structure. In the Great Pyramid however, the opening on the inlet pipe is almost certainly on the south side, possibly near the south-west corner of the structure, but it may be even further west than this. In the Middle Pyramid there is undoubtedly a grand gallery, an antechamber and an upper chamber similar to those in the Great Pyramid.

In the Middle Pyramid at Giza we also find the lower chamber at, or near, ground level. The builders didn't have the benefit of a head of water on the feeder canal here to work with (relative to the opening of the outlet pipe) such as that in the Great

Pyramid and as a result, the opening on the outlet pipe on the north side of this structure is much nearer to ground level than the opening on the outlet pipe in the Great Pyramid. This is probably the main reason as to why we see the lower chamber here at ground level. However, if the pattern of the construction here mimicked that of the Great Pyramid, then the builders at some point would have blocked the opening at the top of the descending corridor here to redirect the flow of water up into an ascending corridor (there are two descending corridors on the north side of this structure, the upper one was the outlet pipe). We discovered earlier that they had to create an ascending corridor in the Great Pyramid as this was the pipe that was later extended all the way up to the top of the grand gallery. But if the Middle Pyramid does have a gallery and an upper chamber, then doesn't it follow that the lower chamber almost certainly performed the same function in this pyramid as the lower chamber in the Great Pyramid? In fact, as we discovered with our reconstruction of the Great Pyramid, there would have been no need to create a lower chamber at all if there had been no need to pump water up to an inner lock beyond the grand gallery, since it was in this chamber that the secondary pulse was generated when the pump was operated. There was therefore no need to create a lower chamber in the Middle Pyramid if there had been no need to pump water up an ascending corridor and then up through the grand gallery to an inner lock beyond.

As I mentioned earlier, the layout of the pipes and chambers at the lower levels in the Middle Pyramid varies greatly from those in the Great Pyramid, but nonetheless, we can still recognise the pipes and chambers here for what they are. We know, for instance, that the chamber at ground level is indeed the lower chamber as the counterweight of the hydraulic crane (the granite coffer) once used in this distribution hub is still to be found within this chamber. But as this chamber is at or near ground level, the limestone used to build up the lower platforms of this structure would have been transported right into this chamber on barges. We can see evidence to support this in the chamber itself as there are four large blocks of masonry on the floor of the chamber. With limestone blocks having been transported right into this distribution hub on barges – as opposed to low trolleys in the Great Pyramid – the hydraulic crane (shadouf) had to be propped up off the floor of the chamber here in order to hoist the limestone blocks up a similar distance from the decks of the barges as the blocks hoisted up from the decks of the trolleys in the Great Pyramid. That is why we find a granite coffer here and four blocks of masonry on the floor of this chamber.

If you can cast your mind back to when we constructed the lower chamber in the Great Pyramid, you will no doubt remember that the builders created a shaft and a ramp on each side of this chamber, prior to its use as a distribution hub. However, when they went on to complete the chamber, they blocked up these shafts as the completed chamber had to be air and watertight. Needless to say, the builders of the Middle Pyramid would also have blocked up the shafts in the lower chamber here when they went on to complete it, since this chamber would undoubtedly have performed the same function as the lower chamber in the Great Pyramid (these chambers were expansion chambers). However, the shafts (water pipes) in the lower chamber of the Middle Pyramid would have been set at a higher level than those in the lower chamber in the Great Pyramid. The landings on the sidewalls of this chamber would also have been at a much higher level than those in the Great Pyramid because the water level in this chamber when the crane was in use would have been much greater than the water level in the lower chamber in the Great Pyramid. So, although the openings to these shafts are likely to be found just off to the west side of the passage into this chamber, they will be a greater distance from the floor of this chamber than those in the Great Pyramid due to the fact that the hydraulic crane had been propped up off the floor here.

The discovery of these concealed shafts will confirm that this chamber did indeed function as a central distribution chamber when the perimeter platforms were being built up in the Middle Pyramid. But their discovery will tell us much more than that for when these shafts (pipes) are discovered, they will confirm that this chamber was also completed to play the role of an expansion chamber. When they are discovered they will confirm that the builders of this pyramid went on to create a gallery and an upper chamber here also, as there would have been no need for them to complete this chamber – the expansion chamber – had they not done so. (The existence of these shafts could easily be determined by electronic means without the need for any destructive measures.)

Before we move on, I would just like to mention that there is one feature of the Great Pyramid that we won't find in the Middle Pyramid and that is the dual channel entrance tunnel. Although the dual channel canal was extended as far as the north side of the Middle Pyramid, it was not extended into this structure; there are no gables above the upper opening on the north side of this structure. Due to the layout of the known chambers and pipes within the Middle Pyramid I suspect that the entrance tunnel here is shorter than the entrance tunnel in the Great Pyramid and the builders may have decided that there was not a great deal to be gained by taking a dual channel canal into this pyramid, considering the time it would have taken to construct such a tunnel. Taking a single channel canal into a pyramid was a much simpler proposition than that of a dual channel canal as the walls of a single channel tunnel could be stepped out (corbelled) over a few courses; there was no need to haul large limestone beams into the structure to create a gabled roof here. In other words, the cost in time and energy may have outweighed the gains here.

Sooner or later archaeologists will gain access to the gallery, the upper chamber and the antechamber in the Middle Pyramid, and in turn, the pump room and the "well shaft" (for want of a better name). As Egyptologists didn't know that these chambers existed, there was probably very little pressure put on the Supreme Council of Antiquities to open up these structures to further excavation and investigation, but now that we can quickly and easily determine for certain that these chambers and pipes do exist, I would hope that there will be some further investigations conducted here in the near future. After all, this presents Egyptologists with the ideal opportunity to find out just what the builders left behind in this structure when they exited its inner chambers and passageways, as no one could have gained access to these pipes and chambers since the ancient builders sealed them up. Hopefully, in light of my discoveries at Giza, we will see the dawn of a new age of exploration and discovery on the Giza Plateau in the not too distant future.

Chapter Eight

The Small Pyramid

Although the title of this book is The Great Pyramid – The Inside Story, I would never have made nor confirmed many of the discoveries within this structure without doing extensive research on all of the Super Pyramids on the west bank (those pyramids built of large stone blocks). I thought I knew most of what there was to know about the pyramids at Giza before I made my last attempt to discover the secrets of the pyramid builders, but I knew very little about the other Super Pyramids (as I would later refer to them) on the west bank. When I eventually made my great breakthrough in the Great Pyramid though, everything changed; not only did I then view the Great Pyramid from a completely different perspective, I saw all of the Super Pyramids of the hydraulic age in a new light – all of the large, stone built pyramids on the west bank.

As you are also now aware, the Great Pyramid and the Middle Pyramid at Giza were constructed from the same basic design plan; it is only the inlet and outlet pipes on these two structures that differ greatly from one another. This is entirely due to the relative positions and elevations of these structures on the plateau. But as time went by, I became intrigued by the layout of the underground chambers and passageways in the smallest of the three principal pyramids at Giza as they differ so much from those in both of its much larger companions. There were many puzzling features within the many underground chambers and passageways in this small structure and I don't mind admitting that I got it all completely wrong when I first tried to make sense of its layout. However, having started out on the wrong foot, so to speak, I then went on to further complicate matters and found myself back at square one, having made no progress whatsoever in my attempt to interpret the layout of the chambers beneath this structure. I therefore abandoned my first attempt to make any sense of this structure and began to concentrate again on my work in the Great Pyramid.

As I worked on my project, something kept pulling me back to this small structure and one day, when I was checking out one of its features, it all suddenly fell into place, well, eighty per cent of it did; I had to work on the other twenty per cent. However, having made these discoveries in the small pyramid, I realized that I would have to include all of my discoveries here as some of the best evidence I have discovered so far as to how these structures were constructed is to be found in this small structure. As my main objective in writing this book is to enlighten you as to the true capabilities of the ancient pyramid builders, and to explain the true methods of large, stone built, pyramid construction, I realized that I had no option but to devote a chapter of my book to the smallest of the three principal pyramids on the Giza Plateau.

The complex layout of the chambers and pipes below ground level in the small pyramid at Giza differ so greatly from the two other principal pyramids that we simply have to set aside some time to better understand this structure and what the builders achieved here. Simply by studying the layout of the Great Pyramid, we get very few clues as to how things developed when work first began on the small pyramid. However, knowing how the two largest pyramids at Giza had been constructed, I found it much easier to understand what had taken place here, once I had discovered where water had entered the hydraulic system in this structure. There was no dual channel supply canal here as the dual channel supply canal was never extended this far. However, if you ever had any doubts that a lock was constructed at the entrance to the descending corridor in the Great Pyramid, you need look no further than the Small Pyramid to have it confirmed. But as usual, I have gotten way ahead of myself again, so let's take it from the beginning.

Although I am now certain of the order of construction of the two largest pyramids at Giza, I have found it difficult to determine when the smallest of the three pyramids was constructed. However, the construction process would have been very similar to that of the two others on the site once the foundation level had been established. But what a time it must have taken the builders to get to that stage, as the Small Pyramid has undoubtedly the most complex arrangement of chambers and pipes below ground level of the three principal pyramids at Giza.

After a branch of the canal system had been put in place to transport limestone to the site where the small pyramid was to be established, some of its water would have been drawn off and used to check that the foundation was level before work began on the structure above ground level. However, the internal layout of the smallest of the three pyramids at Giza varies greatly from the internal layout of both of its companions, and this pyramid is unique in that there is a very extensive network of pipes and chambers below the foundation level, many more than in the two larger pyramids here. Although archaeologists have yet to discover most of the pipes and chambers above the foundation level in the Small Pyramid, we can now be certain that these chambers and pipes must exist, for we now know that the builders could not have completed this small structure without them. Orthodox Egyptologists believe this pyramid to have been the last of the three major pyramids constructed here and they have attributed its construction to Menkaure, a king of the fourth dynasty. It is certainly possible that this small pyramid was dedicated to Menkaure at some point in the past, but I suspect that this would have been long after this pyramid had been constructed, since, like its two companions, the evidence points to it having been constructed long before the fourth dynastic period.

It is obvious from the layout of the structures on the plateau at Giza that the whole site had been surveyed and the footprints of all three pyramids clearly determined, prior to construction work beginning on the plateau. This was an absolutely essential first step as the very extensive canal system that the builders installed on the plateau prior to the construction of any of the structures here had to service all three of the principal pyramids when they were under construction, not to mention the many satellite structures associated with the principal pyramids here also. It was certainly not by accident that the layout of the site was configured in the way that it was and I believe that it is generally accepted now that the three large pyramids at Giza almost certainly represent the three stars of Orion's Belt. An overhead view of the Giza plateau shows that the two largest pyramids are set out along a diagonal running at 45degrees to the south-west from the north-east corner of the Great Pyramid. The Small Pyramid lies slightly to the east of this diagonal. Although they are of a similar size, there are also variations in the dimensions and angle of the sides of the two largest pyramids here. The second or Middle Pyramid is slightly smaller than the Great Pyramid, but it is built at a slightly higher elevation than the Great pyramid and this makes it look just as tall. The steeper angle of incline of the Middle Pyramid also contributes to this illusion, as does the fact that the Great Pyramid is now ten metres or so shorter than it would have been when it was first constructed.

Do they represent the stars of Orion's Belt, as suggested by Adrian Gilbert and Robert Bauval in '*The Orion Mystery*' published in 1994? Or is there a simpler, more obvious explanation? It is unlikely that we will be able to either prove or disprove this theory until we learn much more about the pyramids at Giza, but it is certainly the best theory put forward so far. Discoveries made more recently – much further south at Nabta Playa – certainly seem to confirm that the ancient inhabitants of this region aligned monoliths to these three stars long before the dynastic period. Hopefully, in time, more evidence will emerge to back up what at the moment is just a theory, albeit a very credible one. All I can say is that my discoveries at Giza have neither confirmed nor disproved this theory as I have found no new data that relates to the configuration of these three structures. What we can be certain of though, is that the plateau had been surveyed and the footprints of each of the structures here clearly determined, long before work began on the structures themselves. It simply couldn't have been any other way since the plans for the extensive canal network could not be finalised until this had been established. It was the canals that made all of this possible, for not only were they used for the transportation of masonry to the sites of each of the monuments the water in the canal system was actually channelled through the three principal structures on the plateau. It would have taken many years just to put this canal network in place and this could only have been done once the positions of the principal structures had been determined.

The development and adaptation of the general pyramid design to take account of the topography of the site at Giza can be easily discerned when we study the internal layout of the pipes and chambers in the three pyramids in detail. The obvious modifications that we see in the design of the Great Pyramid over its predecessor, the Middle Pyramid, are plain to see. The water inlet and outlet are on different sides of the Great Pyramid, whereas the inlet and outlet are on the same side in the Middle Pyramid, the north side. The floor of the lower chamber in the Middle Pyramid is just below the foundation level, whereas the floor in the lower chamber in the Great Pyramid is on, or above, the eighteenth course of limestone masonry. In the Small Pyramid however, no chambers have been discovered on, or above, ground level so far.

You will see from the drawing (Fig. 35) on the next page that the layout of all the known subsurface shafts and chambers in the

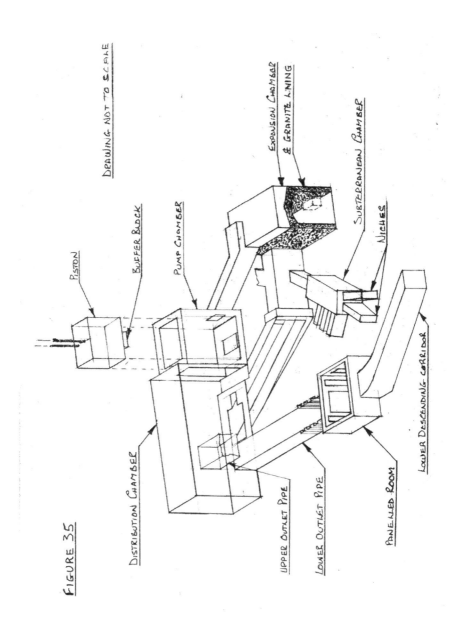

FIGURE 35

DRAWING NOT TO SCALE

PISTON

BUFFER BLOCK

PUMP CHAMBER

EXPANSION CHAMBER
& GRANITE LINING

SUBTERRANEAN CHAMBER

NICHES

DISTRIBUTION CHAMBER

UPPER OUTLET PIPE

LOWER OUTLET PIPE

PANELLED ROOM

LOWER DESCENDING CORRIDOR

smallest of the three pyramids varies considerably from those of both of its larger companions. In fact, the system of pipes here is so complex that I found it very difficult indeed to determine how the smallest of the three pyramids had been constructed initially. I at first had assumed that both the inlet and outlet pipes were on the north side of the structure like those of the Middle Pyramid, as that is how it first appears; however, when trying to make sense of the rather strange internal layout of this structure, I then realized my error. What I was looking at here was not the inlet and outlet pipes of this pyramid; the two 'descending corridors' on the north side of this structure were in fact two outlet pipes. This was a discovery that came very late on in my quest to discover how these structures had been built and I am not aware of any other Super Pyramid that had two outlet pipes to feed the supply canal at different stages of its construction, either at Giza or Dashur. Although, it has to be said that there are still many pipes and chambers yet to be discovered in many of the Super Pyramids on the west bank, this discovery however, did go a long way to explaining why many of the internal pipes and chambers in the small pyramid are so different from those that we see in the other two large pyramids here. (It could be said that the Great Pyramid had two outlet or feeder pipes, but one of these, the ascending corridor, was simply a branch of the other. That was not the case in the Small Pyramid.)

You can't, of course, have two outlet or feeder pipes unless you have an inlet pipe and I am now reasonably certain of the location of the inlet pipe. The outer opening to this pipe is most likely to be discovered somewhere near the south-west corner of the small pyramid as the feeder canal skirted the west side of this pyramid when it was under construction... and probably for a long time after. The reason I am so certain of where the opening to this pipe is likely to be found, has to do with the position of what is undoubtedly the subterranean chamber in the Small Pyramid, or, to be more accurate, the chamber that played the same role here as the subterranean chamber in the Great Pyramid (there are many underground chambers in this small pyramid and all of these would be classed as 'subterranean.' In this case, however, I am referring to the chamber that the water from the inlet pipe rushed into initially.) The only access to this small chamber is at its south end. In addition, there are four niches on the eastern side of this chamber and another two niches at its northern end. It was these cavities or niches, and the baffles between them, that disrupted the flow of water as it surged into this chamber from the inlet pipe – its inner opening being just across the small passageway from the opening to the subterranean chamber. The walls of the niches, the baffles, in this chamber absorbed much of the energy of the turbulent water surging into the chamber before the water was forced back out of the chamber through the same opening. Like the subterranean chamber in the Great Pyramid, this chamber acted as a choke in the hydraulic system to temper the flow of the surging water before it reached the outlets and the supply canal on the north side of the structure. (The supply canal here was in fact the single channel canal that I referred to as the feeder canal when we were reconstructing the Great Pyramid as the dual channel supply canal was never extended as far as the Small Pyramid.) There was only one opening into this small chamber and the walls of the chamber had to withstand the full force of the water surging into it from the inlet pipe and absorb much of its energy; that is why it is located deep in the bedrock beneath the structure.

As you will see from the drawing (Fig. 35), the outlet pipes originate in a rectangular distribution chamber that is also carved out of the bedrock beneath the structure and this chamber is oriented east-west. It is up into this chamber that water from the subterranean chamber would have flowed, and then on through the openings in the north wall of the chamber to the outlet pipes on its north side. You will see from the diagram of the corridors and chambers that the two horizontal sections of the two outlet pipes have their openings on the north wall of the distribution chamber, one above the other, and although much of the upper pipe has been excluded from the isometric drawing in the interest of clarity, I must point out here that water did not flow through the distribution chamber and into both of these outlet pipes at any time. It was only the opening to the lower outlet pipe that existed in the north wall of the distribution chamber when water first flowed through this chamber, and the upper outlet pipe was only brought into use after the lower outlet pipe had been blocked up.

Looking at the isometric drawing (Fig. 35), you will notice that in a small section of the horizontal corridor of the lower outlet pipe there is a portcullis chamber. When I was doing some research on the Small Pyramid early on in my reconstruction of the Great Pyramid, I had assumed that this feature was a chamber similar to the antechamber in the Great Pyramid (I do not refer here to the larger chamber further along this corridor with the decorative panels carved into its walls). However I couldn't understand why it had been cut out of the bedrock beneath the structure and the only conclusion I could draw at the time was that this was possibly an experimental antechamber. It was only later, when I had completed my reconstruction of the Great Pyramid and had taken another look at the internal layout of the Small Pyramid that I realized what this chamber was all about. It was only then that I realized that the builders had in fact created two outlet pipes in this pyramid. (Although I have referred to this feature as a chamber it is not in fact a chamber, it is simply a section of the horizontal pipe where three pairs of vertical channels have been cut into its sidewalls.)

There is no doubt that the three pairs of vertical channels in the walls of the horizontal section of the lower outlet pipe have at one time held three stone slabs, this is, in fact, where the lower outlet pipe was sealed when the builders had no further use for it. Just like the other two large pyramids here, the Small Pyramid was constructed in a number of distinct stages, and the lower outlet pipe here was sealed up after the first stage of the construction was complete. This occurred after only a few courses of the structure had been put in place. This pipe had to be sealed off after the first stage of the construction was complete, as the flow of water had to be directed into the upper outlet pipe at the next stage of the construction. Work on the second stage of the construction could not begin until the water to feed the supply canal on the north side of the structure had been routed through the upper outlet pipe. In the Great Pyramid, the builders blocked the top end of the descending corridor to channel water up through the ascending corridor at this stage of the construction. In the Small Pyramid, however, the lower outlet pipe was blocked off and water was then channelled through the newly created upper outlet pipe to feed the supply canal on the north side of the structure.

I then realized that at long last I had discovered a corridor (pipe) that had been sealed using three slabs of masonry – the elusive 'portcullis slabs'. I then began to wonder, had it been here, in the lower outlet pipe in the Small Pyramid that this whole idea that portcullis slabs had been used to seal burial chambers had originated? Was it with the discovery of the three slabs in this pipe that would indeed have blocked the access to some of the chambers here that Egyptologists mistakenly came to believe that these slabs were lowered into position to seal a burial chamber? After all, at some point in the past, someone had obviously smashed their way through the three slabs that blocked this pipe and gained access to the pipes and chambers beyond; it was therefore not unreasonable for someone to conclude that this had been their true purpose despite the fact that there was no obvious mechanism to verify such a conclusion. But when Egyptologists and pyramid enthusiasts had no knowledge of how these structures were constructed it was almost impossible to determine how, why, or when, most of the chambers and passageways in these structures were created. Although they had almost all of the pieces of the jigsaw puzzle to hand there was no picture on the lid of the box... no key to how it all went together. It is only now, when we have gained possession of that key, that we can say for certain that these portcullis slabs were installed in the lower outlet pipe not long after the builders had begun to construct the Small Pyramid at Giza. Although they did block the access to the passageways and chambers beyond, these slabs had been lowered into this pipe for a purely practical reason – to seal it – during the early construction phase of the pyramid.

Before we go on, perhaps I should mention that I do believe that the granite chamber in the small pyramid was indeed a burial chamber of an early king of Egypt, and that the sarcophagus found in this chamber had almost certainly contained a mummy at some time. As I mentioned earlier, although I do not believe that the pyramids themselves were built to house the burial chambers of early kings of Egypt, I have always been of the opinion that the bodies of the kings responsible for the construction of some of these pyramids were most likely to have been interred in tombs deep in the bedrock beneath these structures. The granite burial chamber in the small pyramid at Giza is one such chamber as it is positioned at the very deepest level in the substructure of this pyramid.

As I mentioned earlier, it is easy to understand why Egyptologists believed that the three blocking slabs in the lower pipe had been lowered into this pipe to seal off the burial chamber. Not knowing how the pyramid had been constructed, they had no idea that these slabs had indeed formed a physical barrier in this pipe, but for an altogether different purpose at the very earliest stages of the construction. However, there is no getting away from the fact that these slabs also cut off the access to some of the chambers deep below the structure, for they did indeed block the access to, what would later become, the granite chamber (the burial chamber) from the northern side of the pyramid after all of the water had been drained from the hydraulic system. Archaeologists had no idea that what they regarded as passageways and corridors in the three pyramids at Giza were in fact the inner pipes of massive hydraulic systems; systems that had been created within each structure in order to facilitate the construction of these monuments. The three slabs that the builders of the Small Pyramid installed in the vertical channels within this horizontal section of the lower outlet pipe played their part in the hydraulic system that was created in this small pyramid. There are undoubtedly some similarities here with the antechamber in the Great Pyramid – the three pairs of vertical channels – but that is where the similarity ends; this was certainly not the bottom end of a lift shaft, nor a chamber of the type we see in the Great Pyramid, it was simply a blocking device to seal a hydraulic pipe.

When water first flowed through the subsurface pipes and chambers of the Small Pyramid, it was only this lower horizontal pipe that was in use, the one above it simply didn't exist at that stage of the construction. When it came time to seal the lower outlet pipe, the builders would have drained down the system and then lowered three stone slabs into the lower horizontal pipe. They would then have poured gypsum or lime mortar into the two cavities between the slabs to seal any small gaps and to consolidate the blocking mechanism; the wet mortar would have flowed into any small gaps between the slabs and the channels, creating a watertight seal and a solid barrier when the mortar had dried. After the slabs had been installed and the mortar had been poured into the cavities, limestone beams would then have been installed across the opening on top of the horizontal pipe above these slabs. These limestone beams would have sealed the roof of the lower outlet pipe completely at this location (a vertical shaft had been excavated above this area prior to the installation of the three blocking slabs). These limestone blocks or beams would have been set down on a bed of wet mortar to ensure a watertight seal in the roof of the pipe, and the area above these blocks, the vertical shaft, would then have been backfilled.

You will see from the drawing (Fig. 35) that there is also a rectangular chamber in the horizontal section of the lower outlet pipe on the north side of where the blocking slabs had been installed. This chamber was carved out of the bedrock here, but it simply didn't exist when the three blocking slabs were lowered into the outlet pipe or when the lower outlet pipe was in use. When the horizontal section of this lower outlet pipe was carved out of the limestone bedrock originally, the pipe would have been of a uniform width and height along its length. The three pairs of vertical channels that later accommodated the blocking slabs would have been cut into its sidewalls after the builders ceased to make use of this shaft and had drained it (prior to the second phase of the construction). The rectangular chamber further along the shaft however, was not created until much later.

The rectangular chamber in the horizontal section of the lower pipe on the north side of the three blocking slabs is unique in that it is the only chamber in all three large pyramids at Giza (that we know of) that has carved decorative panels on its walls. However, this chamber was a later addition and would not have existed when the pipe was being used for the purpose it was originally intended. The lower outlet pipe was later widened to create this chamber, but this could only have occurred after the Small Pyramid had been completed, and after the canal locks on the north face of the pyramid had been dismantled. Due to the fact that this chamber has decorative panels carved into its walls, and no other chambers have been discovered in the two much larger pyramids here with such decoration, leads me to believe that this chamber was created and decorated a long time after the small pyramid had been completed.

The limestone bedrock above the section of the lower horizontal pipe where the three pairs of vertical channels were cut into its walls would have been removed after the lower outlet pipe had been drained. A square or rectangular vertical shaft would have been excavated here to gain access to the roof of the lower outlet pipe. In order to drain the lower pipe, the builders would first have closed the lock or valve on the branch of the feeder canal that supplied water to the inlet pipe, cutting off the water supply to the hydraulic system. They would then have opened a gate valve or sluice at the lowest level of the inlet pipe (on the south side of the pyramid) to drain the water from the system. After the three blocking slabs had been installed in the lower outlet pipe and the spaces between them filled with mortar, the limestone roof beams would then have been placed across the shaft above the three slabs to seal the roof of this pipe. The builders would then have begun to backfill the vertical shaft above the blocking slabs. But the vertical shaft would not have been built back up to the foundation level of the structure – where it had originated – it would only have been backfilled up to the level of the floor in the upper horizontal pipe, a pipe that had still to be created at this time.

When the lower outlet pipe was in use, the pyramid would have been constructed up to the level where the mouth of the lower outlet pipe discharged its waters directly into the lock on the north side of the structure (where visitors enter the pyramid today). After another two or three courses had been added to the perimeter levels of the structure, work on the pyramid would have ceased. It was at that point that the water within the central pond and the lower outlet pipe and chambers would have been drained from the hydraulic system.

The opening to what is now termed the descending corridor (lower outlet pipe) in the smallest of the three principal pyramids at Giza, is only three courses up from ground level. In contrast, the opening to the descending corridor in the Great Pyramid was eighteen or nineteen courses up from ground level when its outer casing was intact. When the first few courses of the Small Pyramid were under construction, the area directly above the horizontal section of the lower outlet pipe, where the three vertical slabs were later installed, would not have been built up beyond the foundation level at this time. When the water was later drained from the pond and the piping system, the aforementioned vertical shaft would then have been excavated down through the bedrock until it intersected the top of the horizontal pipe. As I mentioned earlier, the blocking slabs would have been lowered into this shaft, and then on down into the vertical channels in the outlet pipe. But when the vertical shaft above these slabs was later built up again it would only have been built up to the level of, what was soon to become, the floor level of the upper outlet pipe; it would have been from this landing that the builders began to excavate the horizontal section of the upper outlet pipe out of the bedrock here. They would have tunnelled into the bedrock on the south side of the landing until the rectangular pipe intersected the north wall of the distribution chamber.

In the Great Pyramid the ascending corridor is simply a branch of the descending corridor. However, in the smallest of the three pyramids at Giza, the builders had to create a second shaft, an upper outlet pipe above the lower outlet pipe, in order to channel water to the supply canal within the structure at the next stage of its construction. The opening at the top end of the ascending corridor in the Great Pyramid was where water was discharged into the canal system within this structure. The opening at the top end of the upper outlet pipe in the Small Pyramid was also where water was discharged into the canal system within the structure. Both of these openings are a considerable distance inside the northern perimeter of these structures and work could only have begun on the second phase of the construction in the Small Pyramid after the upper outlet pipe had been excavated out of the bedrock.

If you take another look at the drawing of the pipes and chambers within the Small Pyramid (Fig. 35), you will notice that the horizontal section of the upper outlet pipe is directly above the lower outlet pipe and runs parallel with it. Although I have not shown the complete pipe in the isometric drawing, you will see from the drawing (Fig. 36) below, showing the layout of the chambers and passageways in the Small Pyramid when viewed from the east, that the sloping section of this pipe also lies parallel with the sloping section of the lower outlet pipe.

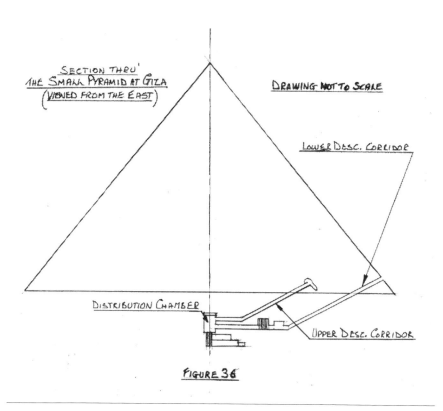

SECTION THRU' THE SMALL PYRAMID AT GIZA (VIEWED FROM THE EAST)

DRAWING NOT TO SCALE

LOWER DESC. CORRIDOR

DISTRIBUTION CHAMBER

UPPER DESC. CORRIDOR

FIGURE 36

However, it is unlikely that any sections of this upper pipe would have been excavated prior to the first phase of the building work ending and the lower outlet pipe having been drained and blocked off. If the builders had begun to excavate sections of the upper outlet pipe prior to the construction work beginning here, they would have had no means of draining these sections of the upper outlet pipe when they drained the hydraulic system after the first phase of the construction. However, when the blocking slabs had been installed in the lower pipe, and the area above these slabs built up to, what would become, the floor level of the upper outlet pipe, the horizontal section of the upper outlet pipe would have been excavated from the landing created after the vertical shaft had been backfilled. The builders would have excavated the horizontal section of the upper outlet pipe, working their way in a southerly direction towards the distribution chamber. Eventually, they would have broken through the north wall of this chamber. They would have excavated the sloping section of this upper pipe – the upper descending corridor, if you prefer – prior to excavating the horizontal section of the pipe and all of the rubble from these excavations would have been hauled up the slope at the north end of the sloping pipe and hauled off to the north side of the structure to be dumped.

Before we continue with our reconstruction of the Small Pyramid, I would just like to mention the descending corridors here and the descending corridors in the two other much larger structures on the plateau. I don't know the degree of precision with which the descending corridors in the Small Pyramid and the Middle Pyramid at Giza were excavated; however, many have referred to the precision with which the descending corridor in the Great Pyramid was excavated and I would just like to clarify the situation with regard to the excavation of this shaft. It would have been almost impossible to excavate this shaft with anything like the degree of accuracy we see here without the use of a mechanical device. When a shaft such as the descending corridor in the Great Pyramid is being excavated by hand, some sort of guide must be used in order to ensure that the shaft is straight and its dimensions uniform. However, this guide can only be inserted into the shaft opening after the first metre or so of the shaft has been excavated by hand and, at best, such a guide can only confirm that each section of the shaft is accurate *after* it has been excavated. There is, however, one way to get around this little difficulty and that is to use a guide that also functions as a cutting machine... an excavator. When using a machine such as this, most of the rock face has still to be cut away by hand, but as each small section of the shaft is later extended by the cutting machine, its roof, floor and sides are perfectly aligned with all of the sections of the shaft previously excavated.

I believe that it was only by making use of such a machine that the builders of the Great Pyramid were able to excavate such a shaft with the degree of accuracy we see in the descending corridor in the Great Pyramid. Whether such machines were used to excavate the descending corridors in the middle and small pyramids at Giza I cannot say, but I have no hesitation in saying that such a machine was used to excavate the descending corridor in the Great Pyramid. The drawings (Figs. 37a, 37b & 37c) on the next page, will give you some idea of what such a cutting machine could have looked like and how it was operated. The leading edges of the machine on all four sides were the cutting blades, whereas the framework behind the cutting blades – the body of the machine – ensured that the cutting head was always aligned with the shaft. The excavators would have removed the bulk of the limestone from the rock face just ahead of the cutting machine, but would have left the last few centimetres of material on all four sides of the shaft *in situ*. The excavators would then have made their way back up the shaft a few metres and then crawled through the cutting machine until they were on the topside of the machine and well clear of it. The cutting machine had been hauled back up the shaft a few metres or so by means of a windlass before the excavators had set to work on the next section of the shaft. When this windlass was then released, the cutting machine would have plunged back down the shaft, where it would have come into contact with the rock face and shaved the last few centimetres of limestone from the sides, floor and roof of the shaft, as the cutting head plunged deep into the soft limestone at the bottom of the shaft. In this way the perfectly aligned shaft, the descending corridor, was extended ever further down into the bedrock of the plateau. As I mentioned earlier, I do not know how precisely cut the descending corridors in the small and the middle pyramids are, therefore I cannot say for sure that such a cutting

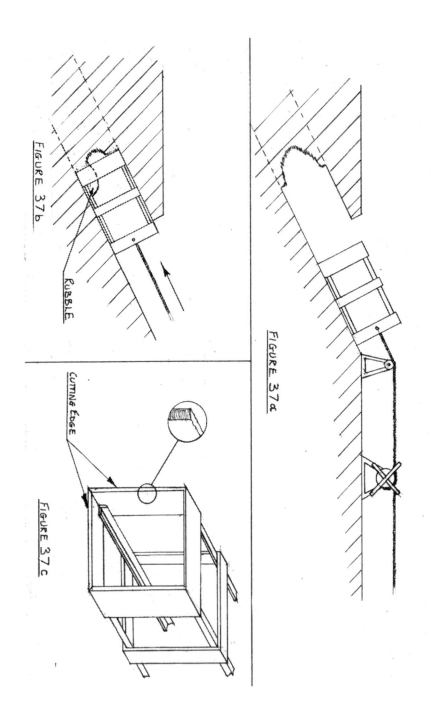

FIGURE 37a

FIGURE 37b

RUBBLE

FIGURE 37c

CUTTING EDGE

machine was used in these structures. However, I think it unlikely that the pyramid builders would not have made more use of this cutting machine elsewhere on the plateau and I suspect that it was probably employed in these two structures also.

As I said, whether or not such a machine was used to excavate the descending corridors in the Small Pyramid I cannot say; but the north wall of the distribution chamber in this small pyramid now had its second opening and the lower outlet pipe had now been blocked, so water could now only flow through the upper outlet pipe when the hydraulic system was brought back into use again. However, there were a few more tasks to be undertaken at that stage of the construction before that could happen. When the walls and floor of the upper outlet pipe were complete, the builders would have had to close the rectangular hole in the roof of this outlet pipe – created when they sunk the vertical shaft here – by placing limestone beams across the sidewalls of the pipe to form the roof here. The area above these limestone beams, the upper section of the vertical shaft, would then have been built up to bring it up to the level of the inner platform – the foundation level – at that stage of the construction. The upper outlet pipe was, to all intents and purposes, ready to be brought into use. The builders now had a new water supply pipe to feed the ponds within the perimeter walls of the pyramid on each level and the supply canal on the north side of the structure. The lower outlet pipe had been used to supply water to the inner ponds and the supply canal as the first few courses of the perimeter had been built up. The lower outlet pipe had been extended up through these first few levels as they were built up until it could be extended no further, when it intersected the north face of the structure. The canal locks on the north side of the structure could be extended no higher than this outlet on the north face of the structure as the builders simply didn't have a head of water at a great enough elevation on this site to supply water to such locks (the foundation level of the Small Pyramid is at the greatest elevation on the plateau of the three principal pyramids). The canal had therefore to be extended into the structure on this level.

Although the builders had now reached the point where we know that they created a grand entrance tunnel in the Great Pyramid and took the supply canal into this structure, the entrance tunnel that they created in the Small Pyramid was a more modest affair. The canal that entered this structure on its north side was a single channel canal; the dual channel supply canal was never extended as far as the Small Pyramid, as it had been constructed purely to service the two much larger structures here. The supply canal at the site of the Small Pyramid was simply a branch of what I have referred to up until now as the feeder canal, with a branch of this canal being extended as far as the opening on the north side of the small pyramid. All the barges that entered the Small Pyramid through the doorway of the entrance tunnel had to exit the structure before another barge could enter. This was also the case with the Middle Pyramid at Giza, but not the Great Pyramid, as the dual channel supply canal had been extended into this structure all the way to the bottom of the grand gallery.

A single channel canal did have some advantages over the two-way system created on the north side of the Great Pyramid. It would have been a much simpler task to bridge the gap above this channel than it was to bridge the gap in the much wider channel in the Great Pyramid. In fact, it's unlikely that the builders of the Small Pyramid would have installed a gabled roof above the inlet channel on the north side of this pyramid, for with such a short span they would almost certainly have put a corbelled roof above the inlet channel here, just as they had done in the Middle Pyramid. The builders of the Small Pyramid did, however, install what could have been the first gabled roof ever constructed at Giza in the granite chamber deep within the bedrock below the structure (depending on whether or not the Small Pyramid had been the first of the three principal structures to have been constructed at Giza). But they also had plenty of experience constructing corbel vaulted roofs in chambers within the pyramids at Dashur prior to the construction of all the principal pyramids at Giza. With such a short span, the inlet tunnel could easily have been bridged within a distance of only two courses, by out-stepping (corbelling) the limestone blocks in the courses above the roof level of the tunnel to bridge the gap. I should of course point out here that the builders had not put the gabled roof on the granite burial chamber when they began to create the inlet tunnel on the north side of the Small Pyramid, for although a chamber had been excavated out of the limestone bedrock at this location prior to the construction of the Small Pyramid, it was not lined with granite until after the pyramid was complete. This chamber could not have functioned as intended if it had been lined with granite prior to the construction of the pyramid (more on this later).

You will see from the isometric drawing (Fig. 35) of the subsurface layout of the chambers and pipes in the Small Pyramid, that there is an odd little channel or pipe that originates above, what eventually became, the gabled roof at the south end of the granite chamber. This channel is oriented east-west and this pipe was created when the much larger chamber here was carved out of the limestone bedrock, long before its granite lining and roof was installed. The only purpose of this small pipe was to channel water from the large limestone chamber at the extreme west end of the lower level up to the pump chamber on the west side of the distribution chamber. You will see from the drawing that there is a rectangular depression in the floor of this small chamber on the west side of the distribution chamber. The piston of the pump was located in this (pump) chamber, but in order to cushion the blow when it reached the end of its stroke, it had a large hardwood buffer fixed to its underside that bottomed on the floor of the chamber when the piston was at the end of its stroke. Although the pump would not have been in use when water flowed through the lower outlet pipe, it would certainly have been brought into use not long after the upper outlet pipe became operational. However, I've got a bit ahead of myself here again, and some explanation is required as to how water flowed through these chambers at various stages of the construction, as its flow was also redirected within these chambers after the lower outlet pipe had been sealed.

When the builders drained the water from the hydraulic system and installed the three slabs in the lower outlet pipe to block this pipe, they did so to redirect the flow of water through the upper outlet pipe. But soon after this pipe had been brought into service, the builders would have needed to pump water up to the higher levels. When they had used the lower outlet pipe to supply water to the canal on the north side of the small pyramid, water would simply have flowed through the piping system and into the canal on the north side of the pyramid; therefore they had no need of the pump at that stage of the construction. However, had they not also taken measures to redirect the flow of water through the pump chamber when they blocked the lower outlet pipe, they would have had no way of pumping water through the upper outlet pipe at the later stages of the construction. Initially, the flow of water had bypassed the pump chamber altogether when it flowed into the lower outlet pipe (the pump chamber is that small rectangular chamber at the western end of the distribution chamber) as the water flowed up the sloping pipe (with the channel up the middle of its floor) from the lower chambers and into the distribution chamber before it entered the lower outlet pipe. In order to be able to pump water into the upper outlet pipe at the later stages of the construction, the builders had to block off the sloping pipe that extends from the lower levels up into the distribution chamber. This redirected the water flow into the large limestone chamber just west of the subterranean chamber, at the far end of this lowest level, then up the short sloping pipe near its roof and on into the pump chamber. Water would have exited the large limestone chamber here through this small pipe up near its roof and it would have flowed into the pump chamber and the distribution chamber beyond. However, as I mentioned earlier, when the first few courses of the small pyramid had been under construction, the water would have flowed up the long sloping pipe in the floor of the distribution chamber from the subterranean chamber, taking the much shorter route, and bypassing the large limestone chamber and the pump room (the piston of the pump would have been bottomed in the pump room at this stage of the construction, blocking the flow of water here). It was only after the sloping pipe in the floor of the distribution chamber had been blocked that all of the water flowing into the hydraulic system was redirected through the large limestone chamber and the pump chamber *en route* to the distribution chamber. The sloping pipe in the floor of the distribution chamber would have been blocked off around the same time as the three limestone slabs had been lowered into the lower outlet pipe after the first stage of the construction was complete, certainly before the inlet valve was opened and water flowed through the hydraulic system again.

When I discovered the purpose of all the underground chambers here I was astonished by the complexity of the hydraulic system that the builders had created in the bedrock beneath this small pyramid. But looking at these empty chambers now, we get little indication of the complexity of the hydraulic system as many of the components are missing, having been destroyed by tomb robbers at some time in the distant past. One of the components that had played a vital part in the hydraulic system had in fact been carved out of the bedrock within the distribution chamber when the distribution chamber was being created. That component was the blocking stone, the one that was later slid down the sloping pipe to block it after the first stage of the construction was complete.

There were three components (five in all, but I have grouped the three blocking slabs together here) that were essential to the proper functioning of the hydraulic system in the Small Pyramid after the first stage of construction was complete. The piston for the pump is the most obvious one, but, as I just mentioned, the very large blocking stone used to block the sloping pipe, had to have been created within the distribution chamber when the chamber was being carved out of the bedrock. This blocking stone remained in the distribution chamber during the first construction phase, and it was only later, after the hydraulic system had been drained, that it was slid down the sloping pipe in the floor of the distribution chamber to seal it at its bottom end. The pump would have been all but useless if this blocking stone had not blocked off the sloping corridor after the first stage of the construction was complete, for the flow of water into the upper outlet pipe would have bypassed the large limestone chamber and the pump room, flowing directly up the sloping pipe into the distribution chamber and the upper outlet pipe. However, with the blocking stone in place, the flow of water was redirected through the large limestone chamber and the pump chamber, via the short sloping pipe section up near the roof of the limestone chamber. After the blocking slabs had been installed in the lower outlet pipe and the blocking stone had been installed at the lower end of the sloping pipe in the floor of the distribution chamber, when the piston was lowered into the small chamber at the west end of the distribution chamber – the pump chamber – water would have been pumped into the distribution chamber and on into the upper outlet pipe. Very little water would have been pumped back into the large limestone chamber by the downward stroke of the piston as there was a greater water pressure in this chamber than in the distribution chamber. This was due to the force of the water entering the hydraulic system from the inlet pipe, the opening to which was opposite the opening into the subterranean chamber, next door to the large limestone chamber. This would have been a very efficient pump.

I have now had a long time to think about how the pump was operated and I can only conclude that a shaft, similar to the lift shaft in the Great Pyramid, was created above the pump chamber. A shaft was required immediately above the pump chamber as the rectangular shaped piston of the pump had to be drawn up into this area before being released. But the pump had to be operated, and the pump operators had to have access to the chamber where the piston lifting mechanism was situated. This chamber, if indeed it was a chamber, had to have been situated some distance above the pump. However, it is entirely possible that the builders did not create a chamber to house the pump lifting mechanism in the bedrock beneath the small pyramid, but instead placed the lifting mechanism above the shaft on the foundation level initially. The piston of the pump would have been lowered down a shaft into the pump chamber at the west end of the distribution chamber when the pump was first set up. The area above this shaft could then have been almost completely covered over as the platforms here were built up, leaving only a slot in the floor or possibly a larger opening for the ropes used to hoist the piston of the pump up to the top of the pump chamber before it was released. If this had been the option chosen by the builders, the workmen on the platforms would not have needed to communicate their instructions to pump operators in a pump room far below, as the pump operators would have been in a position – on the platforms under construction – to see when water needed to be pumped up and into the ponds and locks. I therefore believe that the builders may only have created a small shaft or slot above the pump chamber (for the ropes that were used to lift and lower the piston) and placed the lifting mechanism, a shadouf or a windlass, used to raise and lower the piston of the pump, on each platform of the structure when they were under construction. When the pyramid platforms had been built up to the level of the top of the gallery, a chamber could then have been created on this level to house the pump lifting mechanism as the remaining levels of the structure were built up.

When the Small Pyramid was complete and the water had been drained from the chambers and pipes of the hydraulic system, the block that plugged the sloping corridor in the distribution chamber and the rectangular limestone block – the piston of the pump – were intact, as were the three blocking slabs in the lower outlet pipe. The builders would not have removed these components when the structure was complete, for they had good reason not to. These three components blocked the access to (what later became) the burial chamber from the passages on the north side of the structure. Therefore there is absolutely no doubt that these components would have been left *in situ* when the builders exited the structure.

Which begs the question; when were these components removed? It seems obvious why and how they were removed as I have no doubt that these limestone slabs and blocks would have been hacked to pieces by tomb robbers. After they had smashed their way through the blocking slabs in the lower outlet pipe, they would have entered the distribution chamber. They would have suspected that any burial chambers were somewhere deep within this labyrinth and no doubt realized that one of these large blocking stones, they did not know which, that they discovered at the west end of the distribution chamber, barred the way to their ultimate prize. Eventually, they were successful in their endeavours for both the piston of the pump and the blocking stone at the lower end of the sloping corridor were smashed to pieces, but as to when this occurred I have no idea.

As I mentioned earlier, I have never visited the pyramids nor been to Egypt, but if some accounts are to be believed much of the rubble from when these components were smashed to pieces still lies within the distribution chamber in the small pyramid. However, it is not what is now missing from the pump room that interests me, it is what is to be found there that I am really interested in; and that is the roof of the pump chamber here. Looking at the isometric drawing (Fig. 35) of the sub-surface chambers and pipes, it's possible that this small chamber may have had a ceiling installed when the pump was no longer needed. I have been unable to discover if this chamber has a ceiling and if so, is it comprised of one or more limestone slabs. Either way, if there is a ceiling above this chamber similar to the one above the antechamber in the Great Pyramid this ceiling had to have been installed after the pumping operations had ceased here.

Once again, if Egyptologists have any doubts as to the validity of my conclusions here, they can easily and quickly confirm that there is indeed a vertical shaft and a pump room somewhere above this ceiling, since the builders undoubtedly only sealed the bottom end of this shaft when pumping operations had been concluded here. In order to do that they would have had to enter this shaft from above as there was no way to access it from the pump chamber after the pumping operations had ceased. My conclusions could easily be confirmed by the simple process of jacking up one side of the ceiling slab, or moving it aside, and inspecting the cavity above. However, if two or more slabs have been installed, then it should be possible to simply lever the slabs apart to reveal the cavity beyond. This shaft should certainly be investigated, as we may just discover that there is a route up to the level of the top lock and the floor level at the bottom of the lift shaft in this small pyramid. If the ceiling in the pump room is intact, then it is unlikely that anyone has set foot in this part of the structure since it was completed, almost certainly more than five thousand years ago.

It is clear that a great deal of work went on within the chambers and pipes of the small pyramid after the hydraulic system had been drained and the blocking slabs had been installed in the lower outlet pipe, and it is not difficult to envisage how the pump had been set up here. When the lower outlet pipe had been drained and sealed and the upper outlet pipe created, the piston of the pump would have been lowered down the shaft and into the pump chamber from the foundation level of the structure. This would have been a rectangular block of limestone and it would have had a hardwood block attached to its underside; it was this buffer block that cushioned the blow when the piston bottomed in the chamber at the end of its down-stroke. (The piston and the buffer block can be clearly seen in the drawing (Fig. 38) on the next page.)

I eventually realized that a wooden buffer block must have been secured to the underside of the piston; it then followed that the ropes that the piston was suspended from, must have gone all the way through the limestone block and been looped under and through this buffer block to ensure that this wooden block always remained in position below the piston during the pumping operations. The builders could not simply have placed a hardwood block on the floor of the pump room to act as a buffer as this would have been buoyant and it would have floated away. The only way to ensure that it remained in position below the piston at all times was to attach it to the underside of the piston. With the buffer block in place, the lower end of the piston would have stopped short of the floor of the pump chamber at the bottom of its stroke. The top end of the piston would have been well above the opening in the top of the pump chamber when the piston bottomed the seal between the piston and the walls of the shaft above would have been maintained, preventing any great volume of water from flowing up into the shaft above the piston.

A pump mechanism would have been installed in a chamber somewhere above the pump chamber and this was most probably a

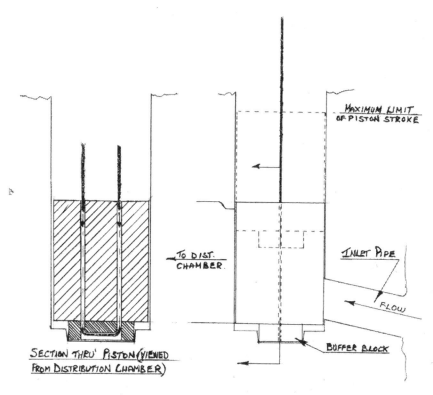

SECTION THRU' PISTON (VIEWED
FROM DISTRIBUTION CHAMBER)

MAXIMUM LIMIT
OF PISTON STROKE

TO DIST.
CHAMBER

INLET PIPE

FLOW

BUFFER BLOCK

FIGURE 38

shadouf operated by one or two men. But as I mentioned earlier, the pump in the Small Pyramid was not needed to pump water into the supply canal when the lower outlet pipe had been in use, as water would have flowed freely through this pipe and on into the supply canal on the north side of the structure. This was also the case when water first flowed up the upper outlet pipe and it was only when the builders began to construct a series of locks up through a gallery here – having blocked off the top end of the upper outlet pipe – that the piston would have been lowered into the pump chamber, cutting off the flow of water through the large limestone chamber and the distribution chamber. The builders didn't have a great head of water to work with here and the supply canal on the north side of the small pyramid was simply a branch of the feeder canal on the west side of the pyramid. But it was water from this canal on the west side of the small pyramid that flowed down into the inlet pipe after the builders diverted a branch of the feeder canal through the Small Pyramid. The feeder canal on the west side of the Small Pyramid was at a much greater elevation than the foundation levels of the two much larger pyramids here, hence the reason why their entrances are a greater distance from ground level. But the canal was only a few metres above the foundation level of the Small Pyramid that is why the opening on the north side of this pyramid is only three courses up from ground level. The foundation levels of the two large pyramids are at much lower elevations on the plateau than the foundation level of the Small Pyramid, therefore the head of water entering these structures was at a much greater elevation, relative to their foundations, than the head of water available at the site of the Small Pyramid. The builders just didn't have the same options with the Small Pyramid and that is why its subsurface chambers and pipes had to be more complex than those in the two larger pyramids at Giza.

The upper chambers and pipes

We have taken a look at the internal layout of the chambers and pipes that have so far been discovered in the Small Pyramid at Giza, but it is clear from the drawings (Figs. 35 & 36) that the layout of these chambers and pipes bears little resemblance to those in the Great Pyramid. However, what we also have to bear in mind is that all of the chambers, those that have been discovered so far, are below the foundation level of the Small Pyramid. We now know, of course, that in order to construct the pyramid, the builders had undoubtedly to create more chambers and pipes within the body of the structure itself. But although these chambers and pipes have yet to be discovered in the Small Pyramid, we can still get a pretty good idea of where they are likely to be by studying the layout of the known pipes and chambers below this structure.

In the Great Pyramid, the builders created the ascending corridor before the descending corridor intersected the north face of the structure. However, they chose not to create a similar ascending corridor in the Small Pyramid branching off from the sloping section of the lower outlet pipe here. In the Small Pyramid the entrance tunnel was created just above the third course of masonry, but here they used a different configuration of internal pipes to provide the secondary water supply to the supply canal (the ascending corridor in the Great Pyramid) that was extended into the structure on this level. That was the purpose of the upper outlet pipe.

After the lower pipe had been sealed off, water flowed up into the ponds and the supply canal through the upper outlet pipe. The canal on the north side of the pyramid was extended into the structure as far as, and beyond, the opening of the upper outlet pipe at this second stage of the construction. But why did they choose to do it this way when they could so easily have created an ascending corridor – similar to the one in the Great Pyramid – that branched off from the descending corridor in the lower outlet pipe? This puzzled me for a long time as I could see no reason why they could not have created an ascending corridor branching off from the lower outlet pipe. In the end, I could only conclude that the Small Pyramid was an earlier, less well developed, pyramid design. In other words, the Small Pyramid was built to a more primitive design therefore it was most likely to have been the first of the Super Pyramids constructed at Giza.

When the builders were constructing the last sixty five metres of the Great Pyramid all the blocks of masonry to complete it were being hauled up the lift shaft to the platforms under construction. When we look at the layout of the outlet pipes in the small pyramid (Fig. 36), we can clearly see that the upper outlet pipe is positioned to supply water to the supply canal on the north side of the pyramid, after it has been extended into the structure. However, this opening on the upper outlet pipe is still fairly close to the north side of the pyramid, so the builders must have extended the canal much further into the pyramid in order to transport the building blocks to the bottom of a lift shaft, for we now know that this shaft had to be positioned on, or near, the east-west axis of the structure. The lift shaft has not yet been discovered in the Small Pyramid but we know enough about the construction of the Great Pyramid to know that it needed to be much nearer to the centre of the structure than the top end of the upper outlet pipe here. Knowing this to be the case, I am certain that a gallery was created in the Small Pyramid to extend the supply canal further south – and up to a much greater elevation within the structure here – as a flight of locks would undoubtedly have been installed within this gallery. It is simply the only conclusion that can be drawn when we know that the builders installed a pump in this pyramid, since they had no reason to do so if they did not install a flight of locks here.

There would have been no need for a lower or upper chamber in this small structure such as we see in the Great Pyramid, for instance, as these chambers had been created in the two much larger structures in order to transport the much larger limestone blocks – used to construct the vast bulk of the lower sections of the large pyramids – up and onto the inner stepped levels and the perimeter platforms of these structures. But the Small Pyramid at Giza is smaller than the two pyramid structures installed above the perimeter platforms in the two much larger pyramids here, where all of the masonry required to complete them had been hauled up the lift shaft. There was therefore no need to create a central hub in this structure as barges would, at all times – at least until the lift shaft was required – have transported all of the masonry blocks used to build up the platforms of the structure, as near as possible to their final destinations.

We discovered earlier that the builders of the Super Pyramids had constructed a gallery on a small scale in one of the satellite structures at Dashur prior to the construction of the Small Pyramid at Giza. Due to the fact that the builders installed a pump in the Small Pyramid, I therefore have no hesitation in stating that a gallery and a lift shaft were also created within this structure. We know this to be true as this was the only way to build a pyramid on this scale using large blocks of limestone and granite (I suspect that the Small Pyramid may have been completely encased in granite when it was completed). As we now know from our reconstruction of the Great Pyramid, the outer casing blocks of these structures had to be installed on each level first. We can therefore now say for certain that there has to be a smaller version of the grand gallery in the Small Pyramid and that it must originate somewhere near the top end of the upper outlet pipe. However, as you will no doubt remember, the pipe running up the centre of the floor in the grand gallery is simply an extension of the ascending corridor; therefore it is almost certainly the case that a short ascending corridor branches off from the sloping section of the upper outlet pipe in the Small Pyramid, with a gallery beyond.

Is the end cap below the plugs in this ascending corridor still intact? Who knows! But if the shaft above the pump chamber is wide enough for a man to pass through (it must be if the builders managed to seal the roof of the pump chamber when operations ceased here), then hopefully archaeologists won't need to bypass the plugs in the ascending corridor to gain access to the gallery for they may be able to access the top end of the gallery and the lift shaft via this shaft above the pump chamber.

So why did they choose to create an ascending corridor and branch it off from the upper outlet pipe and not the lower pipe? Well, it would have been impossible to block off the top end of the lower descending corridor as it exited the north face of the structure just above the third course of masonry. You will no doubt remember that after the ascending corridor in the Great Pyramid had been plugged, the blocking stones were removed from the top end of the descending corridor, or to be precise, the pipe was extended up through this masonry. But the builders of the Small Pyramid were using smaller blocks of masonry and the top opening of the descending corridor in the lower outlet pipe was just above the foundation level. As it was, the builders would only have managed to complete five, possibly six, courses of the perimeter walls before work on the perimeter walls of the structure stopped and the hydraulic system was drained. As you will no doubt remember, when we blocked the top end of the descending corridor we slid the blocking stones / beams down the basement sheet. This pipe was blocked well inside the perimeter of the structure. As I mentioned earlier, the pyramid builders did not have the options here that they had at the construction sites of the two much larger pyramids. Here, in the Small Pyramid, it would have been impossible to block and seal the lower descending corridor since the lower outlet pipe exited the bedrock very near to the perimeter of this structure. This was not the case with the descending corridor in the Great Pyramid, as many of its courses had been established before the builders had to block the top end of the descending corridor here.

When we also consider that the entrance tunnel in the small pyramid was a single width channel, then long heavy beams such as those used to block the descending corridor in the Great Pyramid could not have been used to block this pipe. They got around this little difficulty by creating lower and upper outlet pipes and then opting to block the top end of the upper outlet pipe deep within the body of the structure. This diverted the water flow up the ascending corridor that branched off from the upper outlet pipe. It was therefore not because the Small Pyramid was a more primitive design that its subsurface chambers and pipes were so different from those in its larger companions, as I had earlier assumed, it was simply because the foundation level of the Small Pyramid was only a few metres below the level of the canal here that it had to have two outlet pipes.

Although the layout of the subsurface chambers and pipes in the Small Pyramid varies greatly from those in the Great Pyramid, the purpose of these chambers was exactly the same as those in the Great Pyramid; they were all created to facilitate the construction of these pyramids. When the pump was operated in the Small Pyramid water would have been pumped up the upper outlet pipe, or descending corridor, if you prefer this term. An ascending corridor would have been created within the structure and this would have branched off from the upper outlet pipe. Above this pipe a gallery would have been created. The water supply pipe (ascending corridor) would have been extended up to the top of this gallery under the wooden floor of the locks here, just as the builders had done in the Great Pyramid.

Can we expect to see chambers similar to those in the Great Pyramid when we discover the gallery? I think it is highly unlikely that we will find such chambers in this small pyramid. After all, if we compare this structure to the top section of the Great Pyramid, then its foundation level would be 25 metres or more above the peak of the gabled roof on top of the stack. All of the limestone to complete the Great Pyramid above this level was hauled up the lift shaft to the platforms above. I therefore believe that we will only find a lift shaft at the top of the gallery in the small pyramid and beyond that, a pump room, or access shaft to the pump room. However, I have been unable to determine if the block sizes used to construct the top section of the Small Pyramid were of a similar size to those used in the lower sections of the structure. I can therefore only conclude that if a larger block size was used to construct much of the lower section of this structure, then the builders would most likely have set up a distribution hub near the top end of the gallery, similar to the one they set up in the partially constructed lower chamber in the Great Pyramid. This would have enabled them to haul the larger sized blocks up to a much greater elevation on the perimeter platforms before they began to haul smaller blocks up the lift shaft. But I think it unlikely that this was the case here, and I suspect that the gallery was created simply to extend the canal locks up to a docking station at the bottom of a lift shaft. There would have been no real need for a distribution hub to be set up as the top end of the gallery in the Small Pyramid should be much nearer the top of this pyramid than the top end of the grand gallery in the Great Pyramid.

When we were reconstructing the Great Pyramid you will no doubt remember that after the builders had established the lower and upper chambers here, they then used these strategically placed chambers as distribution hubs. It was in these two chambers that the much larger standard blocks, used to construct the great mass of the lower sections of the structure, were hoisted up onto the sidewalls of the chambers, and then hauled up ramps on either side of the chambers to the platforms under construction. The builders needed to construct as much of the structure in the two largest pyramids using the much larger blocks of limestone they had used in the lowest courses of these structures. It was all about time. When they finally had no other option but to haul the much smaller blocks up to the platforms using the hoist, the rate of construction dropped dramatically; so it was in their interest to construct as much of these structures using the larger sized limestone blocks. However, the limestone and granite blocks used to construct the Small Pyramid are much smaller than those used in the two large pyramids; therefore there was probably no need to create a central distribution chamber with ramps on either side to haul larger blocks up to the perimeter levels. These hubs, for the distribution of the largest blocks of limestone up to the perimeter levels of the two largest structures at Giza, are almost certainly only a feature of the two large pyramids here.

I have been unable to discover if the entrance to the lower outlet pipe (descending corridor) in the Small Pyramid is offset to the east of the north-south axis of this structure. But if this is not the case and the entrance to the lower outlet pipe is on the north-south axis, then the builders would probably have extended the top end of the gallery beyond the east-west axis, to place the lift shaft some 6 or 7 metres beyond this axis (possibly less as they were using smaller blocks here). This would have given them the offset that was needed from the centre of the structure when they came to install the pyramidion on top of the Small Pyramid, and enabled them to transport the greatest volume of masonry into the pyramid in bulk.

That is how I believe that the internal layout of the shafts and chambers above the foundation level were most likely configured. But as we have yet to discover these shafts and chambers, we can't be absolutely certain as to their configuration. The only way that we will be able to say for certain how these chambers and pipes are configured is when we gain access to this area of the inner structure.

There are some quite startling differences between the Small Pyramid and its two much larger companions, apart from the size of the structures. For instance, the supply canal entered the Small Pyramid just above the third course of masonry on the north face of the structure (a much lower level than the supply canals on the two larger pyramids); the builders of the Great Pyramid created an ascending corridor and extended it in a southerly direction up to the level of the horizontal passageway to feed the supply canal deep within the structure; the builders of the Small Pyramid, however, had to create another outlet pipe (descending corridor) to feed the supply canal when it was extended into the structure. But the differences don't end there. In the Great Pyramid, for instance, water was pumped up the descending corridor and then the ascending corridor to feed the supply canal with the ascending corridor later being extended up under the floor of the locks to the top of the gallery; in the Small Pyramid, the builders pumped water up the upper outlet pipe and then into an ascending corridor and a gallery. When the supply canal had to be extended deeper into the Small Pyramid, the lower outlet pipe (descending corridor) had to be drained and sealed and the water then redirected through the upper outlet pipe to feed the canal; when it came time to extend the feeder pipe for the supply canal in the Great Pyramid farther into the structure however, the builders simply blocked up the outlet at the top of the descending corridor to redirect the flow of water up through the ascending corridor.

The granite casing blocks of the small pyramid are unfinished, unlike the smooth limestone blocks that originally encased the Great Pyramid and its immediate neighbour. Many believe that it was only the lower courses of the small pyramid that were encased in granite, and this may indeed have been the case as the heavy granite blocks may have been too heavy to haul up the lift shaft. But it's also possible that the builders may have used smaller granite blocks in the top section of the structure and encased the whole structure in granite.

The burial chamber

There are no two ways about it; this is an odd little pyramid no matter which way you look at it. For instance, after the Small Pyramid was capped and the canal lock on the north side of the structure had been dismantled, a chamber was created in the horizontal section of the lower outlet pipe. A section of the pipe was widened here to create a rectangular chamber which was then decorated (in the palace facade style) with carved panels on its walls. So far this is the only chamber discovered in any of the three principal pyramids at Giza that has any carvings or decoration and I have no idea why it was created or what purpose it served. Indeed, I have no idea how long after the completion of this pyramid that this chamber was hewn out of the bedrock. But the anomalies don't end there; after the Small Pyramid was capped and the entrance tunnel sealed, the builders then created a granite burial chamber at the very deepest level in the bedrock below the pyramid (it was here that the sarcophagus was discovered). As we discovered earlier, there had been a chamber at this location before the granite burial chamber was created and water flowed through this limestone chamber *en route* to the pump. But this chamber had been purely utilitarian in nature and the builders obviously wanted to create something much more impressive here.

The burial chamber is oriented north-south and the builders undoubtedly installed the granite linings and the gabled roof in this chamber from its south end, because we know that the inlet pipe / canal had to have been positioned on the south side of the subterranean chamber and this chamber is just next door to the granite chamber. It is therefore very likely that there exists a substantial chamber on the south side of the south wall of the granite chamber, as the builders would have required some space here to manoeuvre the barges that transported the granite slabs used to line the walls and roof of this chamber, into the limestone chamber. This space behind the south wall of the granite chamber however, may have been built up with limestone to consolidate this section of the structure after the granite slabs had been installed in the south wall of the chamber. If this is indeed the case, then the consolidation of this space could only have occurred after the king's mummy had been interred in the burial chamber as the only access to this chamber was via the water inlet pipe / tunnel on the south side of the pyramid after the structure was complete.

At this stage of the construction, there was only one way in and out of this underground warren and that was via the inlet pipe / tunnel, since the builders had long ago blocked the lower outlet pipe and sealed the lower end of the sloping corridor in the distribution chamber. The builders would therefore have had to work from the north end of the granite chamber back towards its south end as they installed its granite lining and gabled roof. The north wall of this chamber would have been the first wall to be installed. The sidewalls and the gabled roofing slabs would then have been installed. All of the granite linings on both side walls of the chamber could have been installed before the granite gables were installed; however, it's more than likely that the builders installed each pair of gables above each section of the granite wall linings as each section of the walls was completed. Either way, they would have worked from the north end of the chamber back towards its south end, and the last wall to be installed would have been the south wall of the chamber.

The granite chamber has a vaulted ceiling and although it was possible to create the vaulted ceiling after the granite gables had been installed, it is not easy to do this kind of work lying on your back, chipping away at the roof above. The builders of the pyramids were precision engineers and I think it is much more likely that the arcs on the underside of the vaulted ceiling had been formed on each pair of roofing slabs before they were installed in the chamber. Had they chosen to do it this way, then the slabs could have been stood on end so that what would later become the undersides of the slabs were vertical faces. The edges of each pair of slabs would have been prepared (machined) first and then each pair of slabs set down on one of their ends in a jig, in the vertical position. The two sides of the gable would have been brought together at the same angle as they would later have been installed in the limestone chamber. The undersides of each pair of slabs could then have been carved – or, more than likely, machined – as a vertical face. The masons would have used a wooden or metal template to ensure that the arcs on the underside of each pair of gables were uniform before they were installed, but whichever way the builders chose to do it, the vaulted ceiling in the granite chamber would have been complete before the wall at the south end of this chamber was installed.

Before we move on, I would like to point out here that the granite gables in the burial chamber are yet another example of very accurate and consistent reproduction of components used here at Giza. The finest examples of this are the coffer in the Middle Pyramid, and most probably the sarcophagus that was discovered in the Small Pyramid at Giza. Studies have been carried out on the coffer found in the Middle Pyramid at Giza and these have confirmed that advanced machining techniques had been used to produce this artefact, since it is simply impossible for the human hand to produce such consistently accurate work. I believe that the vaulted arches in the granite chamber are yet another fine example of this work and I am also certain that the granite slabs that form the vaulted ceiling were machine cut prior to their installation in this chamber.

I don't want to delve any further into this subject here, but for anyone interested in the subject I can recommend an article by Christopher Dunn which was first published in 1984 titled: *Advanced Machining in Ancient Egypt.* Chris has now written a number of articles and books on the subject of manufacturing methods in ancient Egypt that clearly involved the use of machinery and, although I don't always agree with some of Chris's theories on other matters, on the subject of advanced machining in ancient Egypt, I am in total agreement with what Chris has to say.

When the builders of the Small Pyramid were withdrawing from the gallery and the inlet tunnel they blocked up the tunnel to consolidate the structure, just as they had done when they withdrew from the inner passageways of the Great Pyramid. Finally, they dismantled the locks that had been erected in front of the entrance tunnel on the north side of the structure when the construction of the pyramid had first begun. When any water that had found its way into the lower outlet pipe had been removed, this pipe would have been readily accessible. As I mentioned earlier, I don't know when the lower outlet pipe was widened and the rectangular chamber created in the horizontal section of the pipe on the north side of the blocking slabs, but the carved panels on the walls of this chamber are in the palace facade style of the early dynastic period. It is therefore entirely possible that this chamber was created soon after the pyramid had been completed. But it may also have been much later as the pyramids at Giza may be much older than we have been led to believe.

When researching the pyramids of the west bank, I made regular visits to the guardians website (www.guardians.net) and found it invaluable. It is a mine of information, with many diagrams and photographs of the pyramids. But one photograph in particular really grabbed my attention and that is the photograph of the doorway on the north side of the Small Pyramid. If you still have any doubts that a lock was constructed at the openings on the north side of the three pyramids at Giza, then you need look no further than this photograph. You can plainly see from the photograph that the granite facing blocks around the doorway on the north side of the Small Pyramid are very smooth, unlike the other granite blocks here. Indeed, the doorway at the entrance tunnel in the Small Pyramid is totally unique as far as the principal pyramids at Giza are concerned. It is only in the Small Pyramid that the facing stones around the doorway have survived to this day. In this photograph on Andrew Bayuk's excellent website, you can clearly see that the granite blocks around the doorway in the small pyramid (attributed to Menkaure) have been dressed to a smooth finish. This was an absolute requirement here, for the builders had to ensure that they got a good seal between the face of the lock and the north face of the structure. It is only in the Small Pyramid at Giza that this feature has survived, but what a testament it is to the true methods of the ancient builders who constructed these magnificent structures.

How lucky we are to find this unequivocal proof that a canal lock was constructed here. If the builders of the Small Pyramid had chosen to encase the small pyramid with smooth casing blocks, like those used to encase the two larger pyramids, then this area around the doorway would have looked no different to any other section of the north face of the structure. But when the builders chose to leave the outer faces of the granite casing blocks on the north side of the Small Pyramid unfinished, they left us proof positive that they had constructed a canal lock at the entrance to this structure.

I mentioned earlier that a sarcophagus was discovered in the granite chamber in the Small Pyramid by Colonel Howard Vyse during his explorations here in 1837-38. A fragment of a wooden coffin was also discovered at this time, along with some bones and some cloth wrappings. These relics could only have been placed in the granite chamber long after it had been completed as they did not date to the period of the fourth dynasty. The bones were found to be from the early Christian period, and the wooden relic dated from the

Saite period (26th Dynasty 685 – 525 B.C.E.). It is therefore most obvious that various groups had been able to gain access to this chamber on a number of occasions in the past and this could only have occurred after the three blocking slabs in the lower outlet pipe, and the blocking stone at the bottom of the sloping pipe in the distribution chamber, had been breached.

Unfortunately, we can learn nothing from the sarcophagus now; it ended up at the bottom of the Mediterranean Sea when the ship that was transporting it to England sank. Although we can't be one hundred per cent certain, it is, however, almost certainly the case that this sarcophagus was contemporary with the structure and had been placed in the granite chamber before the south wall of the chamber had been completed and sealed. The later relics though, could only have been placed in the burial chamber after the blocking slabs in the lower outlet pipe and the blocking stone at the lower end of the sloping channel in the distribution chamber had been breached. I have, however, been unable to discover when the blocking slabs in the lower outlet pipe were first breached, but the relics were undoubtedly taken into the burial chamber by this route a long time after the Small Pyramid had been completed, and some time before the Vyse exploration of this structure in 1837-38.

The only other possibility here is that access to the granite chamber could have been gained via the inlet tunnel, but if that had been the case then we would undoubtedly have discovered this passageway by now. I believe that the opening to this inlet pipe / tunnel is most likely to be found somewhere near to the south-west corner of the structure, probably near the western end of the south side of the structure. This is where the three small satellite pyramids were constructed and a branch of the feeder canal would have been created here in order to transport the building materials to these structures; the water inlet pipe would simply have been an extension of this branch of the feeder canal.

The temple priests would have known how to gain access to the burial chamber by this route for if this was a true burial chamber (the granite chamber), as I believe it was, and a king's mummy had indeed been interred here, this could have occurred many years after the pyramid had been completed. However, having knowledge of the access tunnel, and being able to access it long after the king's mummy had been interred in the burial chamber, are not one and the same thing, as the burial chamber was almost certainly sealed after the king's mummy had been interred in the chamber. In order to ensure that this chamber would not be disturbed later, the builders would almost certainly have blocked up the entrance to the inlet tunnel and disguised it so that it looked no different to any other section of the foundations. They may even have blocked up the tunnel completely, from end to end, to ensure that no one could gain access to the burial chamber by this route ever again. This inlet tunnel has not yet been discovered and it is almost certainly the case that it was sealed after a king's mummy had been interred in the granite chamber, possibly not long after the structure had been completed. Based on these facts, I have to say that the relics mentioned earlier could only have been placed in the granite chamber after access had been gained through the lower outlet pipe and the distribution chamber.

So what of the sarcophagus? Was the granite chamber really the tomb of a king that had been robbed in antiquity? As you are aware, I have stated more than once that I do not believe that the pyramids were constructed as tombs for kings or pharaohs, so surely the Small Pyramid contradicts this statement? Not at all, the burial chamber is a chamber located deep in the bedrock below the Small Pyramid. That to me is the most logical location for such a tomb to be sited and I do not doubt that other tombs of kings will be discovered deep below the foundation levels of the two much larger pyramids on this site.

There is a very real possibility that access to these tombs was gained via the mortuary temples on the east side of these two pyramids. After all, wouldn't it have made perfect sense to have direct access to the burial chambers from the mortuary temples themselves – where presumably the bodies of the kings would have been taken after death? I've always believed that the tombs of the kings responsible for the construction of the pyramids at Giza would be found very near to these pyramids, but that these tombs would most likely have been created in the bedrock deep beneath the structures here. This is exactly what we see in the small pyramid at Giza, as the granite chamber is on the deepest subterranean level within the warren of pipes and chambers beneath this small structure. But we also know that both here, and in the Great Pyramid, there are inlet tunnels that have yet to be discovered. If the inlet tunnel in the small pyramid was almost certainly the access tunnel for the burial vault here, is it not therefore possible that a burial chamber could have been created somewhere along the inlet tunnel deep within the bedrock beneath the Great Pyramid also? Whether that burial chamber was accessed from the opening to the inlet tunnel south and west of the Great Pyramid, or from the mortuary temple on the east side of the structure, I do not know; but I am certain that burial chambers will one day be found below the two largest structures on the Giza Plateau.

Now I want to take you back to the Great Pyramid as I clearly stated earlier that it was the last of the three principal pyramids at Giza to be constructed. I believe that the water reservoir for the feeder canal on the west side of the Small Pyramid, and on the north sides of both the Small Pyramid and the Middle Pyramid, was somewhere west or south-west of the Giza Plateau. However, I think that it's highly likely that this same water reservoir also supplied water to the canal system at Dashur, south of Giza, for I believe that a canal – the orientation of which was north-south – was constructed to the west side of both of these pyramid fields, and it would almost certainly have been in use when the pyramids were under construction at both of these sites. This canal may not only have supplied water to the pyramid sites at Dashur for limestone may also have been quarried somewhere in the hills west of the canal and it is possible that masonry was also transported south to Dashur along this canal when the pyramids there were under construction. (This canal would have skirted the eastern edge of the hills on the west bank of the Nile and it may have been extended as far south as Meidum, as a vast quantity of quarried limestone was also required for the large pyramid constructed there.)

It is fairly easy to discern the route of this canal on the Giza Plateau itself, for we know that all of the building materials were taken into the Small Pyramid on its north side via this canal. But the feeder canal also supplied water to the inlet pipe on the north side of the Middle Pyramid, and to the inlet pipe that originated somewhere south-west of the Great Pyramid. The single channel canal would also have been extended beyond the east side of the Middle Pyramid to the stone quarries there, and as far as the massive lock / dry dock constructed on the east side of the Sphinx Enclosure. A supply of water was needed for the locks here and this is the most likely source of that water supply. It is also likely that barges would have been able to enter and exit the single channel canal system through the locks on the eastern edge of the plateau here (Fig. 33).

For a number of reasons I had believed that the builders would have constructed the Small Pyramid first. When I later realized that the builders had diverted a branch of the feeder canal through the Great Pyramid, I could only conclude that the Great Pyramid had to have been constructed after the Middle Pyramid. But when I later began to make some headway with the pipes and chambers in the Small Pyramid – after I had completed my reconstruction of the Great Pyramid – I then realized that the Small Pyramid could indeed have been the last of the three principal pyramids to be constructed here as Egyptologists believe. Unlike the two largest structures, the dual channel supply canal was never extended as far as the Small Pyramid. The single channel feeder canal however, would most probably have been in operation long after the dual channel supply canal had been decommissioned, and as it was a branch of this canal that was diverted through the Small Pyramid when it was under construction, this pyramid could therefore have been constructed before, or after, the two much larger pyramids here.

I mentioned earlier that work could have gone on for many decades on the plateau after the Great Pyramid and its nearest companion had been completed. This was possible because a great deal of limestone was quarried on, or near, the plateau itself and what I had termed the feeder canal on the south side of the Great Pyramid would in fact have been used as the supply canal to transport building materials to a number of locations on the plateau where the peripheral structures were under construction. Water from this canal system would have been discharged from the locks on the eastern side of the plateau to the River Nile.

Before work began at Giza however, we know that an extensive canal system already existed at Dashur. It is entirely possible, and highly likely, that it was this canal system that was extended north to the Giza plateau. I believe that the builders would have used the same water reservoir to provide the water resources for both of these projects via this canal. If this had indeed been the case, then the builders of the Small Pyramid and the peripheral structures would have had the option of transporting granite and other building materials to the construction site at Giza from Dashur or from quarries on the west bank. The barges carrying these materials could have entered the canal system at the locks at Dashur, and then made their way north to the site of the Small Pyramid at

Giza. As limestone was also quarried on the plateau itself, much of this limestone could have been used to construct the Small Pyramid. I therefore have to conclude that the builders of the pyramids at Giza could have postponed the construction of the Small Pyramid and most of the peripheral structures on the plateau until they had constructed the two much larger structures here, as they had no shortage of options when it came to the transportation of building materials after the dual channel supply canal had been decommissioned.

When I first realized that a dual channel supply canal had been constructed on the north side of the Great Pyramid I had believed that this was the supply canal for all three pyramids at Giza. It was this misconception that led me to believe that the Small Pyramid had been constructed first. It was only later, when I realized that the dual channel supply canal had only been extended as far as the Middle Pyramid, that I realized that the Small Pyramid could have been built at any time before, during, or after the construction of the much larger structures here.

There is one thing that does trouble me about the Small Pyramid though, and that is the unfinished nature of the granite casing blocks at the lower levels of the pyramid. This could be an indication that this was a much less refined structure than its two companions and therefore, possibly an earlier structure. But although the outer faces of these blocks are, to our eyes, unfinished, this may in fact have been the effect the builders desired here, for if the outer casing of the Small Pyramid had originally been encased in granite it would have been very impressive indeed when it was complete, despite the rough texture of its faces. All we know for certain when we look at what remains of the granite casing today, is that most of the casing blocks were installed when the lower courses of the structure were being built up; the smooth finish on the granite casing blocks around the doorway is testament to this. These blocks had to be dressed to a smooth finish here for this is where the canal entered the structure, and a good seal was needed between the sides of the lock and the north face of the structure.

When I first set out on this final quest to discover how the Great Pyramid had been constructed, and for a long time after, I concentrated all of my efforts on the Great Pyramid itself. It was only later, when I began to compare the internal layouts of the other two structures at Giza with the internal layout in the Great Pyramid, that I became fully familiar with the internal layout of the small and middle pyramids. For a long time after, I believed that the design of the internal pipes and chambers within the Small Pyramid was of a more primitive nature and this certainly led me to believe that the Small Pyramid had been constructed much earlier than its two companions. Years later, when I had completed my reconstruction of the Great Pyramid and had more time to study the Small Pyramid, I realized that the Small Pyramid had two outlet pipes on its north side, not an inlet and an outlet pipe as I had first assumed. As I slowly began to understand what part the various pipes and chambers in the Small Pyramid had played in its construction, I began to realize that the internal structure of this small pyramid had been laid out in the way that it was, simply because of the limitations of this site.

Although its chambers and pipes are configured very differently from those in the Great Pyramid, all of the elements of the hydraulic system that we see in the Small Pyramid, with the exception of a distribution chamber, are present in the Great Pyramid. The descending corridor(s), the subterranean chamber and the pump are common to both structures. However, the builders of the Small Pyramid could not create an ascending corridor as a branch of the lower descending corridor here, as the descending corridor exited the north face of the structure at a very low level, too near to ground level for this to be possible. It would not have been possible to cap and seal the lower outlet pipe in order to divert the flow of water into an ascending corridor at this stage of the construction and still establish the first few courses of the perimeter wall here.

As we now know, the builders got around this little difficulty by creating a second outlet pipe above the level of the original outlet pipe to provide a feed for the supply canal well within the northern boundary of the structure. This is the reason that a distribution chamber exists within the underground chambers and pipes of the Small Pyramid and not in the Great Pyramid, for a second opening on the north wall of this chamber had to be created when the upper outlet pipe was created. Before the valve on the water inlet pipe was reopened and water flowed through the hydraulic system again, the lower outlet pipe was blocked up, and the sloping pipe in the floor of the distribution chamber was also blocked up. With these actions, the builders not only redirected the water from the lower of the two outlet pipes to the upper pipe, they also redirected the flow of water through the large rectangular chamber (the chamber that was later lined with granite facings after the upper structure of the pyramid was complete) and the pump chamber. They were then set up to pump water up into the ponds and the supply canal when it became necessary to do so. When they later created an ascending corridor and a gallery to extend the supply canal up to the lower end of the lift shaft, water would have been pumped up under the floor of the locks in this gallery, just as the builders had done (or would do) in the Great Pyramid. (I don't know which of these structures was constructed before the other.)

So the Small Pyramid at Giza is not so very different from its two larger companions after all, as the builders used their great knowledge of hydraulics and the exact same construction methods to construct the Small Pyramid, as they did to construct the two much larger structures here. But the limitations of this site and the much smaller size of the Small Pyramid is what most influenced the configuration of its chambers and pipes. This makes it impossible to determine if this really is a more primitive structure, and therefore an earlier structure than the Great Pyramid, based on the layout of its chambers and pipes.

Pyramid dating

Between the years 1984 and 1995 over 450 test samples containing organic material were collected from monuments of the Old and Middle Kingdoms. The lime mortar used in the construction of these monuments contains small pieces of charcoal. This charcoal was from the fires that burned in the limekilns and this organic material can be carbon dated. (Limekilns were used to produce quicklime used in the manufacture of lime mortar.) However, although a good number of these samples were submitted, not all of the 450 samples taken from these monuments were suitable for testing.

Although a great deal of organic material was collected from many of the monuments of the Old Kingdom and the Middle Kingdom it was the results of the samples taken from the three principal pyramids at Giza that I was most interested in. The compilers of the data in *The 1995 Radiocarbon project* included all of the results – those regarded as reliable – of the samples tested over the period 1984 – 1995, and they used these results to determine the mean age of each monument based on the average test result. I'm sure that many Egyptologists would have been surprised by the test results but I'm glad to say that those results were entirely consistent with the discoveries I have made at Giza.

The mean date for the charcoal samples taken from the Great Pyramid was 4,147 B.C.E. However, the mean age of the charcoal found in the mortar samples taken from the Middle Pyramid at Giza was 4,174 B.C.E. – twenty seven years prior to the mean date of the samples taken from the mortar in the Great Pyramid. The test results therefore showed that samples taken from the mortar in the Middle Pyramid were slightly older than the samples taken from the mortar in the Great Pyramid.

I must point out here, however, that this was the mean dates of the wood (charcoal) used to produce the mortar in these structures, not the mean construction dates of the pyramids themselves. We therefore can't read too much into this as the age of the wood used in the limekilns could have varied considerably. Given that there are only twenty seven years mean difference in the mortar samples from both of these pyramids, we therefore cannot use this data to confirm that the Middle Pyramid was the first of the two major pyramids to be constructed at Giza as the degree of error could be many times greater than this. All we can say for certain at this time is that this evidence doesn't contradict my findings.

To establish an order for the construction of the three principal pyramids at Giza however, we need to know when the Small Pyramid was constructed. This was, after all, the one that I was not sure about as it could have been constructed prior to the others, or later, as we discovered earlier. The carbon 14 dating of the mortar samples taken from the Small Pyramid produced a mean date of 4,132 B.C.E. – fifteen years after the mean date for the mortar samples taken from the Great Pyramid.

Once again, the dating did not prove that the Small Pyramid had been constructed after the Great Pyramid – or the Middle Pyramid – but, based on the mean date of 4,132 B.C.E. it is certainly possible that the Small Pyramid could have been constructed after the Great Pyramid. However, with such small differences between the mean dates of the charcoal samples taken from all of the principal pyramids, we can only conclude that the dating of the charcoal samples provides no real positive evidence as to the order of construction of the principal pyramids at Giza, as the ages of the wood used in the limekilns could have varied greatly. (Egypt would have had forests and woodlands of its own when the pyramids were built; it would have had a very different and much wetter climate then.)

I cannot say that the carbon dating results have brought any clarity to the issue of the Small Pyramids' construction date, since the margins of error in such dating methods are far greater than the time differential between the earliest mean date and the latest mean date we have for the three principal pyramids. But they are nonetheless very interesting and that is why I have mentioned them here for the mortar samples show that the pyramids at Giza could have been constructed a thousand years or more before the time of Khufu, the supposed builder of the Great Pyramid.

As I had discovered during my quest, the Small Pyramid at Giza was the only one of the three principal pyramids where the builders had the option of deciding when they would construct it. The Great Pyramid however, had to be constructed after the Middle Pyramid, as the building material for the Middle Pyramid was transported all the way from the basin below the escarpment on the north side of the plateau to the Middle Pyramid along the dual channel supply canal. This supply canal would undoubtedly have cut across the site where the Great Pyramid was later constructed for the pyramid builders would have made great use of much of this supply canal infrastructure when they came to build the Great Pyramid. This was the most logical and most efficient way of making use of the canal infrastructure and the builders certainly wouldn't have constructed two branches of the supply canal when one was all that was needed. The water from the single channel feeder canal south and west of the Great Pyramid, on the north side of the Middle Pyramid, was only channelled down through the bedrock beneath the foundations of the Great Pyramid to feed the supply canal on the north side of this structure (via the subterranean chamber and the descending corridor) after the Middle Pyramid had been completed.

When the Great Pyramid was complete, the dual channel supply canal on the north side of the structure became redundant as the builders had no further use for it. The basin below the escarpment on the north side of the plateau had been created to accommodate the supply barges used to transport building material up to the two largest pyramids on the plateau. The flight of locks and the supply canal on the north side of these pyramids had been two lanes wide to accommodate two-way traffic all the way to the bottom of the grand gallery in the Great Pyramid and to the doorway of the entrance tunnel in the Middle Pyramid, prior to work commencing on the Great Pyramid. The single lane system on the west side of the plateau, and the east-west branch of this canal on the south side of the Great Pyramid, was not up to the job as a supply canal when the two largest structures here were under construction. It would have taken a much longer time to complete these enormous structures using only a single channel system. By setting up a two-way system on the north side of the two largest pyramids, a continuous flow of building material was transported to both of these structures when they were under construction.

As we discovered earlier, it's possible that the small pyramid was indeed constructed after its two much larger companions. This was made possible simply because the granite and any other building materials used in the construction of this small structure could have been transported from the locks at Dashur along the canal on the west side of the pyramid fields, all the way to the construction site at Giza. As you will no doubt remember, this is where the Super Pyramid builders constructed what were, quite possibly, the very first flight of locks from the River Nile up to the plateau on the west side of the river. It was here that they also constructed two very large Super Pyramids prior to the construction of the pyramids at Giza.

The pyramid builders at Dashur had to tap into an existing water source or, more than likely, a water reservoir was created in the hills west, possibly north-west, of this pyramid field. An extensive canal system had to have been created at Dashur in order to supply water to the locks for the transportation of the building materials up to the plateau to build the pyramids here. However, the builder's ultimate goal was to build at Giza and they would almost certainly have created a water reservoir in the hills that would have provided the water for the canal systems at both Dashur and Giza. The canal system at Dashur therefore was almost certainly part of the same canal system that served Giza. The locks at Dashur could have been in constant use until the builders had completed all of the Super Pyramids on the west bank. In fact, much of the granite masonry, and possibly some limestone masonry, could have been transported north along the canal on the west bank from the locks at Dashur for many of the smaller structures at Giza.

But this was not the only option when it came to transporting building materials up to the plateau on the single channel canal system. The section of the single channel feeder canal, the orientation of which was east-west on the northern side of the Middle Pyramid – and on the northern side of the limestone quarries on the plateau east of the Middle Pyramid – could also have been used to transport masonry in either direction. There was undoubtedly a flight of locks on the east side of the plateau near the Sphinx and Valley Temples where barges could enter and exit the single channel canal system. In his book *Egyptian Dawn*, Robert Temple draws the reader's attention to points he had made earlier in his book *The Sphinx Mystery*. On page 343 he states;

> "I also explained that the reason why there is no access to the Sphinx through the west wall of the Sphinx Temple is because it acted as the eastern barrier to a moat..."

He goes on to say:

> "In the *Sphinx Mystery* I suggested that the Sphinx pit in which the Sphinx sits was in Old Kingdom times a moat filled with water."

He later writes;

> "I also published a series of detailed photos showing the evidence of sluice-gate bolt holes and other indications of water control mechanisms that were used in the passage between the two temples..."

Robert Temple may be correct in his assertion that the Sphinx was surrounded by water in ancient times but he is probably unaware that the two temples here were constructed within an enormous lock / dry dock. The huge monoliths used to construct these temples could only have been moved from the quarry (Sphinx Enclosure) to these construction sites on barges as they were much too heavy to be moved by any other means. As I mentioned earlier, the passageway created between these temples was a channel that formed part of the canal system constructed on the plateau, prior to the construction of the pyramids here. It was through this channel that barges would have entered and exited the canal system and there would indeed have been lock gates (sluices) at that time in this channel. When all the construction work on the plateau had been completed, the sluices located in the channel between the two temples may indeed have been used to retain water in a small lake within the Sphinx Enclosure, as proposed by Robert Temple.

A tremendous amount of limestone was quarried on the plateau, just east of the Middle Pyramid and all of this limestone would have been transported to the various construction sites of the smaller peripheral structures on the plateau via the single channel canal system. However, some of this limestone could also have been used in the construction of the smallest of the three principal pyramids here.

Although the carbon dating of the charcoal found in the mortar of the pyramids at Giza tells us little about the possible order of construction of the principal pyramids, it does provide us with a very strong indication that the pyramids at Giza could have been constructed long before the time of Khufu, as all of the mean dates are considerably earlier than the dates that most Egyptologists attribute to the construction of the pyramids at Giza by a very large margin. As I mentioned earlier, we have to bear in mind that these are the mean dates of the wood (charcoal) used in the mortar making process and not the mean dates of the mortar itself; but the balance of probability surely puts the dates for the construction of the pyramids at Giza well into the fourth millennium B.C.E. This dating is clearly at odds with the theory that Khufu, Khafre and Menkaure were the builders of the pyramids at Giza, unless these kings reigned much earlier than the currently accepted dates for them. However, if these structures were very old in Khufu's time, it is entirely possible that the monuments here were simply repaired and restored during the reigns of these three fourth dynasty kings. They could, as Graham Hancock has suggested, simply have claimed these temples and pyramids as their own after this restoration was complete. Although this is not the view of the Egyptological establishment, I am certainly not alone in believing this to be the case.

Now that we know what was required to put these structures on the plateau, in my opinion it is much more likely that these monuments were constructed sometime around the middle of the fourth millennium B.C.E. – a thousand years before Khufu.

However, we are unlikely to discover the true builders of the three principal pyramids at Giza until we discover an intact tomb under one of these structures.

The Super Pyramids at Dashur and Giza had to be constructed at a time when rainfall was plentiful in Lower Egypt and my research had shown that the consensus of opinion was that the climate in this region was almost certainly much too dry in the middle of the third millennium B.C.E. How much earlier these structures could have been constructed we do not know but it had to have been at a time when there was ample rainfall to replenish the water levels in the water reservoir(s) on a regular basis. I was certainly not surprised to discover that the carbon 14 dating seems to indicate that most of the structures at Giza were probably constructed sometime in the early to mid fourth millennium B.C.E. and I was certain that by the time of Khufu (2589-2566 B.C.E.), the age of the Super Pyramids was part of the ancient past. However, the carbon 14 dating of the mortar samples to the early part of the fifth millennium B.C.E. is not the only evidence that we have that indicates that the monuments at Giza could possibly be much older than previously thought. In the 1990s, John Anthony West and Robert M. Schoch, Ph.D. produced research data indicating that the Sphinx at Giza was rain-weathered and therefore much older than what we had previously been led to believe. Schoch has stated that he believes that the Sphinx dates back to at least circa 5,000 B.C.E. based on his scientific studies at Giza. Furthermore, since West and Schoch first went public with their findings there have been at least two other independent studies undertaken at the Sphinx Enclosure to determine its age. These studies support most of the analysis and many of the conclusions drawn by Schoch in his earlier study of the Sphinx and the Sphinx Enclosure.

I also believe that the Sphinx and the Sphinx and Valley Temples are the oldest structures on this site as it is only here, and in part of the foundations of the Middle Pyramid, that we find enormous monoliths used in the construction of these structures. I have reason to believe that these structures are much older than all the pyramids on the west bank and hope to prove to you later that the ancient builders of the Sphinx and Valley Temples scaled down the block sizes that they had used in these earlier structures in order to build the Super Pyramids; it would have been impossible to build these structures using such huge monoliths. When we further consider that a channel was created between these two temples during their construction, and that there is evidence to indicate that a canal lock or sluice was installed in that channel, we can be almost certain that these two temples were constructed prior to some, possibly all of the Super Pyramids here.

When we consider all of this evidence, and the fact that the Super Pyramids of Dashur and Giza simply couldn't have been constructed without the use of hydraulic power, then there is little doubt that the Giza complex as a whole is very much older than the fourth dynastic period. It is also very clear that Lower Egypt was host to a highly developed people with great scientific knowledge and great technical skills long before the historical period. These people could only have gained this knowledge over many generations. The ancient Egyptians attributed their civilisation to 'the gods' and to the Shemsu Hor, the 'Followers of Horus'. We don't know the people responsible for the construction of the Super Pyramids of the west bank and the monuments on the Giza plateau but it's certainly possible that these structures were created long before the dynastic period?

There are a great many questions to be answered with regard to the pre-dynastic period and I'm sure that most of the answers will elude us for a long time, if not forever (the further back that we delve, the less we find in the way of physical evidence). We can only hope that now that the Great Pyramid has given up its secrets, new discoveries will be made in the near future that shed more light on this very obscure period and the people who built these magnificent structures. Due to the work of a few intrepid investigators who continually challenge the orthodox position with regard to the Giza Complex, work will continue until the evidence is so overwhelming that the orthodox position on the structures at Giza will become untenable. Real headway will only be made when all of the misconceptions and misdirection of the past have been swept away by the avalanche of evidence that has built up over the last few decades. It can't come soon enough.

Although we know so very little about the people who built the Super Pyramids, there is no shortage of evidence of advanced machining techniques, advanced mathematics and geometry, and phenomenal astronomical and geodetic knowledge relating to the pyramids at Giza. Hopefully it won't be too long before many more pieces of the puzzle fall into place and we gain a much better understanding of this ancient civilisation.

The carbon 14 dating results I referred to earlier clearly show that the Small Pyramid could in fact have been the last of the three principal pyramids to be constructed at Giza. However, as there is only fifteen years between the dates of the mortar samples from the Small Pyramid and the dates of the samples from the Great Pyramid, we can't consider this to be proof of anything as the margin for error in this type of testing is many times greater than this small differential. There is a forty four year differential between the age of the mortar samples from the Small Pyramid and the mortar samples from the Middle Pyramid and, once again, this is still a smaller differential than the margin of error in this method of dating (about plus or minus 75 years if I have interpreted the data correctly). So as I mentioned earlier, all that we can really say for sure is that these dating results do not contradict the true order of construction of the two largest pyramids at Giza.

There was however one really surprising result from the carbon 14 dating of the mortar samples. If the mean dates of the samples are accurate, then the structure attributed to Djedfre at Abu Roash (mortar samples radiocarbon dated to circa 4229 B.C.E.) is older than the pyramids at Giza and Dashur. Unfortunately, not very much of this structure survives as its masonry has been plundered for centuries and it is difficult to glean very much from the bare bones of the structure that remains. However, whether this was a pyramid or some other structure we can only conclude that the canal system constructed on the west bank of the Nile must have been extended as far as this structure north of Giza, as hydraulic power was the only way to construct these monuments built with large dressed blocks of stone.

What we can now say for certain though, is that a very extensive canal system was created on the west bank of the Nile long before the Super Pyramids at Giza were under construction. Now that we know for certain that such a system existed, hopefully it won't be too long before archaeologists begin to build up a picture of this network from evidence on the ground, if it is still to be found. The topography of the area west of Giza and Dashur should provide a good clue as to the possible sites of reservoirs. Hopefully, we won't have to wait too long before this very important site is discovered as none of the Super Pyramids on the west bank could have been constructed without it. Although we have already learned a great deal about the canal system from the discoveries we have made at Giza, the discovery of the site of the reservoir would give us a much better understanding of the layout and possible extent of this ancient canal system on the west bank.

As we have discovered, the Small Pyramid at Giza differs from the two much larger pyramids in many ways. I cannot, for instance, offer any explanation as to why the builders decided to encase the lower courses in granite, or to why these granite casing blocks were not dressed to a smooth finish, like the casing blocks of the two much larger pyramids. We know that the builders had to dress the granite blocks around the doorway to a smooth finish to ensure a good seal between the lock and the north face of the structure yet they left all the others in a rough state. I'm sure they must have had their reasons but this seems to be completely at odds with the great lengths they went to in the Great Pyramid to dress the granite blocks in the upper chamber to a superb finish; all the more so when we consider that the granite blocks that comprise the walls of the upper chamber were never intended to be seen again after the structure was complete. However, it is very difficult for us to understand such things when we live in a time so far removed from the time of the pyramid builders and, as I mentioned earlier, it could simply be that the builders wanted to create a certain visual effect or contrast when they did not dress the granite casing blocks of the small pyramid to a smooth finish. Without an understanding of the mindset of its builders we are unlikely to discover why these granite blocks were not dressed to a smooth finish. However, as I mentioned earlier, I believe that there is overwhelming evidence of advanced machining techniques having been employed by the ancient pyramid builders and it is almost certainly the case that much of this machining would have taken place at the quarries; before the masonry was transported to the various construction sites. This would almost certainly have been the case with the granite blocks and beams used in the construction of the upper chamber in the Great Pyramid and here the sides of these blocks are at right angles to one another and to the ends of the blocks. However, that is not the case with the granite facing blocks around the doorway of the Small Pyramid and it is entirely possible that the sloping faces of the granite blocks here were hand dressed after they had been installed. There are some blocks here that have only part of their sloping outer faces dressed to a smooth finish and this may be an indication that these blocks were hand dressed on site, after all, surely if these faces had been machined prior to the installation of these blocks the builders would have machined the whole face of these blocks after they had gone to the trouble of setting up a machine for this cutting operation? Fortunately, this is something that can easily be determined as it is impossible to hand dress a piece of granite to a smooth flat surface such as a machine would produce.

It may have been the smallest of the three principal pyramids at Giza but until we discovered how it had been constructed this small pyramid was just as great a puzzle to us as its two much larger companions. It's most likely that the sarcophagus was placed in the granite chamber around the time of the completion of this pyramid when the rectangular chamber was lined with granite, but I am certain that this was long before the time of Menkaure. I believe that the relics found in this chamber were placed in this chamber long after the blocking slabs in the lower outlet pipe had been breached. This would have been a very long time after the reign of Menkaure, in fact, it is possible that these relics were taken into this pyramid within the last two hundred years. Either way, they tell us absolutely nothing about this structure whatsoever.

I am certain that there would have been a small gallery created within the Small Pyramid, similar to the one constructed in the small pyramid on the south-side of the Bent Pyramid. When we looked at the pyramids at Dashur, we could clearly see that the builders of the Super Pyramids were adept at constructing corbel vaulted ceilings in some of the chambers there, both on the horizontal plane and on an angled plane. This was undoubtedly a standard method of construction by this time and I have no doubt that the entrance tunnel and the gallery in the Small Pyramid at Giza were constructed in this same manner. I do, however, appreciate that until we discover these features in the Middle Pyramid and the Small Pyramid at Giza there will be some who will doubt their existence.

The Small Pyramid certainly has some pipes and chambers yet to be discovered, as has its companions, but we now have a great understanding of how all the principal pyramids at Giza were constructed, and a much greater understanding of the abilities of the people who built them. But I suspect that these structures may yet spring a few more surprises on us before we have fully explored all of their internal pipes and chambers.

It is very difficult to determine when the climate in northern (lower) Egypt became too dry to provide the water resources to construct Super Pyramids but this is undoubtedly the reason why we see no more of these large, stone built structures after Giza. However, in April 2012, I watched part one of an excellent BBC series on ancient cultures titled *Ancient Apocalypse, The Fall of the Egyptian Old Kingdom,* and I discovered that Professor Fekri Hassan had discovered the true cause behind the collapse of the Egyptian Old Kingdom c. 2200 B.C.E. To quote Professor Hassan:

> "the initial breakdown of the Old Kingdom was caused by a sudden, unanticipated, catastrophic reduction in the Nile floods over two or three decades. This was so severe that famine gripped the country and paralysed the political institutions."

It is plain to see from Professor Hassan's research that the climate in Egypt was very dry by the time of the sixth dynasty and that Egypt relied upon the annual inundation – the Nile floods – each June to provide the water resources to irrigate their crops. We certainly can't say for certain on the basis of his research that the climate was too dry two or threecenturies earlier during the time of the fourth dynasty when the pyramids at Giza were presumed to have been constructed, since we just don't know when it became too dry to construct large, stone built pyramids – Super Pyramids. But Professor Hassan's research clearly indicates why we don't find any Super Pyramids after the end of the Old Kingdom.

We must not presume, however, that later dynasties did not use hydraulic power and canals to transport massive obelisks and huge blocks of masonry from quarries to construction sites; it is just that all of these later constructions were on much lower ground where the canals were simple extensions of the River Nile. The annual inundations did return after this long period of drought and famine at the end of the sixth dynasty and I do not doubt that the builders of many of the great monuments during the Middle and New Kingdom periods exploited this annual increase in the river levels to both transport, and aid the installation of many obelisks, statues and monoliths at many ancient sites. In fact, many of the huge obelisks and statues that were installed at many of these ancient sites on the east bank of the Nile could only have been transported to these sites by canal barge as they are much too large to have been hauled overland to these sites from the quarries. Each year, with the annual inundation, builders had the opportunity to trap great quantities of water in huge canal locks at these sites and position the barges with these great obelisks within the locks in such a way that, when the waters receded and the water in the locks drained away, the lower ends of the obelisks were lowered into a previously prepared pit or socket. The obelisks would then have been hauled up into the vertical position and the lock then dismantled. These later builders, however, could not consider building their great temple complexes and monuments up on high plateaus like the ancient builders of old, but just like those builders of old they used their ingenuity and the resources that were available to them to build some of the most magnificent structures the world has ever seen.

Before we move on, I would just like to point out that the smallest of the three principal pyramids at Giza has eight sides, just like the Great Pyramid. Does this mean that it was also constructed after the builders encountered problems with the middle pyramid? I certainly think that the balance of probability favours a construction date after that of the Middle Pyramid.

Chapter Nine

Early development

At some time in the very remote past there was a period of rapid development in pyramid construction in Egypt and the main contributing factor was the harnessing of water power for the transportation of large quantities of building materials. The River Nile had long been used for transportation and its flood waters had probably been contained and distributed by means of dams, dykes, sluices and canals for irrigation purposes long before the dynastic period. But at some point prior to the dynastic period the canal lock was invented.

Before the completion of the Aswan High Dam in 1970, the River Nile annually overflowed its banks in June. This was the annual inundation and the farmers along the banks of the Nile understood that the fertility of their soil was directly linked to the silt that the Nile's floodwaters deposited on their land each year. But the annual flood was also a time of great concern for the farming families of the fertile lands that flanked the Nile, for they had no way of knowing in advance how small or how great these floods would be. If the floods were poor, then little silt (nutrients) was deposited on the farmlands (it was only the fields nearest the river that would receive any nutrients in the years when the floodwaters were very low). But some years the flood levels could be much too high, devastating the farming communities along the banks of the river. The farmers of the fertile land that straddled the river had no way of knowing how far from the river the floodwaters would extend each year, but this same annual flood event had played out year after year for millennia and the families living in the fertile belt had to cope as best they could, no matter how great the flood.

I don't want to go into this in any great detail here as numerous articles and essays have been written on the subject but I have raised it simply to make the point that on numerous occasions, when the Nile floods were very high, they would have carried vessels that slipped their moorings on the riverbank far inland. Indeed, anything that floated, anything that was not firmly secured would have been carried away by the devastating floods when they were exceptionally high. On some of these occasions, it's very likely that some vessels would have been left high and dry (stranded) far from the river as the floodwaters receded.

People living in this fertile belt that straddled the Nile must have witnessed the phenomcnal power of the Nile's water time and time again as it moved objects of considerable size and weight up to much greater elevations far from the riverbanks. Some of these people would also have been responsible for the care and maintenance of the myriad of small dams, sluices and irrigation channels that were used to trap much of the floodwater for irrigation purposes when the floodwaters of the Nile receded. It therefore doesn't take a great leap of imagination to understand how the canal lock came into being, for if large vessels could be lifted up to these higher elevations by the power of water, then surely the opposite was true also.

A controlled release of water from one level to another in a narrow channel was what was needed in order to get these vessels back down to the river when the waters receded. The farmers here had probably been doing just that for thousands of years on a much smaller scale with their sluices and irrigation channels, and the channels and sluices they later created for the purpose of transportation were simply larger, more robust versions of the former. The only prerequisite for a system of locks where barges could be transported up to higher ground when the river was not in spate was a water source, a reservoir, at a greater elevation.

About 50 kilometres south of Cairo lies the Faiyum depression and there is a small lake here (Birket Qarun). There was once a much larger lake here (Lake Moeris) and this lake was first recorded around 3,000 B.C.E. The small salt water lake that exists in the Faiyum today is 43 metres below sea level; however, when the climate was much wetter there was a much larger lake here, a freshwater lake. The land around this freshwater lake was some of the most productive farmland in Egypt. Most years the flood waters of the Nile would overflow into the Faiyum depression, greatly increasing the water level of the lake. Records show that around 2,300 B.C.E. the channel from the Nile to the lake was widened and deepened, creating the canal that is known today as the Bahr Youssef. Unfortunately, due to those widening and deepening operations, we now have no way of determining how early the people of this region first created a canal and locks here; the later work to widen the channel would have obliterated any evidence of such prior activity here. It is, however, most likely that it was in this channel that the very first locks – wide enough for barges to pass through – were installed. When the water levels in the lake were high, barges would have been able to gain access to the lake through the canal locks. These same barges would then have been used to transport grain and produce from the fertile areas around the lake, through the narrow channel to the River Nile beyond. This once fertile area has supported human cultures for more than 8,000 years and the experience gained from the earliest hydrological works here; the containment of the floodwaters; the controlled release of those waters; the use of locks to facilitate the transportation of barges into and out of the lake, would inevitably have led to the realisation that any body of water contained at a greater elevation could be used to feed such a canal system.

Because the climate in Egypt is now so dry it is difficult for us imagine the country when it had abundant rainfall as its landscape would have been very different to the landscape we see here today. There would undoubtedly have been other small lakes that existed when Egypt had a high rainfall and abundant grasslands and forests, but many of these smaller depressions are simply not noticeable today as they would have been filled with sand as the grasslands slowly turned to desert. It's also likely that some of these small lakes would have been situated in the hills west of the Nile. These lakes, if they existed, would have provided a ready source of water for the first canal systems used by the ancient pyramid builders to construct many of the pyramids on the west bank of the Nile.

If, on the other hand, a plentiful supply of water was not readily available in an area where the ancient builders wished to construct their canal system, but the topography of the area was suitable for such a project, then a dam would have been constructed across a valley and a reservoir created to provide the water resources to feed such a canal system. I have no doubt that just such a reservoir was created in the hills west or south-west of the Giza Plateau and that this was the source of the water that fed the very extensive canal system at Giza and Dashur. The builders would, in all probability, have constructed a dam across an existing water course or outlet from a small lake to increase the volume of water that could be retained there; this water would then have been slowly released into the canal system to maintain its water levels.

The ancient canal builders realized that if rainwater and run-off could be contained in large enough volumes in reservoirs at greater elevations than the canal systems, then barges could be used for the transportation of goods and raw materials to and from areas far from the River Nile. With the construction of dams and the creation of reservoirs and locks, supply barges were no longer confined to the canals at the river level; goods and materials would have been transported considerable distances from the river, and transported up to much greater elevations – way beyond the highest flood levels of the river – by means of the locks incorporated into these canal systems.

Before the Super Pyramid builders came to develop the site at Giza, water had been used as a means to transport building materials to the construction sites of the early Super Pyramids further south, at Meidum and Dashur. At Dashur, as at Giza, there are the unmistakable remnants of engineering works undertaken to facilitate the flight of locks that was needed for the transportation of barges up to the plateau. I have no doubt that in time we will discover where the ancient builders found, or created, the reservoir to supply water to these canal systems and locks that existed on the west bank 5,000 or more years ago. At Dashur, the sloping channel cut down through the face of the escarpment to facilitate the locks, is considered to be a natural feature of the landscape that the builders of the pyramids took advantage of when hauling masonry up to the plateau above. When Egyptologists refer to the transportation of building materials by barges, no reference is made to the use of locks, or of water resources other than those of the Nile itself, and a few channels that were simply extensions of the river. Yet this is undoubtedly how so much masonry was transported up to such elevations, both here and at Giza, for without such a canal system the Super Pyramids could never have been constructed. It was simply impossible to transport and lift such huge blocks of limestone and granite without the use of hydraulic power.

It was the development and introduction of the canal lock that made it possible to build large, stone block pyramids away from the banks of the Nile at higher elevations. But it was the introduction of a revolutionary new method of construction that saw both the pyramids themselves, and the projects in particular, become even more ambitious. At some point, someone realized that canal locks could be utilised, not just to transport barges and their loads up and onto higher ground, they could be utilised to transport barges up and into the structures themselves if the canal was routed through these structures. Apart from the invention of the canal lock itself, this was the first, and arguably the most revolutionary idea of what became a torrent of new ideas that sprang forth from the development of the canal lock and the transportation of building materials into pyramids. It culminated in the greatest feat of building construction in ancient times that remained unparalleled for thousands of years; until the modern era. This was the age of the Super Pyramid.

The new canal systems and the harnessing of hydraulic power offered many new possibilities, the main one being the increased size of the masonry blocks that could be used in the construction of these new Super Pyramids. An increased block size had not one, but three advantages. It reduced the number of blocks required to build the pyramid, drastically reducing the time required to build the structure. But it also resulted in a reduction in the labour force (more than likely a redeployment of the labour force) at the quarries, as it took less man hours to produce a given volume of limestone masonry quarrying large blocks than it did to quarry much smaller blocks. The third great benefit was in the structures themselves; the much greater block size produced more stable structures. This was a huge leap forward in pyramid construction for the pyramid builders were now able to construct larger, more stable structures using less manpower and in a much shorter time.

But other, more subtle changes occurred at this time. This new method of pyramid construction must have brought about a fundamental shift in responsibility for the success or failure of these new larger structures. The design of these structures – and the infrastructure required to build them – became very complex as water had now to be channelled, controlled and manipulated within the pyramid structures themselves. In order for this resource to be fully exploited a great degree of collaboration was required between the masons, the engineers and the architects at the design and planning stages of these new structures. But the complexity of the new structures – and the transportation and distribution of the building materials within them – meant that the opportunity for errors to occur at the planning and design stages was greatly increased. The success or failure of these Super Pyramid projects was therefore greatly dependent on the skill, knowledge and ingenuity of the designers and planners employed on the projects, more so than on the actual builders of the structures, the masons. Architects and engineers had a much greater role to play in the construction of the new Super Pyramids of the hydraulic age, whereas most of the responsibility for the success or failure of the much simpler clay brick and rough stone pyramids (that may or may not have preceded the Super Pyramids) had been with the builder. This new hydraulic age was the age of engineers and architects, a new technological era.

Dashur

We can clearly see from what we know of the internal layout of the pipes and chambers in the two large Super Pyramids at Dashur, that the builders of these pyramids could vary the configuration of the internal structure yet produce consistent results. One of the pyramids at Dashur, the Red Pyramid, so called because of its now exposed red sandstone core masonry, is the third largest pyramid in Egypt. It is over 100 metres tall. This pyramid has a complex internal structure including a 60 metre long descending corridor that lies at a 27 degree angle from the horizontal. This corridor (pipe) is accessed by means of an opening set high on the north face of the pyramid, as are the openings in the two largest pyramids at Giza. The descending corridor levels out at the bottom and a short distance farther on we find the first of three corbel-vaulted chambers.

It is however the pyramid believed to have been constructed just prior to the Red Pyramid that has the most complex internal structure discovered so far at Dashur and it is in this pyramid, and in its small satellite pyramid, that we can see almost all of the elements contained within the internal structure of the Great Pyramid. The internal features of the Bent Pyramid do not have the refinements we see in the Red Pyramid, or in the later pyramids at Giza, but it has all of the features necessary to manipulate and control the flow of water within the structure, and to provide hydraulic power for the transportation of masonry within the structure when it was under construction. Apart from its various chambers and tunnels, the Bent Pyramid also has two entrances, one on the north face, and another on the west face of the pyramid, a prerequisite if you have to divert a watercourse through a pyramid. As we now know, one of these openings (on the west side) was the entrance to the inlet pipe, and the other, the exit of the outlet pipe (descending corridor) on the north face of the pyramid. The Bent Pyramid also has two gate valves in a tunnel (pipe) that is oriented east-west, one either side of a tunnel that intersects it at right angles from a northerly direction. Also to be found within this complex series of tunnels and chambers is what I believe to have been a pump chamber.

The move from clay brick to large, dressed block, stone construction also made it much easier for the builders of these new type pyramids to create the complex internal chambers and pipes that were required when water power was harnessed for the actual construction process, and not just as a means of transporting materials to the site. But with the installation of a pump in the Super Pyramids, the canal system was extended up to much higher levels than the head of water entering the hydraulic systems could naturally support. This took pyramid design and construction to another level altogether. This was not just a small step forward; it was a great leap forward in pyramid design and construction.

It was the construction of the Bent Pyramid at Dashur that laid the groundwork for what would become the most ambitious project ever seen in Egypt. However, before the builders could embark on the Giza Project they had to refine their designs and their techniques and raise the quality of their workmanship. To do that, they moved just a short distance north of the site of the Bent Pyramid to construct the next Super Pyramid and it was here that they created the first, fully integrated, true pyramid.

The supply canal would simply have been extended northward from the Bent Pyramid to the site of the new pyramid, where, once again, the supply barges would have transported the building materials up and onto the platforms of the new structure, just as they had done at the Bent Pyramid site. The Red Pyramid was the last and the largest pyramid of the hydraulic age constructed on this site, but before we take a look at this pyramid in more detail we need to take a look at the small satellite pyramid that was constructed on the south side of the Bent Pyramid as it has a very interesting feature.

The small pyramid on the south side of the Bent Pyramid looks quite insignificant next to its much larger neighbour. It was originally just over 30 metres high, about half the height of the smallest of the three principal pyramids at Giza, but it is not its size that makes it one of the most important pyramids on our itinerary, it's what's inside.

As you will see from the drawing below (Fig. 39), this small pyramid contains both a descending and an ascending corridor, but it is another feature that I want to draw your attention to for this pyramid also contains what is possibly the first sloping chamber (gallery) incorporated into a pyramid. The gallery in this small pyramid is on a much smaller scale than the grand gallery in the Great Pyramid, but that is to be expected for this is a very small pyramid. However, with the creation of a gallery here, we can see in the pyramids at Dashur, in some form or another, nearly all of the components that we have now become so familiar with in the internal structure of the Great Pyramid at Giza. Although we have yet to discover many of the chambers and pipes in most of the Super Pyramids on the west bank, I suspect that there are also large galleries to be found in both the Bent Pyramid and the Red Pyramid. After all, why would the builders create such a feature in a very small pyramid, yet not incorporate the same feature into the much larger pyramids nearby?

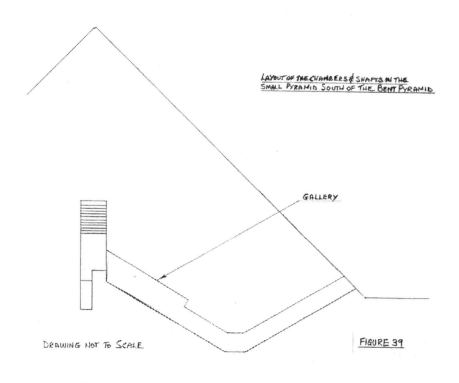

LAYOUT OF THE CHAMBERS & SHAFTS IN THE SMALL PYRAMID SOUTH OF THE BENT PYRAMID

GALLERY

DRAWING NOT TO SCALE

FIGURE 39

The small satellite pyramid and the Bent Pyramid were designed as complimentary structures; therefore it is very unlikely that a gallery isn't part of the internal layout of the two much larger Super Pyramids here – given that the builders went to all the trouble of constructing such a gallery in the smallest of these three structures.

It was almost certainly at Dashur that all of the internal components that we see in the pyramids at Giza were developed and refined as the builders honed their skills and improved the designs and the quality of their structures. The two Super Pyramids here undoubtedly have more pipes and chambers in the upper part of the structures that we have yet to discover; the chambers and pipes that we have discovered in the Great Pyramid indicate most strongly that this is almost certainly the case. It was at Giza that we discovered that these Super Pyramids had to be built from the inside out as the outer casing blocks could not be installed any other way. We can therefore be certain that each of the large pyramids at Dashur has a central vertical shaft where the masonry for the upper sections of these structures was hoisted up to the platforms when they were under construction. If they had a central shaft, the builders had to have gained access to this shaft; therefore there are almost certainly galleries and pipes still to be discovered within these structures.

By the time the builders had completed the Red Pyramid at Dashur, they had proved to themselves that they could build high quality, fully integrated, true pyramids in stone. Their next project would be on a massive scale, for not only would they build the greatest pyramids ever constructed here, they would also build many other structures and causeways, a great complex of structures that would take many decades, possibly centuries, to construct. This was to be a whole complex of temples and monuments that would endure for thousands of years, but before they could contemplate the construction of the two largest pyramids they intended to build at Giza the designs for these structures had to be further refined. Here, at Giza, they would introduce the largest blocks of masonry ever used to build a pyramid. Never before had they built pyramids using such massive quantities of large blocks of masonry, and in order to reduce the time it would take to transport such massive quantities of masonry to the construction sites of the two largest structures here, the builders constructed a dual channel canal system on the north side of these structures.

There was also another aspect of the structures that had to be carefully considered before any of these pyramids could be built at Giza; that was the position of the pipes and chambers within these enormous pyramids, for the builders had to take account of the topographical conditions at the construction sites of each structure when determining the internal layout of the pipes and chambers within the structures. The foundations of the three principal pyramids at Giza were established at different elevations on a sloping site so the greatest head of water was available at the lowest foundation level, that of the Great Pyramid. Hence the reason that the opening on the north side of this pyramid is at the greatest elevation, relative to its base, of all three principal pyramids here.

The surveyors of the site at Giza would have had to work very closely with the architect(s) and the canal builders in order to accurately determine the routes of the canals that had to be constructed on the plateau, and to determine where, and at what elevation, the openings of the inlet and outlet pipes would be created. A great deal of responsibility was placed on the shoulders of the canal builders at Giza and it would have taken all of their knowledge and skills for them to overcome many of the difficulties they would have encountered on this project. Engineers had designed efficient hoists and lifting mechanisms to ensure the smooth flow of masonry within these structures, however, all of this technology would have been of no use whatsoever if the hydraulic engineers couldn't deliver the masonry to the hubs where these lifting mechanisms were to be installed. The new technical innovations employed in these structures would further reduce the time it would take to construct the two massive pyramids on the new site and help to keep the cost of this massive project under control, but only if the masonry could be delivered to where it was required at each stage of the construction, and in a timely manner. The more large blocks of masonry that they could transport up and on to the platforms in bulk using only the power of water, and the nearer to its final destination that the masonry could be transported, the less time it would take to construct these massive structures.

The design the architect finally came up with for the Great Pyramid was a design *par excellence*. The ingenuity of the architect who designed the internal structure of the Great Pyramid had no equal. He overcame obstacle after obstacle to facilitate the construction of this pyramid and he used hydraulic power to transport the greatest number of large masonry blocks that it was possible to put into this structure. By any measure he was a genius, for he fully understood the capabilities and limitations of both the men and the technology that was employed on this project to bring his creations to fruition. In fact, I eventually ran out of superlatives to describe the many wonderful innovations that were incorporated into the structure of the Great Pyramid and the technological innovations employed in the actual construction process. In a few short stages, these builders took pyramid construction to a level way beyond anything that had ever been done before, or done again. It has taken us until the 21st century just to figure out *how* they were constructed; whether we would ever be able to reproduce them, however, is another matter altogether.

In the chapter that immediately preceded this one, we looked at the carbon 14 dating of the mortar samples taken from some of these Super Pyramids. Although I concluded by saying that the dates for the three principal pyramids at Giza did not contradict the order of construction of the two large pyramids, neither did they confirm them; the margin of error in such tests is much greater than the difference between the lesser and greater dates of these structures. These dates however, should not be viewed as the dates of the construction of the respective Super Pyramids from which these samples were taken, they simply indicate the approximate age of the organic material in the samples, the age of the remains of the charcoal / wood used in the production of the lime mortar. It is the mean age of the trees cut down to produce firewood for the limekilns, and the age of these trees could have varied widely, possibly by a few hundred years. This fact alone means that we cannot read too much into the dates of the various test samples.

A tremendous quantity of lime mortar would have been required for just one of these Super Pyramids and a great volume of timber would have been used to produce the mortar for each structure. It's very likely that timber from a number of sources was used over the period when these Super Pyramids and their peripheral structures were under construction, a period that lasted possibly not much more than two or three hundred years.

Anyone who has studied in detail the Super Pyramids of the west bank, can't fail to see that the Bent Pyramid and the Red Pyramid are more primitive constructions than the pyramids at Giza; there is undoubtedly a clear progression in the design and quality of these structures as the builders moved northwards. The Great Pyramid and its immediate neighbour, however, are quite simply in a league of their own. Their sheer size, their complexity, the creation of a two-way transportation system that extended from the basin below the escarpment, to the bottom of the grand gallery in the Great Pyramid, all of these things and more set them apart from the pyramids that preceded them.

The design and construction of the two largest pyramids at Giza was a great developmental leap forward. There had never been anything like them and there will be no more like them ever again, for each of these structures is unique. When we look closely at what the pyramid builders achieved at Giza, there is simply no way that these builders built such magnificent structures and then took a retrograde step and built some inferior Super Pyramids. The mean dates of the mortar samples taken from the Super Pyramids on a number of occasions tell us absolutely nothing about the order of construction of these structures, but we can clearly see if we take a close at the structures at Dashur and Giza how these structures evolved and that is the best indication of the order of construction. The mean dates of the mortar samples taken from the Super Pyramids on the west bank does, however, clearly indicate that these structures are more than likely to be much older than Egyptologists believe them to be. That is entirely in keeping with the fact that the builders of these structures required vast volumes of water in order to construct them.

Giza

As I mentioned earlier, I was of the opinion that the Small Pyramid at Giza was the oldest of the three principal pyramids. This was based purely on the inferior finish on the exterior of this structure and on what I believed to be a more primitive internal structure. However, when I finally discovered how its pipes and chambers had been put to use, I realized that it is quite simply impossible to make such a judgement based on the design of the inner layout of this pyramid, and I came to realize that the Small Pyramid is a very different structure from its two neighbours. These structures certainly all have that distinctive pyramid shape in common, but that is where the similarity ends, as the constraints of this site (Small Pyramid) were very different from that of the other two pyramid construction sites. It was those constraints that had determined the layout of the pipes and chambers in the Small Pyramid. In fact, I am of the opinion that it was the limitations of this site that led to the construction of a much smaller pyramid here. Even if the space had been available, which it was not, it would have been impossible to build a pyramid of a size approaching that of the Great Pyramid at this elevation with such a small head of water, since the canal here was only a few metres above the foundation level of this structure.

The most visible clue as to the constraints of this site is the opening on the north face of the small pyramid. At the outlets on the north face of the two largest pyramids at Giza, water flowed freely into the supply canal. This was also true for the outlet on the north face of the Small Pyramid, but here the outlet on the north side of the structure was just above the third course of masonry, only a few metres above ground level. In the Middle Pyramid and the Great Pyramid, the outlets were above the tenth and the sixteenth courses of masonry respectively, but it was only possible to have these outlets on these levels because the foundation level of these two structures were at a much lower elevation on the plateau than that of the Small Pyramid, and, more importantly, than that of the single channel canal system. It was simply impossible to increase the height of the outlet on the north face of the Small Pyramid and have water flowing naturally out of this opening as the feeder canal on the west side of this Small Pyramid was only a few metres above the foundation level of this structure. By the time the first four or five courses of the structure had been installed, the builders would have had to pump water up into the ponds to feed the supply canal. On a pyramid of this scale this was manageable, but on a pyramid approaching the scale of the two largest structures here, it would have been next to impossible to keep the ponds topped up with water using only the pump as these ponds were so large at the earliest stages of their construction.

To build a much larger pyramid at the location and elevation of the Small Pyramid at Giza, the builders would also have had to extend the dual channel supply canal as far as the north face of the Small Pyramid. This is something that would never have been considered by the pyramid builders for it would have been impossible to pump enough water to keep the water level in such great ponds topped up, and also to feed a dual channel canal system. In fact, if there had been little or no gradient on the plateau, the three principal pyramids here would all have been the size of the Small Pyramid that we see at the south west corner of the Giza Complex.

But it is not just the two largest pyramids at Giza that prove this point, for the two large pyramids constructed at Dashur are at much lower elevations than the elevation of the canal that skirted the hills west of the plateau here also. In fact, the general rule was; the greater the size of the structure, the greater the differential between the foundation level of the structure and the elevation of the feeder canal. That is why the largest of the three principal pyramids at Giza is at the extreme eastern edge of the plateau, and the smallest of the three pyramids here is on the higher ground at the south-west corner of the plateau.

When we look at the Great Pyramid today without its outer casing stones, it looks like a series of stepped and ever smaller platforms placed one on top of the other... and it is. But most of us have no experience of just how difficult a task it is to raise blocks of stone weighing just a few tons up onto a platform five or ten metres or so above ground level. Even if we were to somehow achieve this feat, there is then the matter of how we would transport these blocks to their final destinations to consider. The base of the Great Pyramid covers an area of approximately thirteen acres and by anyone's reckoning this is a massive site. Even if it had been possible to manually haul the smallest blocks of limestone up an incline to the lowest platforms – and then haul those blocks to their final destinations – the time it would have taken to carry out those operations would have been considerable. However, even if we overlook the time aspect we are still left with the problem of how to raise this masonry up and onto two hundred platforms, the highest of which is 146 metres above ground level. Just to make it a little more interesting, we would have to install the polished outer casing blocks first on each of those platforms as we built the structure up, since it was impossible to install these blocks later.

These are just some, but not all, of the difficulties that were faced by the builders of the Great Pyramid and we have not even considered how we would haul granite blocks and slabs weighing 50 tons or more up to 50 metres or more above ground level. Oddly enough, we never ever see archaeologists explaining how this was achieved on television documentaries or reconstructions; they like to play safe and stick to dramatizations of ancient workmen cutting limestone and hauling 2 ton limestone blocks up ramps. They all carefully avoid any mention of how the massive granite blocks and slabs were raised up to these levels and then installed, for it is absolutely impossible for men to haul such huge blocks of granite up even the slightest of gradients. We can't do it, and the ancient pyramid builders couldn't do it either. But then again, they didn't need to, for they had become master manipulators of hydraulic power long before they began to build the Super Pyramids; it was only hydraulic power that made it possible to build such structures. Even today, we would undoubtedly find it impossible to build such structures without the use of hydraulic power.

Without the early hydrological experiments, pyramid development would not have progressed much beyond the primitive mud brick mastabas and stepped pyramids. Any structures built in stone would have consisted only of manageable sized blocks that could be easily handled manually. The Super Pyramids – those fully integrated pyramids built with large, dressed, blocks of limestone – could never have been constructed if the ancient builders had not discovered how to harness and master one of the most powerful forces on the planet. Hydraulic power made the Super Pyramids and that is why we see this great leap forward in pyramid construction that most probably began at Meidum and culminated at Giza. If anyone has any doubts about this great technological development, they only need to take a look at the pyramids that were (supposedly) built prior to the hydraulic age and then look at the pyramids that were built after the hydraulic age ended. Hydraulic power made it possible to construct these large, stone built pyramids and when the water resources used to build these structures disappeared, the construction of Super Pyramids ended also.

The pyramid builders discovered how to manage and manipulate this power source for their own ends, and for a fairly short period of time – probably just prior to the early dynastic period – there was a frenzy of pyramid building activity. But time was running out for the Super Pyramid builders as fate dealt a devastating blow to the region and the climate changed forever. No sooner had they grasped this new source of power, than it was snatched away from them again. How cruel and unpredictable Mother Nature can be.

We have no way of knowing if they were aware of what nature had in store for them when they set out on this building programme at Giza, but it is certainly possible that the rainfall levels had begun to decrease before the construction work at Giza was complete. However, what was to come would completely change the landscape of Lower Egypt and beyond forever, at least until the present day, and result in the mass migrations of both people and animals as the grasslands of the region slowly died and the land turned to desert. Whether the Super Pyramid builders were aware of climatic changes at the time of their construction we do not know, but they certainly made the most of the water resources that were available to them while it was possible to do so. Through a series of innovative design features, the builders made the most of this power source. They learned to pump water up to ever greater heights within the new structures they had designed to obtain the maximum benefit from the new methods of construction. The lower chamber, the grand gallery and the upper chamber in the Great Pyramid were all designed to take full advantage of the new construction methods that the controlled flow of water through these structures had made possible. Water was channelled into, and pumped through, these Super Pyramid structures when they were under construction and it was undoubtedly this ability to transport the vast quantities of masonry required on each project – from its source to its final destination within the structures – that led to the construction of the vast complex at Giza.

But it wasn't only pyramids that this new technology was used to build. In *Keeper of Genesis (The Message of The Sphinx)* by Robert Bauval and Graham Hancock they write, with reference to the huge monoliths used to construct the Valley Temple that sits alongside the Sphinx Temple at Giza:

> "The problems are manifold but stem mainly from the extremely large size of the blocks – which can be envisaged as a series of diesel locomotive engines stacked one on top of the other."

There are no small blocks in the walls of this temple and many of the largest blocks are estimated to weigh in excess of 200 tons. There is only one way that such monoliths were transported to these locations, and that was by barge. As I mentioned earlier, the limestone used in the construction of many of the peripheral structures around the three principal pyramids at Giza was quarried on the plateau itself. There is a large area just to the east of the

Middle Pyramid where a great deal of limestone was removed from the plateau; this was undoubtedly a quarry that would have been flooded after a quantity of masonry had been quarried here and hauled onto the decks of barges that had been grounded on the stepped levels of the quarry, prior to the loading operation (this lock / dry dock was continually extended as more and more masonry was removed from the quarry). The masonry from here would then have been transported to the site of each structure under construction through the single channel (feeder) canal system. Walls would have been constructed around the sites where the temples and small pyramids were to be established and lock gates would have been incorporated into the walls of these locks. The water levels within these locks would then have been increased as each course of the structures was put in place and the perimeter walls of the enclosure extended upwards. All of these structures once had perimeter walls and it was these walls that would have retained the water in the locks at these sites when the buildings were under construction. The water from these locks and the feeder canal would have been discharged to the Sphinx Enclosure, and ultimately to the River Nile on the east side of the plateau as the water levels in these locks was reduced.

The area around the Sphinx, the Sphinx Enclosure, was the quarry for the large volume of limestone used in the construction of the Sphinx and Valley Temples, just east of the Sphinx. Although the Sphinx Enclosure served as a quarry when the two temples here were under construction, it would also have been set up as an ever expanding lock / dry dock as more and more limestone was removed from the area around the body of the Sphinx – the enclosure – and transported to the nearby construction sites of these temples, east and south-east of the Sphinx. I believe that this whole area around these temples and the Sphinx Enclosure was walled off and set up as one great dry dock / lock where huge monoliths weighing 200 tons or more were simply moved from one area of the lock to another. It is possible that the masonry used in the construction of the walls of the dry dock could have been put to good use elsewhere when the temples were complete. However, it was more than likely that these walls were left *in situ* to provide the perimeter wall for this temple complex when work on the plateau was complete.

It is not possible for human beings to move such enormous blocks of limestone and pile them one on top of the other by brute force. The ancient builders had many ways of moving and lifting smaller blocks of masonry as they proved time and time again when they set up hoists in the Super Pyramids, but hydraulic power is the only possible and credible explanation for the fantastic engineering feats that we see in the upper chamber of the Great Pyramid and in the walls of the Valley Temple.

The Great Pyramid was so far ahead of its time that for thousands of years no one ever came close to figuring out how it had been constructed. With hindsight, we were naive in the extreme to believe that Egyptologists would ever discover the secrets of these very complex structures as a great many architects, engineers and builders have studied these structures in the past and been completely puzzled by them. It has been obvious for a very long time that the designers and builders of the pyramids at Giza had skills and technology far beyond anything that was believed to have existed in the early or pre-dynastic periods. I believe that I have now provided incontrovertible proof that such technology and skills were indeed employed by the ancient builders of these structures in this fully comprehensive account of how the ancient Super Pyramid builders put these magnificent structures on the Giza Plateau. Hopefully, it will satisfy all but the most hardened sceptics.

When I set out on this, my last quest, I did not have a theory of my own, nor did I set out to prove the theory of another; it was simply the desire to understand the Great Pyramid that kept drawing me back time and again to this enigmatic structure. In the end though, it was the Great Pyramid itself that revealed the secrets of its construction. I have simply had the wonderful privilege of being its interpreter.

Prime position

Before we move on, I would just like to state that I don't ask you to take anything at face value and I urge you to do your own research if you have the slightest doubt as to the validity of any of my statements; I don't doubt that I have made mistakes with some of the finer details. I also have no doubt that, in time, others will discover things I have overlooked, or see other, simpler, ways of achieving some of the outcomes that I have identified. But there is absolutely no mistaking that the pyramid builders constructed the Great Pyramid in the general manner that I have described here, since the evidence for this is overwhelming. Before we take a look at the origins of the pyramids at Giza however, I want to relate to you something that I came across some time after I had made some early breakthroughs on this project.

In 1997 a book on the origins of freemasonry, *The Hiram Key*, was published and its authors were Christopher Knight and Robert Lomas. Although I am not a freemason myself, I was greatly interested in this subject from the historical perspective and bought a copy of this book not long after its launch. Although my own project does not compare with their exhaustive investigation, I soon discovered that there were some similarities. Their project had involved them in a tremendous amount of investigative research and although my own project involved a good deal of research also, I was trying to get to grips with a physical puzzle, as opposed to the purely historical one that Knight and Lomas were grappling with. To cut a long story short. I came across an astonishing statement in Appendix I of this book that was so relevant to my own situation at that time that the authors of *The Hiram Key* could have written it for me. They write:

> "Earlier on in our research we had had frequent celebrations as we came across some artefact or gem of information that locked in another section of the growing picture. By this stage however, we were starting to accept that remarkable pieces of evidence would keep cropping up because our core thesis was correct and we were mining a continuous and endless vein of historical truth."

I was completely taken aback by this extraordinary statement and by how their experience mirrored my own. This was a time when it seemed that, as I realized how each feat had been accomplished, it altered my perception of what lay ahead and pointed me in directions that I had not previously envisaged. But some of the time I was not conscious of this and it was only when I set about tackling the next problem, and began to get a handle on it, that I would make a connection and then realize that it was my slightly altered perception of the structure that had led me to make the connection. There was a natural progression, a flow, but it was so obscure at times that often I would only become conscious of it after I had solved a problem. It was an uncanny, yet wonderful feeling and I eventually concluded that I had finally gotten into the heads of those ancient builders and began to think like them.

I agree completely with the authors of *The Hiram Key*. Something very strange does indeed happen when we pick up a trail and follow it to its logical conclusions, even if most of the time we are not aware of where we are heading. I certainly couldn't have expressed this extraordinary experience nearly as well as the aforementioned authors, though, as I don't have the command of the English language that they clearly possess. I am therefore grateful to them for expressing those wonderful experiences so eloquently.

Another man I will be eternally grateful to is Graham Hancock, for without his *Fingerprints of The Gods* I would never have made my initial breakthrough. For years now I have had three reference books sitting on my desk that I could easily refer to when necessary. One of those books is a dictionary, the other a thesaurus and the other, *Fingerprints of The Gods*. In fact, without *Fingerprints of The Gods*, I doubt that I would have made very much progress on my quest at all for it has been an invaluable source of information. The section in *"Fingerprints"* titled: *Part VI The Giza Invitation, Egypt I,* is packed with so many facts and observations that it was always my first point of reference when I encountered some difficulty. I had read this section of the book three, possibly four times, before I set out on my final quest and I should have known it off by heart, yet time and time again it came to my rescue when I got bogged down with one problem or another along the way. Graham's great attention to detail in *"Fingerprints"* was invaluable. I have no hesitation in saying that Graham Hancock's *Fingerprints of The Gods* is singularly responsible for my initial breakthrough and for many of the subsequent discoveries that I made on my quest to discover the secrets of the Great Pyramid. I doubt that I would ever have made my breakthrough if this book had never been published.

I'm sure that this book must have inspired many amateur pyramid enthusiasts and it certainly rekindled my interest in this subject after a very long absence. Without *Fingerprints of The Gods,* what became my final quest to discover the secrets of the ancient pyramid builders would probably have ended up like all of my previous quests, where I made little or no progress at all. After studying the Great Pyramid for decades, I finally got lucky thanks to this book. Within the Great Pyramid the secrets of the ancient pyramid builders had been there for all to see for centuries, but with *"Fingerprints of The Gods"* Graham Hancock shone a much needed light into the gloomy interior of this great structure and laid out the bare bones of it. All that was then missing was the key.

The Great Pyramid, as we have discovered on our journey, all slots together like those interlocking three dimensional puzzles that, as kids, we found so easy to take apart, yet so difficult to put back together again. Just like those puzzles, every section and every feature of the Great Pyramid is essential and interdependent on all the others for its very existence. That is the great truth about this structure. Unfortunately, since the birth of archaeology many archaeologists have been sticking labels on the features and chambers of the Great Pyramid as if they had some great understanding of it. But they did not... they were deluded. They had no idea why any of its features had been created so they constructed a fantasy, a fantasy that became ever more removed from the truth as time went by.

I now fully understand why historians say it is so difficult to understand the mindset of ancient peoples, for I truly became aware of this towards the end of my quest, when I suddenly realized why we had made so little progress over so many years. We had been studying all of the spaces within the Great Pyramid and trying to figure out why they had been created, when in fact, we should have been trying to figure out how the solid parts of the structure had been put together; after all, that's what its builders had been focussed on. We couldn't understand how the Great Pyramid had been constructed because we had assumed that it had been constructed to house the chambers and corridors (pipes) created within it. But the plain truth is that its builders didn't create any of its chambers and pipes for any purpose other than to put this great structure on the plateau; the chambers, pipes and tunnels they created within the structure were simply the means to that end. The greatest clue of all that this had been the case was the fact that the builders sealed up most of these chambers and pipes when they had no further use for them. But this was only one of many clues that we failed to understand the significance of.

In trying to figure out how to build a pyramid like those at Giza, we looked at it from a modern perspective; we didn't try to put ourselves into the shoes or the minds of the ancient pyramid builders. When I eventually realized that it was only by doing so that I would have any chance of completing my quest to discover how the Great Pyramid had been constructed, the pieces of the puzzle that had eluded me up to that point finally began to fall into place. Looking back, I now realize that this was a major transition point on my journey, for when I'd begun to look at the structure through the eyes of its builders, I gained a much deeper understanding of the structure and the difficulties its builders faced. What I still don't understand, though, is why it took me so long to realize this. However, all that matters is that I got there in the end.

In 1301 the Great Pyramid lost its mantle. Now, 700 years later, we have finally managed to mentally rebuild it from scratch. Along the way, when looking for clues as to how this enormous puzzle had been put together, I discovered many facts about the other two large pyramids on the Giza plateau and I unearthed facts about the plateau itself that I had been unaware of when I first set out on my quest. I'm sure you will agree that the picture that has now emerged from the mists of time is a very different one from that widely promoted by orthodox Egyptologists, or portrayed on television over the last few decades. Nonetheless, it is one that is totally compatible with the landscape of the Giza plateau and the archaeological record.

Theories are all well and good but only if they can be tested. I never set out to prove or disprove any theories; I just wanted to better understand this structure. As it turned out, all of the evidence as to how this structure had been constructed had been there all the time we just couldn't see the bigger picture. It had been buried in a sea of inaccurate data, flawed theories that had been trailed out so often they were regarded as fact, and conclusions that had been drawn based on very selective data. At the end of the 20th century – before *Fingerprints of The Gods* had been published – it was almost impossible to separate fact from fiction when it came to the Great Pyramid and the Giza complex for it seemed that everyone and their grandfathers had expressed their opinion on it. I had long been convinced that a canal with a flight of locks rising up from the basin below the escarpment had been used to transport the building materials up and onto the plateau, but when I got lucky and realized that the original doorway had been the entry point for the canal to reach right inside the Great Pyramid, I instinctively knew that this was the beginning of the end. I realized immediately that this was the route to the top of the Great Pyramid and I set out to discover how the ancient pyramid builders had achieved this seemingly impossible feat.

And what a journey it's been. I set out to understand one pyramid, the Great Pyramid, but found that I could not look at it in isolation, since its construction was inextricably linked to its companions and the pyramids that had preceded them. As I slowly made my way up through the Great Pyramid I realized that, although the pyramids at Giza were in a league of their own, some of the earlier pyramids held many of the clues as to how the Great Pyramid and its companions had evolved into the phenomenally complex structures they had become. In fact, the link between some earlier pyramids and those at Giza became perfectly clear when I fully understood the common purpose of their internal layouts.

The principal pyramids at Giza represent a great leap forward in pyramid design and construction and no doubt most of this can be put down to major advances in technical innovation, hydraulic engineering and precision machining. But when I discovered that these large, stone block pyramids could only be constructed using huge volumes of water at each and every stage of the process, it immediately called into question the true age of the Super Pyramids. As far as I have been able to ascertain, the climate in the middle of the third millennium B.C.E. was almost certainly much too dry to construct these Super Pyramids.

If the Super Pyramids at Giza and elsewhere were constructed much earlier than supposed, I then realized that some of the more primitive pyramids, supposedly constructed before the Super Pyramids, may actually have been constructed after the Super Pyramids of the hydraulic age. However, we are not primarily concerned with the chronology of these pyramids here as it is the Super Pyramids on the west bank that is the focus of our attention, but in light of my discoveries it is plain to see that the chronology of the pyramids will need to be fully re-examined.

I'd soon realized that the large, stone block pyramids at Giza were the last of their kind simply because the much drier climate that had set in after their construction had made it impossible to construct any more of these enormous complex structures in Egypt ever again. Hydraulic power had made it all possible, but without the water resources to provide this power, the designs for these Super Pyramids were absolutely worthless.

But it doesn't really matter if the pyramids at Giza were completed by 3,500, 3,000 or 2,500 B.C.E. because pyramid construction in Egypt did not end at Giza. It was certainly the end of the Super Pyramids of the hydraulic age, but there was more than one way to build a pyramid. In fact, later kings and pharaohs continued to construct pyramids but these were the much simpler, stepped pyramids, with slanting accretion layers and an outer casing consisting of small blocks of masonry to create the true pyramid shape. The pyramids that were constructed after the Super Pyramids therefore were not fully integrated structures like those at Giza they were of a more primitive construction. But now that we know that the Super Pyramids were possibly built much earlier than we had assumed – and that the hydraulic age probably came to an end not long after the pyramid builders had mastered this new power source and used it to construct the Super Pyramids – then there may have been very few of the more primitive style of structures built before the Super Pyramids, if any at all. But we must be very careful here for it is possible, though unlikely, that the rainfall in the delta region around the middle of the third millennium B.C.E. was indeed sufficient to provide the builders of the Super Pyramids with the water resources needed to construct them in the middle of the third millennium. Although that area of North Africa, just south of the Mediterranean Sea had possibly become much drier prior to the third millennium B.C.E., it is entirely possible that a micro-climate existed in the delta region, a climate with more precipitation than the Western Desert region. However, I think it extremely unlikely that this was the case and the only way that we are likely to be able to determine when the Super Pyramids at Giza were constructed is when we discover one of the tombs below the two largest structures here. Until then it is purely a guessing game.

I believe that the carbon 14 dating of the charcoal in the mortar of the Super Pyramids and the vast volumes of water required to build these structures indicate most clearly that they were most likely constructed sometime during the fourth millennium B.C.E., not in the middle of the third millennium as we have been led to believe. But now that we understand why the age of the Super Pyramids came into being, and why it came to an end, we can clearly understand why later pyramid builders had to resort to other methods of construction with the many pyramids that were constructed after Giza. A major change in Egypt's climate – an unforeseen event – brought an end to the construction of large, stone built pyramids and it was this catastrophe that put an end to the linear development of the pyramids on the west bank, and no doubt put an end to a way of life for tens of thousands of people across North Africa and the Middle East. But although it did not bring an end to pyramid construction in Egypt, it certainly turned everything on its head and forced later pyramid builders to adopt the low tech approach to pyramid building. (Pyramid building was by then an intrinsic part of the culture in Egypt and they continued to construct pyramids century after century.) However, now that we know that the Super Pyramids of the west bank could be much older than previously believed, it is indeed possible that the Super Pyramids were the very first pyramids ever constructed here and that all of the more primitive structures came later.

I believe that it is entirely possible that the Super Pyramids of the hydraulic age could have been constructed by a people who settled in the delta area and introduced this new technology to the region prior to the dynastic period. However, it is also possible that newcomers who settled in the delta region just realized the potential of the hydraulic systems already in use by the indigenous population. The Super Pyramids, of course, may have no connection whatsoever to migrants; they could just as easily have been developed by the indigenous peoples of the region after they began to construct dams at higher elevations to provide water resources for a canal system on the west bank of the Nile. But although we cannot determine at this moment in time who built the Super Pyramids, we can be absolutely certain that hydraulic power was the driving force of the Super Pyramid age in Egypt.

Before we move on, I would just like to mention that hydraulic power was undoubtedly the driving force behind another major construction project at an altogether different location in the eastern Mediterranean region. Archaeologists have been unable to determine when this structure was constructed also, but it is surely too much of a coincidence to believe that there is not some connection between this structure and the Super Pyramids on the west bank. I don't want to go off at a tangent here, but I did want to mention this other project when we were looking at some of the possibilities for the origins of the super pyramids, as it may be relevant. (We will take a closer look at this structure in a later chapter.)

When I had first began to research what I believed at that time to be the forerunners of the large stone pyramids – the mastabas and the early step pyramids – I soon became aware that, if these structures had preceded the super pyramids, at some point in the evolutionary process the objectives of the builders of these structures must have changed (if we are to believe that pyramids were built as tombs for kings of Egypt, as orthodox Egyptologists would have us believe). I accept that the mastabas had been constructed above burial chambers and that this was probably the most effective way to protect a tomb, by putting a large mass on top of it. But I do not agree with the common belief among Egyptologists that these mastabas and stepped pyramids had been constructed using ramps. In my opinion, there is more than enough evidence to suggest that many, if not most of these structures, had been built using tunnels and central shafts for the transportation of building materials into the structures, and then up to the platforms under construction. The common belief seems to be with these structures that the body of the deceased was lowered down the central shaft of the mastaba after it had been almost complete, the shaft having then been backfilled after the burial chamber had been sealed. But tunnels have been discovered in many of these structures at, or near, ground level. These tunnels had been part of the original structures and later backfilled by the builders, most likely after the structures were complete and the body of the deceased had been interred in the burial chamber. Is it therefore not reasonable to assume that these tunnels would have been the most convenient way of transporting the body of the deceased into the structure prior to its interment in the burial chamber below the mastaba?

Transporting the building materials into these constructions and then hauling them up vertically to the platforms under construction, is quite simply the most efficient way to build one of these structures. Ramps are all well and good at low levels and I am quite sure that they were used when the lower courses of these structures were under construction, but these ramps either have to become much steeper or much longer the higher the structure becomes. A point is soon reached where it becomes much more efficient to hoist the building materials up to the top level of the structure than to extend the ramps. I am, in fact, now certain that it is only a matter of time before it is discovered that all of these primitive structures had at least one tunnel at, or near, ground level as more becomes known about them.

Now I'm sure you don't need me to point out the theme common to both structures here – the mastabas and the pyramids. As we have now discovered, the only way to construct the Great Pyramid and the other Super Pyramids on the west bank, was to take the building materials into the structures through a tunnel at a fairly low level, then hoist those materials up to the platforms that were under construction. The fact that the builders of some of the mastabas chose to take building materials into these structures through a tunnel, and then hoist those materials up a central shaft, simply indicates that this was the most logical and efficient way of doing it (ramps are not an efficient way of using labour and materials). However, if we accept that there was a logical progression from the simplest structures, the mastabas and stepped pyramids, to the most complex, the Super Pyramids, at some point along the way the objectives of the builders must have changed... if Egyptologists are to be believed. The mastabas had begun life as simple constructions built over burial chambers to protect the tomb of the deceased king or nobleman from tomb robbers, but Egyptologists tell us that the burial chambers were not below the Super Pyramids, they were inside these structures. But why on earth would the builders of the pyramids entomb the mummy of the king within such a structure when his tomb would almost certainly be much safer below the great mass of the structure? After all, wasn't the great mass of the mastaba placed above the tomb of the deceased to protect it from grave robbers? Why on earth then would you change the system and create a burial chamber within the structure when you could put an even greater mass of masonry above the tomb to protect it?

We have been here before, of course, and as we discovered with our reconstruction of the Great Pyramid, all of the chambers and pipes in this structure are fully accounted for as being essential components of the construction process. As we discovered earlier, there was a burial chamber discovered in one of the Super Pyramids at Giza, but in keeping with the practice of the mastaba builders, this chamber was not created within the body of the structure; it had been created deep within the bedrock below that structure. In fact, this chamber is at the very deepest level beneath the Small Pyramid. We also know now that this chamber could only have been accessed via the inlet tunnel on the south side of the chamber when the pyramid was complete, for we know that the two outlet pipes on the north side of the structure were blocked up by then, one during the early stages of the construction and the other after the pyramid had been

374

capped and completed. So rather than bolster the Egyptologist's theory that the mummies of ancient kings were interred within pyramids, this clearly indicates that the pyramid builders were of the same opinion as the mastaba builders; the safest place for these tombs was deep in the bedrock below the Super Pyramids of the hydraulic age.

I'm absolutely certain that the builders of the pyramids at Giza did not expend so much time, energy and natural resources building these large, stone built structures to function solely as mausoleums for ancient kings. If that had been their intention surely it would have been much more obvious. We need only take a look at the richly decorated burial chambers that have been discovered elsewhere on the west bank to realize that the chambers within the Great Pyramid must have served some other purpose. If the builders had constructed these wonderful pyramids as tombs, I believe that the chambers within these structures would undoubtedly have been more in keeping with the richly decorated chambers we see in later tombs. We would possibly have had inscriptions and possibly some type of decoration on the tomb walls, possibly even an elaborate sarcophagus, a sarcophagus that is absent in the Great Pyramid. (The sarcophagus that was removed from the burial chamber under the Small Pyramid did fall into this category, for we know that it had some intricate carving on its sides and its lid in the palace facade style.) But the most telling clue in my opinion is the fact that there was no way for a funeral party to gain access to any of the inner chambers in the Great Pyramid anyhow for it is plain to see that the entrance tunnel and the ascending corridor were blocked up after the builders completed their tasks within the structure and withdrew from the inner chambers and passageways.

When the Great Pyramid was complete, the only chamber that could be accessed was the subterranean chamber, but no elaborate sarcophagus – or any other – has been found here. The only access shaft to this chamber that we are presently aware of is the descending corridor. Can we really believe that the king's successor, other members of the royal family, and priests and dignitaries would have used this pipe in the Great Pyramid to gain access to this chamber to see the king's mummified body laid to rest? Of course not! If that had been their intention, the builders we have encountered on our journey up through the Great Pyramid would not have found it difficult to create access corridors suitable for such a purpose. Nothing about the chambers and pipes that we have so far discovered within the Great Pyramid indicates that they were used for such a purpose.

Aside from the issue of where the burial chambers were located in these structures, when we look at the early Super Pyramids we can clearly see that the objective of the Super Pyramid builders changed after they had constructed the two large pyramids at Dashur. Up until the completion of the Red Pyramid at Dashur, the builders seemed content to construct one-off structures with some smaller peripheral structures. Each of these pyramids was a great improvement on the pyramids that had preceded them and it's plain to see that the Super Pyramids at Dashur were evolving into the complex structures that we later see at Giza. But Giza is something entirely different, for here the builders undoubtedly set out to create a pyramid complex with three large Super Pyramids at its heart and a host of other structures besides. As we discovered earlier, Giza didn't just come about because a succession of kings did their own thing and constructed a pyramid on this site. The planning that went into this project was way beyond anything we could have imagined only a few years ago. However, once we fully understand what the builders had to do to construct these pyramids on the Giza Plateau, and the restrictions of the site, it's plain to see that the builders of the Giza complex set out to build the largest, most refined, structures that it was possible to put on the plateau. The planning that was needed in order to make this happen doesn't bear thinking about. The three principal structures here also seem to be a mirror image of three stars in the constellation of Orion, the three stars of Orion's Belt. If any more proof were needed that this was a pre-planned project and not a series of random constructions, this surely is the clincher.

There are of course many smaller pyramids at Giza, as well as the remains of a number of temples and causeways and I have no doubt that the grouping and the positions of these structures on the plateau, relative to the principal structures, was also of significance to the builders of the complex. This was plainly not a series of random acts by a number of individuals; it was a pre-planned complex of structures, each of which was an intrinsic part of the whole.

The earliest structures

The complex, true pyramids constructed at Giza are in an altogether different league from the primitive mastabas and stepped pyramids on the west bank and I can't shake off the feeling that there is much more to this than we fully understand at present. Just the fact that these pyramids were constructed at such an early period makes it very difficult to determine their origins and the true course of their development. As I mentioned earlier, it is entirely possible that a race of people who migrated to the delta area before the dynastic period introduced this technology to Egypt. Egyptologists, after all, have told us for longer than I care to remember that it was simple farming people who built the pyramids, but we now know for certain that either the indigenous population here were a highly advanced people or the technology needed to put the Super Pyramids on the west bank was introduced by a race of people who migrated to Lower Egypt, probably sometime before the middle of the fourth millennium B.C.E. However, we know so very little about this very early period that it is unlikely that we will ever discover who built the Super Pyramids unless, of course, one or more of their tombs are discovered deep below the pyramids on the Giza Plateau. We can only hope for such good fortune.

All we can truly say for certain about this very early period is that when a means of raising heavy loads up to higher elevations was devised (the canal lock) it made the construction of large, stone block pyramids – on high ground away from the flood plain – possible for the very first time. The building materials could be quarried far from the construction sites and transported to these elevated sites on barges. Once the pyramid builders had set out on this path, it is fairly easy for us to follow the trail that ultimately led to the pyramids at Giza. But before the ancient pyramid builders began to transport masonry up to elevated sites they first had to tap into, or create, a water reservoir at a greater elevation to supply the canal and its locks with water. Once they had secured a water source for one of these projects, it wouldn't have taken them long to realize that, if the canal was channelled through the actual structures, it could also be used to transport the masonry up and onto the platforms of the structures as they were being built up. These new type pyramids, the Super Pyramids, were designed specifically to exploit this new power source.

The very first pyramid they constructed using large blocks of stone, however, was not a true pyramid; it was a stepped pyramid, its stone core having survived the ravages of time remarkably well. I believe that the collapsed pyramid at Meidum (Fig. 40) was the first attempt by the early pyramid builders to construct a pyramid using hydraulic power within the structure itself. They undoubtedly used a canal to transport stone into this structure for the inlet and outlet pipes on its north side provide the clues here. At the lower end of the lower pipe there is a chamber, and at the lower end of the upper pipe, two small chambers. There was undoubtedly a channel or pipe between these chambers originally and together they acted as the choke in the piping system, to slow the flow of water coming up the outlet pipe into the supply canal. (The core of the collapsed pyramid at Meidum is of brick construction which was then clad in stone.)

When the pyramid builders had completed the pyramid at Meidum they then moved north to Dashur where they constructed a flight of locks to transport masonry up and on to this elevated site. I'm not sure if the River Nile played any part in the transportation of masonry when the pyramid at Meidum was under construction; it is possible that both the water resources and the quarried stone for this project was sourced in the hills just west or north-west of this pyramid. I have, unfortunately, been unable to confirm if this was definitely the case, but the fact that I have been unable to unearth any reference to what may have been the foundations of a flight of locks from the Nile up to the higher ground near to the collapsed pyramid at Meidum, does not really mean very much, as the foundations for the flight of locks at Dashur and Giza have not been recognised for what they truly are by Egyptologists either. It is therefore very unlikely that a similar feature would have been recognised for what it was and recorded by Egyptologists as such if such a feature exists near the site of the pyramid at Meidum.

The pyramid builders had a new, phenomenally powerful system to transport and lift very large blocks of masonry up and onto the platforms of the structure at Meidum, but they used it here to construct a stepped core pyramid, a new system to construct a flawed pyramid design. They simply had not realized at this very early stage of Super Pyramid construction that this new power source had the potential to totally transform pyramid construction, if indeed any pyramids existed prior to the development of the Super Pyramid, as we now cannot be certain that they did. What we see at Meidum and later at Dashur could, in fact, be the development of the very first pyramids in Egypt if these pyramids prove to be much earlier than originally thought. If they are far older than Egyptologists believe them to be, there may have been no pyramids in Egypt at all before the Super Pyramids were constructed on the west bank.

The ancient pyramid builders used hydraulic power at Meidum to construct a stepped brick core and then clad it in stone. It is very easy here to assume that the ancient pyramid builders took an archaic design and adapted it in order to exploit the new found power source. But what if this pyramid is a thousand years older than those attributed to Snefru, the king who founded the fourth dynasty? We could in fact ask the question here: are any of the more primitive style of pyramids, with their stepped cores and accretion layers, earlier than the super pyramids? Or are they just the best that later pyramid builders could do when hydraulic power was no longer available? It is certainly possible for the Super Pyramids to have been constructed a thousand years before Snefru, who is thought to have reigned for 24 years or more (c. 2613 – 2589 B.C.E.) since the dating of some of the charcoal samples from the super pyramids is 1500 years prior to the reign of Snefru. Given that vast quantities of water were needed to build the Super Pyramids, the evidence certainly points to the pyramids at Meidum and Dashur as not only having been the first of the Super Pyramids to be constructed, they may in fact be the very first pyramids ever to have been constructed in Egypt. Egyptologists may in fact have drawn the wrong conclusions when they assumed that the more primitive style of constructions, the stepped core with the accretion layers, came first. As I mentioned earlier, only the discovery of a king's tomb beneath the two largest structures at Giza is likely to determine the true age of these Super Pyramids.

Hydraulic power brought with it many new possibilities but it's plain to see that the builders of the pyramid at Meidum had yet to fully realize the true potential of the power source they had tapped into. At Meidum, they simply hadn't figured out that this new power source could be used to revolutionise pyramid construction, that it could be used to construct full width, fully integrated, true pyramids from the foundation course up. The new power source provided the early pyramid builders with the opportunity to construct large Super

Pyramids using very large blocks of stone for the first time, but a complete rethink of the construction process was needed after the construction of the pyramid at Meidum if they were going to create a fully integrated structure. If the new technology was to be exploited to the full, then completely new designs for these structures were needed; there was simply no point in building a pyramid with a very stable core and an unstable outer casing when you had the technology to do otherwise.

After the construction of the stepped core pyramid at Meidum, we can see that the builders had begun to rethink their whole building strategy and in doing so they created for the very first time a fully integrated pyramid. The very first pyramid of this type was the Bent Pyramid at Dashur. Here, instead of constructing a stepped core and then building up the outer casing to create the pyramid shape, they built each complete course of the pyramid up from ground level. It's clear that they did not have the confidence or the experience at this stage to set down all of the masonry blocks of each course on the horizontal plane but each course was complete on all four sides before the next course was begun. (The blocks nearest the outer edge of each level on the Bent Pyramid were installed sloping inwards. When the structure reached the level where the angle of the sides decreased, they then set all of the blocks down on the horizontal plane.)

The design of the stepped core pyramid at Meidum was structurally unsound simply because all of the masonry on each level could not be fully interlocked. At Meidum the builders had used hydraulic power to construct a very stable stepped core from brick and large blocks of stone, but they built up the outer casing of the structure with small bricks and stones. They may have believed that a very stable core was all that was required to give this structure the strength and rigidity it needed, but the design of this structure was flawed as the outer casing could not be bonded to the inner core. They had, in fact, not thought far enough ahead when they designed this structure and seemed to be content to use hydraulic power to construct the core of the structure from brick and large blocks of masonry, and to transport the vast quantities of brick and stone used in its construction into the structure on barges. However, the builders learned a very valuable lesson when they constructed the first pyramid of the hydraulic age, for it was here at Meidum that they must have realized that they could install large casing blocks on each level of these new structures as the structures were built up. (As we discovered at Giza, it was impossible to install these casing blocks in fully integrated, large stone block pyramids after the core blocks had been installed.) After Meidum the builders did not make the same mistake again; with the next pyramid they constructed, they laid down full width courses on each level using large blocks of masonry as the structure was built up.

In failing to look far enough ahead before harnessing hydraulic power to build a pyramid, they built a structure with two major design flaws. The main problem was that they were constructing two different types of structure. They built a solid core structure and then encased it within another. But since they had no effective way of bonding these two structures together, they could not create a fully integrated structure. But this design flaw was greatly compounded by the fact that the outer structure was built up using much smaller blocks / bricks. The fact that the more robust inner structure could not be bonded to the less stable outer structure was a recipe for disaster. The outer casing of this structure was much more prone to collapse than its solid core, so it was inevitable that the most stable part of this early structure would survive long after the unstable outer structure succumbed to the ravages of time. That is exactly what we see at Meidum today (A photo of this pyramid can be found on the guardians.net website).

I have no doubt that the builders learned many lessons at Meidum and discovered, among other things, that in order to build a fully integrated structure using large stone blocks you simply have no other option than to take the masonry into the structure at some point, then haul it up to each of the platforms. There was simply no way to encase the structure they built here at Meidum using large masonry blocks after they had completed the solid core of the structure.

After the completion of the Bent Pyramid, the next step in the development of the Super Pyramid was the construction of a pyramid using dressed rectangular blocks of stone set down in horizontal courses from the foundation level up. The Red Pyramid at Dashur was the first of the Super Pyramids to be constructed in this manner. This is a pyramid where each course was constructed using fully interlocking, large masonry blocks set down on the horizontal plane from the foundation course. All of the aforementioned features are easy to see when we look at these early super pyramids in detail, but these structures were not only being transformed externally, because the internal layouts of the structures were evolving – they had to evolve to accommodate the new construction methods. Canal locks, in combination with pumps, were used to such great effect inside these new, technologically advanced structures that they completely transformed pyramid construction and drastically reduced the time it took to construct such pyramids. However, a few more refinements were needed before the evolutionary process was complete, and only then were the pyramid builders in a position to put the finest pyramids ever constructed on the Giza Plateau.

Looking at the topography of the area north-west of Dashur and west of the Giza plateau, I am now certain that the builders of the Super Pyramids constructed a dam and created a water reservoir somewhere in this area to feed the canal system that they undoubtedly created to the west of the pyramid fields. Although the site of this dam / reservoir does not seem to have been discovered yet, it is in fact possible that the site of the dam has actually been discovered, but it has been mistaken for a quarry site. We know that dams were being constructed during the fourth dynastic period, for instance, for the site of one such dam was discovered east of the Nile, and south of Dashur, at Wadi al-Garawi. This dam is believed to have been constructed c. 2600 B.C.E. (I don't know how this approximate date of its construction was arrived at or how accurate it is.) This is believed to be the earliest dam ever constructed. However, if the dressed stone used to construct many early dams was later taken from these locations and re-used long after the dams had been in use, it would be very difficult to determine whether these sites had been quarries or the foundations of dams. Hopefully, in light of my discoveries, any quarry sites that have been discovered in the hills west or north-west of Dashur will be re-examined to determine if any of these sites could actually have been the site of the dam where the Super Pyramid builders created their water reservoir prior to the construction of the Super Pyramids at Dashur and Giza. I am certain that all of the early Super Pyramids on the west bank were built with Giza in mind; therefore it's logical to assume that the builders created a water reservoir and a canal system that would serve both Dashur and Giza, and possibly Meidum. Unfortunately, not long after the Super Pyramids at Giza had been constructed, the climate became very dry, so for the past few thousand years sand has blown across the western desert. This will have built up in the valleys and low lying areas and will undoubtedly have buried many ancient sites that would be of interest to archaeologists. The reservoir that supplied water to the canal system on the west bank is almost certainly in one such valley.

Now that we know that the pyramids at Giza and Dashur were most probably constructed long before the middle of the third millennium B.C.E., it is a distinct possibility that all of the more primitive pyramids on the west bank, presumed to have been constructed prior to the pyramids at Giza, were in fact constructed long after the age of the Super Pyramids. Hydraulic power was not an option (away from the river) for the pyramid builders in the dry climate that followed the age of the Super Pyramids; the builders of these more primitive structures therefore had to rely solely on manpower and draught animals to transport the building materials to the construction sites. The hydraulic age was well and truly over by then and all of the plans and designs for the Super Pyramids, if they still existed, were absolutely worthless by the middle of the third millennium B.C.E. The fifth and sixth dynasty pyramids at Saqqara for instance, are not built of massive blocks of stone, but with a core consisting of rubble. This great decline in the quality of the pyramids built after those at Giza has puzzled many archaeologists but they were completely unaware that the builders of the technologically advanced pyramids, built earlier on the west bank, had harnessed the phenomenal power of water to construct them. Knowing what we now know about the Super Pyramids and the hydraulic age, it is plain to see that the deterioration in the standards of pyramid construction had been brought about by natural causes – by climate change. It was no longer possible to move and lift the massive blocks of masonry used in the construction of the Super Pyramids during the Hydraulic Age, for the age of hydraulic power was long gone.

It is now obvious that the Great Pyramid is unlikely to have been constructed during the reign of Khufu, unless he reigned at a much earlier time than is currently believed. However, it is possible that the three principal pyramids at Giza were restored long after they had been constructed, possibly around the middle of the third millennium B.C.E. If so, it is then possible that the kings responsible for their restoration, maybe Khufu, Khafre and Menkaure, adopted these structures and made them their own after this restoration. If these kings were responsible for the restoration of some of the structures at Giza, they could easily have claimed the principal pyramids as their own, or the mortuary temples on the east sides of the three principal pyramids as their own. However, there is little, if any, evidence to suggest that Khufu, Khafre and Menkaure had any connection whatsoever to the three principal pyramids at Giza and I believe that we are now entering a period when much of what we previously believed to be true about this early period will be turned on its head, for many new discoveries have come to light in recent years that call into question much of what we have been told about this very early period and the pyramids at Giza. Although we have now discovered how these structures were constructed, it is still a very blurred picture when we come to the question of those responsible for the construction of these structures. Hopefully, in the not too distant future, we will be able to answer this big question and discover who was truly responsible for their creation. However, as I have previously stated, we are only likely to discover the answer to that question if, and when, we discover one or more of the tombs of those responsible for their construction. Now that we know for certain that the Great Pyramid has another shaft or pipe in close proximity to the subterranean chamber, Egyptologists may be that little bit closer to discovering a burial chamber in the bedrock beneath the Great Pyramid (and possibly beneath the Middle Pyramid also, if the burial chamber here was accessed from the same inlet tunnel).

It is almost certainly the case that the ancient people of Egypt had established an observatory on the Giza plateau, or possibly at Abu Roash, just north of Giza, long before the Fourth Dynasty came into being. In fact, it is now very clear that ancient astronomers had been observing and recording the movement of the stars over a phenomenally long period in Egypt prior to the construction of the pyramids at Giza. For instance, in 1972, potsherds were discovered in the Nubian Desert 800 kilometres south of Cairo, indicating that there had once been human settlements here. Later, archaeological explorations uncovered ancient stone circles in this area. In 2002, one time NASA physicist Thomas Brophy noted the calendar circle correlation here with Orion's Belt in his book *The Origin Map*. Using a software program adapted for the purpose, he determined that the correlation of the calendar circle with Orion's Belt occurred between 6,400 and 4,900 B.C.E. This was entirely consistent with the radio carbon dating of organic materials found in the remains of campfires unearthed around these stone circles.

From this evidence, it is very clear that the ancient peoples of this region were plotting the movements of the stars long before the dynastic period. But it goes much deeper than that; it was the study of astronomy over a phenomenally long period that almost certainly gave birth to the advanced geometry and mathematical formulae used by the builders of the Super Pyramids, for astronomy is at the very heart of the Giza Complex.

Most of us are completely unaware of how incredibly difficult it is to create an accurate four sided pyramid even on a very small scale. The builders of the Great Pyramid had undoubtedly developed surveying methods and techniques, at least on a par with the very best methods in use today, to have produced such an accurate geometric structure as the Great Pyramid. It is easy for us to look back a few hundred years and see the scientific progress that man has made over this time, but this is as nothing compared to the progress the builders of the Great Pyramid had made since man first gave up the nomadic way of life and began to form the first settlements in the near east. He would undoubtedly have been aware of the ever changing movement of the stars long before he settled in one place and began to farm, but it was only when he was settled at a fixed location that he could begin to accurately observe and plot their movement over time. It was probably not long after the very first settlements had been established and farming had become a way of life for these former nomadic peoples that they first began to construct stone circles. These were the first calendars used to mark the passage of time from one season to the next.

The people who were settled in Lower Egypt when the pyramids at Giza were under construction must have gained their great knowledge of the celestial sphere, and developed the geometry and mathematics necessary to fully understand and record it, long before they began to build pyramids on the west bank. But the evidence from the Nubian Desert also suggests that the indigenous people of what has now been long known as Egypt had also acquired a great knowledge of the celestial sphere thousands of years prior to the construction of the Super Pyramids. However, we don't need to know how the builders of the Super Pyramids at Giza acquired their knowledge of the movements of the celestial bodies and precession to understand that they were scientists, mathematicians, builders, engineers and surveyors of the highest order; the monuments at Giza stand as testament to their phenomenal skills and knowledge. I truly hope that in the fullness of time the world will come to understand just how much their great achievements at Giza and elsewhere on the west bank have been underestimated by scholars. Maybe then we will begin to appreciate just how much our modern society owes to this ancient culture.

When I set out on my quest, I was unconcerned about the purpose of these structures on the plateau as it was not relevant to the task that I had set myself. However, along the way I found myself comparing the Giza complex to the Great Exhibition at the Crystal Palace in Hyde Park, London, in 1851. This was billed as *The Great Exhibition of the Works of Industry of all Nations*. Anyone who has taken the time to get to know the Great Pyramid and its companions cannot fail to grasp that here are structures designed to exhibit the phenomenal capabilities and knowledge of their creators. Like the exhibits of the Great Exhibition, the structures at Giza must have been viewed as a giant showcase of all that could be achieved by human endeavour, skill and intellect, even if this had not been the intention of its builders. This would have been the stuff of legend, and travellers in Egypt must have been completely overawed by the magnificent splendour of these wonderful structures sitting atop the plateau, as indeed we still are today.

Although we can no longer see them in all their glory, the pyramids are still a very impressive sight to behold, and the Great Pyramid has certainly fared much better than the Crystal Palace, constructed more than four thousand years later for the Great Exhibition, and now long gone. The three principal pyramids, of course, are only three out of the many structures that were built on this very sacred site and I cannot even begin to understand what this place meant to the people who built it. Fortunately, my objective was to discover how they were constructed and I was completely focussed on that goal when I was able to pursue it. I simply couldn't afford to explore other avenues of research that were not relevant to the goal I had set myself for I had in fact doubted for a long time that I would ever manage to complete this project. So I simply viewed the pyramids at Giza as repositories of knowledge, knowledge carved in stone. I knew that I had to find a way to tap into that ancient store of knowledge to understand it if I was to be successful. I was, quite literally, the apprentice pyramid builder who turned up a few thousand years too late to learn directly from the masters who built these structures. I could only study their work long after the event and use the key to interpret it to the best of my ability. Although I have been rewarded greatly for my diligence, there is no discounting the fact that lady luck played a major role in these events. There is still much to be learned.

Chapter Ten

In the beginning

Although the main focus of my attention over many years has been the Great Pyramid, it is impossible to consider any of the structures on the Giza plateau in isolation as they are all interconnected in so many ways. All of the major pyramids have their satellite pyramids, and they all had temples on their eastern flanks. The three pyramid temples also had covered causeways that linked them to three valley temples on the west bank of the Nile. The complex covers a huge area – the Great Pyramid alone has a footprint of almost thirteen acres – and the Sphinx and the Sphinx Temple are situated on the eastern edge of this incredibly sacred site. The orthodox view is that the three principal pyramids at Giza were built by three successive kings – Khufu, Khafre and Menkaure – but whether this was the case or not one thing is certain, this was no piecemeal project that was subject to the whim of any one individual. Chance played no part in the construction of this sacred complex.

The more I studied this subject, the more I came to realize that, if the three principal pyramids here were indeed built during the reigns of three successive kings, they were all working toward the same goal, the completion of a complex, predetermined plan. In my view, everything about this historic wonder points to it being a religious site that was designed, planned and constructed over a tremendously long period of time as if it was the ultimate goal of this great sovereign state. But whatever they represent, with the completion of the pyramids at Giza and its complex of temples and lesser pyramids, Egypt's rulers seemed to draw a line under their seemingly obsessive compulsion to construct ever larger pyramids. It was as if all of the experiments and the early developments at Meidum and Dashur were just early prototypes for the ultimate super pyramids that were to be constructed on this, their most sacred site.

Did they wait until they knew they could construct the finest pyramids that the world would ever know, and then build them on the place of the first time, the mound that arose from the primordial waters? Who knows, but what I do know is that the planning, surveying and construction of the canal system alone – used to transport unbelievable quantities of masonry and other building materials – was a tremendous undertaking on its own. This canal system, however, was not only used for the transportation of the masonry used in the construction of these structures on the plateau, for its flow was also routed through the three principal structures to transport masonry right into the heart of them. I therefore do not believe that the success of this whole project would ever have been put at risk by simply giving anyone the option to just "do their own thing."

The canal system at Giza was designed to deliver vast quantities of water to specific locations at various elevations on the plateau. The layout of the canal system had to take account also of the order of construction of the various structures and the head of water that was available at each location. In other words, the canal system had to be designed three dimensionally. The branch of the feeder canal that was channelled into the inlet pipe south and west of the Great Pyramid, for instance, had to have been at a higher elevation than the opening of the descending corridor on the north side of the structure. This ensured that water would flow freely through the structure and up the descending corridor to feed the supply canal on its north side.

The outlet for the supply canal in the Middle Pyramid is also well above ground level, so the head of water on the feeder canal had to have been at a greater elevation than this outlet also. However, the foundation level of the Middle Pyramid at Giza is at a higher elevation than the foundation level of the Great Pyramid and this is the reason why the upper opening on the north side of the Middle Pyramid, the outlet, is a few courses lower than the opening on the north side of the Great Pyramid. The builders simply did not have the same head of water to work with here as they had at the site of the Great Pyramid. Although I have been unable to determine if it is indeed the case, the openings on the north side of both large pyramids are possibly at, or very near, the same elevation, as both of these outlets would only have been just a few metres lower than the head of water on the feeder canal that supplied water to both systems.

Now I have a confession to make, for I had originally assumed that the Middle Pyramid would also have had a grand doorway and a dual channel entrance tunnel after I discovered that this had been the case with the Great Pyramid. I had not paid very much attention to the opening on the north side of the Middle Pyramid until I had completed my work on the Great Pyramid and it was only then that I realized that the opening to the outlet pipe in the Middle Pyramid is now set back well beyond, what would have been, the north face of the structure. Unlike the Great Pyramid however, there are no gables to be seen above the opening to the outlet pipe in the Middle Pyramid, so it is almost certainly a corbelled roof that was constructed above the entrance tunnel here. If that is indeed the case, then it is much more likely that the entrance tunnel on the north side of the Middle Pyramid was only wide enough to support a single channel canal and not a dual channel canal, like the one that was later created in the Great Pyramid. The dual channel supply canal therefore would only have been extended as far as the opening to the entrance tunnel on the north face of the Middle Pyramid, not to the bottom of the grand gallery, as had been the case with the Great Pyramid.

I have to say that I was puzzled as to why the builders had not created a grand entrance tunnel, a dual width channel in this pyramid when they had done so in the Great Pyramid. But when I considered the fact that the construction of the Middle Pyramid had begun long before work began on the Great Pyramid – the reasons for which I have stated earlier – I wondered if this could explain why they didn't create a dual width channel in the Middle Pyramid. After all, up until then all super pyramids had been constructed with a single channel entrance tunnel, so why would this one be any different? In the end, I came to the conclusion that the dual channel entrance tunnel in the Great Pyramid was a later development, an evolutionary step beyond that of the Middle Pyramid.

It is entirely possible, for instance, that during the construction of the Middle Pyramid the builders realized that the time it took to construct one of these enormous structures could be substantially reduced if they extended a dual channel supply canal into the structure itself, to the bottom of the grand gallery. I believe this to have been the likeliest scenario; after all, the builders and architects had many years to improve and refine the design of these structures before work on the next structure began. The Great Pyramid therefore could easily have been the first and the last of the Super Pyramids to have had a dual channel entrance tunnel.

Can we therefore say for certain that the Middle Pyramid at Giza did not have a dual channel canal system in operation within the structure? Certainly not, for the builders could possibly have put a corbelled roof on the entrance tunnel to bridge across a dual width channel. However, if they did indeed create a dual channel entrance tunnel here, then they most likely would have used much larger blocks above the channel to create the corbelled roof, or stronger granite blocks or beams. We know, for instance, that the grand gallery in the Great Pyramid has a corbelled roof and there are chambers in other Super Pyramids that are wider than the grand gallery with corbelled roofs, so we certainly can't rule out the possibility that such a roof once existed above a dual channel entrance tunnel in the Middle Pyramid. However, the only way that we are likely to ever know for certain is if further explorations are done in the area around the opening of the outlet pipe on the north side of the Middle Pyramid. At the end of the day however, it doesn't really make much difference to the overall picture as the same methods were used to construct both large pyramids. It just means that it may have taken a little longer to construct the Middle Pyramid if a single channel entrance tunnel had been used.

Before we move on, I would just like to mention the large chamber that was created within the Middle Pyramid at, or near, ground level. The fact that the floor of this chamber is just a few metres below the foundation level is not an indication that the Great Pyramid was an evolutionary step beyond that of the Middle Pyramid. This chamber in the Middle Pyramid almost certainly served exactly the same purpose as the lower chamber in the Great Pyramid, and it was from this chamber that the first stepped levels were built up. In the Great Pyramid, however, the floor of the chamber where the builders first began to build up the first of the stepped levels was sixteen or more courses up from its foundation level, clearly an improvement on the layout of the chambers in the Middle Pyramid. But the lower chamber central distribution hub in the Middle Pyramid did have one advantage over the lower chamber in the Great Pyramid, because the limestone masonry was transported right into this chamber in bulk on the decks of barges. When we consider that the entrance tunnel on the north side of the Middle Pyramid was at a much lower level than the grand entrance tunnel in the Great Pyramid, it is obvious that the builders were never going to be able to put the floor of this chamber fourteen or fifteen courses above ground level. So rather than have it seven or eight courses up from ground level and have the limestone blocks arrive in the distribution chamber one at a time, it was probably more advantageous to have it at ground level, where a number of limestone blocks could be transported right into the chamber on each barge, proving once again that the basic design of the internal chambers and pipes was very flexible as it could be modified to accommodate the limitations of each site.

We also discovered earlier that the only reason the lower chamber in the Great Pyramid exists is because it performed another function after its lower section had been used as a distribution hub. This chamber had to be completed after it had been used as a distribution hub as this was the expansion chamber and it was a vital component of the hydraulic system when the builders brought the pump into use. It therefore follows that the same must also be true of the lower chamber in the Middle Pyramid for this chamber must only exist because it performed a function other than that of a central distribution hub; it would not exist otherwise. But as I mentioned earlier, the concealed shafts here are likely to be at a much greater distance from the floor of this chamber, and probably slightly farther from the east wall of the chamber than the openings in the sidewalls of the lower chamber in the Great Pyramid. This was because the limestone blocks did not arrive in the lower chamber in the Middle Pyramid one at a time as they did in the Great Pyramid, as the limestone blocks were transported into the lower chamber in the Middle Pyramid in bulk on the decks of barges. When in due course these pipes are discovered in the lower chamber in the Middle Pyramid, they will be proof positive that this chamber performed the exact same functions as the lower chamber in the Great Pyramid, and proof positive that there is a pump room still to be discovered in the Middle Pyramid, as this expansion chamber wouldn't exist otherwise.

I don't know at what point most of the subsidiary structures on the Giza plateau were constructed but if they are contemporary with the large pyramids on the plateau – and I don't doubt that they are – it is impossible to determine the order of their construction at this time. A great quantity of limestone was quarried on the plateau itself, just east of the Middle Pyramid, and I believe that at least one quarry has been found west of the Giza plateau. The limestone used in the construction of the peripheral structures would have been transported to the various construction sites here using only what I have come to think of as the feeder canal (the single channel canal system on the west bank of the Nile). It is therefore possible that work on some of the small pyramids, temples and causeways could have been on-going when work on the three principal structures was underway, but we have no way of knowing for sure if this was the case. However, the Mortuary Temple on the east side of the Middle Pyramid is on the south side of the limestone quarry just east of the Middle Pyramid, and I have no doubt that some of the limestone removed from the quarry here was used in the construction of this Mortuary Temple. You will see from the drawing (Fig. 33) of the probable layout of the single channel canal system on the plateau, that a branch of this canal would have been routed through this quarry and a number of locks would also have been created within the quarry here as more and more limestone was removed from the bedrock of the plateau.

When the Sphinx Temple and the Valley Temple were under construction, and the Sphinx Enclosure was being created, a water source would have been a requirement here, for the construction of the two temples and the creation of the enclosure all happened within a great lock / dry dock. As you will see from the drawing, I believe that the single channel canal would have followed the course of (what would later become) the causeway that connected the Valley Temple with the Mortuary Temple on the east side of the Middle Pyramid. I believe this to have been the most obvious course for the single channel canal, as most of the canal infrastructure here would later have been incorporated into the covered causeway.

There is evidence to indicate that a lock gate (sluice gate) was in use in the channel between the Valley Temple and the Sphinx Temple at some time in the remote past. Whether this indicates that the canal system was still in use here after the temples had been constructed, we cannot say for sure, but it is also possible that a small lake was created in the Sphinx Enclosure, as Robert Temple has suggested. Whether this was the case or not, I believe that the discovery of evidence of a sluice gate / lock in the channel between the two temples here is a very good indication that barges entered and exited the canal system for some time after the two temples on this site had been constructed. As far as I am aware, Robert Temple was completely unaware that a very complex canal network had been constructed on the plateau prior to the construction of the pyramids when he came to the conclusion that the Sphinx had been surrounded by water in ancient times. Had he been aware of this, he may have come to a very different conclusion. That is not to say that I believe him to be wrong on this matter, for it is entirely possible that the canal system here was used for such a purpose long after the canal network on the plateau had been decommissioned. Indeed, the quarry on the east side of the Middle Pyramid could have been later used as the water catchment area (reservoir) to provide the water for this pond at the Sphinx Enclosure.

In earlier chapters, I have referred to the pyramids at Giza as fourth dynasty pyramids but this was simply because it was easier to do so at the time. It would only have added a further complication if I had questioned the date of their construction, or speculated as to when they possibly had been built each time I had to refer to the construction of the Great Pyramid and its companions. Even now, I do not intend to speculate as to the last time the climate could have been wet enough to provide the water resources for the construction of these large, stone built pyramids on the west bank. I will leave that to the climatologists to determine. But I do strongly suspect that it was long before the supposed time of Khufu.

As I mentioned earlier, Dashur is where these large, stone built pyramids first evolved into true pyramids and it was here that a flight of locks was undoubtedly constructed for the transportation of barges up and onto the plateau here. There is a deep channel cut down at an angle through the face of the escarpment at Dashur. This 'ramp' is regarded as a natural feature of the landscape here and Egyptologists believe that it was used by the pyramid builders when the pyramids at Dashur were under construction. The Egyptologists, however, believe that the pyramid builders hauled limestone blocks up this ramp from barges moored on the river below. This was simply not the case, and although I have never seen this channel on the escarpment, I know for certain that limestone blocks were not hauled up this ramp. It may well be that a natural cleft in the face of the escarpment existed here before the Bent Pyramid and the Red Pyramid were constructed, but the builders of these pyramids almost certainly engineered this cleft to the angle and width that would best accommodate the flight of locks they undoubtedly constructed here, prior to the construction of the large pyramids at this site. Just as they would later do at Giza, they transported building materials on barges up onto the plateau here from the River Nile below. They then transported those materials up and onto the platforms of the pyramids themselves as these pyramids were built up. Just as at Giza, the evidence for this is overwhelming and unequivocal. Indeed, the pyramids at Dashur stand as testament to this as these pyramids could only have been constructed using hydraulic power, and their inner pipes and chambers confirm that this was how they were constructed. These were the first true Super Pyramids of the hydraulic age; the first two pyramids where each full width course was built up from the foundation level using hydraulic power to transport the building materials into the pyramid structures. There was simply no need for the ancient pyramid builders to haul limestone blocks up ramps when they could construct a series of locks to lift the masonry up onto the plateau at Dashur, just as they did with the pyramid structures themselves.

Both of the large pyramids at Dashur have an extensive pipe system and a number of chambers have been discovered in both of them. Both of these pyramids have what are currently termed descending corridors on their north sides. Both of these pyramids also have inlet channels or pipes on their west sides, the sides nearest the water reservoir and the feeder canal. Although the configuration of the pipes and chambers in these two pyramids differ from those of the Great Pyramid, it is plain to see that the waters of the feeder canal were channelled into, then through, both of these pyramids. The builders constructed the feeder canal on the west side of both of these pyramids as the reservoir that supplied water to the canal system was situated somewhere in the hills west or possibly north-west of the canal system at Dashur. Undoubtedly, the reservoir and the canal system on the western side of these pyramids would have been used to supply water to the canal that was routed through each of these structures, and a branch of this canal would have been extended to each of the construction sites here.

I recently came across an article in *Forbidden History* written by J Douglas Kenyon, titled: *Pushing Back the Portals of Civilisation* where the writer recounts a visit to the Red Pyramid at Dashur in the company of John Anthony West. A number of photographs accompanied this article but I was absolutely taken aback when I viewed the three photographs of the so called 'burial chamber' in the Red Pyramid. The masonry in the lower section of this chamber (the author refers to this as the pit) is in disarray, but it was his comments about this chamber that really caught my attention. I quote:

> "The stones in the pit were clearly of a different type
> from those of the structure above. Moreover, while the

pyramid had been built with great precision, the arrangement of the pit was chaotic. And even though the stones were doubtless cut artificially, their edges had been rounded in a way that suggested water weathering."

West and Kenyon's conclusions were that this had once been an older structure that had been exposed to the elements for a long period of time before it was incorporated into the lower courses of the Red Pyramid. Had I not known otherwise, I would have believed this to have been a very logical conclusion for them to draw here. However, I was delighted that I had discovered this article, not because I agreed with the author of the piece and John Anthony West, but because I recognised this chamber for what it truly was.

The 'weathering' that had puzzled John Anthony West and J. Douglas Kenyon had not occurred earlier as they had presumed; it had occurred during the construction of this pyramid. It was not weathering caused by exposure to the elements over a long period of time; it was water erosion that had occurred during the construction of the pyramid. Water from the feeder canal had once tumbled down into this pit and then flowed through the chambers and pipes of the structure to feed the supply canal on its north side. This chamber was the Red Pyramid equivalent of the subterranean chamber in the Great Pyramid. It may not have been below the foundation level of the Red Pyramid but it had undoubtedly played the same role as the subterranean chamber in the Great Pyramid.

The subterranean chamber in the Great Pyramid has been carved out of the bedrock far below the foundation level of the structure and the effects of water erosion are plain to see in this chamber also. But there is no disarray here, such as we see in the pit in the Red Pyramid. These two chambers served exactly the same purpose but it's plain to see that when the builders came to construct the pyramids at Giza they had learned from the mistake they had made in the Red Pyramid. Water surged down into both of these chambers through inlet tunnels. The vortex created in these chambers acted like a choke, absorbing much of the energy generated as the feed waters surged into the chambers and then through the piping system. This is what regulated the flow in the outlet pipe that fed the supply canal via the descending corridors in both of these pyramids. The disarray in the pit in the Red Pyramid, however, only occurred because this chamber had been constructed of blocks of masonry within the body of the pyramid; it had not been carved out of the bedrock below the structure. Many of the blocks were dislodged by the tremendous forces at work here as water surged into this chamber from the inlet pipe above. Much of the damage on the masonry in this chamber has been caused by blocks that had been dislodged by the powerful force of the water as it surged down into the chamber. The blocks that were dislodged would have been caught up in the vortex created in the chamber as the feed waters surged into it, and as long as water continued to flow into the chamber, these blocks, and the pieces that had broken off, would have been spun around and around, bouncing off the sides of the pit, dislodging yet more blocks, and chipping away at the exposed edges and corners of other blocks in the walls of the chamber. Had this chamber been carved out of the solid bedrock below the foundation level of the Red Pyramid, there would have been no blocks of masonry to be dislodged.

When the pyramid builders came to construct the three pyramids at Giza, it is therefore very significant that all three of the chambers of this type – and their respective inlet pipes – are carved out of the bedrock below the foundation level of each pyramid. It is plain to see that the builders had learned at least one very valuable lesson at Dashur and that is why we see these chambers excavated out of the bedrock deep below their respective pyramids. The incoming water was channelled down into chambers well below the foundation level to prevent damage occurring within the chambers themselves, and by carving these chambers out of the bedrock there were no blocks of masonry to be dislodged in these chambers.

The birth of the Super Pyramid

When I first set out on my quest to discover how the pyramids had been constructed I was of the opinion that the grand gallery in the Great Pyramid was unique. I had not come across any references to similar features in other pyramids, although I was aware of chambers with corbelled roofs in pyramids elsewhere on the west bank. However, as you are now aware, it was when I was doing some research on the pyramids at Dashur that I discovered that there was a small pyramid here with a sloping chamber just like the one in the Great Pyramid. As I pressed on with my study of the pyramids, I discovered that almost all of the components of the Great Pyramid's internal structure existed in some form or other at Dashur. In the Bent Pyramid, for instance, there is what looks like a pump room and a vertical shaft off to one side of it where a plunger, a piston, could have been installed. Although I have been unable to determine for certain that a pump had been installed here, there is nonetheless no shortage of evidence at Dashur to indicate that this was where the true Super Pyramids came into being; this is where we see the first flight of locks from the River Nile up to the plateau; this is where the pyramid builders first constructed pyramids from large blocks of masonry and this is where we first see chambers, pipes and valves being created for the manipulation of water within these structures. All of these essential elements were present at the birth of the Super Pyramid here.

Dashur is where the ancient pyramid builders first began to construct true pyramids from large blocks of masonry and it is here that we see pyramid design and construction in a form very similar to what we later see at Giza, albeit less refined. It was also here, for the very first time, that someone routed a canal through a fully integrated pyramid – as opposed to one with a stepped core structure – and a great revolution in pyramid design and construction began. These new Super Pyramids have almost nothing in common with the many primitive pyramid structures to be found on the west bank. In fact, true, fully integrated, stone block, pyramid construction began at Dashur and if these structures are much older than Egyptologists believe them to be, these are quite possibly the very first pyramids ever to be constructed in Egypt.

Nowadays, the small satellite pyramid on the south side of the Bent Pyramid at Dashur with the sloping chamber (gallery) is in a pretty poor state as much of this structure has collapsed. We are therefore unlikely to glean any more information regarding Super Pyramid construction from this small structure. Having now reconstructed our own Super Pyramid, however, we can be absolutely certain that the Middle Pyramid at Giza also has a similar internal structure to that of the Great Pyramid as we can see from its external appearance that it must have been constructed in a similar manner; the perimeter platforms have been built up from two central hubs. In light of this knowledge, we can therefore also be certain that the Bent Pyramid and the Red Pyramid at Dashur must also contain more pipes and chambers than we have so far discovered. Can we really believe, for instance, that the pyramid builders created a miniature grand gallery within a small satellite pyramid here in order to construct it, but didn't think it necessary to put such chambers in the nearby much larger structures? Of course not!

While I was researching this early period in pyramid design, I came across a paper written by Bonnie M. Sampsell. It was titled: *Pyramid Design and Construction – Part I: The Accretion Theory.* The paper was originally published in 2000 and Bonnie kindly agreed to let me reproduce the paragraph below.

> "I am devoting this first paper of the series to this point regarding the pyramid internal structure because this knowledge is necessary before one can discuss construction methods. I believe that the change in the method of building a pyramid's nucleus signalled an improvement in ancient technology and materials. By Dynasty IV, the pyramid builders found a way to quarry, move, and set in place really enormous blocks of limestone. It was this capability that changed their entire approach to pyramid construction and not any disasters or problems encountered during the construction of any particular monument. Engineering of true pyramids relies on different principles than used with step pyramids."

I couldn't agree more. But, as I mentioned earlier, I am not completely convinced that what we are seeing is a straightforward evolutionary process from mastabas, to stepped pyramids and then to true pyramids. It may not be nearly as clear cut as that, for it's possible that we are seeing pyramids here at Dashur, Super Pyramids, constructed long before the more primitive stepped core pyramids were constructed. The mud brick structures on the west bank may not pre-date the Super Pyramids either as they may just have been the simplest solution to pyramid construction when hydraulic power was no longer available. At Dashur and Giza we can clearly see the linear progression of pyramid development, the evolution of these structures, but when the hydraulic age came to an end, so did this linear development as the pyramid builders had to adopt much simpler techniques to construct pyramids without the use of hydraulic power. As I mentioned earlier, it is only when we finally gain entry to a sealed tomb or chamber beneath one of the Super Pyramids and discover organic materials that we can carbon date, that we are likely to get a much better idea of when these pyramids were constructed for the picture is not nearly as clear as we have been led to believe.

We know, of course, that many of the more primitive style of pyramids and mastabas on the west bank were built long after the true, fully integrated, Super Pyramids at Dashur and Giza. The pyramid age didn't come to an end at Giza, it was the hydraulic age that came to an end after the Giza complex had been constructed and the climate had changed dramatically. The ancient Egyptians went on to build pyramids long after those at Giza but all of those later pyramids had to be constructed without the use of hydraulic power. Without hydraulic power, it was no longer possible to construct pyramids using large blocks of masonry, such as those used in the construction of the Super Pyramids, on high ground away from the river. It was only manpower and primitive lifting devices that the builders of these pyramids had at their disposal. That is why these later structures were such simple constructions compared to the pyramids at Giza, the Super Pyramids.

But there was something more happening on the west bank south of Giza when the ancient pyramid builders began to construct large, stone built, true pyramids here for as Bonnie M. Sampsell quite rightly pointed out in her paper on pyramid construction methods;

> "the pyramid builders found a way to quarry, move and
> set in place really enormous blocks of limestone."

However, it's also plain to see that by the time the builders had completed these new, fully integrated pyramids at Dashur and had moved north, they had an altogether different agenda. The Super Pyramid builders had been developing grander and more complex structures at a remarkable pace and they were clearly on a mission for when it came time for them to build at Giza, they set out to construct a whole pyramid complex laid out in a pre-determined grand plan.

When I now look at the early pyramids of the hydraulic age that were constructed south of Giza at Meidum and Dashur, I cannot help but believe that these early structures were all about Giza. In a few short steps the pyramid builders went from constructing the first Super Pyramid using large blocks of masonry, to designing and building fully integrated, incredibly refined and phenomenally complex, true pyramids with a degree of accuracy that we would have great difficulty in reproducing today. In a few short steps from its inception, they produced the most stable, true Super Pyramid ever constructed and put three of these structures on the Giza plateau. This was a phenomenal achievement in such a short period of time, but when we consider that it all took place five thousand years ago, it is almost beyond belief. Yet, as you have now discovered, the evidence for this is unequivocal; the internal features of the Great Pyramid are a testament to the method and manner of its construction. Clearly, the time has come for us to re-evaluate what we thought we knew about these early pyramid builders, as the people who built the Super Pyramids bear little resemblance to the Egyptological establishment's view of the builders of these monumental structures.

I mentioned earlier that all of these Super Pyramids were constructed on the west bank of the River Nile. However, if we look at a map of northern Egypt (Lower Egypt), we can also see that none of these Super Pyramids were constructed south of Dashur, with the exception of the collapsed pyramid at Meidum, although this was not a fully integrated, true pyramid, as it was only part of its core that was constructed using large, dressed blocks of masonry. Whether or not we include the stepped core pyramid at Meidum, what is immediately obvious when we look at all of these structures in detail is that each evolutionary step was taken as the builders progressed steadily northward. The stepped core pyramid at Meidum, probably the first pyramid of the hydraulic age, was the furthest south of all these structures. The Bent Pyramid was the next evolutionary step in pyramid design and this pyramid was constructed at Dashur, north of Meidum. Although the Red Pyramid, the next step in pyramid design after the Bent Pyramid, was also constructed at Dashur, it is located just north of the Bent Pyramid. This was the first fully integrated pyramid where all of the limestone blocks were set down in horizontal courses from the foundation level.

The next project the builders undertook was not just the construction of a pyramid it was the construction of a series of pyramids and many smaller satellite pyramids and temples on a gargantuan scale, the most famous pyramid complex on the planet. The pyramids at Giza were not simply the next evolutionary leap forward in pyramid design and construction; something new and momentous happened here. The Super Pyramid builders constructed a whole, pre-planned, pyramid complex on a grand scale.

We can clearly follow the course of pyramid development that had begun at Meidum, with two further stages of development occurring at Dashur, before the builders moved north and began the construction of the pyramids at Giza. But prior to Giza, all that these other pyramids had in common was their sequential development and their pyramid shape, for the fact remains, that these were three individual pyramids that seem unrelated to each other in any other way. (I must point out here that the pyramid builders possibly constructed another pyramid just prior to the pyramids at Giza and this was north of the Giza complex. However, masonry from the structure north of Giza, at Abu Roash, has been plundered for centuries and it is now difficult to determine if this structure was in fact a complete pyramid. That is why I have not included it in the sequence of events above. There is also the possibility that this structure may have been the last of the Super Pyramids and it may indeed have been constructed after the Giza complex had been completed.)

The pyramids and the many peripheral structures at Giza, on the other hand, are all part of a grand plan and each and every one of the structures here played its part in the overall scheme. The three largest pyramids tower over all the other structures on the plateau and it's plain for all to see that they form the nucleus of the Giza complex. What must not be overlooked here though is the almost unimaginable amount of planning and organisation that went into this project long before a single block of limestone was ever set in place. We have looked at the phenomenal amount of planning and preparatory work that had to be undertaken before work could begin on the foundation course of the Great Pyramid, but this was just one of many structures here. Although the work undertaken in the bedrock below the Great Pyramid was more complex than the work undertaken in the bedrock beneath the Middle Pyramid at Giza, there was also a very considerable amount of preparatory sub-surface work undertaken in the bedrock below the Small Pyramid. Also, in the case of the Small Pyramid, a further two phases of work were undertaken in the bedrock below the structure after work had begun on the structure itself. One of these phases occurred not long after work had begun on the above ground structure (when the lower outlet pipe was sealed and the upper outlet pipe created). The other operations below ground level did not occur until the structure was complete (the creation of the granite chamber and the creation of the rectangular chamber in the horizontal section of the lower outlet pipe, although the latter may have occurred long after this pyramid had been completed).

This is what makes Giza so different from any other pyramid fields on the west bank. The builders designed, planned and surveyed this site long before they began the construction of the first of the many structures here. This site didn't develop piecemeal like some of the other pyramid fields; every structure in the Giza Complex was built exactly where it had been envisaged prior to the construction of the very first structure here. That is why I believe that the pyramids of the hydraulic age, constructed prior to those at Giza, were all experimental Super Pyramids. They were one-offs, and I believe that Giza is what they were all about. (I have referred to the pyramid situated between the Great Pyramid and the Small Pyramid at Giza as the Middle Pyramid. I cannot refer to this structure as the Second Pyramid as it was clearly constructed before the Great Pyramid. Neither can I refer to it as the pyramid of Khafre as I believe this structure was at least thousand years old when Khafre ruled Egypt.)

When we look at the bigger picture, we can also see that the builders made the most of the site at Giza for they constructed the three largest pyramids that it was possible to construct in this configuration on the plateau. They couldn't have made the three principal structures larger, as they couldn't have risked putting the Great Pyramid any nearer the escarpment on the eastern side of the plateau. They couldn't have constructed a bigger structure where the small pyramid sits today for this was the biggest structure they could build here, given the head of water they had to work with at this location. If they'd gone any further west to build this pyramid, the small pyramid would most probably have been smaller still. In other words, we have to look at the Giza Complex three dimensionally to see the limitations of the site for this is what determined the position and size of the principal structures here.

I have not been able to make sense of the configuration of the more primitive pyramids constructed after Giza and it certainly looks like each of these structures were not constructed as part of a grand plan, like those at Giza. These pyramid fields seem to have developed randomly over time for as far as I'm aware there is nothing to indicate that they were configured according to a pre-conceived plan. It is therefore very unlikely that we will discover patterns in these pyramid fields if there are none to be found.

Giza is unique and about the only thing that the pyramids of the hydraulic age have in common with the more primitive pyramids on the west bank is their geometric shape. Giza was undoubtedly a very sacred place to the ancient builders, if not the most sacred, and I have no doubt that a few early royal tombs may yet be discovered here. But now that we have accounted for the inner chambers and passageways of the Great Pyramid, and can clearly understand their purpose, we know that these chambers were not created as tombs. However, I don't doubt that the mummified bodies of ancient kings of Egypt were interred in tombs somewhere on this very sacred site and hopefully archaeologists will discover some of those tombs in the fullness of time. If the pyramids at Giza are memorials to ancient kings, then I believe that their tombs are most likely to be found under these structures. But that is clearly not just what the pyramids at Giza were all about, for the structures we see here were configured according to a pre-determined plan. There may be tombs under, or near, the two largest structures here, as it was almost certainly the case that there was one such chamber in the bedrock beneath the small pyramid. But the structures themselves were not just constructed as cenotaphs because they so obviously form part of a much greater grand plan.

We now know that the smallest of the three principal pyramids at Giza and the Great Pyramid had inlet tunnels that have yet to be discovered. As I mentioned earlier, the granite chamber in the smallest of the three principal pyramids here was almost certainly a royal tomb, so we are unlikely to discover another tomb when we gain access to the inlet tunnel in this pyramid. (We cannot rule this out completely until we gain access to this inlet pipe; it is possible that other burial chambers could have been carved out of the bedrock somewhere along this tunnel).

There was once a substantial chamber behind the south wall of the burial chamber in the Small Pyramid, and we know that the inlet tunnel was extended as far as the opening in the passageway opposite the opening to the subterranean chamber here. There is no opening in this wall now for it was sealed up when the builders completed the structure and installed the south wall of the granite chamber, but it may be possible to gain access to that inlet tunnel at this location if the tunnel itself still exists (there may be no chamber here now if the space behind the south wall of the passageway was built up after the granite chamber was completed). This is certainly one area of the structure where some non-destructive testing may prove fruitful. If a chamber still exists here, it should certainly be easier to gain access to the chamber from the south wall of the passageway, rather than to try and gain access via the opening to this pipe on the south side of the structure, for the external opening to this tunnel is likely to have been blocked up over a considerable distance in order to safeguard the burial chamber(s).

We have not yet discovered the location of the inlet tunnel in the Great Pyramid and it may very well be the case that a tomb was created deep below the structure somewhere along this tunnel. When the structure was complete, and the water had been drained from the piping system, a burial chamber could easily have been created somewhere along this pipe. The inlet pipe would have provided access to the tomb until such times as a king's mummy could be interred in the chamber. It would then have been backfilled and consolidated over some of its length and the entrance to the tunnel sealed. It remains sealed to this day.

This was just one of the options available to the builders of these structures and it was almost certainly the case that this was how access was gained to the burial chamber in the Small Pyramid after the pyramid was complete. When we discover the inlet pipe in the Great Pyramid, we may find that it is nothing more than an inlet pipe, for the builders could have created burial chambers almost anywhere beneath these structures. However, if these structures were built over a tomb to prevent tomb robbers from desecrating the burial chambers of kings – as was the purpose of the mastabas – then surely the inlet pipe in the Great Pyramid would have provided the perfect access tunnel for such a tomb – as was the case with the smallest of the three principal pyramids here. When the deceased king's mummy had later been interred in the burial chamber and the access shaft sealed there would have been no outward indication that an access shaft had ever existed.

The largest limestone blocks used at Giza are to be found in the Sphinx and Valley Temples, just east of the Sphinx, but these blocks were quarried from the area around the Sphinx itself, the Sphinx Enclosure, and transported the short distance to these temples. The feeder canal that was oriented east-west would have been extended as far as the Nile on the eastern side of the plateau and barges would have entered the canal system just east of the Sphinx and Valley Temples through a series of locks. The dry dock / lock here needed a water supply and it was this branch of the feeder canal that provided the water for the huge lock that had been constructed here prior to the construction of the two temples. Very large barges would have been needed to move the 200 ton monoliths from the Sphinx Enclosure, to the walls of the Valley Temple where they were to be installed. These barges would have been much wider than the feeder canal on the plateau; therefore the locks east of the Sphinx and Valley Temples were the most likely entry point for these barges. These very large barges would only have been used in the lock that had been constructed around the site of the Sphinx and Valley Temples and the Sphinx Enclosure. This is as far as these barges would have travelled within the canal system east of the Middle Pyramid, and south of the Great Pyramid. The walls of the massive lock that were constructed prior to the building of the temples would have been left in place when the temple complex was complete; these would then have become the perimeter walls of the temple complex.

Perhaps we will never discover why the structures at Giza were configured as they were. However, I think that the discoveries made by Thomas Brophy at Nabta Playa, certainly go a long way to bolstering the Orion Correlation Theory put forward by Robert Bauval and Adrian Gilbert in their book *The Orion Mystery*. This theory proposes that the three principal pyramids at Giza are an image of three stars in the constellation of Orion, the three stars of Orion's Belt. However, the three large pyramids at Giza are only three of many pyramids and structures on the plateau and clearly there is a lot more to the Giza complex than this correlation with Orion. Hopefully it won't be too long before we get a better understanding of these structures and their relationship to one another.

In my research I stumbled upon many statements by others that backed up my findings at Giza and on the west bank. In *The Egypt Code* by Robert Bauval, in Appendix 2, page 214, I came across a quote by Giulio Magli on the possible discovery of precessional effects in ancient astronomy.

He states:

> "I have therefore proposed that the error in the orientation of the 'second pyramid' actually shows that it was constructed before Giza 1 or, more precisely, the two projects were conceived together..."

Professor Magli goes on to say:

> "It is very well known that the main pyramids of the fourth dynasty (the main three at Giza and the two Snefru pyramids at Dashur) were oriented to face the cardinal points with a high degree of precision. The precision achieved by the pyramid builders was so high that it is absolutely certain that the orientation method used was based on stars and not on the measurement of shadows".

Professor Magli is a cutting edge physicist and a passionate astronomer who teaches physics and mathematics at Milan Polytechnic. His work has been quoted by many authors, many of whom refer to him as 'the only scientist who understands the role of astronomy in antiquity.' I've never met Professor Magli, but it's good to know that an academic of such high standing agrees with me on the order of construction of the two largest structures at Giza.

The Bent Pyramid and the Red Pyramid at Dashur were the first of the new Super Pyramids to be built using hydraulic power. This was not a small step in an evolutionary process it was a major leap into the future. In fact, it is difficult to accept that it was the same people who were involved in the construction of these new type pyramids as those involved in the construction of the more primitive types that supposedly preceded them. I had long been convinced that most, if not all, of the really large pyramids on the west bank were not constructed as tombs for kings or pharaohs, but when I discovered how the true Super Pyramids had been constructed, and realized the true purpose of their pipes and chambers, I was then absolutely certain that they were not constructed as tombs. If it was the same people who were responsible for the construction of some of the earlier, more primitive, type structures – if indeed any of them were earlier than the Super Pyramids – then it seems obvious that at some point the goal of the pyramid builders must have changed by the time they began to construct pyramids at Giza, as no mummies have ever been found in any of the super pyramids. However, I later discovered that many of the more primitive type pyramids had been constructed as cenotaphs and not as tombs either. This seemed to be totally at odds with the orthodox view that pyramids were built as tombs and Egyptologists never seem to tire of telling us that this was the case. However, most Egyptologists must be aware that the primitive pyramids were not always constructed for this purpose.

Egyptologists also maintain that a number of kings or pharaohs have been responsible for the construction of more than one pyramid and I always thought that this did not sit well with the theory that these pyramids were built as tombs. In fact, it is totally at odds with it, for why would a pharaoh need more than one tomb? I have since discovered, however, that it was the custom at times for some pharaohs to construct pyramids at both Saqqara and Abydos. It is thought that these pharaohs built one pyramid over their tomb and built the other as a cenotaph. However, if this was indeed the case, it is impossible to discover which one was the tomb and which one the cenotaph, as no bodies (mummies) have been found in either of the structures ascribed to these pharaohs. This begs the question: why do some Egyptologists promote the "tombs and only tombs theory" when they talk about the pyramids at Giza when they know that this was not the case with many pyramids?

This really is an abominable state of affairs. More has been written about the pyramids of Egypt than any other type of structure on the planet, yet all we have at the end of the day is conjecture, obfuscation and misinformation. Some Egyptologists have stated so often that pyramids were built as tombs that I think they have actually come to believe it themselves. But it doesn't have to be this way, for much of the confusion that surrounds this issue could easily be swept away if Egyptologists simply dealt with the facts, as opposed to promoting their own pet theories. When archaeologists refer to specific pyramids, they should state quite clearly if the body of a pharaoh or anyone else has been discovered within the pyramid. If there is no record of any mummy being discovered in the pyramid, it should be clearly stated that "there is no indication that this pyramid was built as a tomb." To say otherwise, or say nothing, simply muddies the waters and perpetuates the myth that all pyramids were built as tombs.

A distinction should also be made between the pyramids that contain a coffer, those that contain – or contained – a sarcophagus and those that contain neither. A coffer is a plain, usually rectangular box; a sarcophagus on the other hand would normally have some decoration and possibly an inscription and could never be mistaken for a plain coffer. Once again, it is simply misleading to refer to a coffer as a sarcophagus if there is no evidence to indicate that it was ever used as such. We expect archaeologists to give us a true and accurate account of the facts; when they are less than honest, confusion is the result.

While we are on the subject of coffers, I would like to bring to your attention the fact that at least two sealed coffers were found in chambers within pyramids on the west bank in the twentieth century. Coffers have been found in a good many pyramids and some pyramids actually contain a number of coffers. However, it is the discovery of sealed coffers that I want to bring to your attention here as the granite coffer in the Great Pyramid was once a sealed coffer with a granite lid. When I was researching this subject, I discovered that at least two coffers had been found that had been completely sealed at the time of their discovery. One of these coffers was made of alabaster and the other of limestone, I believe. When these sealed coffers were opened they were found to be completely empty. This begs the question: why seal an empty coffer?

It should have been patently obvious that something was going on here that had nothing to do with the interment of a pharaoh's mummy. Even if we assume that this was the intended purpose of any sealed coffer and another coffer was substituted, why would anyone go to the trouble of sealing the empty coffer? Having just reconstructed a Super Pyramid however, we now know of at least one reason why the ancient pyramid builders would seal such vessels.

When coffers were used as counterweights in the hydraulic cranes of the day – the shadoufs – these simple machines could be used in confined spaces where it wasn't possible to use a shadouf with a longer beam to increase the leverage. These machines enabled men to raise much heavier loads in confined spaces as long as the water levels within those spaces could be manipulated and controlled. As we now know, the buoyancy of these counterweights, when the water level was increased within the working area, enabled the workmen to lower the lifting end of the beam to pick up a load.

They could not have done so if they had had to raise such a counterweight as a dead weight. These counterweights were therefore essential parts of hydraulic lifting machines – hydraulic cranes – used in confined spaces where increased leverage was not possible. It may also be the case that some coffers were used in conjunction with other types of lifting mechanisms, such as an elevator for instance, as a great many of them were produced. All that we can say for certain is that sealed coffers were an essential part of the hydraulic lifting machines used by the ancient pyramid builders, and these were undoubtedly used to great effect in the two largest pyramids at Giza when they were under construction.

The step core pyramid at Meidum was probably the first pyramid to be constructed using canal locks to raise barges with building materials up and onto the platforms of the structure as it was built up. The layout of the internal chambers and pipes so far discovered in the stepped core pyramid at Meidum bears a resemblance to the inner pipes and chambers so far discovered in the Middle Pyramid at Giza. In the drawing (Fig. 40) of the Meidum pyramid on the next page you will no doubt see that the inlet and outlet pipes are both on the same side (north side) of the structure, as are those in the Middle Pyramid at Giza. These pipes in the Meidum pyramid were created one above the other, as were those in the Middle Pyramid.

The lower pipes in both of these structures were the inlet pipes and water would have flowed down into the system through various chambers, then up and out of the mouth of the upper pipes, and on into the supply canals at both sites. There is a chamber that is referred to as the burial chamber and two so called relieving chambers are shown at the lower end of the upper pipe in this sectional drawing of this pyramid. However, I have changed these misleading labels to terms that we are more familiar with, and more in keeping with their true purpose. Although the subterranean chamber in my drawing is not technically a subterranean chamber, it would have served the same purpose as the subterranean chamber in the Great Pyramid.

The three chambers here would probably have been interconnected and together they would have acted as a choke in the system to slow the flow of water entering the supply canal. Looking at the drawing of this inner layout, it is also possible that an ascending corridor was created up near the top end of the upper

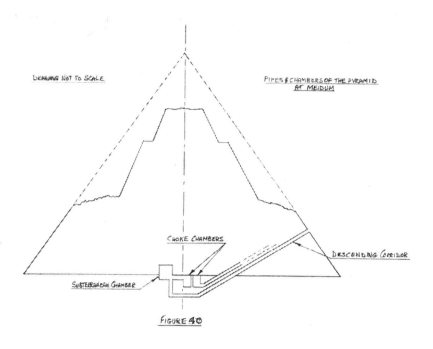

CHOKE CHAMBERS

DESCENDING CORRIDOR

SUBTERRANEAN CHAMBER

FIGURE 40

descending corridor (as is certainly the case in the Middle Pyramid at Giza). It is also possible that a sloping gallery was constructed deep inside the structure at Meidum but this is by no means certain, for the inner core was not constructed of large limestone blocks but much smaller bricks. If these features do indeed exist in the earliest pyramid of the hydraulic age, however, it almost certainly means that most of the classic elements of the inner structure of the Great Pyramid exist in all the pyramids constructed at this time, including the Bent Pyramid and the Red Pyramid at Dashur. We also know that a smaller version of the grand gallery was created in the small satellite pyramid on the south side of the Bent Pyramid; therefore it is inconceivable that such galleries should not exist within the two much larger structures at Dashur.

The pyramids at Giza and Dashur could only have been constructed when the climate was favourable for the collection of large volumes of water to supply the canal systems, without which it would have been impossible to construct these massive structures. As we discovered earlier, the grand gallery in the Great Pyramid was created so that the builders could extend the canal system all the way up to the top of this gallery. As we then discovered, hydraulic power was also used to construct the upper chamber and the stack above it, in fact, this free-standing granite structure would not exist if hydraulic power had not been available at this elevation. This was only achieved by extending the canal system beyond the grand gallery into the inner area. By designing the free-standing and very complex upper chamber and stack, and by extending the canal system into this inner area around the upper chamber, the builders of the Great Pyramid were able to construct much of this inner section of the pyramid using very large blocks and slabs of masonry. More importantly, by constructing the free-standing upper chamber beyond the gallery, they were able to construct much of the mid-section of the pyramid – beyond the 50th course of the structure – using the large limestone blocks they had used to construct the lower section of the structure. Had they not constructed the upper chamber and the stack, then much of the mid-section would have been constructed using the much smaller limestone blocks used to complete the upper section of the structure. This would have greatly increased the time it would have taken to complete the Great Pyramid as all of this masonry would have been hauled up the lift shaft from the 50th level, one block at a time.

When I look at the earlier structures at Dashur, I can't help but wonder at what evolutionary stage the builders realized they could extend the canal system way beyond the top of a gallery. In other words, were the free-standing upper chambers and inner locks beyond the galleries in the Great Pyramid and its large companion the only Super Pyramids to have such design features? Perhaps one day we may find the answer to that question.

There has been a lot of speculation as to why the angle of the sides of the Bent Pyramid was altered and many theories have been put forward, but I noticed something about this pyramid recently that I had not been aware of earlier. I noticed that the limestone blocks used to construct the top section of the pyramid, from the level where the angle changes, were much smaller blocks than those used to construct the much greater lower section. This level, where the angle changes, is also the level where the builders began to set the blocks down horizontally across the full width of the platforms. This clearly indicates that it was probably when the construction had reached this level that the builders first began to hoist the much smaller blocks up a central shaft within this structure (a lift shaft). .

However, when they began to use these much smaller blocks of limestone, the rate of construction would have slowed considerably as these blocks could only be hauled up to the working platforms one at a time. I then began to wonder if, as I suspect, these early pyramids of the hydraulic age were experimental prototypes, did the builders just want to complete this one as quickly as possible by this stage of the construction and move on to the next prototype structure – the Red Pyramid? By this time, it is entirely possible that new, advanced design features had been included in the plans for the new structure, features that would greatly improve the rate of construction of these large, stone built pyramids.

This is all pure speculation of course, for we have no way of determining why they chose to change the angle of the sides when they did. But it is certainly not beyond the realms of probability, and at this moment in time we do not know when the builders introduced lower and upper chambers to the internal structure of the super pyramids. This is something else that we will only be able to determine when we discover all of the pipes and chambers in the upper sections of these early structures.

This was just another of those little things that led me to believe that the ancient builders were perfecting their skills and experimenting with new designs and building methods at Dashur, specifically with the Giza project in mind. Was it only when they had come up with a design where they could put the biggest pyramids it was possible to construct on the Giza Plateau in the shortest possible time that their focus shifted to Giza? It's unlikely that we will ever know for sure but I certainly don't think we can rule this out.

The grand doorway of the Great Pyramid was the zero point where all the mysteries of the past converged and the possibility of a final solution to the puzzle emerged. We have been staring at those double gables for hundreds of years and didn't recognise that they were only the first of many. This was the way into the heart of the Great Pyramid and to the heart of the great mystery that its construction posed. Not long after I made my initial breakthrough – when I realized that the builders had to have employed technology way beyond anything we had ever believed possible – I came across a quote from Arthur C. Clarke that I would like to share with you.

He states:

"Highly advanced technology is indistinguishable from magic".

I couldn't help but think that most of the ancient observers who witnessed the construction of the magnificent pyramids at Giza must indeed have believed that they were witnessing magic at work. Within the Great Pyramid, the builders created three different types of chambers; chambers cut out of the bedrock below the structure – the subterranean chamber; chambers which were created within the limestone body of the structure – the lower chamber and the grand gallery fall into this category; and chambers created as free-standing structures within the Great Pyramid – the upper chamber. We now know that there is an expansion chamber in the Middle Pyramid for that is undoubtedly what the large chamber directly below the peak of the structure at ground level is. But this pyramid almost certainly has a grand gallery and an upper chamber, as it's plain to see that the builders used large limestone blocks to construct the greater part of this structure also (the perimeter levels here had to have been extended farther from an upper chamber). If we also consider why the pyramid builders created the lower chamber in the Great Pyramid, then they had no reason to create a lower chamber in the middle pyramid at all if they did not go on to pump water up to much higher levels here also.

Djoser's Step Pyramid at Saqqara is regarded as the first known stone built pyramid on the west bank. This may or may not be the case but this pyramid was not built using large stone blocks like those used in the pyramids at Giza. The original structure here has also been added to on a number of occasions therefore this pyramid should not be confused with the Super Pyramids of the hydraulic age.

In the paper by Bonnie M. Sampsell that I quoted from earlier, I also came across another very interesting quotation. She writes:

"Interestingly, the size of blocks employed for non-pyramidal structures tended to increase in the late Dynasty III to early Dynasty IV period. Goneim reported that limestone blocks in the "White Wall" surrounding the tomb of Sekhemkhet southwest of Djoser's tomb at

Saqqara were twice as high as those in Djoser's temenos wall, and he remarked: "It is certain that already in Djoser's reign there had been a tendency to increase the size of the stone blocks, as the builders ultimately came to learn that an increase in size meant an economy in the work of cutting out the stones, and lent more strength and a greater degree of cohesion to walls" (Goneim 1956:46).

Sekhemkhet is believed to have been a king of Dynasty III but scholars can't agree on the length of his reign... or if he even existed. It is thought by some that this may just be another name for Djoser. However, what we have at this site is what remains of a primitive step pyramid. It is thought that work stopped on this pyramid not long after it had begun; that at least, is the official version. However the white walls to which the quote refers have been built using much larger dressed limestone blocks. It is almost certainly the case that these walls were constructed right at the beginning of the hydraulic age when builders began transporting large, dressed, limestone blocks to construction sites. These blocks would have been transferred from the decks of the barges directly onto each course of the temenos wall as it was built up.

I have to admit though to having been puzzled as to why Egyptologists believe the pyramid here to have been unfinished. If work on this structure had stopped not long after it had begun, why would the builders have constructed such a substantial wall around an unfinished pyramid? The answer, of course, is that the temenos wall was constructed around the site of the pyramid here prior to the construction of the pyramid, since this structure would have been constructed within a large lock just like many of the peripheral structures at Giza. The only reason that I have mentioned this site is the fact that we probably had a combination of the old and the new here; a temenos wall built with large blocks of limestone that were almost certainly transported to this location on canal barges, with a stepped core pyramid constructed using small, roughly hewn, blocks of limestone. I seriously doubt however, that this pyramid was not completed, as it is more than likely that this small, stepped pyramid was encased within an outer shell of large, dressed limestone blocks like those used to construct the temenos wall. As this was a small pyramid constructed within a large lock, it would have been a fairly simple matter to build up the courses of the outer casing using barges to transport and raise these blocks up to their respective levels; therefore it is very unlikely that it was never completed. Being a fairly small pyramid though did have its drawbacks as these small structures would have been the first structures to have their dressed stone plundered by later builders. This, I would suggest, is a more likely reason for the rather dilapidated state of this structure today.

The pyramid builders may possibly have begun to build pyramids using large blocks of limestone soon after this temenos wall had been completed, but only after they discovered how to take a canal and barges into these structures. Here they had used canal barges to take the building materials to the construction site, and taken the first tentative step on the road that would ultimately lead to Giza and the construction of the greatest Super Pyramids ever constructed. As was the case at Giza and all of these ancient pyramid sites, many of the dressed limestone blocks that were most accessible have been plundered since medieval times as this was a ready source of dressed stone for later builders. Many of these sites were still being used as stone quarries in more recent times as it was much easier to haul pre-cut and pre-dressed stone blocks away from these sites than to quarry such blocks from the bedrock of a stone quarry.

Finally, I just want to say that I didn't conjure up the technology that I suspect was used in the construction of the pyramids at Giza; I simply set out to discover how the Great Pyramid had been put together, just as I had done on previous occasions. Along the way, I realized that the Old Kingdom Egyptians had to have been more technically advanced than we had otherwise understood them to be. I had long suspected that canal locks had been used to bring masonry up to the plateau, but when I discovered that the grand doorway was the entrance to a tunnel I immediately realized that the supply canal had been extended into the structure. These so called primitive builders had used hydraulic power to get the building materials up to the plateau but they also made use of that power within the structure itself. In time, I realized how the builders had transferred the masonry from the barges through to the lower chamber, the first distribution hub created within the structure. I then discovered that they had made use of the constantly changing water levels to power a hydraulic shadouf, a crane to lift large limestone blocks up onto the sidewalls of a partially constructed lower chamber, the central distribution hub on this level. I discovered that the inner stepped levels and the perimeter platforms of the structure had been built up from this hub and then I realized that the upper chamber had most likely been created for the same purpose. There was then a very long period of time when I made no progress beyond this stage of the construction. I was certain that the builders must have taken masonry up to the upper chamber on the 50th level and hauled it up ramps from this hub, but I could not figure out how they got the masonry up to the top of the gallery. After many months of getting nowhere, I put the problem to one side and forgot about it for a while. I hoped that when I came back to it I would look at it anew and discover a clue as to how it had been done, a clue that I could not see at that time.

As you are well aware by now, that is exactly what happened, but when I first realized that the builders might have constructed a flight of locks in the gallery, I couldn't put it all together. I couldn't figure out how they had pumped water up to the top of the gallery to feed the locks within it. Eventually, when I figured out how it had been done, I then knew for certain that they had transported large limestone and granite blocks and slabs up to the top end of the grand gallery. The upper chamber had indeed been a second distribution hub, just as the lower chamber had been before it and from here the builders built up the inner stepped levels and pushed the perimeter platform up to the greatest elevation possible.

Having solved the problem of how the builders transported these blocks up to the 50th level, I then hoped that the way forward would be clear and, although I didn't know it then, my greatest challenges were still ahead of me. I made many attempts to move beyond the area at the top of the gallery but it was more than two years before I finally understood how the upper chamber and the stack had been constructed, and why it had been constructed in the manner it had been. Just trying to figure out what had taken place at what stage of the construction in the area just beyond the top end of the grand gallery was a nightmare, and I went down many dead end paths in my search for the truth. Eventually, I discovered that the builders had constructed an inner lock at the top end of the gallery on the 50th level long before they installed the step-stone and the floor of the antechamber. I then hoped that most of my difficulties were behind me.

After the difficulties I had encountered at the top of the gallery, and now knowing why the upper chamber had been constructed of granite, I thought that the construction of the upper chamber and the stack would be straightforward. How wrong I was. The problem here was that the upper chamber and the stack had to be completed before the limestone blocks could be transported into this chamber. These, as we know, were then hauled up the ramps to the platforms above to build up the inner stepped levels and extend the perimeter levels to the greatest elevation possible using the large limestone blocks. This was not how it had been done in the lower chamber and I began to despair that I would ever solve all of the problems here. It was so difficult trying to visualise how this inner area of the structure looked at each stage of the construction and I gave up trying to remember how many times I had reconstructed a part of the structure, only to realize later that it couldn't be done in the manner I had reconstructed it. Eventually though, I managed to complete the upper chamber and the stack and build up the inner levels, using the large blocks of masonry that had been used to construct most of the structure. At that point, I really hoped that the antechamber wouldn't pose so many problems as I didn't have the mental stamina to go through such a long process of trial and error again.

Fortunately, it didn't, at least not its construction. But that was the easy bit for I hadn't given enough thought to the area directly above the antechamber and the wall at the top end of the gallery. I got bogged down here again. However, there was good reason for my short-sightedness as I was trying to figure out how the hoist was set up at this time and I was wrestling with the problems of completing the top end wall of the gallery and building up the area above the antechamber. If this had been all that was distracting me I might have solved some of the problems here sooner, but I simply couldn't get it out of my head that I was once again heading down (or up) a dead-end street. I knew that there was no other way to go, yet I couldn't see how the builders could have completed the pyramid by this route. It just didn't make any sense!

Was it a two-way street? Did they somehow use the lift shaft to complete the pinnacle of the pyramid, seal the top of this shaft and exit via the antechamber? These were some of the thoughts rattling around in my head when I was constructing the antechamber and the area above it and I didn't have any answers. Maybe it was just fatigue after spending so much time trying to solve all of the problems of the reconstruction of the upper chamber but I hadn't a clue as to how the builders had overcome this one. I vowed that when I got the hoist set up and I had built up the inner areas around the upper chamber that had still to be completed, that I would take another long break from the project. I hoped that the break would do me good and I would come back to it with a fresh pair of eyes.

The hoist proved to be a lot more complicated than I had first thought. Once I had discovered the true configuration of the hoist, it all seemed so straightforward, so obvious. But it was a long drawn out process before I finally managed to interpret the features within the antechamber and began to understand how the hoist had been set up and how the cradle had functioned. Many of the problems I had at the beginning with the hoist were down to the visualisation of the inner area above the antechamber when the hoist was first set up. As you are now aware, the inner platform around the east end of the upper chamber had still to be built up at this stage, including the areas above the ramps on the north and south sides of the upper chamber. The rig was also sandwiched between the top end of the grand gallery and the north wall of the upper chamber and the stack for such a long time also, at least until the inner platform had been built up beyond the level of the top of the stack. I had great difficulty visualising how the various operations had been undertaken and when I did manage to get a good idea of what the builders were up against, I realized that many of the options I had at first assumed were available to the builders (with the set-up of the hoist) were not available at all. Having then realized the limited extent of their options, I slowly began to determine the configuration of the components purely on the basis of the clues in the antechamber walls. The hoist mechanism is therefore not something that my imagination conjured up; it was determined purely by the constraints on the original builders and the physical evidence within the antechamber itself... the little chamber of secrets.

We cannot deny the existence of the pyramids and I believe the evidence to support my conclusions as to how they were built is overwhelming. The ancient builders built these structures and all the evidence as to how they did it is there in front of our eyes. If they hadn't done what I have described to the best of my ability here, then the pyramids at Giza and elsewhere would not exist in their present form, could not exist in their present form.

If they hadn't taken the canal into the structure; if they hadn't constructed a flight of locks in the grand gallery; if they hadn't created the inner lock to construct the upper chamber and the stack; if they hadn't constructed a hoist, then none of what you see at Giza today would ever have existed. I have absolutely no doubt that in the fullness of time this fully comprehensive account of the construction of the Great Pyramid will be accepted by academics as there was simply no other way to construct these magnificent structures.

I didn't come to the Great Pyramid in search of treasure; I came in search of truth. In the end I discovered both, as we had no idea that such a treasure trove of information had been hidden in plain sight.

Chapter Eleven

Fact and fiction

For as long as I can remember I have been fascinated as to how things worked and that is probably why I became an engineer. However, with the pyramids at Giza the picture that had been painted for us by academics was a diametrically opposed one. On the one hand, they told us that the Dynasty IV king Khufu was responsible for the construction of the Great Pyramid sometime around the middle of the third millennium B.C.E., on the other hand they claim that the pyramids were built by a farming people with only a primitive level of technology available to them, copper chisels and earth ramps, for example. Something was badly wrong with this theory and many of us knew instinctively that the orthodox explanation of how these complex structures had been constructed was badly flawed. Unfortunately, we could not prove otherwise.

In later life I realized that I had been conditioned to think of the Great Pyramid in the terms that Egyptologists referred to these structures and that it was this way of thinking that was holding me back from making any real progress with my attempts to discover the secrets of the ancient builders. So I began to deconstruct the conditioning in order to see the pyramids as they are, rather than as how I had become conditioned to think of them. I began this process by looking at a cross-section drawing of the Great Pyramid and tried to imagine that I was viewing this image for the very first time with no prior knowledge of its internal structure. Gradually, I created my own terminology for most of its passageways and chambers (much of the terminology currently in use is grossly misleading and based on the misconception that the Great Pyramid is a mausoleum). I also realized that I had to be focussed completely on *how* the pyramid had been constructed and not on the possible reason(s) for its construction. I had no way of knowing who was responsible for the construction of the Great Pyramid or to what ends they had built it, but this was of no great importance to me as it would only detract from my real objective, which was to discover *how* it had been constructed.

When I set out on, what turned out to be my last quest to discover how the Great Pyramid had been constructed, I had done so having discarded almost all of the unwanted baggage of the past. But although this quest turned out to be an experience beyond my wildest dreams, at the end of it all I still cannot tell you when this structure was constructed; I cannot tell you who it was that commissioned this structure; I cannot tell you what race of people were responsible for its construction. All that I can say for certain is that the structure itself holds almost all of the clues to its own construction. I have carefully examined and considered all of the evidence that I had access to and I can only conclude that this structure was put together by a highly skilled and technologically advanced people. I cannot tell you when it was constructed but I do believe that the evidence clearly points to it having been constructed long before the middle of the third millennium B.C.E. (This is entirely in keeping with the Sphinx, as a number of studies have also confirmed that it must be much older than was previously supposed.)

The evidence that points to the internal features of the Great Pyramid having been created to facilitate its construction is, in my opinion, overwhelming and unequivocal. It simply cannot be interpreted any other way as it all fits together perfectly like the pieces of a jigsaw puzzle. Whether the subterranean chamber was used for purposes other than its primary purpose I cannot say, but I cannot believe that those chambers and pipes within the body of the structure itself had a secondary role to play after the completion of the pyramid, given that the passageways here had been sealed by its builders and these passageways remained sealed until Caliph Al Ma'mun tunnelled his way into its inner pipes and chambers in the ninth century. These chambers simply had to be sealed before the pyramid could be completed.

There is certainly no doubt in my mind either that it was its original builders who sealed it up when they completed the structure (with the exception of the descending corridor and the subterranean chamber). Most of its chambers therefore could not have been accessed or utilised after its completion and, as you have now discovered, all of these chambers and pipes were created for practical purposes during the construction of this magnificent structure. (I believe that the various attempts to link the shafts in the upper and lower chambers to particular stars were just attempts by others to make sense of these shafts from a symbolic perspective, since we could see no practical reason for their existence.)

It is the Great Pyramid itself that has at last revealed how it was constructed and the clues have been there for all to see for centuries, we just couldn't interpret them. We had been told what it was, and how it had been built so often by those who considered themselves to be experts that we couldn't see what had been staring us in the face for more than a thousand years. We had been grossly misled.

When I eventually set out to write this account of my discoveries in the Great Pyramid, I wanted to get across just what was involved in the creation of this enormous structure. I realized that I risked boring the more technically minded reader but I wanted to lay out the bones of it all so that every schoolboy could understand how it had all been put together. It was when I was a schoolboy that I first became fascinated with Egypt and the pyramids, but they were all so mysterious then and no one had much of a clue as to how they had been built except in the fantasy world of motion pictures. But I wanted everyone to understand how advanced our ancient ancestors really were long before the time of classical Greece and the Roman Empire. There have been many discoveries made in the countries around the eastern Mediterranean in recent years that attest to the level of technology in use at very early periods indeed. It is abundantly clear from these discoveries that some technologies were developed much earlier than we previously had reason to believe, yet children are still being taught that the pyramids at Giza were built as tombs by Old Kingdom Egyptians, despite the fact that there has never been any tangible evidence to back this theory up. I can only hope that my discoveries finally put an end to this rampant speculation that has been presented as fact for far too long by those whose job it is to interpret the evidence without venturing into the realms of fantasy.

The Great Pyramid was constructed by a highly developed people who possessed technical skills far beyond any that we had been led to believe existed in Egypt's distant past. I have now discovered how the ancient builders constructed this wonderful structure and it is far from the picture painted by orthodox Egyptologists. The plain truth is that we never came close to understanding how it had been built because it was utterly impossible to build it given the level of technology believed to have existed at the time. I have absolutely no doubt that the Great Pyramid was constructed in the manner that I have now described, as it simply wasn't possible to build this structure by raising the limestone blocks up the outside of the structure. Neither was it humanly possible to raise granite blocks weighing fifty tons or more up to the upper chamber on earth ramps. It certainly wasn't possible to cut hundreds of granite blocks and slabs with copper chisels.

These are the main reasons as to why we didn't crack this problem before now. There was no way of doing it with external ramps and we didn't understand how it could have been done otherwise. We had a Catch 22 situation.

The Iron Age

So how do we explain it? Well, I think the likeliest scenario of all is that the Iron Age, and undoubtedly the hydraulic age, came to the Eastern Mediterranean much earlier than archaeologists believe, certainly much earlier than orthodox Egyptologists believe it to have occurred. The iron plate discovered during the Howard Vyse expedition is contemporary with the structure and we know that it was wrought (hammered) iron, not meteoritic iron. As I said earlier, iron would most probably have been a very expensive material and highly prized, therefore it would have been continually recycled when tools or implements were no longer of any use due to wear, or simply because they had been broken. There is archaeological evidence to show that copper smelting was being carried out in settlements near the southern shore of the Black Sea as early as the sixth millennium B.C.E., more than 2,000 years before the time of Khufu. Recent discoveries in this area show that ancient peoples were proficient in metallurgy long before the time of dynastic Egypt. In Western Turkey, for instance, an iron sword was discovered in a tomb dating from around the middle of the third millennium B.C.E.

Based on the scant evidence that we do have, it is not at all clear when the Iron Age began in Egypt, since we only have a very scattered picture of how the peoples of the Eastern Mediterranean migrated, intermingled and traded at such an early period. If the advent of the Iron Age in a region is determined as the time when the people of the region began to work with iron, then that gives us little clue as to when iron was first available in that region. Those who first discovered how to extract iron ore and smelt or work it would have done everything possible to keep the process secret and to safeguard the source of the raw materials used to produce the iron. The ability to smelt or work iron ores would have brought great wealth to those who controlled its production; therefore it could have taken a very long time for this process to become widely known. No doubt a great export industry grew up around these early iron production facilities, and as the material became more plentiful, it would have been exported and traded far and wide.

In time, more people would have become familiar with the smelting process and iron production would have spread throughout the Middle East and into Asia and Europe. However, knowing what the process entailed was one thing, but it was quite another to be able to secure the ores required to produce iron. Undoubtedly, many rulers would not have had a source of iron ore available to them within the territory they controlled, so they would have had no choice but to import iron long after the knowledge of how to produce it had been widely disseminated. This being the case, I presume that the Iron Age was said to have come to these regions when iron was being imported and used in sufficient quantities to satisfy the demand of those who could afford it. But iron could have been imported into these regions for many centuries before iron implements and weaponry became commonplace. If iron was only available in small quantities, or was very expensive, then the odds are greatly against us ever discovering such material in most archaeological excavations. When we also consider that it would have been a very valuable commodity, and, as such, it would have been recycled time and time again, then we are unlikely to discover any iron until its usage became much more commonplace.

We have also to bear in mind the limitations of archaeology for we only get a very tiny snapshot of a vastly greater culture or age when an archaeological site is excavated. In other words, we have no way of establishing extensive knowledge about a culture or a pre-historical period based on the information gleaned from one archaeological site. To take a small amount of data and make sweeping generalisations about a people or a particular period based on that data, or lack of it, is a great error, as we can only begin to build up a true picture of a culture or age when we get corroborative evidence to back up the original data. Most of the corroborative evidence, with regard to the earliest Egyptian culture – and the pyramids at Giza in particular – is simply not there. The further back in time that we go, the less physical evidence archaeologists tend to discover for it is usually only stone utensils and potsherds that survive the ravages of time when we go back four millennia or more. However, now and again we discover artefacts that have survived simply because of a unique set of circumstances, or because the conditions were just right for the preservation of those artefacts. The iron plate from the Great Pyramid is one such artefact.

Some excellent archaeological discoveries have been made in recent years that have helped us to gain a better understanding of how ancient peoples, their technology and their skills, spread out to the south and west of the Black Sea. However, it is likely to be a very long time before we can accurately chart the spread of metallurgical skills or accurately determine the introduction of iron to specific regions. At Catal Huyuk, at the southern edge of the Anatolian Plateau in Turkey c. 6,400 B.C.E., craftsmen were smelting copper and lead. We don't know how or where the people who lived here first learned how to smelt these metals – or how widespread this knowledge was at this time – but it is unlikely that the smelting of metals was confined to Catal Huyuk. Over time this knowledge would undoubtedly have spread to other areas of the near and middle-east and beyond where the raw materials, the ores, were to be found. After 5,500 B.C.E., when the land bridge collapsed at the north end of the Sea of Marmara and the Bosphorus Strait was formed, trading ships could navigate all the way from the Mediterranean Sea, through the Aegean Sea and the Sea of Marmara, to the Black Sea. I certainly do not mean to imply that iron smelting occurred this early in Anatolia or on the Black Sea coast, but if primitive furnaces were in use at Catal Huyuk in the middle of the seventh millennium B.C.E. can we really believe that it was another four millennia or more before iron was traded throughout the eastern Mediterranean?

Like copper and bronze, iron would have been recycled as it would have been very expensive to produce. It would also possibly have been in very short supply for many centuries after its discovery, as it was a much more difficult process to produce good quality iron than it was to produce copper and lead; much higher temperatures are required to extract iron from its ore. In order to generate those higher temperatures a new form of fuel was needed one that didn't occur naturally. Nowadays, iron smelters use coke to get the high temperatures needed to smelt iron but in historical times it was charcoal that was used as the fuel. Until such times as our ancestors learned how to produce a fuel that burned at a much higher temperature than wood, there would have been no iron smelters. This was where the smelting of copper, lead and tin differed from that of iron; these metals could be extracted from their ores at much lower temperatures. We should therefore not be surprised that the odd iron artefact turned up out of the blue at a time and place where archaeologists tell us it shouldn't be, as iron could still have been extremely rare in areas not so far from those of its manufacture, even a thousand years after it was first worked.

The iron plate in the Great Pyramid survived for so long simply because it had been incorporated into a structure that had survived for thousands of years after its construction. The only section of this plate to survive was the section that had been sandwiched between two limestone blocks and therefore it had not been exposed to the elements during the thousands of years that the structure has stood on the Giza Plateau. That is why this particular artefact survived and why we don't find other examples of smelted or wrought iron from this early period. It was not because iron couldn't be produced in this early period; it is simply because this particular object had been incorporated into a structure that has survived for thousands of years that we have this iron sample today, a unique set of circumstances. This plate, in my opinion, is an artefact that speaks volumes about what we don't know of this period for it tells us that iron could be sourced by those who could afford to pay for it. Unfortunately, it does not give us any clue as to how rare or how widely used iron may have been at this time. It may be the sole iron artefact from this period, although this is highly unlikely given the technology that was obviously in use at this time, but it is proof positive that smelted or wrought iron was available to the builders of the super pyramids.

The availability of iron would certainly have provided the builders with an excellent material for making chisels and tools and for fabricating mechanical contraptions, but without their phenomenal hydraulic skills it would never have been possible to build any of the super pyramids using large stone blocks weighing several tons. The builders of the super pyramids were highly skilled canal builders and hydraulic engineers. If they'd had limited experience of hydraulic engineering before they began to build super pyramids, then they certainly learned how to take full advantage of hydraulic power very quickly, for by the time they were ready to put the two largest structures on the Giza Plateau they were absolute masters of this craft.

In the Great Pyramid the ancient builders achieved almost impossible feats of hydraulic engineering when they installed the upper chamber and the stack above it, but we must not forget that it's highly likely that they would have installed just such a granite chamber and stack in the Middle Pyramid also. It was the creation of this advanced pyramid design that made it possible to build such huge structures within an acceptable time frame and that is the only reason why we can see two such structures on the Giza Plateau. It was only their mastery of hydraulics that enabled these builders to transport and lift gigantic monoliths such as those that we see in many of the structures at Giza. Hydraulic power is without a doubt the only explanation as to how such feats were achieved.

If Giza was unique, in that it was the only place where huge monoliths had been transported and raised up to higher elevations, we could certainly say that this was likely to have been the work of one particular culture, at one particular location, at a specific period in time. However, that is not the case, for there are a number of sites in countries bordering the Mediterranean where very large monoliths have been used to construct buildings and walls. At one such site, some of the monoliths are many times greater in size than the largest blocks we see at Giza. It is beyond the scope of this book for us to take a look at all of these sites but we will take a look at the site where the largest monoliths of all were quarried and transported in ancient times. Interestingly, this structure was built in an area that had very strong links with Egypt during the early dynastic period and most probably in pre-dynastic times also. It is to be found in the country we know today as Lebanon.

Baalbek

The temples at Baalbek were constructed on a platform at a site in the northern Bekaa Valley in Lebanon by the Romans. What remains of the grandest temple ever built by the Romans – the Temple of Jupiter, one of the wonders of the ancient world – is to be found here. The Romans built a huge temple complex here using millions of stone blocks in the process, but it is not the Roman constructions that I found so interesting; it is an outer wall of the platform that these structures stand on, for the Romans undoubtedly did not build the original walls here. In all probability these walls had existed on this site for millennia before the Romans built their structures here.

In the west wall of the platform at Baalbek is what is known as the trilithon, three massive stones each weighing around 800 tons. This is not what I would normally think of as a trilithon – which more often consists of two uprights with a great lintel on top – for these three dressed blocks of stone lie end to end in the west wall of the platform six metres up from its base. The platform at Baalbek is undoubtedly much older than the Roman period but its construction is shrouded in so much myth and mystery that it could be impossible to figure out when it was constructed. The walls around the platform have been added to on at least two occasions, but it is easy to discern that the oldest section of the west wall is of a much greater age than the later additions for the huge monoliths used to construct the lowest sections of the west wall are deeply pitted and weathered due to their great age. This is not the case with the later additions.

Although the three 800 ton blocks in the west wall are the largest blocks used in the construction, there are many others in the west wall that weigh between 300 and 500 tons each. These truly are walls of gargantuan proportions (the original walls, not the later additions). But it is the sheer size of the blocks that make up the trilithon that is so impressive; they are 4.4 metres high, 3.6 metres thick and have an average length of 19.5 metres, building blocks of gigantic proportions that were once believed by the primitive peoples of the region to have been put here by giants. You will have no doubt realized that these three monoliths are many times larger than any of those to be found at Giza, but what is most astonishing about Baalbek is that these are not the largest dressed stone blocks to be found at this site.

As its name would suggest, 500 metres or so south of the platform is the "Stone of the South" which weighs in at an incredible 1,000 tons. The Stone of the South however is not part of any structure here for it still lies in the quarry from which it was hewn when work stopped on this project. The monolith lies at an angle of 30 degrees or so from the horizontal and it is still attached to the parent rock at its lower end, but it is the length of this huge monolith that is so astonishing; it is 30 metres long. One French scholar actually calculated that it would have taken 40,000 men to haul this 1,000 ton monolith to the site of the platform. However, this was a pretty useless exercise as this monolith would never, could never, have been hauled the 500 metres or so to the construction site.

We certainly don't need to speculate now as to how these huge monoliths were transported and raised up onto the walls of the platform at Baalbek for there was only one power source available to its builders that would have enabled them to move such huge blocks of stone. It was, after all, this same power source that the builders of the Super Pyramids had harnessed to build the greatest single structure on the planet. In fact, it is the same power source that we, more often than not, employ today when we have to lift very heavy loads. The builders of these ancient structures had only one option available to them when it came to lifting and transporting very heavy objects, for it was only hydraulic power that was capable of lifting and transporting such phenomenally large monoliths. We can therefore only conclude that the original structure at Baalbek was constructed when vast water resources were available to its builders.

In Egypt, the much drier climate brought an end to the super pyramid age. The water resources that had made their construction possible were no longer available in the much drier climate that set in after the Giza complex was complete. The drier climate that turned the land of Egypt to desert so long ago is still with us today. Unfortunately, we will never know what brought the project at Baalbek to an abrupt end but we have been very fortunate that this project did end prematurely, for it has provided us with a very good insight into how the builders quarried these huge monoliths. However, our good luck does not end there, as the Stone of the South also provides us with the key to how these huge monoliths were loaded onto barges and transported to the platform wall 500 metres or so from the quarry.

The first thing we have to understand about the Stone of the South is that such an enormous monolith would not have been hauled to the site of the platform; this was impossible, given the resources available to its builders. However, it didn't matter that these monoliths could not be hauled by men, for the masons cut these very long rectangular columns of masonry from the top levels of the quarry and then undercut them in order to facilitate the loading of the monoliths onto barges, just as the ancient pyramid builders at Giza had done when they removed the 200 ton limestone monoliths from the Sphinx enclosure. There would originally have been more of these columns cut down into what was probably the natural sloping face of the rock here and it was from the topmost mass of the rock here that the blocks used in the trilithon would have been cut. I sincerely doubt that the builders of the platform at Baalbek could have mustered tens of thousands of men to haul these blocks onto the decks of barges, but this would have been totally unnecessary anyway for the builders here, just like those at Giza, used their intellect instead of their pulling power to both load and transport these huge monoliths. The builders of this structure devised a method of quarrying here where they would quarry the smaller blocks used in the walls of the structure from the area underneath the top slab, the slab that the massive rectangular monoliths were cut from. These smaller blocks would then have been hauled from the ledges onto barges bottomed on the ledges below, using the dry dock system that we encountered at the Aswan quarries and at the Sphinx enclosure. The builders would have been well aware of the maximum block size that could be hauled by the men employed on the project, but they also had the intelligence to know that much larger blocks could be quarried and transported using methods that did not involve hauling the blocks on and off the decks of barges. Instead of quarrying the smaller blocks in the usual way, where the stone that was removed created a series of ledges cut into a vertical face of a quarry from the top down, the quarry at Baalbek was set up in such a way that, when the smaller blocks of masonry were removed, they undercut a very deep sheet of limestone. It just so happens that the sheet of limestone the Stone of the South was cut from lies at a slight angle to the horizontal, 30 degrees or so, and it's more than likely that more rectangular columns had been cut from this same top sheet of limestone at the highest level of the quarry. The long columns of limestone used to construct the platform wall would have been cut from the top sheet of stone after it had been undercut – after the smaller blocks of masonry had been removed from the horizontal levels beneath it. When the final cut was made at the lower end of the column to sever it from the parent rock, the monolith would have been ready to be lifted out of the quarry and transported to the construction site.

When a block of stone is so large that even a thousand men cannot haul it onto a barge, there is only one way around the problem; you have to position the barge underneath the block then use hydraulic power to lift the monolith up and out of the quarry. That is how the builders of the platform wall at Baalbek managed to get these huge monoliths onto the barges. It was no simple matter, but it is undoubtedly the reason why we see these limestone beams cut from the topmost layer of rock in the quarry. When the builders removed the smaller blocks of stone from the horizontal levels below the top sheet of limestone they created a channel – or extended the existing channel – beneath each of these columns. The width of this channel would not have been much wider than the barges themselves, which in turn were narrower than the length of the monoliths cut from the quarry. The lengths of the monoliths in the west wall at Baalbek vary though; therefore the builders would have used barges of varying widths to remove these monoliths from the quarry.

Each of the monoliths would have been attached to the parent rock when the channel underneath the monolith was excavated, and each monolith would have been supported on its underside by two columns of rock, one at either end, until it was almost ready to be cut free from the parent rock. Freeing the monoliths from the parent rock at the lower end was a slightly different procedure from that at the higher end, as the blocks at this end would have been undercut in one operation. As can be seen in the drawing (Fig. 41a) on the next page, a 'V' shaped undercut would have been made at the lower end of the blocks and then a channel would have been cut across the beams down through the rock from above, and at right angles to the top and side surfaces of the monoliths. This would have freed the monoliths from the parent rock at their lower ends.

The operation to free the monoliths from the parent rock at their upper ends had involved the cutting away of the limestone columns supporting this end of the monoliths. Part of the supporting rock columns under the top end of these monoliths would have been cut away and huge hardwood beams would have been rammed into the gap between the underside of the monoliths and the ledge that had been cut into one side of the supporting column. These beams supported the higher end of the monoliths as the last part of the supporting parent rock columns were cut away to free the monoliths at this end.

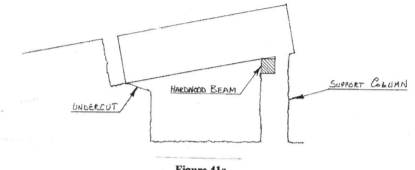

Figure 41a

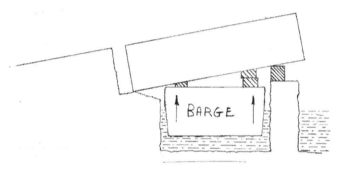

Figure 41b

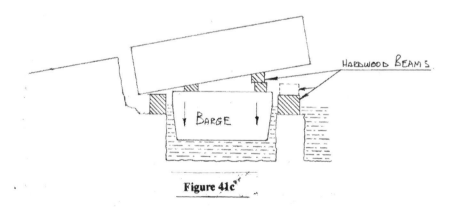

Figure 41c

When each of the monoliths had been finally cut free from the parent rock, water would have been released into the channel / lock and barges would have been manoeuvred into the channel and positioned beneath each of the monoliths. Before the water level was increased, hardwood beams would have been placed on the decks of the barges. To compensate for the slope of the underside of the monoliths, more of these beams would have been placed on the side of the barges at the high end of the monoliths than at the other, so that the wooden beams would make contact with the underside of the monoliths at about the same time when the barges were raised. When the water level was increased farther, the barges would have slowly raised these monoliths up off of their hardwood beams and ledges that had supported them (Fig. 41b).

The next task would have been to cut a horizontal ledge where the "V" shaped undercut had been made at the lower end of each monolith. When this had been done, the height of the supporting column at the other end of the monoliths would also have been reduced and hardwood beams placed on top of the columns to support the monoliths as they were lowered down onto the columns again (Fig. 41c). This was possibly done in two stages (you will see that I have shown the outline of another hardwood beam on top of the support column at the higher end of the monolith). When the sluices were opened and the water level in the lock decreased, the underside of each monolith would have come to rest on these hardwood beams.

By jacking the monoliths up in this way and then lowering them onto hardwood beams, the monoliths were brought into the horizontal position in two manoeuvres. The hardwood beams on the decks of the barges would then have been removed before the sluices were closed once again and the water level in the channel / lock increased. The monoliths were now ready to be transported to the construction site.

Although it has been estimated that the Stone of the South weighs around a thousand tons, it's possible that the cut to free it from the parent rock would not have been made at the extreme lower end of this column. It's more than likely that a stump would have been left on the parent rock and this would have formed the top end of the next column to be carved out of the top sheet of bedrock. However, if a shorter monolith had been cut from the limestone columns, then the builders would have had to support the underside of the monolith with the barge before it was cut away from the parent rock. I suspect however, that the underside of the Stone of the South (a.k.a. the "Stone of the Pregnant Woman") may be much shorter in length than the top face of the monolith, giving an impression that this column of limestone is much longer than the other monoliths used in the construction of the west wall at Baalbek (the lower end of this monolith is below ground level). Although I have no photographs of my own showing the west wall at Baalbek or the stone quarries here, photographs of this site are to be found on the earth-mysteries.com website where you will also find an excellent article by Alan Alford titled: *The Mystery of The Stones at Baalbek.* There are also many other photographs of this ancient site posted on the internet that clearly show the arrangement of the blocks in the west wall here.

These limestone monoliths lay across the decks of the barges with their ends overhanging the sides of the barges when they had been lifted up off their supports. Work on these blocks however, was not complete at this stage for the underside of the monoliths had still to be dressed at either end where they had been supported by the columns. It's also possible that some material had to be trimmed off of what had been the lower end faces of each monolith to square them off, and to ensure that the end face was flat before it was installed. These were gargantuan limestone blocks and massive barges would have been required to transport them to the site of the platform wall that was under construction a few hundred metres from the quarry. Although this was not nearly such a complex structure as the Great Pyramid at Giza, a great deal of planning, surveying and laying out would also have been required at Baalbek prior to the construction of the west wall. If the builders had made errors here, many man hours of hard physical labour could have been wasted.

The width of the various barges that transported the monoliths to the construction site was important also, as they had all to be considerably narrower than the length of the monoliths they transported. The barges had to be narrower by a good margin, for the ends of the monoliths had to overhang the sides of the barges in order for them to be installed on their supporting piers in the west wall. These piers had been constructed earlier and the gaps between them were just wide enough to accommodate the barges. As there were a number of different lengths of monoliths that make up the courses of the west wall, a number of different sized barges would therefore have been required for this operation.

Each stage of the construction of the west wall had to have been planned very carefully as the monoliths had to be installed in a specific order. A number of observers have noted the seemingly odd configuration of the blocks in the west wall as the blocks in the courses below the two courses of colossal blocks in the wall are much smaller than those in the courses above. On first inspection, this odd configuration of the blocks may not make much sense, but we discovered earlier that the builders of the super pyramids at Giza had very good reasons for creating, what many had regarded as anomalies, simply because we didn't understand their purpose. If we therefore assume that the builders of the west wall at Baalbek also had very good reason to construct the wall in this manner, and hold that thought while we ponder the difficulties they would have faced in their attempts to install these monoliths, the configuration of the blocks in the west wall (Fig. 42) makes perfect sense and it provides us with the clues as to how this wall was constructed. If you also consider for a moment how the masonry was quarried and removed from the quarry, you will find that there is also a clue here as to how the wall was constructed.

In the quarry, the builders had to remove the smaller blocks of masonry from the lower levels before they cut the long columns (beams) of limestone out of the top sheet of rock. There was good reason for this, as the huge monoliths cut from the top sheet of rock were simply too massive to be hauled onto barges. The much smaller blocks, on the other hand, could be hauled from the quarry ledges onto the decks of the barges by the quarrymen, possibly even by draft animals such as oxen. The colossal monoliths cut from the top layer of stone in the quarry though could only be raised up out of the quarry using hydraulic power. So if this was the only way to lift these monoliths up and out of the quarry, it also follows that the same was probably true in reverse when the builders came to install these huge monoliths. In other words, it was only hydraulic power that could have been used to raise such colossal monoliths up and onto the west wall of the platform at Baalbek.

That is the sole reason why the blocks in the west wall of the structure are configured in the way that they are, since barges were used to transport and lower these huge monoliths into position on the two upper courses of the wall. These colossal limestone beams

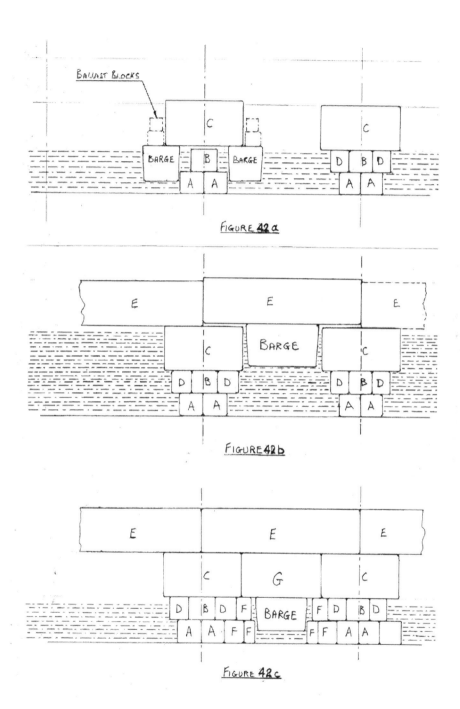

FIGURE 42 a

FIGURE 42 b

FIGURE 42 c

simply could not have been moved by the hand of man after they had been set down; therefore this was the only way to install them in the west wall. Some of the much smaller limestone blocks in the lower courses, on the other hand, could easily have been slotted into the gaps in the lower courses of the wall by the use of a battering ram. This, as we discovered earlier, was how many of the blocks in the upper chamber of the Great Pyramid would have been manoeuvred into their final positions after much larger (longer) monoliths had been installed in the course above them. In other words, the builders had only one option with the largest limestone monoliths but many more options with the much smaller blocks as it was possible to move these blocks in a number of ways.

In the drawings (Figs. 42a, 42b & 42c) showing the order of construction of the west wall at Baalbek, you will notice that I have letter coded the limestone blocks in order to show the various stages of the construction as it was gradually built up. This, in effect, was a wall that was built from the top down rather than in the more conventional manner from the bottom up. Looking at the west wall now we can clearly see that the configuration of the blocks, where huge monoliths sit atop much smaller limestone blocks, makes perfect sense. We can now see that there were good reasons as to why the builders of the platform walls at Baalbek chose to install the limestone blocks in the manner they did, as this was the only way that it was possible to manoeuvre these huge monoliths in the top two courses into position. The monoliths in the top course were lowered onto piers that had been put in place to support them and then the shorter monoliths and the smaller limestone blocks in the courses below were then slotted into position.

After the largest monoliths had been installed in the top course – the trilithon – the gaps in the course below would have been filled to complete the top two courses. You will see from the drawing (Fig. 42c) that these, the smaller of the large monoliths, had also to be floated into position on barges. But these monoliths that filled the gaps in the second top course of the wall could not be lowered into position like the others that had been lowered onto the piers here earlier to support the trilithon, they had to be slotted into position. A great deal of precision was required when these monoliths were being aligned with the openings into which they had to be rammed, but we can clearly see that only a very small area on the underside of these monoliths came into contact with the blocks in the course below. As such a small area of the underside of these monoliths came into contact with the lower course of the wall there would have been very little drag due to friction here when these monoliths were being nudged into the gaps on this level. Wet mortar may possibly have provided the lubrication but I have been unable to determine if mortar was used in the structure at Baalbek. However, if mortar had not been used here, water would most probably have been used as the lubricant when these huge monoliths were being slotted into position in the course below the trilithon.

When the last of the monoliths in the top two courses had been installed, the blocks in the lower courses of the wall would then have been installed and the last of the blocks rammed into place to fill the last of the gaps on each of these levels. As I mentioned earlier, the wall was constructed in reverse fashion from the top course down; it was only some small piers that had been constructed on the lower levels to support the much larger monoliths in the top two courses of the wall prior to the installation of these monoliths.

This anomaly at Baalbek therefore is just like all of those anomalies that existed in the Great Pyramid before we discovered the true reason for their existence. Just like the anomalies in the Great Pyramid, this anomaly ceases to exist when we finally grasp the reason for its creation. I have no doubt that in time we will find it difficult to understand why we could not immediately have understood why these anomalies existed, as it will all seem so logical when we have had time to absorb the true reason for their existence. We will then come to accept that these were never anomalies at all, that this was just the term archaeologists and others gave to features that they couldn't make sense of.

The west wall at Baalbek, however, is a much simpler construction than the pyramids at Giza and it is much easier to see how this structure was put together. If you had still harboured some doubts that hydraulic power had been used to build the super pyramids of Egypt, then the configuration of the blocks in the west wall at Baalbek should surely have blown those doubts away. The configuration of the blocks in the west wall here is proof positive that the ancient builders of this structure used hydraulic power to remove these blocks from the quarry, transport them to the construction site and install them in the west wall of the structure. There is simply no other way to explain the configuration of the limestone monoliths in this wall or how they got here. Once again, the evidence for the use of hydraulic power at a very early period is overwhelming.

We may not yet know who was responsible for the construction of the west wall at Baalbek, or who was responsible for the construction of the super pyramids, but I think that it is far too much of a coincidence to believe that two cultures in the Eastern Mediterranean discovered how to manipulate hydraulic power independently of one another to the extent that they did. At Baalbek we can see the largest blocks of stone ever moved by man, and at Giza we can see the largest single stone structure ever constructed by man. If it was not the same people that were responsible for the construction of both of these structures, then I would say that there was undoubtedly a very strong link between the two groups. Perhaps in time we will discover what that link was.

We now know that the pyramids were likely to have been constructed long before the time of Khufu, as it was almost certainly much too dry a climate at this time to build super pyramids; the water resources would not have been available. I believe that the project at Baalbek was undertaken long before the Roman era and that a rapid change to an arid climate could possibly have been the reason why this project came to an abrupt end, but there could be many other reasons as to why this project ended so abruptly. However, due to the fact that both of these projects would have required huge volumes of water, it is possible that they were both undertaken sometime during the fourth millennium B.C.E. We know that the west wall at Baalbek is much older than the Roman period so hopefully the paleoclimatologists will be able to determine the last time that both of these regions had the water resources to feed the very extensive canal systems that would have been required at both of these sites. However, it may be very difficult to determine the climatic conditions at Baalbek in ancient times as Baalbek is situated in the Bekaa Valley, which sits between two mountain ranges; the weather in the mountains here could have been very different from the weather down in the plain when the west wall here was constructed.

A very extensive canal system had been constructed on the west bank of the Nile prior to the construction of the super pyramids, for they simply could not have been constructed without this canal network. But the same may also have been true for the structure at Baalbek; it may be that the builders of the west wall here had also to construct a very extensive canal system to bring the much needed water resources to the construction site. If that had been the case, then archaeologists may be able to discover the site of the water reservoir or course of the ancient water channel that supplied the water for this project.

In my research I came across an article where the writer stated that the Great Pyramid at Giza could be dated, based on the angle of inclination of the descending corridor – assuming that this passage / pipe was directed at the pole star when construction began. The astronomer has apparently shown that in the year 2,170 B.C.E. the passage pointed to Alpha Draconis at its lower culmination. However, this is much too late for the construction of the pyramids at Giza to have taken place. The astronomer, Mr Richard A Proctor, then adds:

> "If then we regard the slant passage as intended to bear on the pole star at its sub polar passage, we get the date of the pyramid assigned as about 3,350 B.C., with only a probable limit of error of not more than 250 years either way, and perhaps of only fifty years."

If this was the case with the Great Pyramid and its builders did target the pole star with the descending corridor, then the Great Pyramid could indeed be 1,000 years older than the time of Khufu. I can't vouch for the validity of Mr Proctor's theory but I am certainly of the opinion that the super pyramids on the west bank were constructed long before the time of Khufu. The date that Mr Proctor has proposed for the construction of the Great Pyramid is, in my opinion, a much more probable date when we consider the water resources that were needed for this project. As for the construction of the west wall at Baalbek, I have no idea when this early section of the west wall was constructed and I can only conclude that these projects *could* have been contemporary. I should however, point out that this is only a personal opinion.

There is however, some evidence to suggest that some of the earliest work at Giza may have been contemporary with, or come just after, the construction of the west wall at Baalbek as some very large monoliths were used to build up the foundations and the first few courses of the middle pyramid at its south-western corner. These monoliths are estimated to weigh around 200 tons each. As we discovered earlier, some very large monoliths were also used to construct the Valley temple, just east of the Sphinx and there is now a great deal of evidence to suggest that the Sphinx and the Sphinx Enclosure may be the earliest works ever undertaken at Giza. Indeed, the Sphinx may pre-date all of the Super Pyramids on the west bank. But if this is the case, then so do the Sphinx and Valley Temples, as the stone used in the construction of these temples was removed from the Sphinx enclosure.

I am certainly intrigued by the fact that some of the first constructions at Giza were built using massive monoliths. If it was the same builders who later designed and built the super pyramids, it is easy to understand why the block sizes here are, in the main, much smaller than the massive monoliths used to construct the Valley and Sphinx Temples. The massive monoliths used in the construction of the temples adjacent to the Sphinx Enclosure were only moved a short distance within a massive lock by very large barges. These monoliths had been quarried from the very top layer of the bedrock in the Sphinx Enclosure and it would simply have been impossible to build structures like the pyramids using such massive blocks of limestone quarried in this way. It would also have been impossible to create a canal system within these structures big enough to take the huge barges needed to transport these limestone monoliths; therefore the only option was for the block sizes to become much smaller in order to build the Super Pyramids. The Super Pyramids could only be constructed using limestone blocks that could be easily hauled and manoeuvred into position by men. The enormous 200 ton blocks used in some of the earliest constructions here could only be lowered into their final positions using hydraulic power. In other words, the block sizes had to get much smaller to construct Super Pyramids as most of the masonry in the Super Pyramids had to be manoeuvred into position by men. All of the much larger monoliths in the Great Pyramid that could not be manoeuvred into position by men – the granite slabs in the stack and some of the beams in the upper chamber – were installed in an area that could be accessed by barges where they were lowered into position using hydraulic power. The largest of the granite blocks / slabs used in the construction of the Great Pyramid however, weigh much less than half the weight of the 200 ton blocks used in the construction of the Valley Temple and the base layers of the middle pyramid. Is it possible that some of the builders responsible for the construction of the west wall at Baalbek migrated south to settle in the Nile Delta? It's certainly an intriguing thought.

At Baalbek and Giza we can see the phenomenal engineering feats that these ancient builders achieved. Many of these feats are way beyond anything that could be achieved by manpower alone and there is no other physical force that can account for these feats other than hydraulic power. This being the case, we therefore have to accept that these ancient builders managed to harness hydraulic power to achieve these phenomenal feats at a time when archaeologists believe it to have been impossible. Had it not been for the fact that the Stone of the South is still lying in the quarry and still attached to the parent rock, it may have taken us longer to discover how these huge monoliths were loaded onto barges, but we would certainly have had no doubts whatsoever as to how these monoliths had been transported to the construction site for it was simply impossible to do it any other way. If proof were needed, then we only need to take a look at the configuration of the blocks in the west wall of the platform at Baalbek to have it confirmed since no one would choose to construct a wall in this way if there was no valid reason for doing so. There was a valid reason, and it was the only one.

The presence of the Stone of the South in the quarry at Baalbek, and the fact that the west wall was never completed, clearly indicates that this project came to a very sudden end. We now know that it was almost certainly climate change that brought the construction of the Super Pyramids on the west bank of the Nile to an end but we simply don't know if any of the Super Pyramids remained unfinished when the lack of rainfall brought the hydraulic age to an end in Egypt (possibly the pyramid at Abu Roash). The platform walls at Baalbek however, were far from complete when the hydraulic operations ended at this site.

There could have been many reasons why the project at Baalbek came to an abrupt end, which it most obviously did, but although we cannot say for certain when, or why, this project came to an end we can say for certain that what had been achieved at Baalbek had been achieved at a time when there was sufficient rainfall to support a very extensive canal network there. This area today only gets an annual average rainfall of 230 mm. This rapid decline in rainfall eventually affected all of North Africa, the countries bordering the Eastern Mediterranean and many other countries of the Middle East. I have, however, been unable to determine if the decline in rainfall occurred in the Northern Bekaa Valley first and then spread south, or if the arid conditions occurred further south and then spread northwards. I have been unable to find data that shows how this arid climate developed and spread in the Eastern Mediterranean and North Africa. However, it is possible that we may never be able to accurately determine which areas were first affected by the more arid conditions or discover how they developed.

Was it the same people who were involved with the construction of the west wall at Baalbek and the Super Pyramids on the west bank of the Nile? While it is possible that certain individuals took the knowledge of hydraulic engineering from one region to the other, it is also possible that the builders of these projects were one and the same body of people. In fact, this whole region may even have been ruled as one kingdom in pre-dynastic times for we have scant knowledge of life in the Eastern Mediterranean in the fourth millennium B.C.E and beyond. We know, for instance, that Egypt traded with Lebanon and had very strong links with it long before the Roman period, but just how far back into pre-history these links may have extended is impossible to determine at this time. There is an ancient myth that refers to a twinning between Byblos in Lebanon and Egypt that pre-dates the Pharaonic Age. While we can't place too much faith in myths and legends, we can't completely discount them either, for there is often a small grain of truth at the heart of them. Heinrich Schliemann, for instance, would certainly never have discovered Troy had he discounted the stories of this city as myth and legend with no factual basis. (Great discoveries are made by those who have an open mind and don't rule out anything. Those who are blinkered never see the bigger picture.)

I have been fascinated by these structures at Giza all of my life and in awe of those who constructed them. It is now patently obvious that at some time in the distant past the pyramid builders developed hydraulic skills that enabled them to construct pyramids using large blocks of stone and these are the structures that I have referred to as the Super Pyramids of the west bank, for they truly are in a league of their own. When we compare these structures with the more primitive pyramids that supposedly preceded them and those that came after, it is plain to see that something momentous happened in pre-dynastic Egypt that brought about the creation of these large stone-built pyramids. I am now one hundred per cent certain that it was the canal lock and hydraulic power that made it all possible, but whether this came about as the result of outside influence or local inspiration, I cannot say. All I know is that no sooner had these builders discovered how to transport barges up to higher ground away from the flood plain, than they began to channel canals through the actual structures. This enabled them to transport the building materials from their source, right to their point of use. In a few short steps, they had produced the world's first, fully integrated, true pyramid. These were not just new, revolutionary pyramid designs however, for this was a completely new way of thinking about pyramid construction. We therefore cannot rule out the possibility that this new way of thinking was an introduction to Lower Egypt rather than a home grown flourishing of ideas. While we can't completely rule out the possibility that someone local may have had a spark of inspiration and the whole thing snowballed from there, it is very often the case that someone from a different background with a different approach can see the solution to a problem that those up close to it cannot see; they come at it from a different perspective. Owing to the fact that so many technological advances were made in pyramid design and construction in Egypt over a relatively short period of time, I do suspect that these may have been an introduction rather than a flourishing of new ideas by the indigenous peoples of the region. But it's unlikely that we will ever discover the truth of the matter.

The structures on the west bank of the Nile and the west wall at Baalbek are testament to the fact that very early cultures discovered how to manipulate hydraulic power to their advantage. They developed this skill to a phenomenal degree and this enabled them to construct the largest man made structure on earth and to transport the largest monoliths ever created by man. The structures at Baalbek and the pyramids on the west bank of the Nile exist, we either have to waken up to the truth of the matter and accept that hydraulic power is the only possible explanation for their existence, or continue to accept the naive explanations regularly trailed out by Egyptologists who have failed at every attempt to prove their naive theories. As I see it, we can continue to listen to those who peddle those failed theories forever and nothing will change, or we can look at what the evidence is really saying about these structures and understand what the ancient builders really had to do to construct them. I have not presented you with theories here that may or may not prove to be true, I have presented you with facts that the structures themselves are testament to. To say that my discoveries turn the establishment view on its head is a gross understatement but that is something that academics will have to come to terms with in due course since we have now begun to understand the true language of these structures. Just as the Rosetta Stone was the key to understanding ancient Egyptian hieroglyphs, the double gables above the doorway in the Great Pyramid are the key to understanding Super Pyramid construction. However, we still have so much more to learn about these structures and I hope that in the fullness of time many more discoveries will be made for I'm sure that there is much that I have overlooked.

There was no shortage of evidence of a technologically advanced people in Lower Egypt having used machines to create coffers and vases, and to drill very large holes in hard rock (granite) prior to my discoveries at Giza. We know that they used tubular drills to hollow out coffers and other vessels and some sort of milling machine was also used to then machine the surfaces of many of these coffers to a degree of accuracy that we would find difficult to improve upon today. But while there are plenty of examples of machine cut artefacts, there are no examples of the machines that created them in our museums, as none of these machines have ever been found. However, drill cores abound and hundreds of these cores have been discovered at many ancient sites in Egypt. Thousands of small vases have also been discovered in tombs and some of these have been machined from very hard materials, such as basalt and granite. Archaeologists have no idea how the insides of many of these vases were hollowed out as the necks of many of the vases are very small in relation to their inner diameters. Some very complex tooling was required to hollow out the inside of these vases. All of these artefacts and more are testament to the technical capabilities of these very skilled people and they confirm the existence of such machines in ancient Egypt.

Now that we have discovered the extraordinary lengths that these ancient people went to in order to construct the Great Pyramid using their phenomenal hydraulic engineering capabilities, I am now one hundred per cent certain that it would have been water that was the power source for most of their machines as well, especially when we consider that water would have been used, both as a lubricant and as a coolant during most of these cutting operations in stone (a coolant would have been used to keep the cutting tools cool as their cutting edges would have become blunt very quickly if the metal was allowed to become very hot). As they proved when they put three Super Pyramids on the Giza plateau, they were absolute masters of hydraulic engineering. As water was the source of their power when they came to build these very complex super pyramids, surely they would have made much more use of this power source and used it to power many more of their machines and mills as we ourselves did before the advent of steam power, the catalyst for the Industrial Revolution in Britain.

We are very unlikely to discover any examples of these machines in the future, since any metal or wood that was not recycled in ancient times would have long ago deteriorated to a point where it would be unrecognisable as a machine or part of a machine today. The best we can hope for is to discover a depiction of some of these machines when the tomb below the Great Pyramid (and possibly the Middle Pyramid) or some other vault is discovered in the bedrock of the Giza plateau. But whether we discover such depictions or not, there is absolutely no doubt that man's first great technological revolution occurred in Egypt circa 3,000 – 3,500 B.C.E., when water, the driving force of this great technological age, was plentiful. This is what we have completely failed to understand about this very early period and although there are many reasons as to why most archaeologists have not come to fully accept that these ancient people were technologically advanced, I believe that the foremost reason for our failure to accept this is the fact that the Egypt of today is so far removed from the Egypt of the ancient (super) pyramid builders. It is almost impossible for us to imagine what the Egypt of the ancient pyramid builders would have been like when it had a very different climate to what it has today.

The New Kingdom Egypt of Akhenaten and Tutankhamun, thirteen hundred years before Christ, was so vastly different from the Egypt of the ancient pyramid builders that we tend to think of Egypt as having always been an arid country with vast expanses of desert east and west of the fertile Nile Valley. It is so difficult for us to imagine this country as a green and pleasant land, teeming with wildlife and with an abundance of water resources. But it once was such a land and its ancient people – now almost totally obscured by the mists of time and the desert sands – developed an extensive network of canals, created mechanical and hydraulic lifting devices and constructed water powered machines to cut and quarry stone. Had it not been for these advances, there would never have been the great Super Pyramid age, the Hydraulic Age of 5,000 years ago. As I mentioned earlier, the pyramids at Giza would not exist in their present form if the ancient pyramid builders had not had this technology at their disposal. And there can be no doubt that this technology existed, for the Great Pyramid itself is testament to it. In the course of our reconstruction, we discovered what extraordinary lengths the builders of the Great Pyramid had to go to in order to complete the free-standing granite edifice on the 49th course of the structure. Had the canal not been extended beyond the grand gallery, this granite structure would not exist as it was not humanly possible to construct this edifice without hydraulic power and a super efficient pump.

But like so much of Egypt's long forgotten past, it has taken us such a very long time to unearth the secrets of these ancient builders for much of the evidence of this great technological age has all but been obliterated by the arid conditions that dramatically altered the Egyptian landscape and its pattern of life more than four millennia ago. Ancient Egypt changed forever during the Old Kingdom Period (possibly before) and the desertification of much of the country in the centuries that followed ensured that almost all of the evidence of this once very advanced society having existed at all, has been almost completely obliterated. Fortunately, the large, stone built structures – the Super Pyramids – have survived and it is within these structures that we find most of the evidence of this once great technological age. It has taken us a tremendously long time to finally interpret the language of these structures and to discover the true capabilities of these ancient builders, simply because we never suspected that they had such advanced technology at their disposal. But with the discovery of the key – the pyramid code – each feature of these very complex structures has slowly given up its secrets and we have at long last discovered just how ingenious and technologically advanced the builders of these structures truly were. As far as I'm concerned, academics can no longer deny the existence of advanced technology in ancient Egypt because the Great Pyramid now leaves us in no doubt as to how it was constructed and what it took to put it on the Giza plateau. Sooner or later they will come to realize that logic dictates that this feat could not have been achieved by any other means.

Once you discover how each feature of the Great Pyramid was created; once you discover the true purpose of each of its internal features... and the part they played in the construction of the whole; once you discover that water power was what made it all possible, you can only conclude that this structure was created by a highly intelligent, technologically advanced people right at the dawn of the Egyptian culture. There is no other rational explanation.

Giza and Baalbek are by no means unique; all over the world there are ancient structures that we have no idea how, or when, they were constructed. Some of the stone used in the construction of many of these structures is so hard that we have great difficulty cutting it today with modern machine tools. There is now a great body of evidence to indicate that man has possessed knowledge and skills in the distant past far beyond anything that modern historians accept. The pyramids at Giza are the prime example of this but the Egyptological establishment have so far managed to avoid this issue by conjuring up their own naive theories as to how they were constructed. It doesn't seem to matter to them that they have failed to prove most of those theories, as they go on pushing these same old theories despite their failures. We have grown tired of this dogma that is unchanging decade after decade despite the great body of evidence that now contradicts it. But the issue cannot be avoided any longer for that body of evidence has now grown exponentially and it is overwhelming.

Egyptologists have constructed a fantasy over the last one hundred years and more with regard to the pyramids at Giza, a fantasy that now bears no resemblance to the true facts of this matter. However, now that we can clearly understand the true purpose of all its chambers and passageways – and understand how the Great Pyramid was constructed – this matter must now be fully addressed by those who constructed the fantasy that has been the orthodox position for decades now.

The Great Pyramid has at long last given up its secrets and they are there for all to see. Indeed, it would be a very different structure standing on the plateau today if its builders had not developed their phenomenal hydraulic skills when the abundant water resources were available to them. But it wasn't earth ramps or magic that was used to put these structures on the west bank, it was hydraulic power and ingenuity. Isn't it time that the builders of these magnificent structures got the recognition they so richly deserve?

INDEX

Selected Bibliography

Chapter Three
1. Piazzi Smyth, C., 1877 *Our Inheritance in The Great Pyramid*, 2nd edition, London, Strahan.

Chapter Seven
2. Lemesurier, P., 1977, *The Great Pyramid Decoded*, 1997 Ed., Shaftsbury, Element Books.

Chapter Eight
1. Dunn, C. P., 1984, *Advanced Machining in Ancient Egypt*, Analog Magazine, Worcester, Mass. Davis Publications.
2. Bayuk, A., *Guardians Egypt*. Available at: <http://guardians.net/egypt/pyramids.htm>
3. Bonani et al, G., 1995, Radio Carbon Dates of Old and Middle Kingdom Monuments in Egypt [pdf] Available at: <http://www.2dcode-r-past.com/1995Radiocarbonproject.pdf >
4. Temple, R., 2010, *Egyptian Dawn*, London, Century.
5. Temple, R. and O., 2009, *The Sphinx Mystery*, Rochester, Vermont, Inner Traditions.
6. Hassan, F., 2012, Ancient Apocalypse, The Fall of the Egyptian Old Kingdom, BBC series first shown in the UK April 2012.

Chapter Nine
1. Bauval, R. and Hancock, G., *1997, Keeper of Genesis,* London, Arrow Books.
2. Knight, C. and Lomas, R., *The Hiram Key*, 1997, London, Arrow.
3. Hancock, G., *Fingerprints of The Gods*, Pub. Heinemann 1995.
4. Brophy, T., 2002, *The Origin Map*, Bloomington, Indiana, iUniverse.

Chapter Ten
1. Kenyon, J. D., 2005, *Forbidden History, Pushing Back the Portals of Civilisation*. Rochester, Vermont, Bear and Company.
2. Sampsell, B. M., Autum 2000, *Pyramid Design and Construction – Part I: The Accretion Theory*, Paper first Published in The Ostracon, Vol II, No.3,.

3. Bauval, R. and Gilbert, A., 1994, *The Orion Mystery*, London, Mandarin.

4. Bauval, R., 2006, *The Egypt Code*, London, Century.

5. Magli, Professor G, Akhet Khufu: archaeo-astronomical hints at a common project of the two main pyramids at Giza, Egypt, 2009, Nexus Network Journal – Architecture and Mathematics 11, 35-50. (www.springerlink.com).

6. Magli, Professor G, 2010, Astronomy, Topography and Dynastic History in the Alignments of the Pyramid Fields of the Old Kingdom, Mediterranean Archaeology and Archaeometry, Vol 10, No. 2, pp. 59-74.

7. Magli, Professor G, 2009, Mysteries and discoveries of Archaeoastronomy, New York, Springer-Verlag, (Originally published as Archaeoastronmia, 2005, Rome).

Chapter Eleven

Alford, A., 2002, *The Mystery of The Stones at Baalbek* (article copyright of Eridu Books) Available at: <http://www.world-mysteries.com/mpl_5b1.htm>

Robert Carson is the author of this, his first book. He is 64 years of age and he lives with his wife in West Central Scotland. His background is in engineering and he has had a lifelong interest in ancient peoples and the structures they left behind.
More information can be found on the website. (www.thegreatpyramidstory.net)

Made in the USA
Lexington, KY
11 April 2013